THE

AMERICAN ALPINE JOURNAL

1976

Published By

THE AMERICAN ALPINE CLUB

113 EAST 90TH STREET

NEW YORK, N.Y. 10028

*Articles and notes submitted for publication
and other communications relating to*
THE AMERICAN ALPINE JOURNAL
should be sent to the office of
THE AMERICAN ALPINE CLUB

The American Alpine Journal

VOLUME 20 • NUMBER 2 • ISSUE 50 • 1976

CONTENTS

Cover Photo: K2 seen from Concordia
Photo by H. Adams Carter

Committees of the Club for 1976

AMERICAN ALPINE MOUNTAINEERING FELLOWSHIP.
Samuel C. Silverstein, *Chairman*; Yvon Chouinard, Eiichi Fukushima, Andrew C. Harvard, Edward A. Johann, Joseph C. LaBelle, James Wickwire, Michael Yokell

AMERICAN ALPINE NEWS. Christopher A. G. Jones, *Chairman/Editor*

CLIMBING AREAS. John Christian, *Chairman*; Robert C. Anderson, Robert H. Bates, Alex Bertulis, Nicholas A. Dodge, S. John Ebert, Richard M. Emerson, Keith W. Evans, Bill E. Forrest, Eiichi Fukushima, Dick Jablonowski, George H. Lowe, Tom A. McCrumm, Louis W. Pearson, Philip C. Ritterbush, William Q. Sumner, Joe H. Wagner, H. Bradford Washburn, Kurt Wehbring, Richard French Wilcox, Jr.

CONSERVATION. T. C. Price Zimmermann, *Chairman*; William H. Babcock, David L. Beckstead, Eric Bjørnstad, Ken Boche, Mary Lou Combs, Fred L. Dailey, John Dalle-Molle, Charles C. Grier, Robert S. Hyslop, Vera Komarkova, William H. La Fontaine III, Darvel T. Lloyd, John D. Mendenhall, Malcolm Moore, Daniel L. Osborne, Rick Reese, Robert H. Schneider, Ira Spring, John Stannard, Ralph H. Tingey, James W. Whittaker, Paul W. Wiseman, Kenneth R. Wyrick

ENDOWMENT AND FUND RAISING. Robert W. Craig, *Chairman*

EQUIPMENT. Helmut F. Microys, *Chairman*; Gerald B. Abad, Michael B. Dent, Daniel K. Eaton, Arthur H. Fitch, Edward A. Johann, Tom A. McCrumm, Bradley J. Snyder, Arnold Wexler

EXPEDITIONS. James F. Henriot, *Chairman*; George I. Bell, Arlene D. Blum, H. Adams Carter, Stanwood Armington, Tom Frost, Thomas A. Nash, Leigh N. Ortenburger, William A. Read, Jeffrey B. Salz, Samuel C. Silverstein, William E. Siri, Daniel Taylor-Ide, Fritz H. E. Wiessner, Glenn E. Porzak

GRAND TETON CLIMBERS RANCH. David B. Dornan, *Chairman*; Nicholas B. Clinch, W. V. Graham Matthews, Cleveland M. McCarty, Leigh N. Ortenburger, Elizabeth D. Woolsey

GUIDES. Raffi Bedayn, *Chairman*; Alex Bertulis, Michael M. Covington, Glenn Exum, Lou Whittaker

INSURANCE. John E. Taylor, *Chairman*; Daniel K. Eaton, Robert S. Hyslop, William G. May, John A. Woodworth

LEGAL. Edward E. Vaill, *Chairman*; T. E. Calleton, Jack Dozier, N. Michael Hansen, William V. Lahr, James P. McCarthy, Martin Mushkin, Alan M. Rubin, Griffith Way

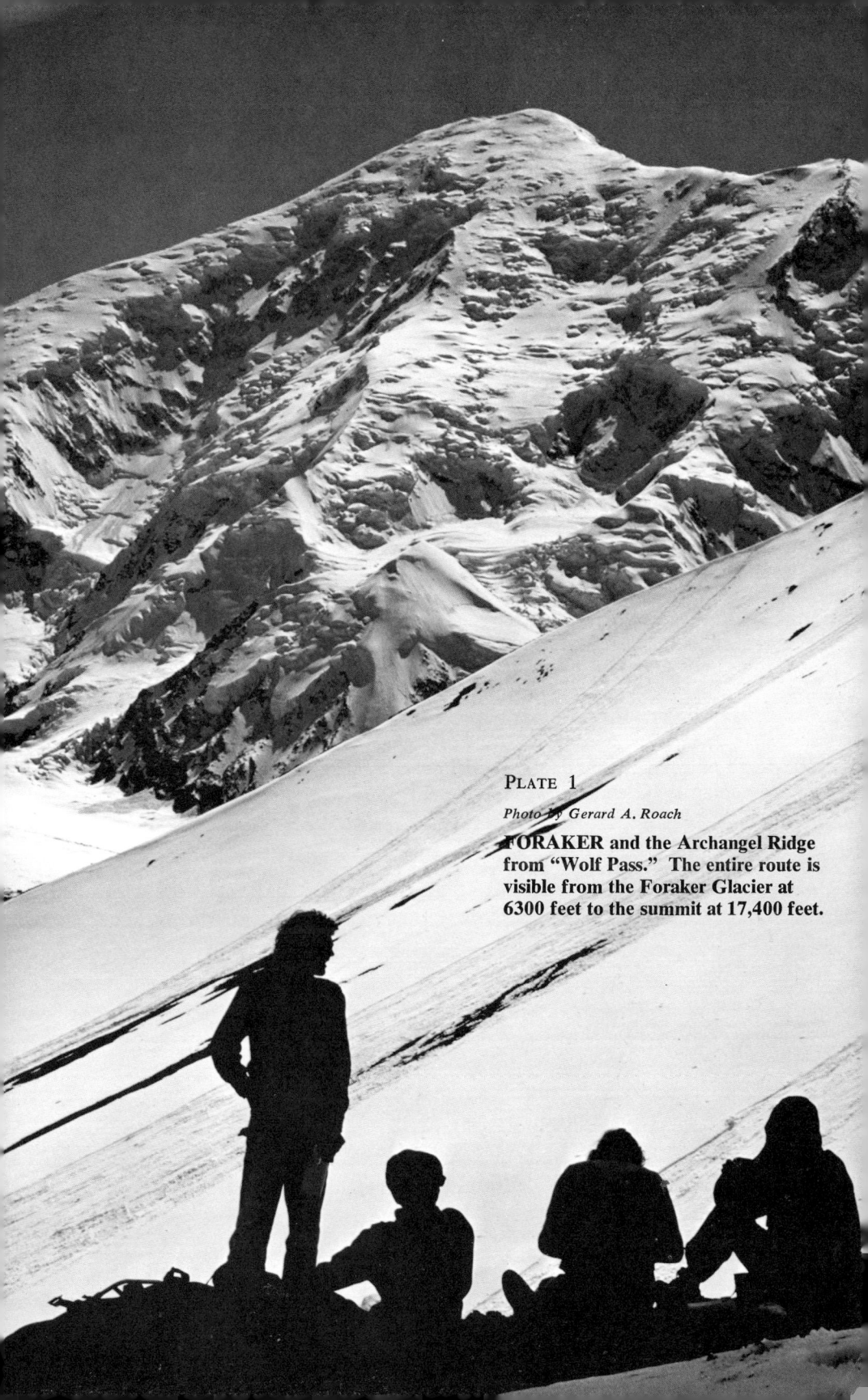

PLATE 1

Photo by Gerard A. Roach

FORAKER and the Archangel Ridge from "Wolf Pass." The entire route is visible from the Foraker Glacier at 6300 feet to the summit at 17,400 feet.

The Archangel—
Foraker's North Ridge

GERARD A. ROACH

AS we approached the pass, we instinctively speeded up. Soon we were running pell mell with giant strides across the scree until the entire peak came into view. It was fantastic. We were gazing up at the beautiful 11,000-foot-high north face of Mount Foraker. Right in the center of the face and rising directly from glacier to summit was the ridge we had come to climb. THERE IT WAS!!

Our approach to this pass was almost as much fun as the climb itself. No climbing party had approached this cirque in 41 years, since 1934 when Charles Houston and party made the first ascent of Mount Foraker. They rode horses out from Wonder Lake, packed loads up the Foraker Glacier under the north face and ascended the west ridge. At the beginning of 1975, Foraker had seen another six ascents, all by routes from the south or east and involving air support. The west and north flanks are well within McKinley National Park and regulations prohibiting the use of aircraft plus the distance from roadheads make access to these faces more difficult.

We hired Berle Mercer, an excellent horse packer, to pack our supplies and we hiked from Wonder Lake to the snout of the Foraker Glacier in three days. On the fourth day we went four miles along the east side of the Herron Glacier, then an additional three miles southeast into "Caribou Valley" (seen and named by the '34 party). By using horses to this point, we cut the load-humping distance to half what it would have been from the snout of the Foraker Glacier. Our approach hike had covered 60 miles and we had crossed 16 major creeks and rivers.

Finally alone with our pile of gear, we contemplated our situation. For our gamble with the horses to work, we had to cross the 6300-foot pass connecting Caribou Valley with the upper Foraker Glacier. What if the pass wouldn't go? We found the approach slopes to the pass beset by avalanches pouring in from both sides. This gave us pause until we spotted a set of wolf tracks across the debris and over the pass. This supplied the courage we needed and soon our pile of gear was on a beautiful meadow just above the Foraker Glacier.

Our "Wolf Pass" had worked and we felt rather smug as we sat on the tundra just three miles from the bottom of our north ridge. And

277

PLATE 2

Photo by *Bradford Washburn*

MOUNT FORAKER from the North.

PLATE 3

Photo by Gerard A. Roach

The Archangel Ridge from Glacier Meadows Camp, three miles from the foot of the mountain.

what a ridge! It rose in one great unbroken sweep from the Foraker Glacier at 6300 feet to the 17,400-foot summit of Foraker with an average angle of 35°. We had studied Washburn's aerial photo of this ridge long and hard, but the reality of sitting underneath it was over-powering.

We took advantage of a spell of good weather to push the route up 2000 feet to a tiny platform for Camp I. This was the most dangerous part of the climb. The first 1000 feet was exposed to séracs above and the debris that we climbed over gave mute testimony to what could happen. On the slope above we found a thin layer of snow over hard ice. This slope was ever changing and always in bad condition and we dubbed it the "Target." Above the Target was a 30-foot rotten ice head-wall. While Dave was leading this pitch there was a sharp settling crack and we felt the whole wall move. We were in instant terror at this dis-play of the mountain's power. And so the pitch became known as the "Shock Wave Wall."

Back in our Base Camp at the base of the route we felt rather sobered by this first day's climbing. Doubt was there. Obviously, we would have to climb at night, but since the route basked in the sun from two A.M. to ten P.M. this would only be a partial solution. Before we could make another move however, we were battered by a violent storm. The wind sprang from nowhere and whisked three airing sleeping bags out across the glacier. We recovered them only after a mad "keystone-cops" chase of 600 yards! The storm came on in earnest and camped on the bare glacial ice, we were very vulnerable. Two of our three tents went down, and all six of us ended up shivering in the third, which only survived because it bent down like the proverbial reed before the wind. The storm blew itself out in 24 hours, but it took over two days to recover from it. We had soaked sleeping bags, and ripped tents to contend with, and this wretched camp soon became an energy sink. As fast as we would laboriously chop a tent platform out of the ice, it would melt out. During this period our resolve to climb this route strengthened and doubts vanished. Nothing could be worse than our energy sink Base Camp! We escaped up the mountain.

After a series of night maneuvers, we were safely established in Camp I above the danger zone. The climbing above Camp I was beautiful. A series of ridges, ramps and walls led up 1000 feet to the Apex, an important and spectacular point where the north ridge becomes well de-fined. Standing on the Apex, we had the feeling of being suspended from a skyhook. There were great voids on 3.9 sides! The only connection with reality and the rest of Mount Foraker was an incredibly sharp knife-edged ridge. It curved and danced away from us, climbing gently. Up to this point we had traded the lead like gentlemen, but now everybody wanted to be up there on the "Angel's Way". After complicated negotiations, Dave, Stu and Brad went up to do the honors. It turned out to be more hard work than glory.

We had been having good weather, and it was just plain hot. Our igloo at Camp I sagged and collapsed under the onslaught of the sun. We repaired it; it melted again; we gave up. Many nights were spent sleeping out, a practice followed even at High Camp.

The snow condition along the beautiful Angel's Way was generally rotten. In the morning the sun would beat in on the left or east face and the steps on that side would shine blue from underneath. In the afternoon the other side would get the same treatment. We had to resort to more nighttime tactics before we were established safely in Camp II, nestled in a wide spot on the ridge just beyond the Angel's Way. Each time we traversed the Angel's Way was special. Its perfect form and spectacular setting more than compensated for the rotten snow.

Camp II was at 10,000 feet; and with most of the major difficulties below us, there was a growing feeling that we could dispatch the upper part of the peak in short order. But we had been having perfect weather —it couldn't last. The barometer would drop more each day, and we resisted the temptation to bolt for the summit.

Above Camp II the ridge continued curving upwards—more steeply now. Higher still it became more of an edge than a ridge, and we had several hundred feet of bare ice to contend with. Above in a slight basin at 11,800 feet, we found good igloo snow. At last! We left the tents at Camp II and moved up to stay. After several hours of labor, we had a magnificent igloo. It was over 8 feet high, and all six of us could stand up and walk around in it together.

We had had 11 days of good weather since the Sink Camp storm, and we had climbed ourselves into a frazzle trying to keep up with it. Now poised in our igloo one day from the summit, the weather went out. This provided us with a much needed rest before our long push for the summit, still 5600 feet above us.

Two days later it looked as if it might clear. We started with the theory that if there was any chance, we should start and go until it became obvious we should turn around. We went up 1000 feet to the beginning of the broken rock band, and it was obvious we should turn around. It was not summit weather. Back in the igloo the barometer kept going down, and we wondered.

The next morning I rolled over in my sleeping bag and checked the barometer again. Down some more. It was now the lowest we had seen it on the trip. A shout filtered in from outside the igloo, "Hey, it's clear!"

"Clear?"

"Clear!"

McKinley danced in the sun as we moved up through the rocks and onto the vast upper slopes of the mountain. Up, up and up for ten hours,

PLATE 4

Photo by Gerard A. Roach

Dave Wright leading the Shock Wave Wall below Camp I on FORAKER.

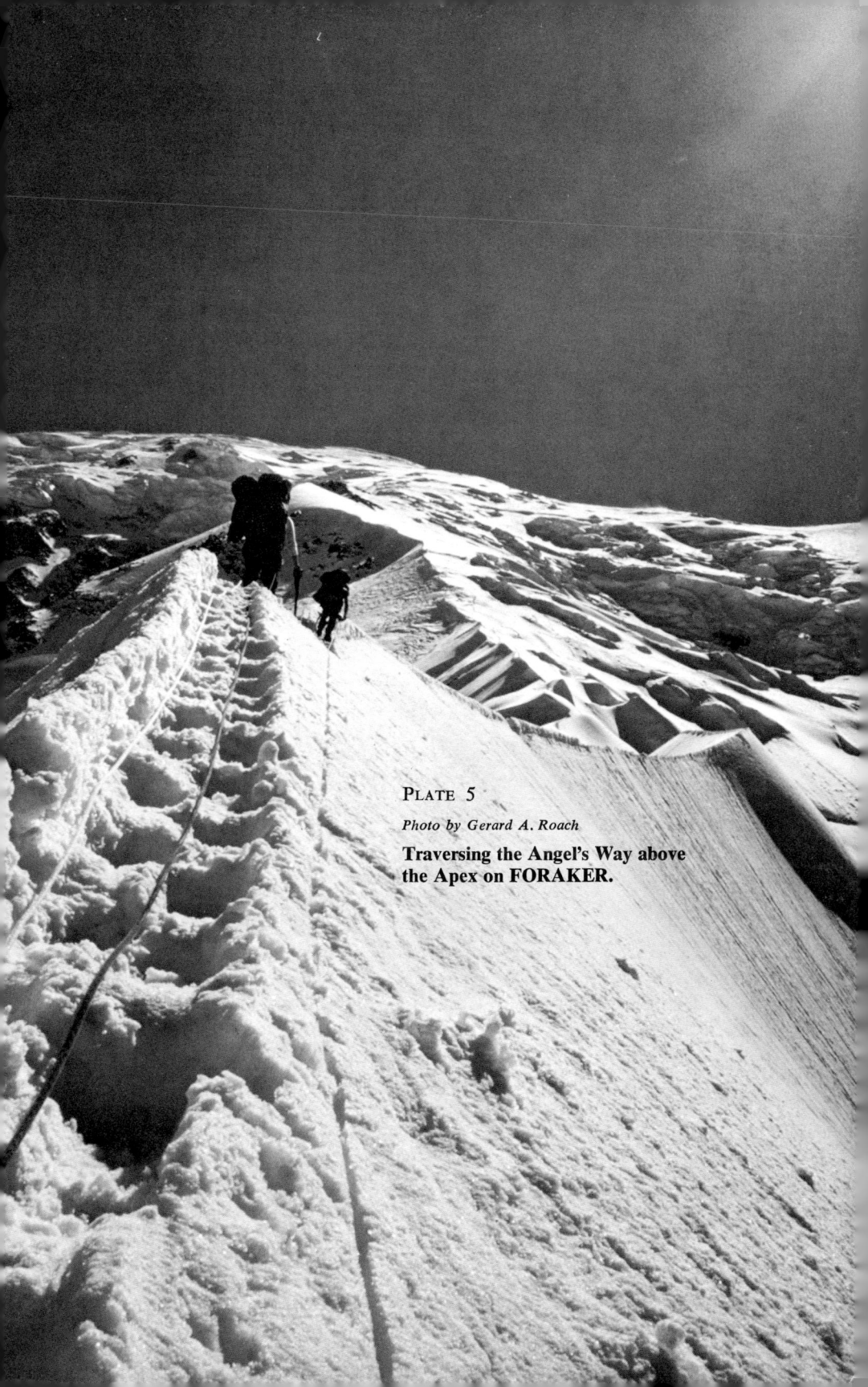

PLATE 5

Photo by Gerard A. Roach

Traversing the Angel's Way above the Apex on FORAKER.

and then we were capering on the flat summit of Foraker. We dashed from edge to edge, got the ropes all tangled up and overexposed several photos. We all congratulated Barb on being the first woman to climb Foraker and soaked up the incredible view.

Back in the igloo it snowed about three feet in the next two days. We finally made a break for it and found a lot of changes in the route below. Twenty-five hours later we sank into the tundra and flowers of glacier meadows tired and happy. As we slogged out in the rain, the memories were already playing in my mind. It had been fine.

Summary of Statistics:

AREA: Alaska Range.

NEW ROUTE: Mount Foraker, 17,400 feet, via the North Ridge; left Wonder Lake on June 15, 1975; reached the summit on July 14, 1975 (entire party).

PERSONNEL: Gerard and Barbara Roach, Brad Johnson, David Wright, Stewart Krebs, Charles Campbell.

Ham and Eggs on the Moose's Tooth

JONATHAN KRAKAUER

A new route on Kichatna Spire. The winter and spring had been spent scheming and psyching up for it, but we just couldn't seem to get decent cards. After waiting several days for flying weather, Tom Davies, Nate Zinsser, and I were finally in the air, but by the time we arrived over the Cathedral Spires they were hopelessly socked-in once again. The thought of more days—maybe weeks—in Talkeetna hit hard. My ambition was pickling and coordination growing shaky from endless hours spent compulsively tipping cans of Oly in Evil Alice's and the Fairview.

"Tough break there, boys." Hudson turned the plane around.

"Tom, what would you say about going to try Johnson?"

"Yeah? Tell me about it."

"Really, no jive this time. Looks pretty in the photos. That big, smooth buttress south of Dickey. Steepest part's right off the glacier."

"A map, Jon. How are we going to know asses from elbows there without a map?"

"No sweat, Nate. I've seen a million slides of the Ruth Gorge."

"Mount Johnson. What the hell, why not?"

"What the hell, why not?"

"Sweet Ever-lovin' Mama, I do hope we haven't finally gone over the edge."

The Cessna turned again and we raced the storm front to the Ruth Amphitheatre, eighty miles to the northeast. That night we teetered down the Ruth as far as we could with three ghastly carries each, and there made our Base Camp. It turned out to be right beneath the east wall of Mount Barrille when the clouds lifted. The next day we skied down to Johnson, but didn't see any continuous lines on it and the rock looked bad. No need to fret though—we'd just try that pretty little (if a bit steep) east face of Barrille, conveniently located right above our camp.

Little, like 2500-feet-little, we were to discover. 500 virtually ledge-less feet up on the wall, I got to a seam that was crumblier than I had nerve to try without dipping into our meager bolt kit. Eight hundred difficult, dead vertical feet lay between me, the first apparent bivvy ledge, and the first snow for water. Having planned for Kichatna Spire, we'd flown in only ten bolts, three small water bottles, and one hammock.

285

PLATE 7

Photos by Jonathan Krakauer

Tom Davies on rotten 80° ice on the 11th lead of the MOOSE'S TOOTH.

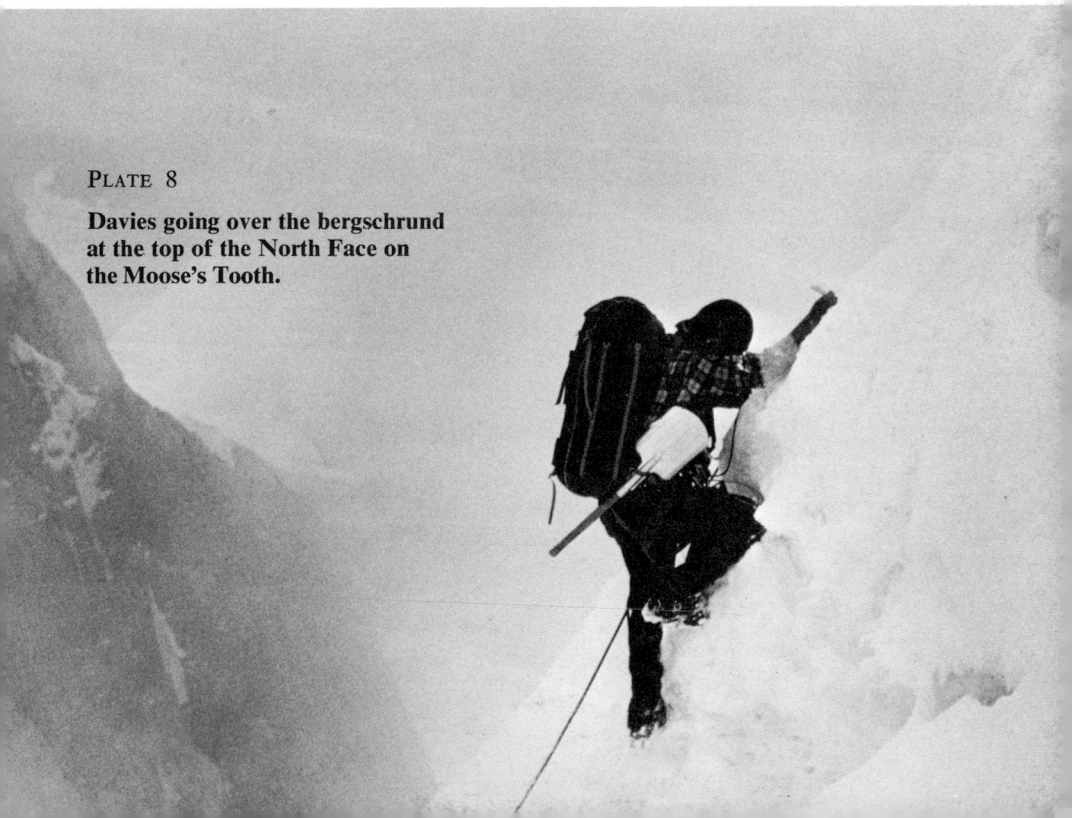

PLATE 8

Davies going over the bergschrund at the top of the North Face on the Moose's Tooth.

No way. I decided not to waste our bolts. ". . . humility to retreat rather than continue in bad style." Right, humility. A nice euphemism, anyhow.

A couple of days later, we did make it to the summit of something: "Mount Cosmic Debris"—an ugly thousand-foot pile of loose rubble and avalanching snow south of the Moose's Tooth, but I'd be a happier soul today never having been on that mountain.

A week was gone and my self-image was not good.

"I'll tell you, Jon-boy, some people are going to laugh pretty long when they hear what happened to our bold, skillfully executed bid on Kichatna Spire, and I don't believe that I'm going to think it's funny at all."

"I think you have a point there."

From the otherwise worthless summit of "Cosmic Debris," though, we had glimpsed an amazing couloir on the south face of the Moose's Tooth. The line caught our eyes immediately: rock at the bottom, then what looked like a hairline of steep, grey ice rising directly to the west ridge, topping out just west of the true summit. A reconnaissance up to the high shelf beneath the couloir reinforced the hope that we'd blundered across a beautiful unclimbed route. On the Moose's Tooth, no less! Nothing to do but give it a go.

On July 11, the last of seven clear and balmy days, we humped a bad load up the easiest-looking icefall on the southwest side of the Tooth. We set up camp on the glacier beneath our couloir after sweating for twelve hard hours over, between, and underneath wild séracs and thin snow bridges. With the glacier's constant groaning and creaking came terrifying thoughts of Jake Breitenbach's end, but our beer- and tobacco-filled histories kept us from moving any faster. From this 7400-foot camp we hoped to make one, go-for-broke, alpine-style attempt.

The next evening we started up the south face under a grey sky. The first lead was a loose dead-end. Tom tried another line, and this one had a future. Three of the first four pitches were rock, thin free climbing that seemed hard in mountain boots and packs, with a bit of aid now and then. Three leads up steep, mashed-potato-like snow followed. This was Alaska—why was it so warm? Even though rock was never far away, anchors were hard to come by in the rotten, frost-riven granite. We used axes and snow flukes in the soft snow. On pitch 8 the couloir turned into a bizarre, two-foot-wide, hollow ice hose. The ninth pitch needed a bolt before I could finish hooking over a very short, but overhanging wall, and that was the furthest up the mountain that crampons were not on our boots.

"Hey, now. A bolt? On an alpine route like that? Doesn't this dude have any yarbles?" I can hear it coming. It was just that a month earlier, on a virgin Yukon wall with Dave Roberts, I had taken a 45-foot nose-dive trying to force the route through a blank section. We had to retreat from seven-eighths of the way up the wall because we didn't have a bolt or two along. Pragmatism has since shaped my alpine mores —in wild mountains the game can be real enough for me without contrived rules.

On pitch 11, rain coming down, we hit the first 90° ice step. Tom took care of it skillfully, front-pointing up the disintegrating ribbon of ice, and eventually aiding on wobbling Warthogs with spectacular cursing. A thick film of water poured over the ice, down Tom's sleeves and into his boots, soaking him. The rain came down harder, but lulled by all those earlier sunny days and reluctant to fold our hand in the face of what was turning out to be a rich pot, we wouldn't believe that we weren't just being bluffed by a passing squall.

By the time I started the twelfth lead the trickle in our couloir was a waterfall. That pitch ended with another 25 feet of rotten 90° ice, and long before I finally aided over the rock at its lip with wooden hands, I, too, was very wet. At a stance out of the water, I yelled down to Nate to come on up. Then something let go. The waterfall doubled in volume. Chunks of ice hummed past from high above. Nate tried to jümar in the torrent but immediately retreated to the belay ledge, drenched from only a few seconds on the ice. Man, who was bluffing whom? A low straight trying to scare four queens up can lose big.

A yell from below: "What are you doing?! Let's get the hell out of here before we get ourselves killed!"

"OK! OK!" I screamed back over the roar, "just clean the pitch and we'll leave!" Nate swung reluctantly back into the water and struggled upwards. A few feet from security, ice-water splashing over his helmet and pouring through his rain gear, he got stuck. In the confusion, Tom had begun jümaring up the same rope, pinning Nate's ascenders under the lip for a few bad minutes.

"WHAT ARE YOU DOING?!!! GET OFF THIS F***ING ROPE! HURRY! PLEEEEASE!!!"

"WHAT? OH! Sorry there, Nate."

"JUST GET *OFF*!!! FAST!!" At this, Tom went quickly down, and Nate shot up to my stance, soaked to the skin, mumbling nonsensical phrases.

We began descending immediately. After ten rappels and some unpleasant down-climbing, exhausted, shivering, and on the verge of hypothermia, we crawled into our tent and wrung out our half-bags.

Sixty hours later, we were still in that stinking, dripping tent, lying in soggy Polarguard amid puddles and filthy dishes, wondering when it was going to stop coming down outside. We inventoried the remains of our food and iron and decided, with some ambivalence, that we had enough of both to give it another shot. All we needed was a two-day break in the storm—time to dry out our bags and clothing and make a light, fast

PLATE 9

Photo by Jonathan Krakauer

Tom Davies halfway up the couloir on the MOOSE'S TOOTH.

push up the 2500 feet to the summit ridge. On the night of the fourteenth it suddenly cleared, but only long enough to fool us into putting our clothes out to dry so they could be buried by a foot of wet snow in the wee hours of the morning.

The break in the storm brought sudden insomnia. I lay with racing thoughts and twitching legs in fear and anticipation of what was to be the morrow's climb. Then the snow came and, at first, I was greatly relieved. Now we couldn't go back up there—I grew euphoric over our good luck. We made a raid on the first-aid kit, and were soon laughing heartily, cheered by a good dose of Percodan and Dalmane. Lovely snow! Let it bury the tent!

The storm continued, snow turning to sleet. I began to think about blowing a chance to put up a good Alaskan route, and how it would feel next fall having washed out to the tune of more than five-hundred dollars. The post-Percodan depression hit and my initial relief became renewed disappointment.

We resolved to ration our food and wait as long as possible for fair weather. Fears of the couloir were intensified by having to sit impotent beneath it for so many wet, wretched hours. Thoughts about the climb were relentless—neither reading nor conversation were successful diversion for long. My morbid imagination got carried away and the waiting got worse. I just wanted to *do* the damn climb, without having to think another thing about it, and then get the hell out to friends, music, and beer.

The sixteenth of July was clear. We dried gear in the sun, packed, and apprehensively started up at eight P.M., with the sky above cloudless, but a faint black line beginning to appear over the southern horizon. Having had the dubious advantage of several days with little to do but ponder each lead we'd done first time around, we flew up the first ten leads, but found pitches 11 and 12, the first vertical ice steps, greatly deteriorated. The ice was now even more hollow and rotten, and it was covered by a crust of rime that oozed water when pierced by an axe or screw. It took more aid this time, but we didn't get as wet, and Nate started up new territory on the 65° to 70° ice of the thirteenth lead.

We were climbing confidently and well. Even though clouds closed in and it began to snow, cutting visibility to a rope-length, we felt well in control. All my fears during the unpleasant wait had dissolved after the first few pitches. I was completely absorbed by the climb. The sense of singular, unwavering purpose, as clear and definite as the straight line of our couloir, was a rare, incredibly good feeling.

Pitches 11 through 15 gave us the hardest climbing on the route. The ice hose here was at times no more than four feet across, frequently at an angle over 65°, and there were four short sections of very rotten 90° ice. Our Jümars no longer held on the frozen ropes, so we broke out the

Gibbs. Pitch 15, the last of the very steep ice, went from 50° to 75° and ended with a twelve-foot vertical stretch that was capped by an over-hanging mushroom of wet, crusty snow. I passed the mushroom, with difficulty, via a bad aid pin in a crumbling flake at its edge. A few feet above I ran out of rope and had to use another bolt for a belay in the blank rock. I didn't trust quickly melting screws in bad ice enough to hang the jümar rope from them.

Nate led around a bend on pitch 16 to find solid, 55°, grey-white ice rising smoothly into the cloud. It stayed that way for six leads. Swing axe, swing hammer. Kick in right front points, step up onto left inside points. Swing, swing. Kick, step. Swing, swing. Kick, step. Now and then stick in something bombproof, occasionally alternate the aching upper foot. It was damn close actually to being fun.

The twenty-first pitch put us abruptly on level snow in a whiteout: the crest of the summit ridge! We sat down happily and brewed some tea, our first rest since leaving camp twenty hours earlier. The mountain seemed in the bag if we could find the top through the pea soup.

"If the clouds would just lift a bit. . . ."

"If we had some ham, we could have ham and eggs, if we had some eggs."

But not ten minutes had passed when the clouds parted and the way to the summit was revealed. For a while we just whooped and yelled at the Ruth Glacier, 5000 feet below. Three hours later, after a cocky false start that had Tom and Nate up on an 80° sérac wall out on the north face, and two short, steep bits over the 'schrund at the juncture of the north face and west ridge, we sat on the corniced summit. We had made the second ascent of the Moose's Tooth.

The descent was no fun. The storm was again on us when we got back to the top of the couloir. We unwisely decided not to bivouac, even though we had been climbing for twenty-four straight hours, and contin-ued down into the cloud. It was hard enough just keeping our eyes open between rappels; little things like placing anchors, tying frozen webbing, and remembering which rope to pull down took real effort. By midnight, Tom and Nate, both bespectacled, were having trouble seeing. Wet snow came down heavily. We began hallucinating: spotlights flashed across the mountain, yells and car horns came from above and below. Nate took a Dexedrine to stay awake, enhancing his hallucinations but not doing much for his judgment. On the eleventh or twelfth rappel, the stiff, frozen ropes refused to come down. I whimpered. They stayed hung-up. More whimpering. Finally I had to go up and free them.

By the fifteenth rappel we were all nodding off frequently. I came down the nineteenth rappel to find Tom sound asleep, bent over a sling he was trying to untie for the next anchor. Finally, at five A.M., thirty-three hours after starting up the couloir, we fell into our beautiful, sagging tent and passed out. We had actually climbed the Moose's Tooth, and put up a fine 2800-foot route in the process. Lord love a duck—we could go home now.

Summary of Statistics.

AREA: Alaska Range.

ASCENTS: The Moose's Tooth, 10,335 feet, second ascent via a new route, the south face, July 16 to 18, 1975 (Jonathan Krakauer, Thomas Davies, Nate Zinsser).

P 7200+ (1½ miles south of the Moose's Tooth and ½ mile east of P 6720; "Cosmic Debris"), first ascent, July 8 and 9, 1975 (whole party).

PLATE 10

Photo by Brian Okonek

**The summit ridge of DEBORAH.
The basal cornices are the prominent
ice pinnacles in the saddle.**

Deborah

BRIAN OKONEK, *Mountaineering Club of Alaska*

W HEN Fred Beckey, Heinrich Harrer, and Henry Meybohm stepped onto the summit of Deborah twenty-one years ago for a first ascent, they came to the "unanimous conclusion that Deborah was the most sensational ice climb anyone of us had ever undertaken." (See *A.A.J.*, 1955, 9:2, pp. 39-50.) The beautiful, awe inspiring, pyramidal mass of Deborah (12,339-feet) located in the Hayes Group of the Alaska Range has since then repulsed many expeditions on her numerous flanks due to bad weather and technical difficulties. Such were the thoughts of our all-Alaskan party, consisting of Pat Condran, Mark Hottman, Dave Pettigrew, Pat Stuart, Toby Wheeler, and myself, as we walked to the preeminent Mount Deborah.

It was on April 2 that we said good-bye to friends and stepped off the Anchorage-Fairbanks Highway at mile 229 to begin our 60-mile slog up the Yanert Fork to Base Camp. Each of us was well loaded down with gear, both on our backs and tagging behind in plastic sleds, but the vast majority of our equipment was hauled by Dennis Kogl and Ford Reeve with their dog teams. With the invaluable help of these two hard-core dog mushers we were able to establish Base Camp without airdrops. Four long days up the braided channels of the Yanert River, now frozen, brought us to the Yanert Glacier. We skirted the lower moraines on the north side in a couple of days, then found ourselves grounded by a three-day storm twelve miles short of intended Base Camp. Was this a hint of the days to come? Late on the twelfth we finally arrived at 6400 feet on the Yanert Glacier, site of Base Camp. With the mushers and dogs gone, we stood alone with Deborah bathed in the pink of a setting sun; the climb had begun!

Our route would be one Pettigrew and Stuart had attempted the year before, but due to the loss of vital equipment in a storm the climb had to be aborted at 11,700 feet. We'd go up the west buttress of the south summit (11,700 feet), then along the crest of the south ridge via the middle summit (12,000 feet) to the 12,339-foot mushroomed top of the north summit. At the saddle between the middle and north summits we would intersect Beckey's route. The route would be long, but not littered with objective dangers.

We spent the next six days under the grip of wind and snow storms trying to force the route to the site of Camp I at 8500 feet.

295

"Little windy ain't it!"

"Damn fixed rope is a mess."

"Hang on, another slough avalanche is coming!"

"Hey Pettigrew, your pack just blew off the cornice!"

"What the hell! Can you see it?"

"Not since it fell off that big cliff."

"Man, the first couple of years out of prep school are always the toughest."

"I give up, the fluke won't stay in."

"Up, up, always up!"

To safeguard load hauling, we used 200 feet of fixed rope up through a cornice; and another 600 feet up an exposed snow-filled gully system and 200-foot ice bulge, the best climbing so far. For several days 8000 feet was as high as we could get as bad weather kept pushing us back to camp. Finally as the snow got deeper, the wind stronger, and the slough avalanches more frequent, we were forced to spend two days in camp. As we lay around the depressing interiors of the storm-bound tents, periodically going out to shovel away the accumulating snow, we began to kid each other on how this was turning out to be "the most sensational snow slog anyone of us had ever undertaken." Finally the skies cleared and we swam and jümared our way up the slope to Camp I.

For four days the weather remained perfect (this was the longest stretch of good weather we had on the trip) and we began to gain altitude a little faster. The snow remained deep though, in one place taking two hours to break 300 feet of trail through armpit-deep, wind-crusted snow.

"This is absurd!"

"Want a shovel?"

"Wheeze, gasp; made it another step."

"Up, up, always up!"

At least we didn't have to rebreak trail this time. A total of 1300 feet of fixed rope was placed on questionable avalanche slopes before reaching a small, well-protected bowl at 10,200 feet where we placed Camp II.

And still the weather remained tranquil. Stepping out of the bowl put us onto the narrowing, wind-exposed ridge that would take us to the "blow hole" (the south summit so named because Deborah appears as the silhouette of a whale from the west, the north summit being its tail and the middle summit its hump) and eventually to the top of Deborah. Luckily, the exhausting powder turned to hard, wind-packed snow on the ridge. In one day, with this much-improved condition, Dave and Toby were able to fix and mark the route all the way to the middle summit where we were going to establish our High Camp. That evening they were in a state of simple elation as they told us of the incredibly corniced summit ridge. We couldn't wait to give it a go!

The ridge walk between the blow hole and middle summit was absolutely fantastic, offering grand views in all directions. Although it is relatively level for a full mile, it has spectacular drops off either side. Where it wasn't corniced we could look straight down through rime-heavy flutings, curled in upon each other, to the crevassed surface of the West Fork Glacier on Deborah's east side 5000 feet below! When I peeked over the middle summit and saw the full sweep of the summit ridge, fantastic wind sculptures of wild-looking cornices met my eyes. It was indeed incredible! Unreal!

We had cached a few loads at the middle summit and the blow hole and were ready to move to Camp III on the twenty-fifth, but instead we were once again storm-bound; this time for three days.

On the twenty-eighth we broke camp and began our move to Camp III in what appeared to be stable weather, but was actually only a lull in the eye of a hurricane. Although wind, clouds, and snow began their attack upon the ridge well before we arrived at our destination, we pushed on. Digging in was first on the agenda when we reached the middle summit. That night three slept in an unfinished cave and three tried to sleep in a wind-battered tent. The following night we were all in the cave, headquarters for the next eleven days. We had been eating half rations every storm day to stretch our food supply, and were once again on half rats. To say the least it was getting old! The monotony of cave life was broken by tall tales, chopping of convex drip demons off the ceiling, the do's and don'ts of the next expy, and herculean struggles to the outside world through a snow-clogged entrance.

Our first impression upon seeing the summit-ridge basal cornices was "incredible"; the second "they'll be slow." It would be necessary to fix the route across them to hasten our try for the summit when the day came. So when it cleared a bit on May 1, Hottman and Stuart took off to do some spectacular ice work. Our intuition proved correct when they labored for the day to fix 300 feet. After falling through the cornices' unstable crest several times, they turned to the painfully slow traversing of 65° ice along the fracture line. Seeing Pat and Mark only as two tiny specks on the huge curled pinnacles made us appreciate the cornices' tremendous size. Another 300-foot section of fixed rope would be needed to complete our hand rail along the basal cornices. When the clouds dissipated the next day Toby and I were off for our stint on the ridge. We found the same slow going as we worked our way across the exposed cornices on ice that was none too perfect: brittle or honeycombed ice prevailed. Poor protection and scratchy were names of the game. In places tube pickets replaced alpine hammers. The airy belays atop protruding cornices were darn near as exhilarating as the climbing. Under the glow of a setting sun we stepped past these huge pinnacles of ice and snow to the somewhat easier ridge beyond. Even though the cornices remained

PLATE 11

Photo by Brian Okonek

**Wheeler on the basal cornices of
DEBORAH. The summit is 1000 feet
higher and a half mile away.**

PLATE 12

Photo by Brian Okonek

The corniced South Ridge of DEBORAH. The East Face drops 5000 feet to the West Fork Glacier on the left.

overhanging, from here we would be able to walk their crest. Perhaps tomorrow would be summit day.

Early the next morning Pettigrew and Condran emerged from the cave, found favorable weather, and began their pilgrimage to the summit. The rest of us were to follow in an hour, but before we got underway Deborah was swallowed by the fury of yet another storm. Disgruntled we crawled back into the cave; we knew Dave and Pat would be back soon. Ten-and-one-half hours later they dragged their tired, snow en-crusted bodies into the cave after being all but lost in the blizzard between the basal cornices and camp! So much for that summit day.

Four days later the weather began to break. Once again we prepared for the summit push. Somehow we knew this was it, it had to be for our food supply was dwindling fast. On the eighth at 2:30 A.M. Pettigrew and Condran were heading for the summit. Watching their progress we judged the amount of time it would require to follow in their steps com-plete with belay points, and left accordingly so as not to get congested on the ridge; Hottman and Stuart at five A.M. and Wheeler and I at 9:30 A.M. The airy, corniced ridge was a little nerve racking at first, but as the hours clicked by and we became oblivious to the impressive over-hangs it was just a little weird. Several ice pinnacles that had appeared troublesome were easily surmounted by the lead pair and we followed quickly in their chopped staircase. Three pitches below the summit Toby and I caught up with the others. Stuart and Hottman were taking over the lead after an heroic ten hours of leading by Pettigrew and Condran. The ridge was blocked by mushroomed cornices that overhung in all direc-tions; Stuart headed out onto the relentless ice of the southwest face to find the secret to the top. Stuart was a pitch below the summit working out a route through the summit mushroom, Hottman was buried in a belay hole, and the rest of us were perched atop a cornice surveying the view, when Cliff Hudson, a bush pilot from Talkeetna, floated by in his Cessna 185 and tipped his wings to us. We waved back thinking how demoraliz-ing it must be for Cliff's passengers if they were being dropped off for an attempt on Deborah. After a couple of dead-end leads Pat finally found a route through the "medieval gargoyles" that guarded the summit.

At 4:40 P.M. on May 8 we all stood on the summit of Deborah after thirty-six days of patient determination on the slopes of one of Alaska's more reputable mountains. Man what a "high," but the feeling came slow-ly as we still had the descent ahead of us. We gazed at our spectacular surroundings, Mounts Hess, Hayes, Moffit: ugh—they were disappear-ing in the clouds of an approaching front. We could see summer taking over the whiteness of winter in the low lands, it was time to head back. Before we descended, a section of the summit cornice with our tracks on it fell off the 6000-foot north face as if the "mountain gods" objected to our treading on them! As we climbed and rappelled down the ridge, clouds moved in upon us obscuring all views. At 11:30 P.M. we reached camp just as the full force of storm number six hit. We had just squeezed in a summit day! Victory was celebrated with a satisfying double-ration supper.

This final storm lasted only twenty-four hours, but was the most violent. It began to erode away our snow cave threatening to expose us to the wild world outside. Deborah wasn't giving up easily!

The storm over, we descended in one long day to the warmth of Base Camp. It was hardly the same place, considerable melting had changed things in our absence. We spent the following day drying gear, reorganizing loads, and drawing cards for team-bought equipment that was divided into six equal-cost piles; what we won we could carry out. Late that afternoon we began our seven-day walk to the road on perfect snow conditions. But as we approached the end of the glacier the snow became rotten and fell out from beneath us until we were showshoeing and dragging sleds across rocks and tundra. "What do you expect in the middle of spring break-up?" We were in such a good mood that it didn't get anyone down. It felt so great to walk around uninhibited by a rope. Summer got closer around each bend of the Yanert River. On a small landing strip 28 miles from the road we cached all but the most necessary of our gear, after finding 100-plus-pound packs a little too heavy for fun. We'd have the stuff picked up later. With this load off our backs we had a most enjoyable trek out. As Deborah disappeared from sight behind us, the trip became a memory, one that will always remain vivid. It had been a spectacular climb!

Summary of Statistics.

AREA: Hayes Group, Alaska Range.

NEW ROUTE: Second ascent of Mount Deborah, 12,339 feet, via the west buttress of the south summit and south ridge and southwest face to the north summit, May 8, 1975.

TECHNICAL DATA: 3000 feet of fixed rope, 18 pickets, 21 ice screws, 23 snow flukes.

PERSONNEL: Pat Condran, Mark Hottman, Brian Okonek, Dave Pettigrew, Pat Stuart, Toby Wheeler.

PLATE 13

Photo by Michael Graber

The Southeast Face of Tatina Spire from the Tatina Glacier, Cathedral Spires.

Ascents in the Cathedral Spires

MICHAEL GRABER, *Buff Climbing Club*

ON June 26, Cliff Hudson flew Hooman Aprin, David Black and me from Camp Creek to the Tatina Glacier in the Kichatna Mountains. We were surprised and slightly disappointed to find a party of Alaskan climbers carrying loads to the base of the same wall that we had anticipated climbing. But eventually we appreciated their company, especially during the long, dreary days when the peaks dissolved into a patchwork of rain and gray clouds and the cold and lifeless cirques rang with the uproarious laughter from our wild, 8-man tea parties. We soon realized that a new friendship can be far more important than climbing.

The next day, under a resplendent Alaskan sky, we began climbing on the southeast face of "Tatina Spire" (P 8200+, 1½ miles northwest of the Monolith Col). We were prepared to make three bivouacs on the 2500-foot face, but after two days of climbing, including 400 feet of difficult aid, we were only 700 feet up. During the second night, a storm struck, blasting us with sleet. We were soon drenched but fortunately we stayed warm in our Polarguard parkas. In the morning it was snowing; we decided to attempt going down. The ropes were badly iced, the rock plastered, but by tying two ropes together, we reached a ledge. We left these ropes fixed over the most difficult aid sections and rappelled the lower, easier pitches with the haul rope. Once on the glacier, we groped our way back to our tent in a downpour.

It rained and snowed for the next three days. On July 3, the sky cleared partially, but a fierce gale swept the glacier. The tent frustration was too much; we had to climb. In wet boots, Dave and I reluctantly set out to climb the south ridge on P 7133. The climbing difficulties had appeared modest from the tent but below the ridge we apprehensively struggled through desperate snow while small avalanches hissed insouciantly past. The ridge, although narrow and exposed, was easier, and when the clouds lifted we were blessed with a spectacular view of the Tatina and Cool Sac Glaciers. The schizophrenic weather held long enough for us to quickly descend from the summit and as we returned to the security of the tent, it began pouring again.

On July 5, warm sunshine slowly filtered through the fog to brighten our spirits and dry our clothes. We timidly returned to Tatina Spire prepared for three days of climbing. The bottom pitches were hurriedly re-led and soon we jümared to our previous high point, "Tempest Ledge." Above the ledge, the climbing was mostly free in cracks and squeeze chimneys. Dave led the crux; an unprotected F9 off-width crack. To take advantage of the clear weather, we climbed through the night, sleeping for a few hours on top of the 13th pitch, the "Tatina-Ahwanne." Early the next morning, Hooman led a diagonal traverse to a gash which we followed for five pitches to the summit ridge. A thousand more feet of 5th-class climbing on the exposed ridge brought us to the summit. We ate the rest of our food and watched the sun melt into a distant storm front before we faced the ugly reality of finding a way back down. It took us all night and 11 rappels to descend the northwest face to a hanging glacier. Two additional rappels were needed to descend an icefall. We returned to our tent after 30 hours of continuous climbing. Inside the tent we collapsed into a narcotic sleep.

Warm sunshine and a rich, blue sky characterized the following days. Again the specious weather lured us onto the walls. After reconnoitering from the Monolith Glacier, we unanimously agreed on the west face of Sasquatch (South Triple Peak), a mixture of a steep, rock face and a long, snow and rock ridge which ended at the summit. The directness of this line brought to mind the name, "Comici Route." In the afternoon of July 10, we climbed a thin crack and then through a series of overhangs. We fixed the first 350 feet and returned to the glacier to sleep. The next morning was cool but clear and we started up the wall. The rock was superlative granite and in the warm sunlight we jokingly imagined being at Tahquitz in mountain boots and supergators. We climbed 900 feet that day, most of which was difficult free climbing, to the base of a chimney which was copiously dripping water. We decided to leave this pitch for the morning. A few hours later, a storm moved in and we remained in our bivouac sacks for 34 hours while the storm raged. The morning of the 13th gave counterfeit promises of clearing. We had climbed one pitch when a wave of clouds broke over the mountain and poured down the wall, inundating us in fog and drizzle. Climbing in parkas and cagoules, we continued up steep aid cracks.

The miserable weather didn't let up. During the night I had dreams about dry towels, after which I would wake, shivering and feeling wetter than before. Our water-soaked and wrinkled hands were abraded and numb. We were running extremely low on food. When would the wall end and the ridge begin? Dave racked the hardware and slowly led into the gloom while Hooman and I shivered continuously. Finally the angle relaxed and after 17 pitches we were off the face and on the ridge. Wearing crampons, I began leading the ridge—a nightmare of rock towers and wet slush overlying 50° water ice. Climbing in the cadaverous mist was a lonely and depressing task. The ridge narrowed and Hooman led a wet,

PLATE 16

Photo by Michael Graber

David Black celebrates on the summit of Sasquatch while snow gently falls.

F9 crack. Suddenly the gray monotone gave way to blue sky. The temperature however, dropped and with the summit in sight, our ropes (including a "waterproof" rope) became hopelessly frozen and we were forced to bivouac; our third in four days.

In the morning, high clouds filled the sky and it was snowing lightly. We drank the last of our food, an "instant breakfast" apiece, and untwisted the stiff ropes. I led through a cornice to a ledge. When Hooman reached the ledge, he decided that he wasn't climbing any higher; the summit had become "meaningless." Dave and I climbed the remaining 600 feet while Hooman waited on the ledge for us to return.

Standing on the summit wasn't much fun knowing we now faced a 3400-foot descent. The first rappel hung up on a flake and Dave magnanimously climbed up to free it. When we returned to Hooman, we began rappelling into a couloir to the south, to where we thought we would find the lower portion of the Robbins' route. The clouds returned and we were soon lost in the fog. After something like 12 rappels, the wall became vertical, the ledges disappeared and the rain turned to wet snow. We dropped from hanging rappel to hanging rappel. We were rapidly losing strength and the ability to think beyond rote behavior. Hooman rappelled leaving his pack hanging on the anchors. He was too apathetic to even unclip the pack and throw it down. More rappels. We had made about 20 already. Where was the glacier? Somewhere to our right an avalanche was pouring down the face. I began seriously wondering if we were going to live and then, meandering up through the mist came Dave's exhausted voice—he was on the glacier.

Summary of Statistics.

AREA: Cathedral Spires, Kichatna Mountains, Alaska.

ASCENTS: P 7133, first ascent via south ridge, July 3, 1975, NCCS III, F6 (Black, Graber).

P 8200+ ("Tatina Spire"), first ascent via southeast face; summit reached July 6, 1975; NCCS VI, F9, A4 (Aprin, Black, Graber).

Sasquatch (South Triple Peak), second ascent, first ascent of west face (Comici Route); summit reached July 15, 1975, NCCS VI, F9, A3 (Aprin, Black, Graber).

PERSONNEL: Hooman Aprin, David Black, Michael Graber.

Fairweather's South-Southwest Ridge

STEVEN GASKILL, *Colorado Mountain Club*

STARTING on June 28 Keith Echelmeyer, Steve Ruhl, Mike Ruckhaus, Mike Berman, Darrell Brown, Chip Mehring and I were flown from Juneau to Cape Fairweather. The next few days saw us begin a discouraging reconnaissance to find a route from the beach onto the Fairweather Glacier. Three days of devil's club, alders, mosquitoes and rain finally yielded a route. The approach up the glacier, 15 miles by eagle and a million or so by foot, took another five days. Base Camp was established at 4700 feet on a small rock outcrop directly above the upper icefall on the south side of the glacier across from Mount Fairweather.

Brief reconnaissance by three of us on the unclimbed south-southwest ridge and by the other four on the south ridge, the first-ascent route, was thwarted by storm. On July 14 Echelmeyer, Ruhl and I reached the cache by eight A.M. and with heavier loads continued up the south-southwest ridge, having already come up the initial snow slopes and scrambled up a loose section of ridge 1800 feet from our Base Camp. The ridge, now a broad snowfield, quickly steepened as we picked our way through a series of ice steps and crossed several gaping crevasses on shaky bridges. The ridge then turned toward the north, becoming a razor-back of mixed rotten rock and loose corn snow. By two o'clock we had reached the first real high point of the ridge at 8500 feet: the same level as the clouds. The next eight hours were spent in the rain and fog as the ridge dropped several hundred feet and seesawed for the next mile. This entire section was quite difficult.

The next morning about ten A.M. the clouds lifted a bit and we could see the next 1000 feet of our route. More mixed rock and snow eventually led to a thin, steep, knife-edged snow ridge. After lunch on the last rock outcrop, we postholed our way up to harder snow, eventually reaching the first ice slopes at 10,000 feet. We pitched another late camp, this time under an ice cliff to protect us from possible avalanches. The third day took us over a straightforward route as we proceeded up the now broad ice slopes, past a steep nose to the West Saddle at 13,000 feet, where we established Camp III.

On July 17 we were off at eight. Though the wind was blowing hard, the weather was fairly good with a cloud cap over the peak and a few scattered clouds below. The snow on the lower part was deep, loose and tiring, but the last 1000 feet to the top were generally ice covered by knobby hoar frost.

On July 18 Ruckhaus, Berman, Brown and Mehring started up the south ridge. Their first day took them past the icefall, across a steep, soft snowfield and up an extremely steep snow couloir to their cache. They ascended another snowfield and couloir and had several hundred feet of rock scrambling to gain the ridge proper. They ascended the long, occasionally broken and steep snow and ice ramp which led to their only high camp at 9800 feet.

After a day of fog and light snow, on July 20 they set off just after midnight and moved up the ice slopes with an occasional belay. At 13,800 feet they had a chance to survey the top portion of their route. What had appeared to be a small bump on the ridge from down below turned out to be the most difficult portion of the climb. The ridge proper was extremely steep green ice. They had to skirt the ridge on the east side, which still involved several leads of 70° ice.

On July 22 I soloed the northwest ridge of "Sabine," the 10,400-foot peak six miles due south of Fairweather. (It had been climbed by Walter Romanes and Fips Broda by its north ridge in 1958. The western summit had been reached by Japanese in 1969. See *A.A.J.*, 1959, pages 297-8, and 1970, pages 115-6.—*Editor.*) From Base Camp I easily climbed to the ridge and followed good snow, though steep at times, up the first 2800 feet to an altitude of 7500 feet. Here I came to the first crevassed section. Rocks on the right and an end-run around crevasses on the left took me up this part to 8000 feet, where the ridge leveled for a long section of rolling knife-edge with occasional wide areas. Near the end of this I was directly under the summit icecap: a section of steep snow and ice crossed by intermittent ice cliffs. I followed the steepening knife-edge for 200 feet onto the face proper. Two hundred more feet of easy front-pointing brought me under the first ice cliff, which had a break to the left: a steep gully. Just as I started up the gully, a section of the ice cliff broke loose, setting off an impressive avalanche down the north face. My tracks of the previous ten minutes had been entirely wiped out! The ice of the gully steepened to where I was in danger of falling. I belayed myself for the next 250 feet with an ice screw and two snow flukes until the angle lessened. I traversed left to the only break in the cornice. Twenty feet of very steep snow, overhanging the 3000-foot north face, led to easy slopes. A quick walk led to the summit bathed in the afternoon sun. In the softer snow during the descent I dropped through a hole into a crevasse. Luckily it was very shallow and I was able to walk along the bottom for 50 yards and climbed out of a low spot where the crevasse had opened. I returned to Base Camp with the last rays of the sun.

(*Editor's Note:* There have been five different routes done on the south

PLATE 17

Photo by Steven Gaskill

**At 13,500 feet on FAIRWEATHER'S
South-Southwest Ridge. The route
ascends the rock ridge in the middle
upper portion, first from right to left
and then straight up.**

PLATE 18

Photo by Bradford Washburn

Looking south from above Mount Fairweather. In the back rise Bertha, Crillon, LaPerouse. In the center is Lituya. "Sabine" is at the right.

side of Fairweather. From west to east these are the southwest ridge, 1973; south-southwest ridge, 1975; south ridge, 1931 and 1975; eastern south ridge, 1958 (The Canadians started up the first-ascent ridge but traversed east at 7000 feet to the ridge descended by Wickwire's party in 1973.); ascent over Mount Quincy Adams, 1973.)

Summary of Statistics.

AREA: Fairweather Range, Southeastern Alaska.

ASCENTS: Mount Fairweather, 15,320 feet, first ascent of the South-Southwestern Ridge, July 17, 1975 (Echelmeyer, Gaskill, Ruhl); ascent via South Ridge, July 20, 1975 (Berman, Brown, Mehring, Ruckhaus).

P 10,400 ("Mount Sabine"), second ascent via new route, the Northwest Ridge, July 22, 1975 (Gaskill, solo).

PERSONNEL: Michael Berman, Darrell Brown, Keith Echelmeyer, Steven Gaskill, Chip Mehring, Steven Ruhl, Michael Ruckhaus.

A McKinley Traverse via Reality Ridge

PETER METCALF

V ISIONS of spectacular mountain spires, steep clean ice, Yosemite-like granite and new routes in an alpine setting filled my mind as I started planning another Alaskan expedition. The south side of McKinley with its incredible array of jagged peaks seemed like a likely place to look for this ideal climb. A visit with Brad Washburn at the Boston Museum of Science and a search through his photo files helped pinpoint good possibilities. As the winter wore on, my temporary inability to climb due to a knee operation somehow made me more confident and summer plans grew ambitious. Even memories of past expeditions did nothing to shake these pleasant fantasies.

After countless flat tires on the Alcan, Henry Florschutz, Angus Thuermer and I arrived at the Anchorage Airport on June 16 just in time to pick up our fourth expedition member, Lincoln Stoller, who like Henry and me, was a veteran of our 1973 Fairweather climb. (See *A.A.J.*, 1974, pages 19-22.) Two hours' drive north of Anchorage took us to the Alaskan frontier town of Talkeetna where we met our bush pilot, Cliff Hudson. He was confident of finding a landing place for us on the West Fork of the Ruth Glacier.

After two days of anticipation, packing and waiting, the weather cleared enough on June 18 for us to be flown in. Cliff Hudson took Henry and Lincoln first, returning within an hour and a half for Angus and me. We should quickly get our gear aboard, he shouted, since clouds were already moving back in on the Ruth.

Barely off the ground, Cliff asked me to pay up the whole round-trip bill for the group in advance. Cliff assured me that my traveler's checks were okay if I would endorse them while we were flying in. Apparently Cliff Hudson had just gotten his first view of what we had in mind to climb and had decided it would be prudent to collect now. I spent the next 15 minutes awkwardly signing some 30 or more traveler's checks on my lap.

When the plane turned the corner of the West Fork, a queasy feeling hit my stomach. Steep walls and fluted ridges rose up at unbelievable angles in numerous thousand-foot sweeps. All were plastered by huge hanging glaciers, menacing cornices and weird snow formations. I was mentally and physically overwhelmed by what I saw. It was hard to find

PLATE 19

Photo by Bradford Washburn

MOUNT McKINLEY. **The South Fork
of the Southeast Spur.**

courage and strength when confronting such an awesome adversary for the first time. Flying in, unlike a slow overland approach, allowed us no time to adjust to the massive scale of the new environment. My fantasies were suddenly dispelled by the stark reality of the frozen landscape.

It wasn't long, however, before we were reconnoitering to determine which ridge we should attempt. Our intention was to do a traverse, climbing semi-alpine style, i.e., fixing and cleaning the climb in sections so we could use our limited supply of rope and hardware several times over. After a rather spirited debate, we chose the unclimbed western leg of the Southeast Spur as our initial objective. This leg rises out of the West Fork of the Ruth Glacier directly across from the west ridge of Mount Huntington at an altitude of 7500 feet and climbs to 13,100 feet before joining the Southeast Spur.

Two days of easy ferrying across the Ruth brought us to our Base Camp site which was set up at an elevation of 7900 feet at the foot of the western leg. The first stage of the attack was to climb and fix ropes where needed up to the ridge crest at 10,370 feet. During the 20 difficult days that followed before we finally reached the Southeast Spur, this became our "Reality Ridge."

We got off to a rather demoralizing start on June 21. With the temperature above freezing, snow conditions on the initial slopes were so rotten that in over two hours barely one pitch was climbed with Henry breaking through to his neck at times. The snow had no consistency, but rather was made up of what seemed like millions of small marbles stacked upon each other. We decided then that climbing at night in colder temperature with our small Sherpa snowshoes would make for faster going. (We had not worn snowshoes the first day due to the steepness of the face and the interspersed rock and ice.) The next three evenings were a repetition of each other. We would awaken each night about nine P.M. only to glance out at a dreary whiteness and the continued falling of heavy wet snow that made climbing impossible.

On the evening of June 24, we rejoiced in the first clear skies of the expedition. Two of us led, fixing ropes, while the other two followed with loads. The climbing on this initial section consisted of steep snow mixed with varying amounts of easy rock and a few little gullies of ice. June 27, moving time, turned out to be the finest evening thus far. The air was crisp, cold, calm and clear, making the climbing in the twilight of the Alaskan night almost magical. At about 9600 feet I turned around to see the moon rising above Mount Huntington while the first orange rays of morning began striking its upper half. At the same time, I could watch the last subdued pastel colors of sunset disappear off the west side of Mount Hunter. This scene alone would have made the climb worthwhile, but it was only a preview of greater glories to come.

The next few days were spent at Camp I, which was set up on a scenic flat spot at the beginning of the ridge crest proper. The last of our supplies were ferried up from a cache a thousand feet below. On June 29 in unusually warm and stormy-looking weather we started to fix the pitches above, which consisted of traversing the ridge over a small hump. In horrendous snow conditions I took nearly four hours to lead two pitches of steep snow interspersed with ice but finally had to call it quits in what had become a full scale blizzard. Fifteen minutes later we were snugly curled up in our two bomb shelters.

By the next evening the storm had blown itself out. Henry led past our previous high point, over the small hump, and back down to a spooky little col that was meringued by large cornices and snow sculptures but offered a good spot for the tents. For the first time we were in an excellent position to view the next thousand vertical feet of the ridge, which was steep and beautifully corniced most of the way with many sections having extreme knife edges. A tight notch appeared at 10,800 feet whose back side consisted of a rock wall capped by steep ice that leveled out to a small col at 11,150 feet.

The first bit of climbing out of our "meringue" camp involved traversing on steep ice beneath some menacing cornices and then up onto the ridge crest, which was so narrow that we could straddle it and look down on both sides some 2000 feet to the glacier below. Memories of photos I had seen of the Southeast Ridge of Dhaulagiri came to mind. While Henry and Angus pulled the old anchors and ropes, Linc and I led on, having to cut through a cornice and drop down to the other side of the ridge when our side suddenly slid off into a void. A little further and we were back onto the 45° to 50° face of the ridge's east side. It was straightforward climbing and traversing on ice overlaid with about a foot of snow. Placing anchors here for the ropes was a tedious job of digging away the snow and trying to get a screw into the often brittle and rotten ice that lay beneath. The last part before the notch was easy rock, but rotten snow lay over it.

On the evening of July 3 under an incredibly clear and cold sky, Linc and I packed camp, ascended the ropes and reached the notch after a frustrating battle with substanceless snow. Our personal gear was dumped into a bivy bag that we suspended from a couple of good nuts so we could pack up the rope and hardware. A rope was then fixed on which Linc rappelled out of the notch by way of an ice gully. While I had visions of freezing to death in this exposed notch, Linc tensioned around to a rock face and competently self-belayed himself diagonally upward, chopping ice from holds as he went. I followed on Jümars, realizing immediately that the pitch would be too difficult to follow in its present form with a pack. I clipped my Jümars onto the haul line and cleaned the pitch by means of a pendulum, making for some exciting rock climbing on this ridge of McKinley.

I then took over the lead and headed up an ever-steepening 300-foot snow runnel that after the first 30 feet turned out to be hard ice overlaid with two inches of snow. It finished with 75° ice before I topped out on the ridge crest. A short descent put us in a beautiful but exposed little col which sank about six inches when we reached it (elevation 11,100 feet). Due to the col's exposure and the ominous looking weather that seemed to be approaching, we decided that a snow cave was in order. It was the only night we spent in a cave. During the whole time we were on McKinley, we never had weather that was violent enough to collapse our tents. But that evening we celebrated the 4th of July in our snow cave with an instant cheesecake, which seemed then like the ultimate creation of American technology.

The climbing up to Camp IV though spectacular and airy was not too difficult, consisting mainly of diagonaling just below the cornices on the ridge crest. The camp was established under continuing fine weather in a depression amidst large séracs and crevasses atop a hanging glacier at 12,190 feet. This unbelievable glacier completely overhung the east side of the ridge, but we deemed that its size made it safe.

The last thousand feet of the ridge was decorated by the most beautiful and awesome-looking ice-flutings and cornices that I had ever seen. Fortunately, the west side consisted of nothing more than moderate ice overlaid with varying amounts of snow. Linc led one rather short but difficult pitch that consisted of 85° climbing on honeycombed ice constructed of large air pockets intermingled with hard ice. Though it was impossible to get an ice-axe shaft fully in and the pick failed to provide anything substantial, the wall was overcome with good balance and chopping. At 12,800 feet our ridge blended into the southern side of the Southeast Spur and it was no longer necessary to fix ropes.

Late in the evening of July 9, we packed up loads for a new cache on the Southeast Spur. An hour or so after leaving our fixed ropes, we joyously stepped onto the 13,100-foot summit of the west leg and our Reality Ridge was completed. The weather was perfect and in the orange light of daybreak the views that stretched out below us were like a fantasy come true. Starting from the north we saw McKinley's East Buttress, then the steep north face of Mount Dan Beard, the rock spires of the Moose's Tooth, the granite faces of the Ruth Gorge, jagged Huntington, the mass of Hunter, and then the impressive summit of McKinley itself. A 360° splendor! Surely this is one of the most impressive and beautiful mountain vistas to be seen anywhere in the world.

A day later ropes and hardware were cleaned and dumped as we left the Reality Ridge for good. Our fine weather lasted long enough for us to make one ferry from the Southeast Spur up to the South Buttress and back, carrying all our remaining food. It was incredibly warm and calm. Wearing just a T-shirt at 15,000 feet on McKinley is hard to believe!

PLATE 20

The South Fork of the Southeast Spur
of MOUNT McKINLEY

We were amazed to see huge waterfalls cascading down several thousand feet to the Ruth Glacier from the Thayer Basin. Unfortunately, the weather broke the next night and it was three frustrating, hungry days before we could climb back to our now buried food cache.

From the South Buttress we traversed into the Thayer Basin and then onto the Thayer Ridge at 15,720 feet which we followed to an elevation of 18,100 feet. From there we moved along the north side of the summit cone traversing the upper Harper Glacier to Denali Pass and then dropping down to the 17,200-foot High Camp of the West Buttress where we met other climbers for the first time in 38 days. It was from here that the summit was reached on July 24 by Angus Thuermer, thereby completing all expedition business. We were really surprised by the hordes of people we passed during the one day it took us to descend the West Buttress on our way to the Kahiltna Glacier airstrip. It was a contrast to the solitude of the south side.

Forty-two days after being flown in we found ourselves back again in Talkeetna with its flowing water, lush green grass, warm earth, delicious food and beautiful people from Oregon. It was like a rejuvenating and hallucinatory drug on my weary body as I experienced the highest high I had ever felt, being truly high on life itself. We set ourselves adrift in time, as memories of a fine new route and a circular traverse of McKinley lingered on.

Summary of Statistics.

ASCENT: Mount McKinley, 20,320 feet, by a new route via the western leg of the Southeast Spur of the South Buttress, over the Buttress, Thayer Basin and Thayer Ridge to Denali Pass and thence to the summit, reached on July 24 by Thuermer.

PERSONNEL: Henry Florschutz, Peter Metcalf, Lincoln Stoller, Angus Thuermer.

Logan Mountains

ANDREW EMBICK

SNOWFLAKES drifted slowly up-
ward, shimmeringly evanescent in the sun. Lines of clouds, some dark
and ominous, had marched toward us all day, but many had turned away
before enveloping us, and the occasional dustings of snow we received
were soon melted. The horizon became more and more distant as we
gained height in the great corner, and more of the myriad of peaks surrounding us became visible. A golden eagle passed silently by us in mist
and sunbeams. The threatening weather and an unknown descent route
added urgency to our efforts but on belays eyes and thoughts turned to
the rough, clean granite studded with feldspar crystals; to the scores of
unclimbed peaks around us; and to the glaciers, wild ridges and deep
valleys we would have to cross on the walk out. Twenty miles to the north
were Mounts Sir James MacBrien and Harrison Smith, and twenty miles
beyond we could see the Stoneflower on a good day. Our route lay on the
1200-foot northwest face of the fin-like peak we called "Scylla," and the
bulk of the Southern Logans, including Mount Nirvana, Mount Savage,
and massive Thunder Dome, was hidden by the great wall.

Below the glacier and its jumbled moraine our tents were pitched beside a beautiful jade-green lake, in a meadow of grass and moss and
flowers, studded with boulders fallen some time past from the peaks of
the cirque. Two days before, Todd Thompson, Al Long and I had tried
to start this route, but numb, unfeeling hands on that cold morning, a
loose handhold which sent Long flying, and a wet, mossy and repellent
corner combined to send us back to camp. Under the guise of making an
inventory of our remaining food, we ate lunch from breakfast to dinner.
Todd and Al were to go out when George Schunk came in and we packed
gear to fly out with them in the helicopter.

Today was the last day before Al left for his lab in Cambridge and
Todd headed back to his bank in Panama. Todd wasn't feeling well, so
it was just Al and I who hopped on familiar boulders around our lake
and trudged up to the base. One route was obvious, and led directly to
the summit: a huge corner, which steepened slightly at the top to vertical. I wondered whether there was a crack in it, and both of us wondered about the weather. Since our arrival, we'd been able to climb only
every two or three days, and during the month we were in the cirque
the warmth of summer progressively faded. During the walk out, on
August 11, ten inches of snow fell behind us. Almost never were there
two good days in a row, so we quickly concluded that our original am-

bitions (and accompanying piles of gear) were unrealistically large. The biggest walls were on peak 37 (all numbers refer to Buckingham's map, *A.A.J.*, 1966 and *C.A.J.*, 1971) and were about 3600 feet, but they were unappealing and would have forced complex and indirect routes up subsidiary spurs and over and down towers flanking the summit.

The haul bags, the hammocks, the bashies and the bolt kit never left camp, and when Thompson and Long did bivouac, they were on the flank of peak 37 close to the top of a beautiful, thousand-foot tower we called "Calypso." They had begun by climbing ropes left on the first three pitches during our retreat in the rain two days previously and had pushed the route all day in a cold rain which began soon after they were on new ground. When darkness made route-finding too hard they stopped, sans duvets, and waited for dawn, clothes wet and snow falling. The new day and a descent much easier than expected gently released them.

. . . gently, but with fingers which were numb for several days. Al's healed more quickly than Todd's and I recovered from a mysterious illness in time to go with him on a day which held for us all the reasons we go to the mountains. A couloir led up from the glacier which tumbled from the flanks of Nirvana and its outliers, but it led up out of sight between the great grey walls and towers of peak 37. No other route on the mountain looked reasonable and "Hydra," as we called it, was so clearly the greatest prize in the area that we didn't want to leave without at least making an attempt. Back in Boston, Bill Buckingham and Lew Surdam had shown us spectacular photographs taken when they were the first to visit the cirque in 1965 and our impressions then and now were that any route would be problematical at best.

I was still weak and not very fast on the approach, but we had eaten and departed within twenty minutes of waking. A sleepy look out the tent at three A.M. generated a startled exclamation and then awe at the spectacularly clear sky under which a light dusting of snow made the summits gleam far above us. Our packs were ready from an abortive try the day before when we'd gotten only a couple of hundred yards out of camp before it began to rain. Today, we were driven by the frustration of staying in camp and led on by the beauty of the peak.

Tiny figures balanced across the stream below camp and jumped and slid down the mossy boulders to reach the goat trail up the moraine. We felt insignificant. John Poizier, our pilot, had been expressive as he described the "great hole" surrounded by rock walls he had set down in with the others before returning to Cantung to pick up Al and me. It was true, we were enclosed on three sides and on the fourth the cirque dropped away to the valley of the Rabbitkettle River. Almost claustrophobic.

When Al and I entered the couloir, rock walls closed around us, quiet, dark and cold. Hard ice lay beneath a thin layer of snow, and we

Plate 21

Photo by Andrew Embick

P 37 ("Hydra") from the Southwest.
Electra Spire on the left.

climbed on front points, unroped, blindly following upward our passage-
way to the sky and marking our gain in altitude by looking across the
glacier to peak 34, the "Minotaur." That peak we'd climbed on our
second day, finding a classic rock and ice route which by-passed huge
rock walls we were to try and fail on later. As the sun rose and grey
turned to pink and then to the blue of a perfect sky, towers flanking us
shone golden and our eyes lingered on an exceptionally beautiful spire,
just left of us as we had begun the route. At the time, it was only one
of many possibilities we might try later, but George and I did return to
it and in 23 hours of continuous climbing reached the summit and descended. I watched amazed as George, bare skin showing through his
thin, tattered sweater, ignored the snow flurries which plastered the rock
and weighted our ropes and forced his way up free climbing. It would
have been hard even with EB's and sunshine. I was content to jümar,
my justification being our real need for haste, only partially redeeming
myself on the descent by climbing up to free a jammed rappel. Luckily
it was the only one in our long series down the wall. A pitch from
this climb, of the tower we called "Electra Spire," sticks in my memory.
George had done some intricate aid, then a big tension traverse and set
up a sling belay in a steep corner high on the wall. From his belay I
led directly up, expecting all the time to be forced into aid because the
rock was improbably steep and unbroken. But a single thin crack rose
above me and miraculously a profusion of knobs and crystals materialized,
creating 160 feet of the climbing we'd come for. The pitch ended at
another sling belay, just below a roof beyond which was the summit.
When I finished cleaning George's lead of the last pitch, he had already
built a cairn and was rigging the first rappel, the last of which brought
us back to our boots and ice gear at the bottom of the couloir.

But all that was yet to come, and Long and I left that tower and
others below us as we cramponed upwards, emerging into the sunlight
on a cornice which overhung the glacier and valley on the previously
unseen side of peak 37. We had seen from below a rock pyramid which
began where the couloir ended, with little hope that it was the true
summit. But now we were almost as high as Nirvana's 9097 feet, and
there couldn't be much more climbing. Indeed there wasn't; the rock
yielded easily, putting us on top at ten in the morning. The sun shone,
there was not a cloud or breath of wind, and though our crackers were
moldy we were happy to sit in the sky, to drink the air, and to stay
for three hours on top of our world of rock and ice.

A small bottle of cherry brandy was employed in the celebration on
our return, but the (just-as-small) bottle of champagne was saved for
skills were brought into play then, including some patience during the
a success on Nirvana a few days later. A variety of mountaineering
slog up the glacier. We used a hodge-podge of implements including rock

hammers, nut prods and 11-point and otherwise deficient crampons to climb the short section of vertical ice at the back of the bergschrund and reached the rock of the north face on which our route diagonalled up and right. On top we found the cairn of Buckingham's and Surdam's first ascent. Around us were the spectacularly wild mountains through which they travelled to reach this mountain and then walk out to civilization. On the descent we made a jump off the bergschrund reminiscent of un-wise childhood leaps from roofs into flowerbeds. But the landing was happily soft and we continued down, entertained at intervals by en-counters with hidden crevasses.

I've digressed, and also jumped ahead. It would be easy to digress more, to rest-day gorges on pancakes and jam, to the magic-carpet-like helicopter ride in and the four-day walk out, to Todd's relaxed equanimity and Kathy Murray's constant cheerfulness, and to the time we thought we were doing a first ascent and on top found a cairn we ourselves had left a few days before. Images perceived intensely are what remain, not a chronology of climbs. We did other peaks: from Nirvana north are "Charybdis," "Scylla," and at the end of the ridge, "Cyclops," facetiously referred to around camp as "Trundle Butte." "Guardian," just northwest of the lake, lacked a cairn until George and Kathy climbed it on a wet day. "Argus" (peak 42) yielded easily though new snow was being sloughed continuously from the ice we climbed. The summit of "Laby-rinth" (peak 43) was a cornice we dared not stand on. The descent was via a couloir we hadn't been able to see from below and by-passed several leads on steep and rotten rock. One lazy day we'd stirred only enough to climb a trio of needles near camp we called the "Eumenides." We didn't manage to try the pair of grotesque and precarious aiguilles which were visible from camp and directly in view from the great corner of Scylla's northwest face. Our climb on that face was the midpoint of the trip. Long and I might have allowed our thoughts to drift in recol-lection and anticipation had we not been so engrossed in the climbing. I was once forced to lead directly past a huge loose block attached only by a few inches at its upper end. Long drew the last hard pitch of the eleven, devious and problematical face-climbing on fragile nubbins and flakes far above a really lousy collection of small nuts. The summit was the highest point of an almost knife-edged ridge, and in fading light we embraced, at peace. Hopes were fulfilled and tension stilled for long moments before we coiled ropes for the descent.

We reached summits, leaving hasty cairns and some loops of rappel sling and often regretting that we'd marked our presence at all. Some days had perfect weather, but more provided an explanation for how the moss could grow so lushly. Time went to placid, convivial games of Hearts and to enjoying the culinary delights Todd's expertise created. We fed unwanted granola to a resident rodent, read *The Godfather* in fragments passed in the rain from tent to tent, and (rarely) bathed at high speed in the lake. An incredibly euphoric immersion in Cantung's hot springs was the transition between the wilds and the "real" world, a transition we were not sure we wanted to make but which was eased by rounds of beer with the miners and geologists in the Cantung bar.

Summary of Statistics:

AREA: Southern Logan Mountains, North West Territories, Canada.

ASCENTS: (All first ascents except as noted. Numbered peaks refer to map opposite page 35, *A.A.J.*, 1966.)

"Cyclops" (last peak on ridge going north from Nirvana) via northwest face, July 15, 1975 (Embick, Long, Thompson).

"Minotaur" (Peak 34) via northwest couloir and north face, July 16, 1975 (Embick, Long, Thompson).

"Eumenides" (three one-pitch needles near lake), July 18, 1975 (Long, Thompson).

"Calypso Tower" (a spur on the south ridge of Peak 37), July 17 and 19-20, 1975) (Long, Thompson), NCCS IV, F8, A2.

"Hydra" (Peak 37), July 23, 1975 (Embick, Long).

Nirvana, second ascent via new route on north face, July 26, 1975 (Embick, Long, Thompson).

"Scylla" (second peak going north from Nirvana) via northwest face, July 28, 1975 (Embick, Long), NCCS IV, F8, A2.

"Argus" (Peak 42), July 30, 1975 (Embick, Schunk).

"Electra Spire" (a spire on Peak 37), July 31 and August 1, 1975 (Embick, Schunk) NCCS IV, F9, A3.

"Labyrinth" (Peak 43), August 3, 1975 (Embick, Schunk).

"Warrior" (Peak 44), third ascent, August 3, 1975 (Murray).

"Scylla," second ascent, and "Charybdis" (peak just northwest of Nirvana) both via northeast couloir, August 6, 1975 (Embick, Schunk).

Guardian, second ascent, August 8, 1975 (Murray, Schunk).

PERSONNEL: Andrew Embick, Alan Long, Kathy Murray, George Schunk, Todd Thompson.

The Cold-Dance Review

Winter Ice Climbing and its Techniques on Kitchener

JEFF LOWE   *"To dance beneath the diamond sky*
with one hand waving free . . ."
—Bob Dylan

Part I — Winter Waltzes

THE dance really started during the winters of 1971 and 1972. Up to that time winter ice climbing in the United States had been a timid affair at best, with climbs such as Mc-Carthy's ascent of Pinnacle Gully on Mount Washington, without chopping steps, marking the limit of adventure. People were aware of the potential for climbing even vertical ice with the new, curved "cheating sticks," yet no one had had the audacity necessary to complete the ascent of a big, steep winter icefall. In March of 1971, however, my brother Greg capped days of practice bouldering on vertical ice with the climb of an obscure but important route on Mahlen's Peak waterfall in northern Utah. Belayed by a partner who seconded on Jümars, he led the 350-foot climb in four pitches. The first 'pitch is 130 feet of 70° to 90° ice, and the second pitch is about 75 feet of 50° climbing. But it was on the third lead that a new standard of free-climbing difficulty on ice was established. Over 200 feet off the ground, one is faced with 60 feet of dead vertical climbing, which in turn is topped by 15 feet of gently impending ice; the ice forms an overhanging bulge as it flows over the lip of a large ledge in the underlying rock.

In the 1971 issue of *Ascent*, Yvon Chouinard wrote about the "Black Gully, Cannon Mountain. A black, filthy, horrendous icicle, 600 feet high. Unclimbed." In the winter of 1972, John Bouchard started up using a self-belay. However, since the ice was rapidly melting, he soon stopped belaying and continued the climb unprotected. Several hours later he climbed the last of the bulges to arrive at the top of this climb that had so impressed one of America's best mountaineers.

That same winter Pat Callis and Jim Kanzler and others in Montana were learning the two-step-and-thunk on the Blue and Green Gullies in Hyalite Canyon. In Colorado, too, people were learning the brittle dance,

PLATE 22

Photo by Michael Lowe

**Jeff Lowe on the second pitch of
Bridalveil Fall, Colorado.**

while out in the Valley fugitives from the rock races began shuffling around, crampon shod and with ice axes in hand. Where previously an overgrown cloud of caution had filled the skies of American ice climbing, a new adventurous attitude was blowing in on the winds of a personal understanding of what is possible. Many of those who had tried the cold-dance were extremely jazzed about the possibility of making great crystal climbs heretofore scarcely dreamed of.

The next winter was a time of maturation of techniques and consolidation of the gains already made. The small ranks of active ice climbers began to swell, but no new climbs were made that surpassed the Black Gully or Mahlen's Peak waterfall in overall boldness, beauty, or difficulty of technical performance required.

Mike Weis and I had both been introduced to the possibilities of steep waterfall climbing by my brother in 1972, and by December of 1973 we felt ready to try something really big. Our first inclination was to make an attempt on the Widow's Tears, a 900-foot waterfall in Yosemite Valley with an average angle of about 75°, but calls to the Valley informed us that there was no ice. However, we knew of a fall closer to our home stomping grounds. Bridalveil Fall, in Telluride, Colorado, is only half the height of the Tears, but much steeper. On completion of the climb on January 2, 1974, we had to admit that it had been a good introduction to a new sort of ice climb.

Mike and I knew from experience that the brittle ice produced by weeks of sub-zero temperatures would not allow tube screws to be placed, or wart hogs to be driven, without completely cracking up. So we made some pitons out of tubular chromemoly stock and bevelled the tips to the inside. These we found worked very well, fracturing the ice only slightly as they were driven in and freezing solidly in place. Their only drawback was the necessity for chopping them out. With these for protection we pushed the free climbing to our limits and managed to free-climb the entire icefall, only taking rests from pitons in a couple of places. Mike led the crux, which was a three-foot roof with giant icicles drooping from the lip. For 20 feet he climbed the slightly overhanging wall below the roof and then knocked a hole in the curtain of icicles. Next he delicately bridged between the base of icicles on either side of the hole, got the pick of his axe in above the overhang and muscled his way up. Following, it seemed equivalent to 5.10 rock climbing. We were both laughing and amazed at our success when we reached the top; we now knew we would never have to consider any ice climb in terms of aid.

At this point let's break away from a chronological recitation of American events, and look in on the dance they're doing up north in the Canadian Rockies, where the music of commitment does not play so loudly.

The technique used for climbing steep ice in Canada is best described by its originator, Bugs McKeith: ". . . faced by pillars of brittle, vertical ice, and lacking the guts to front-point up them, I had attached aid-slings to the shafts of both Terrodactyls and had found that, even on vertical ice, I could relax and spend as much time as I wished clearing rotten ice and placing each axe alternately to my complete satisfaction." * All the big Canadian climbs have utilized this technique, as well as fixed ropes and what is much worse, bolts on some belays. The aid techniques and fixed ropes don't bother me much; they're simply slow and unenjoyable, like climbing in leg irons and trailing a rope that's anchored in fear. But they cause no damage to the mountain, and are therefore a matter of personal choice. The bolts, however, are a different matter. After the pioneer ascent, bolts on an ice climb are not always available for subsequent use, as they are on rock. This is because most icefalls form differently from season to season and even from week to week in the same season. Thus the bolt may be buried under thick ice, unseen and unreachable, during heavy icing, or unreachable and in the wrong place when there is less ice than that encountered on the first ascent. Is each new party to place a new set of bolts, then? That's absurd, of course, and destructive and degrading to the climb. If a climb can't be done without resorting to such tactics, then I don't think it should be made. The big climbs in the Rockies all await first free ascents, and many await first clean ascents, i.e., without the use of bolts.

It's heartening to know that no bolts have been placed on important American ice routes, so that a strong tradition of adventure is developing. Take for example this year's best ice climb: Kevin Worral's and Mark Chapman's first ascent of Widow's Tears. After numerous attempts they finally found climbable conditions and in three days of free climbing with two bivouacs on the climb, they completed America's most beautiful ice climb. They carried no bolts, and this was only the second or third ice climb for either of them! This was the first first-ascent of a Scottish grade 6 accomplished in one continuous push. Another climb made in this style was the Keystone Green Steps, near Valdez, Alaska. John Weilund and I started this 600-foot climb, which consists of six pitches of 75° to 90° ice, on the last day of 1975, and made one bivouac.

So the cold-dance is in full swing. From Frankenstein Cliff to June Lake, from Colorado to Alaska, climbers are waltzing on front points in greater and greater numbers. And the name of the tune they're dancing to is: DON'T FALL OFF THE FLOOR.

Part II — The Alpine Ballroom

Climbing frozen waterfalls offers the ice climber the same sort of opportunity to sharpen his technique as crag climbing offers the rock

---

* *Mountain* 41, Jan. 1975.

climber. But to the alpinist the skills and strength gained on the water-fall are primarily important in their application to major new routes in the high mountains. Actually, normal alpine ice climbing becomes easier for one who has trained on winter icefalls. The proof of this is the first solo ascent of the Black Ice Couloir on the Grand Teton, made by my brother Greg the summer following his ascent of Mahlen's Peak waterfall. And John Bouchard used his experience on the Black Gully to good ad-vantage this summer on his solo climb on the north face of the Grands Charmoz, and on his new solo route this summer on the north face of the Grand Pilier d'Angle, on Mont Blanc, one of Europe's most impressive ice walls. Yvon Chouinard and Mike Covington used their winter ex-perience to advantage on the first direct ascent of the Diamond Couloir on Mount Kenya, which has several pitches of nearly vertical ice. In fact Americans experienced in winter ice climbing had one of the best seasons ever in the Alps. At the same time in the Canadian Rockies, Mike Weis and I were aided by the confidence acquired on Bridalveil Falls and other winter ice climbs in the ascent of a hard new route on the north face of Mount Kitchener. The account of this climb may serve to illustrate that blend of objective hazard, subjective trauma, and technical difficulty that must be overcome in the ascent of a modern alpine ice route.

The story of the first ascent of the 3500-foot north face of Mount Kitchener has already been told in the pages of this journal. (*A.A.J.*, 1972, 18:1, pages 66-9.) For those involved, the "Ramp Route," as I call it, was a terribly satisfying experience, and a difficult climb in its own right. But for me at least, the face held an even greater attraction—the great central couloir that falls from the broad summit of the mountain like the tail of a white comet. I doubt if anywhere else in the Rockies there is a couloir of equal size that is at once so beautiful, and steep, and singularly imposing. Perhaps I should add *dangerous* as well, for it is the natural path for rockfall. Indeed, on my first encounter with the slopes below the couloir, in August of 1970, with my cousin, George Lowe, the weather was warm and the couloir rumbled with the noise of traffic as heavy as Grand Central Station on Christmas Eve. Since that time I have always thought of the big gully as the Grand Central Couloir.

For several years following the climb of the Ramp Route yearly at-tempts on the Grand Central Couloir were made. Brian Greenwood, George Homer, and Bob Beal managed to work a way up the ice and rock buttress to the left of the couloir in 1973. This was actually an attempt on the couloir, but rockfall forced them to follow a more pro-tected line. Then in the winter of 1975 at least two determined attempts were made, doubtless in the hopes that the winter cold would reduce the rockfall. In the end the short winter days, brittle ice, and avalanches confined both attempts to the lower half of the face.

PLATE 23

Photo by Jeff Lowe

**Weis soloing left of the bergschrund
on the Grand Central Couloir,
MOUNT KITCHENER.**

Such was the state of affairs when Mike Weis and I arrived at the Icefield's Campground in mid-August. We were back for yet another of our annual attempts. On our first try this year our now traditional bad luck held, and a snowstorm caught us before we crossed the bergschrund. Soon the avalanches were roaring and we were doing a quick-step to get down out of their range.

Several days later we were back at it. This time the weather looked as if it might hold. We had also adopted new tactics. We carried minimal food, water, and bivouac gear. Starting up at six P.M., we planned to climb through the night with headlamps and finish the following day. By climbing at night we hoped to be above the zone of bad rockfall by the time the morning sun hit the top of the face.

The real climbing began to the left of the lower of the two bergschrunds of the small hanging glacier at the bottom of the wall. The bergschrund itself was impassable without undue exertions. Climbing on ice and rotten snow over ice, we climbed unroped, each with his own thoughts, for four or five hundred feet to about the level of the upper "schrund." At this point the ice got very hard. Mike cried "uncle," so we got out the rope. I'll have to say that I welcomed the added security, too. While the features of the huge amphitheater at the top of the face gradually darkened to a ragged silhouette, for six or seven ropelengths we moved simultaneously but with two screws between us for safety. At the top of the right-hand *rognon* in the lower icefield, we had a bite to eat and drink and prepared our headlamps for the dark hours ahead. I said I thought we would bag the climb this time, but Mike cautiously reminded me that "We've barely gotten started."

From that point on we belayed each pitch. While the leader stomped slowly up with vision limited to the small circle of light projected by his headlamp, the belayer had time for reflection. To spur his thoughts, he could gaze into the infinite darkness of the valley or peer up at the starry sky, his headlamp turned off to save on batteries. For a while the Aurora Borealis flashed. Then, as the gully narrowed and steepened, we bumped into the lowest of two or three polypropylene lines, remnants of an attempt the previous winter.

The eastern sky began to lighten. At the vertical narrowing of the upper couloir, it was six A.M. and full light. We were at the top of the fifteenth roped pitch.

The next pitch looked as though it had been borrowed from a hard Scottish gully. It was my lead. Initially it was almost a chimney. I could bridge with the left crampon on rock and the other on ice, while using the axe to whatever advantage it could be put. This moderate going came to an end all too soon. The couloir widened and forced me to climb the thin face of ice and snow directly. With only knifeblades between frozen blocks for protection, the climbing was extremely nerve-wracking. Seldom would the tools penetrate more than half an inch before meeting rock. The crux was climbing out from under an ice mushroom, crammed into the couloir like a huge marshmallow. It took a couple of hours before I had a hanging belay from wart hogs in the rock at the side of the couloir. We had no jümars or hauling rope. Even with his 30-pound pack, after a couple of pendulums from underneath the ice mushroom, Mike pulled himself over the bulge by amazing brute strength.

The angle eased now, to a "mere" 65°. The ice was thick and held our points well; we made quicker progress for several pitches. Then we came against the final section of the upper couloir, which had looked well-iced from below but turned out to be steep compact rock, thinly veneered with snow. Luck was with us; we found a narrow ice gully leading out to the right onto the rib that borders the couloir. Several hard leads of mixed snow and ice with one or two short but hard rock steps brought us out onto the summit ice cap, just 200 feet short of our goal. In our thirsty and fatigued condition, time had moved faster than we. Our thirst was greater than our fatigue. With the air scratching at our throats, we climbed the last pitches. The first pitch was ice at a moderate angle, and the other a vertical path on rotten snow through the summit cornice. The last few feet had been as difficult as any and were an exhausting capper to 26 hours of intense climbing. It was eight P.M. when Mike and I stood side by side in the sun's horizontal rays on top.

Then we turned, and with the sun a shimmering red disc at our backs we wobbled through deep snow toward the east ridge, which was our descent route. We still had several hours to go before we could rest and drink much needed water that trickled from a snowfield in the saddle below the small peak known as K2.

The best dances are sometimes marathons.

Summary of Statistics:

Subject: Various winter ice climbs, their techniques and application to big, alpine ice ascents.

New Route: Mount Kitchener, Canadian Rockies, Grand Central Couloir on North Face, August, 1975 (Jeff Lowe, Michael Weis).

New Colorado Ice Climbs, 1973-1975

MICHAEL KENNEDY, *Elk Mountain Climbing Club*

THERE was little interest in winter ice climbing in Colorado as an end in itself until fairly recently. Improvements in technique and equipment, and a general keenness to do something different and exciting during the long winter months has led to a greater acceptance of ice as a climbing form equal in interest to rock, and in some ways more fulfilling. Ice offers an infinitely variable and interesting terrain for climbing, and few, if any, of the harder routes are ever crowded. It is also an area with many possibilities for fruitful exploration, and more important, great adventure.

The climbs I will describe are all within a small area of Colorado, centered around Glenwood Canyon and the Crystal River valley. It is an underpopulated area in terms of climbers, and we feel fortunate in having been able to do these climbs in a remote and non-competitive atmosphere.

Things started to happen in 1973. Mark Hesse, Larry Bruce and Lou Dawson climbed an isolated ice pillar near Redstone, netting a long, sustained pitch of near-vertical ice; the route has yet to be repeated. A few weeks later, Dawson, accompanied by Ken Williams, climbed the classic Marble Icefall. This is a very sustained 150-foot frozen waterfall located in a beautiful canyon a mere half-hour from the road. The climb was repeated shortly afterwards by Brian Robertson and Steve Shea. Several ice-bouldering areas were also discovered, notably Hays Creek Falls and the Grotto Icefall.

But the major challenge of the area, the Glenwood Icefall, remained untouched. Several early attempts failed due to the poor ice, which gets a lot of sun. A strong party consisting of Brian Robertson, Mark Hesse, Rich Jack and Steve Shea made a bold attempt on a bitter cold day in February, 1973. They were two thirds up the climb when their attempt was abruptly terminated by Robertson's thirty-foot power-dive off the rotten and brittle ice. So ended the 1973 season.

In 1974, things began to move. Several ascents of the Marble Icefall were made, and several short climbs of note were found. The most interesting of these was the Redstone Ice Pillar, a 70-foot free-standing pillar of rotten, bulging ice. Lou Dawson and I managed it with some difficulty; it has yet to be repeated. Many attempts were made on the

PLATE 24

Photo by Michael Kennedy

GLENWOOD ICEFALL. Routes from left to right by Dawson-Kennedy, Lanbeck-Loeffler, Kennedy-Shea.

Glenwood Icefall as well; I made at least five, with various partners, and several other parties tried as well. These all failed below Robertson's high point.

The most outstanding ascent of the season was made by Michael Loeffler and Bob Lanbeck, who climbed the central ramp line on the Glenwood Icefall. Indeed, the climb was done in such a quiet and unassuming manner (both parties left the area shortly afterwards) that I didn't get full details on the climb till a year later, after making what I thought to be the first ascent of the fall. This line to my knowledge, has not been repeated.

In 1975, conditions were excellent and many ascents of note were made. It was a rare combination of weather, conditions and climbers. Lou Dawson, Steve Shea and I made an attempt on the right side of Glenwood Icefall; we failed after climbing the crux due to a rapid warming and subsequent deterioration of the ice. A few weeks later, Steve and I returned and climbed the route in five hours; we encountered everything from thinly glazed rock, vertical pillars of ice to alternating layers of ice and powder snow. The route was repeated a couple of days later by Mark Hesse and two others.

A week later, Lou and I were back to try the left side. Although it was technically more severe than the right side, it was a bit less sustained. The crux was the last pitch, a 70-foot vertical column; we climbed the entire route in 4½ hours, and it has not been repeated. Shortly after this ascent an unseasonably warm spell melted away most of the ice.

For two years I had been eyeing a mysterious set of icicles high in a side canyon in Glenwood. They were visible from the road, but only if you knew where to look. At the end of March 1975, Dave Wilkinson and I decided to take a look; after an hour of hard slogging up avalanche debris we were rewarded with the vision of the most incredible icefall I had ever seen. The lower section was fully 300 feet across and 160 to 200 feet high. Above, a series of bulges went on for at least another 300 feet before fading into several free-standing icicles hanging from the limestone roofs.

Steve Shea and I returned the next day and climbed the easiest looking line; it turned out to be the hardest pitch of ice either of us had ever done. Fully 165 feet long, it consisted largely of vertical ice, and the top actually overhung by a few degrees. Purists may scoff, but despite my being plastered as close to the ice as I could get, our extra rope hung out at least five feet from the base while I was seconding ten feet from the top. All other possibilities look as hard, and longer and more sustained, than our line on Hidden Falls.

A few brief notes on the techniques employed in climbing these routes follow. Firstly, no fixed ropes were used, and all belay anchors and protection were on ice screws, runners, nuts or ordinary rock pitons. No bolts were placed; it seems foolish to resort to such tactics as they are not only destructive to the rock, but impermanent; ice build-up will vary year to year, and it is doubtful that bolts placed one year will be found the next. Minimal aid was used on all of these ascents. This consisted of tying off the tip of an ice axe to the swami belt, allowing rest and both hands free to place protection. Etriers were not used, nor were steps chopped or protection used for progress. And in many days of climbing, at least among the small group I know, no falls were taken. This technique allows for a fast, clean ascent of ice without excess gadgetry and wasted time.

What of the future? Few major features remain in the area without at least one route, although the Hidden Falls offer at least two more routes that will be harder than anything yet done here. As advances come in techniques, equipment and concepts of what is possible, ascents will be done in better style on established routes, with fewer points of aid or even solo; new routes will be found in remote and untraveled areas. As with rock climbing, these climbs are also stepping stones to big alpine routes, where speed, efficiency and daring make the difference between success and failure.

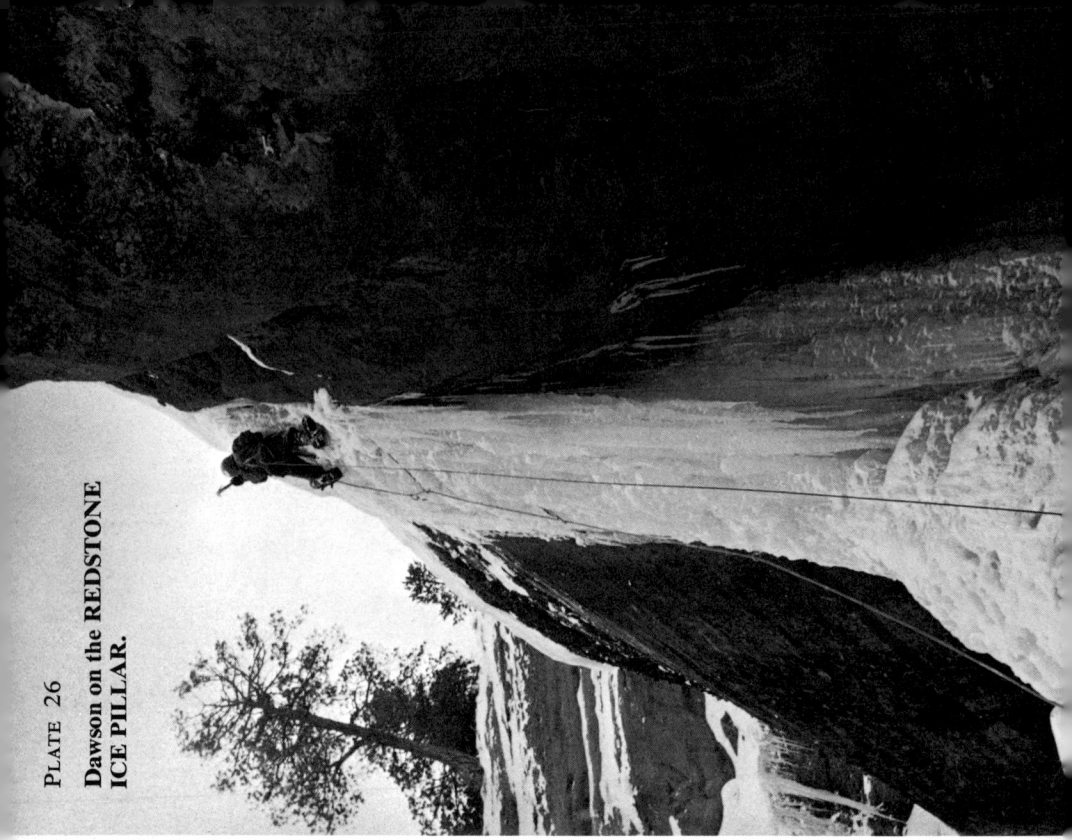

PLATE 26

Dawson on the REDSTONE ICE PILLAR.

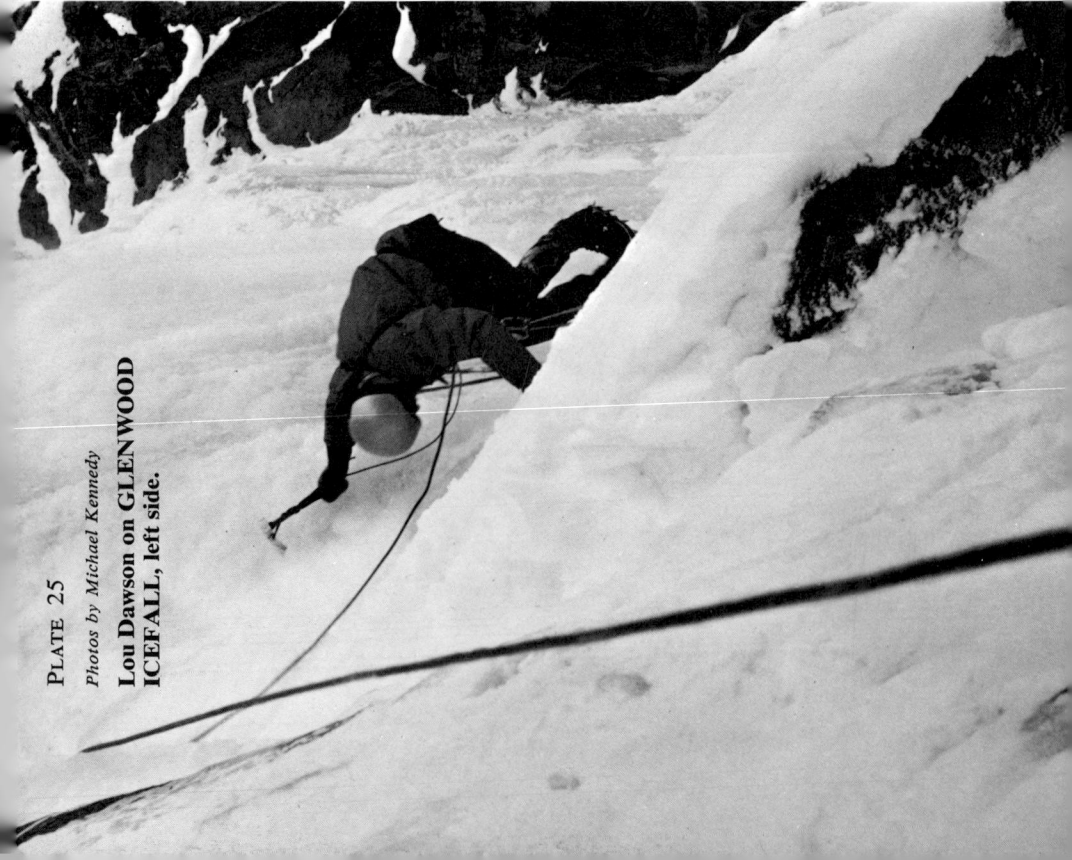

PLATE 25

Photos by Michael Kennedy

Lou Dawson on GLENWOOD ICEFALL, left side.

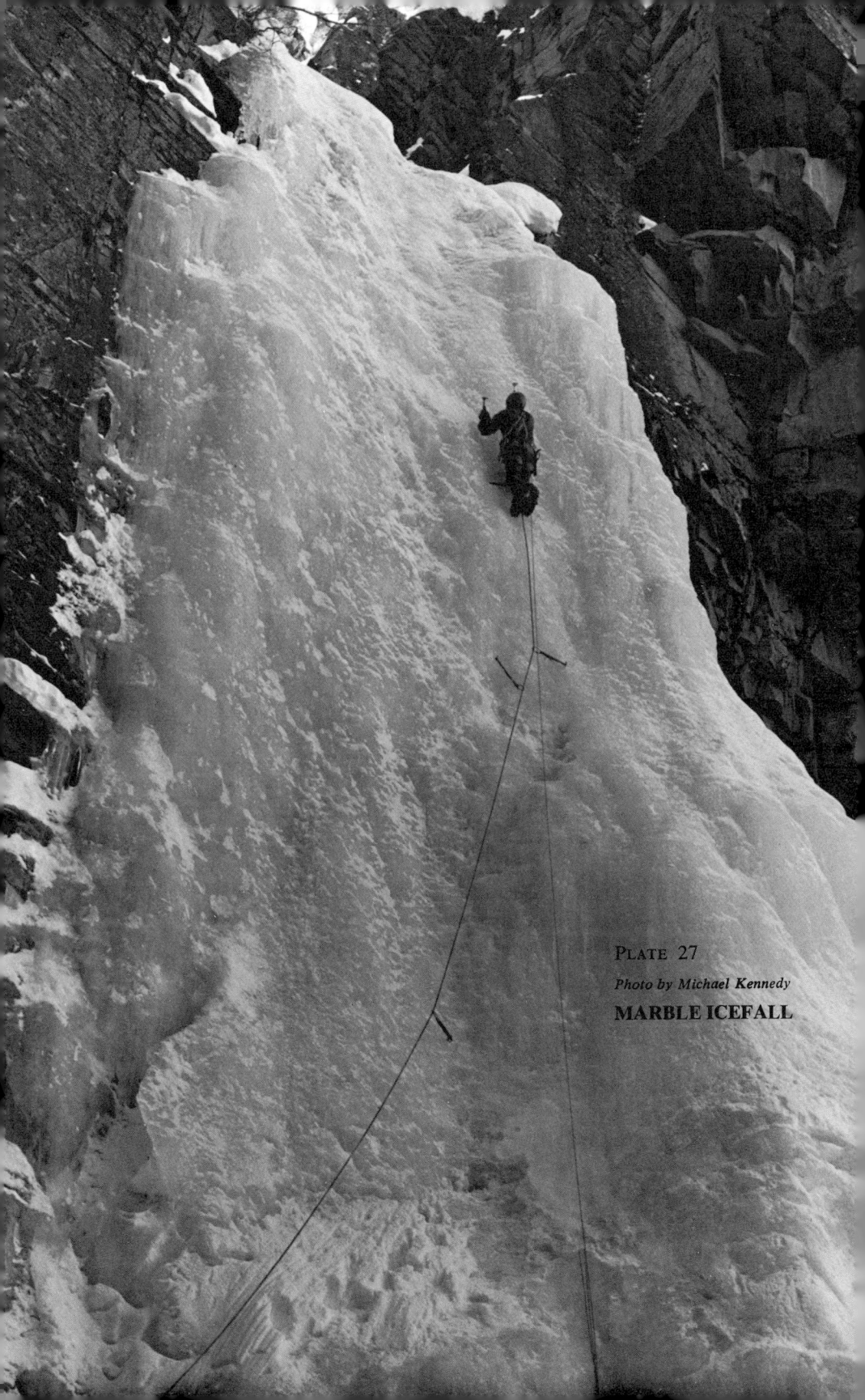

Plate 27

Photo by Michael Kennedy

MARBLE ICEFALL

A Soviet First Ascent in the North Cascades

ALEX BERTULIS

*... when tied to the same rope, there
is more than one bond that transcends
language, culture and ideology.*

WHEN the Soviet team arrived in
Seattle, we met them, for the first time, during a luncheon in the Plaza
Hotel. I arrived a little late and at first glance I could not be sure which
of the fifteen persons at the table were the foreigners. A series of intro-
ductions by Pete Schoening and a round of handshakes quickly acquainted
me with the Soviet guests and some of the Northwest hosts.

About a week later, after a Northwest tour that included an ascent
of Mount Rainier, water skiing on Lake Washington and a visit through
37 departments of the local Sears and Roebuck store, I was advised that,
as a finale, our guests would be interested in a "hard first ascent" in the
North Cascades, but one that involved no more approach difficulties than
driving up in a car and marching off the roadway to the first pitch! Well,
accessibility is not exactly what the North Cascades are famous for but
upon viewing my slides of a 2300-foot, nearly vertical, buttress that was
still unclimbed, the Soviets admitted that the two-hour hike to its base
would not be objectionable.*

Early in the morning of September 10, the "North Cascades team"
(Vitaly Abalakov, Vladimir Shatayev, Vyacheslav "Slava" Onishchenko,
Valentin "Valia" Grakovich, Anatoly "Tolia" Nepeomnyashchy, Sergei
Bershov, all of the USSR and Nina Cvetkovs, Mike Helms, Jim Mitchell
and I) drove over to the east side of the Cascades, sailed forty miles up
Lake Chelan, drove ten more miles over an old mining road in a "wilder-
ness taxi," and after a three-mile hike, arrived at the "Bonanza base camp"
on the north shore of Hart Lake (3935 feet) still early in the day.

After a refreshing swim in the ice-cold waters of the lake (the Soviets
never lost a chance to "skinny dip" in any body of water they happen to
encounter), the rest of the afternoon was spent sorting out food, gear
and tactics for the climb. American freeze-dried food, nylon down gear
and "rip-stop" nylon tents impressed the Soviets very much. The Soviet

---

* The north face of the southwest peak of Bonanza (at 9511 feet, the
Cascades' highest non-volcanic mountain).

340

hardware collection included many innovative designs (mostly by Abalakov) for both rock and ice climbing. Most of their pitons were titanium, which combines the strength of steel and the light weight of aluminum. The drawback of titanium pitons is that they deform quicker, during repeated use, than pitons of chrome-molybdenum steel.

Starting early the next morning we ascended the steep rock and heather terraces to the 7100-foot pass between North Star and Bonanza Peak in about two-and-a-half hours. It was a perfect autumn day. As we reached the pass the north buttress of the southwest peak of Bonanza came into close view. Slava studied it for a while then, gesturing, asked me where the route was? There was no apparent fault system that indicated that the buttress would even "go." I responded, "The route is where you make it. I wish you luck!" I gave them one more opportunity to make it a team of four (Onishchenko, Bershov, Grakovich and Nepeomnyashchy)* but they all insisted that I must climb with them.

As we roped up at the base of the buttress, I was startled to see Slava and Sergei put on petit galoshes that stretched tight over their bare feet! Sergei took the first lead up a narrow chimney and proceeded up the broad face above while Slava belayed. Tolia informed me that I would be on the end of his rope with the privilege of cleaning all the pitches. Valia tied a prussik near the middle of the rope and often climbed simultaneously without a real belay, even over F9 terrain!

As we proceeded upwards, the climbing remained demanding (F7-F9). Sergei and Slava were well ahead and could be seen maneuvering under some major overhanging headwalls. Tolia often remarked to me that he would certainly prefer his gloshes now instead of the conventional climbing boots he had on. Valia, a very strong climber who did not enjoy following as much as he does leading, started shouting up at his compatriots that in his opinion they should be attacking the headwalls directly (with aid) and be done with it! I (politely) squelched his vocal efforts and said, "Give them a chance; they may see something we cannot." My words were prophetic. Sergei and Slava, far from encountering insurmountable impasses, reached a sloping ramp that cut diagonally across the crest of the buttress (from east to west) circumventing two of the headwalls. It was an unexpected and important key to the route!

The next few leads involved some of the hardest that I have ever witnessed under alpine conditions: three consecutive pitches of F10 and sustained F8 and F9. As we reached our bivouac ledge, I learned that Sergei did almost all the leading. His stature as USSR rock-climbing (speed) champion is well earned, I thought.

The setting sun silhouetted the mountains of the Olympics and Van-

---

* Shatayev remained in camp with fever. Abalakov explored the North Cascades via its beautiful valleys.

PLATE 28

Aerial photo by Alex Bertulis

**Southwest Peak of BONAZA PEAK.
The first ascent of the 2300-foot buttress
followed the left skyline.**

PLATES 29 and 30

Photos by Michael Helms

The "Abalakov Cam" is cut from an
industrial flywheel (one-fifth section).
It is designed to fit and lock in a wide
range of crack sizes without adjustment.
The cord produces a rotational force
on the nut to lock it in the crack

couver Island while hot food and liquids were shared. Songs, jokes and stories abounded late into the night. The spirit was contagious and our language differences presented no barrier. We were all slipping off into sleep when the resident "snaffle hound" (Pika) started scavenging through our utensils for dinner leftovers. Anchored loosely to some pitons I remained still and semi-awake as the familiar commotion continued close by. Suddenly, I felt this "monster" running over me! When his feet hit my face I jumped up yelling and cursing. My Soviet buddies thought I had been "attacked by a bear" and my description of the beast supported that impression. A "bear hunt" failed to produce a quarry. I lay back down to sleep with my hammer at hand, just in case. More jokes, at my expense, kept us awake a while longer.

By late the following morning we had surmounted the final headwalls of the buttress and were jubilating on the summit. I asked Slava, who had done some of Europe's hardest climbs, what his impression of the route was? He said that "some of the climbing was very hard and some not so hard, but if the weather had become bad it would have been very difficult to escape the face." Having experienced September blizzards in the North Cascades, our predicament on the face would have been unpleasant, indeed, if the weather had broken. A quick descent over the numerous glaciers and cliffs of Bonanza's 5000-foot south face brought us hot and thirsty to Base Camp and another, most refreshing swim in Hart Lake.

* * *

In cleaning the many pitches (22) I was impressed at the Soviet's expert approach to "clean climbing." During this climb over a hundred chocks, nuts, wedges, etc. were placed for protection whereas only six (knifeblade) pitons were used. Two (titanium) pitons were placed in such difficult (desperate?) positions that I was unable to remove them (as future parties will probably be happy to discover).

By far the most impressive item that the Soviets had was the "Abalakov Cam." This most effective anchor is as ingenious in design as it is simple to use. Almost every belay on this climb was safely and quickly secured by one "Abalakov" rather than several conventional nut and chock placements. This cam is easy to make and Mr. Abalakov expressed the hope that it would be produced in this country without patent restrictions.

Summary of Statistics:

AREA: Cascade Mountains, Washington.

NEW ROUTE: North Face of the southwest Peak of Bonanza, 9511 feet, September 12, 1975, NCCS VI, F 10.

PERSONNEL: Vyacheslav Onishchenko, Valentin Grakovich, Anatoly Nepeomnyashchy, Sergei Bershov, USSR and Alex Bertulis, USA.

Everest Southwest Face

CHRISTIAN BONINGTON

I knew there was something wrong the moment Martin Boysen started speaking on the radio. It was 7:30 in the evening of September 26 and in the last three hours the tension had been steadily mounting at Camp II as we waited for news of three climbers who had pressed on towards the summit of Everest leaving the Top Camp that morning. Martin's voice crackled through the static: "Pete and Pertemba have just got back, but Mick hasn't." Suddenly, an expedition that had been so successful, so lucky, and which had run so smoothly, was caught by tragedy, a harsh reminder of just how fine is the margin between life and death on Everest, however strong the team that tackles it.

We had climbed the southwest face just two days before when Dougal Haston and Doug Scott made their magnificent push for the summit. We had a well-established Camp VI, were well ahead of schedule and I wanted to give as many as possible of our strong team of climbers the chance to savour the challenge and satisfaction of Everest's summit. I therefore had planned to make two further summit attempts of four climbers each on September 26 and September 28 respectively.

That morning of September 26, at 3:30 Martin Boysen, Mick Burke, Pete Boardman and our sardar, Pertemba, had set out from the two small box tents that clung to a ledge carved from the snows of the upper snowfield of the southwest face at a height of 26,600 feet. Even at dawn the wind was gusting strongly, and there was a threat of high cirrus cloud in the sky, warning of a possible break in the weather, but there had been such clouds before and anyway this was their chance of standing on the highest point of earth—and so they set out.

An accident is usually composed of several, often unconnected incidents, which inexorably compound the final tragedy. The first one occurred half way across the snowfield above the rock band. They were following the line of rope that Dougal Haston and Doug Scott had fixed in place just three days before when one of Martin's crampons fell off. He had already had trouble with his oxygen, and now with only one crampon there could be no question of going on. By this time Pete Boardman and Pertemba had pulled ahead, reaching the south summit of Everest by 10:30 A.M., much faster than on the first ascent, because of the consolidated nature of the track. They had seen no sign of Mick Burke and assumed that he had gone back with Boysen. Their own

345

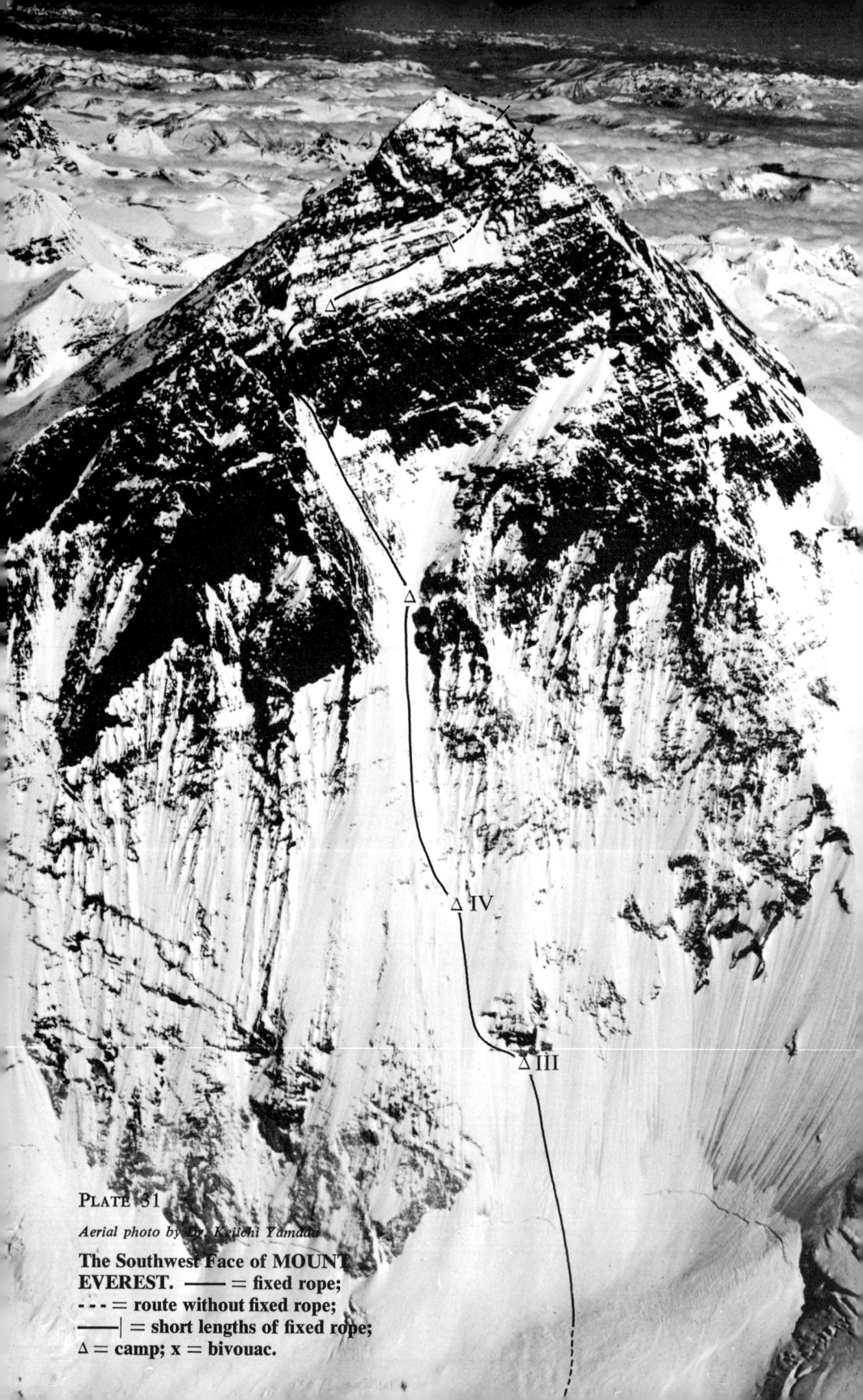

PLATE 31

Aerial photo by Dr. Keiichi Yamada

**The Southwest Face of MOUNT
EVEREST.** ——— = fixed rope;
- - - = route without fixed rope;
———| = short lengths of fixed rope;
Δ = camp; x = bivouac.

ascent was very nearly jeopardized when Pertemba's oxygen system iced up and they spent an hour and a half on the south summit, struggling to clear it, before making their summit bid. They reached it at 1:10 P.M. in what had been an impressively fast ascent. They flew the Nepalese flag in honour of Pertemba's ascent, surely the most difficult attempt ever achieved by a Sherpa, made a tape recording and then started back down.

Just below the summit they were astonished to meet Mick Burke, who was sitting down having a rest. After Boysen had turned back he had decided to carry on by himself. Under the circumstances it was a reasonable decision. There was a well consolidated track and Mick Burke was a very experienced and determined mountaineer. It was he who had forced the rock band, the key to the south face of Annapurna in 1970.

He had been to our high point on Everest in 1972 and had a wealth of summer and winter climbing experience in the Alps behind him, including being the first Briton to climb the Nose on El Capitan. In going on alone he took a calculated risk, something that is an integral part of mountaineering. He certainly was not the first man to go it alone on Everest. At a very similar height on the north face on the north side, before the war, Odell and Smythe had pressed on when companions had been forced to retreat. Although he had been slower than Pete Boardman and Pertemba he had made quite a respectable time and was in good spirits. He even tried to persuade them to go back to the summit with him so that he could film them on top, but you do not retrace your steps lightly at 29,000 feet and Pete declined. He was worried anyway, about the time.

This was more difficult ground than Pertemba had even been on before and he wanted to move one at a time. Pete therefore said that they would make their way to the south summit and wait there. At the time this seemed perfectly reasonable; it was cloudy, but you could see the sun through the clouds, and though it was gusting at about 40 mph, visibility was still quite good. Mick being alone on the way down, would be much faster than Pete Boardman and Pertemba.

And so Mick Burke plodded on alone towards the summit of Everest, the goal of his ambition, and the other pair started down—but within half an hour, weather conditions deteriorated dramatically, with the cloud closing in to form a complete white-out and the snow gusting furiously.

It was all they could do to find the top of the gully leading back down to the upper snowfield. They sat there shivering in the driving wind for an hour and a quarter, hoping desperately to see the vague shape that would be Mick Burke, looming through the scudding snow. But he did not come back. He should have had time to get back down and one can only assume that he missed his footing, or much more likely walked

over one of the cornices which overlook the huge Kangshung face of
Everest which would have been on his left as he came down. I am
absolutely certain that he reached the top of Everest and the accident
would have occurred on the descent.

After an hour and a quarter it became increasingly obvious to Pete
Boardman that unless he and Pertemba started down they would never
get back to the Top Camp that night. Haston and Scott had only just
survived a bivouac in reasonable conditions two nights before. In these
stormy conditions they would have had practically no chance at all.
It was an agonizing decision to make, but the only course open was to
retreat, particularly since he felt responsible for his companion Pertemba
as well as himself. They left the south summit just in time. They had the
greatest difficulty in finding the end of the fixed rope that led back to
Camp VI and only got back an hour after dark.

The next day, September 27, the storm raged unabated. There was
no question of leaving their tent, and anyway Pertemba was suffering
from snow blindness and Boardman had frostbite and was exhausted.
Had the weather been fine, Boysen would have ventured out, at least to
the end of the fixed rope, and we could have pushed Nick Estcourt and
Tut Braithwaite up from Camp V, to have a look as well. But after
another day and another night of storm we had to admit to ourselves
that he was dead; in the unlikely event of Mick not having slipped and
fallen, he could not possibly have survived without oxygen or shelter.

I had spent a year, thinking and planning not just how to achieve
success but also how to reduce the factor of risk—but you can never
reduce it completely. However large and strong the expedition, however
careful the planning, the power of the elements, the personal factor, the
little piece of bad luck, can all combine to wreck the most careful plan—
and yet we must accept this if we go on climbing, for this is the very
challenge and romance that mountaineering presents.

Just one week earlier our expedition had been like a well-oiled machine pushing people, rope, oxygen and food up the southwest face, establishing camps, forging steadily forwards consistently ahead of schedule.
We had established Base Camp on August 25, just three weeks earlier
than in 1972. The experience of the Japanese in 1973 and the French in
1974 had indicated that we should be able to expect settled weather
during this period, with mornings of sunshine and snow in the afternoon.
This had proved the case, and although there was a constant threat of
avalanche both in the Western Cwm and on the face itself, there was
only one day when we were unable to push supplies up the icefall and
the Western Cwm. We had modified our original plan in the face of
the snow conditions during the monsoon, and had completely changed
the positions of Camps IV and V. This had made sound logistic sense
for we had placed Camp IV at a much lower height than on previous

occasions, at about 23,700 feet at a position where it was sheltered from the threat of major avalanches and was in reasonable distance from our Advanced Base. Almost as a direct consequence of this, we put Camp V lower as well, still on the right side of the main gully at about 25,500 feet.

I had moved up there on September 16 to establish camp and assess our future movements. I had never believed in leading an expedition from Base Camp. At the same time it is usually a mistake to get right out in front, for then you become obsessed with the bit of snow or rock immediately in front of your nose, and as a result lose sight of the overall situation. This was a different situation, however. For we were now venturing on to new ground, across the great gully towards the deep gash on the left-hand gully, from a different camp than we had used in 1972.

I felt I needed to get the feel of the situation and so spent nine days at Camp V, working with successive groups of climbers to force the route as quickly as possible up to the mouth of the gully and then through the rock band. I was able to move as far forward as this because of the strength of my organizing team. Dave Clarke was at Camp IV, Adrian Gordon at Advanced Base, Mike Rhodes, our Barclays Bank nominee, at Camp I and Mike Cheney at Base.

Their role was not as dramatic as that of the lead climbers, but in many ways it was more vital, for without the flow of supplies going smoothly up the mountain the people in the higher camps would have had to retreat. I had spent a long time before the expedition working out our logistics, and the fastest time in which we could possibly climb the mountain.

We had consistently stayed in front of this theoretical path, largely because of the tremendous enthusiasm of the Sherpas who carried more, often heavier, loads than from previous experience I had ever thought possible. We were paying them well, but there was more to it than that. It was primarily the spirit and feel of potential success that pervaded the expedition.

It was on September 20 that Nick Estcourt and Tut Braithwaite found the key to the south face of Everest, a ramp of steep snow that crept out of the deep-gashed gully that penetrated the rock band on its left side. Although we had obtained every photograph which we possibly could, none had shown what happened inside the gully; this was one of the big gambles. Mick Burke and I carried loads of rope in support of Estcourt and Braithwaite that day, and we slowly followed up the ropes they had already fixed, into the deep, shadow-enclosed jaws of the gully. A rock plastered with snow, jammed across the walls, formed the first barrier. Tut Braithwaite forced his way up one edge. By the time he had reached the top he had run out of oxygen, but

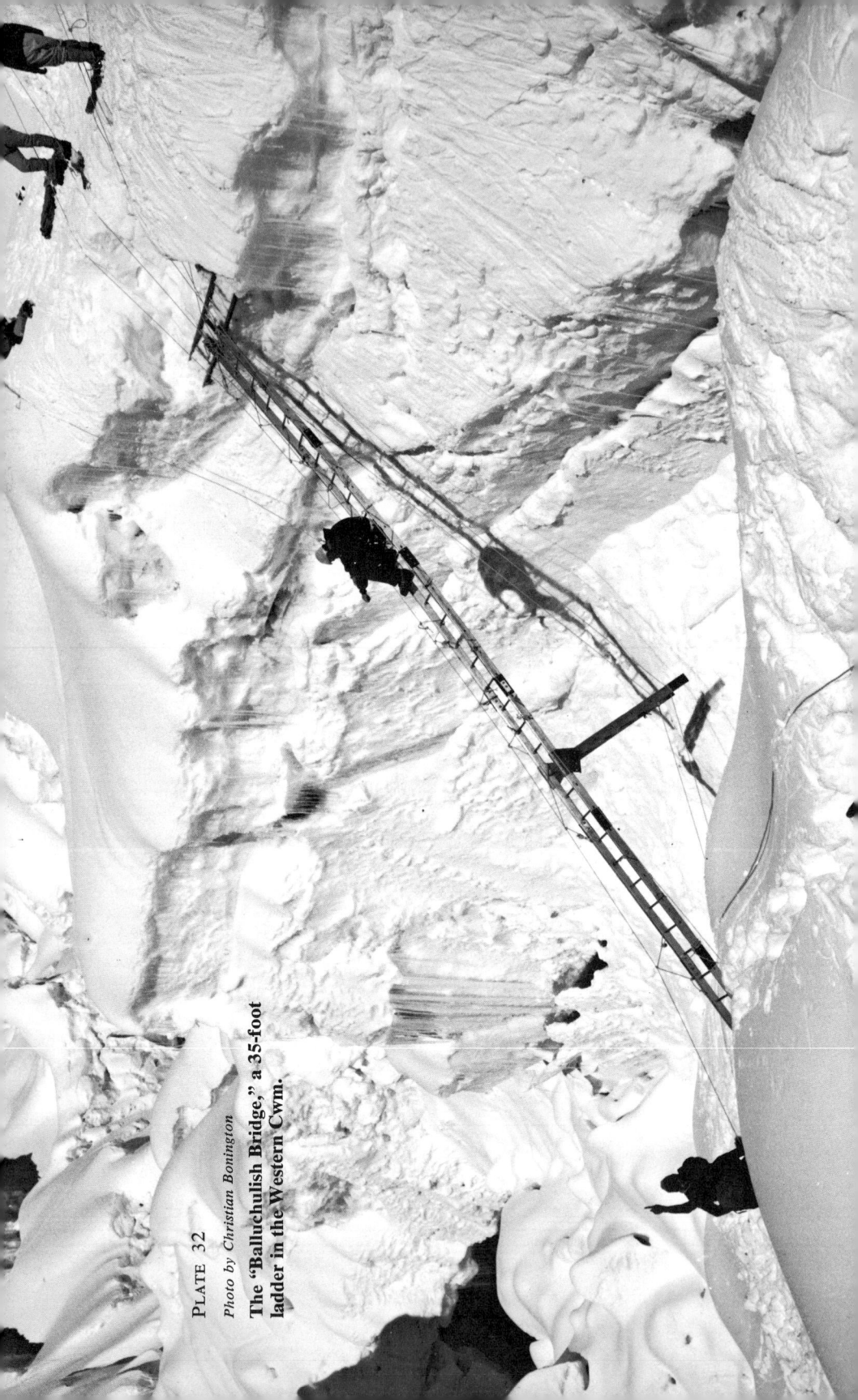

PLATE 32

Photo by Christian Bonington

The "Balluchulish Bridge," a 35-foot ladder in the Western Cwm.

PLATE 33

Photo by Doug Scott

Camp IV at 23,700 feet. The tarpaulins above the MacInnes Boxes act as avalanche chutes to protect against powder-snow avalanches.

he just kept going. Nick, who had already finished his cylinder, climbed up past Tut.

There was a shout from the shadows above, "There's a way through." And we followed on up. By the time Mick and I had reached them, Nick Estcourt was already climbing the ramp. The height was close to 27,000 feet. It was probably the hardest climbing ever attempted at that altitude, and he was without oxygen. The overhanging wall above pushed him out of balance. Afterwards, he said that because of the altitude it was one of the hardest pitches he had ever led. In doing so, he had solved the problem of the rock band.

On our return that afternoon and on the next day, which we used as our rest day, I made my calculations to ensure a smooth summit bid and subsequent ascents or bids. It was an incredibly complex permutation of movement of men, equipment, oxygen and food. I completed it at 25,500 feet, the odd whiff of oxygen to keep my mind working clearly—and at the end of about twelve hours of work, had a plan that worked, with Dougal Haston and Doug Scott making the first bid and two groups of four making the second and third. The next day, on September 22, I had what to me as a leader was the supreme satisfaction of helping Doug and Dougal into Camp VI.

Doug Scott writes:

For Dougal and me here were three incredible days of mountaineering on this our third expedition to Everest. On September 22 we moved up the gully by way of Tut's fixed ropes and then out of it right by the way of the ropes left by Nick. We were both amazed at the simplicity of the solution of the rock band and at the change of perspective—a veritable "devil's kitchen" of a gash so unusual on the open slopes of Everest. There was another 300 feet of ground to climb and rope to fix before we were out of the gully system and had found a site for Camp VI.

This was on a narrow arête of snow made possible only by hacking out a notch in its profile. Ang Phurba brought up the heavy tent with surprising ease. This splendid Sherpa went off down just as Chris, Mike Thompson and Mick Burke arrived with other vital supplies—rope, food and oxygen. Their magnificent carry up to 27,300 feet gave Dougal and me the wherewithal to continue our upward progress.

They went down, Chris weary from nine days' hard effort above Camp V. Mike Thompson gave us his best wishes, trusting us to make good his unselfish ferry. We would not let him down or Chris or any of the other lads below who had worked hard and fast to put us in this position.

The MacInnes box (a special tent named after its designer, Hamish MacInnes, the expedition's deputy leader) took a lot of erecting. Hacking out snow at that height was hard work without oxygen. We had just enough cylinders for climbing and none to waste on static activities around camp. Just before dark we snuggled into our sleeping bags and began brewing mugs of tea and a billy full of sausage and mash.

Before light Dougal left the tent to lay the first of our three 400-foot lengths of fixed rope. It was his turn as I had completed the route of the gully the day before. It was slow going for him in the cold early morning light as the ground became increasingly steep and for 20 feet there was even vertical rock lightly powdered with snow—hard work at 27,500 feet. My lead ran over easier ground and by sun up we had 800 feet fixed. Dougal continued diagonally upwards across more difficult rock shale bands, dipping the wrong way and uncomfortably loose. We also ran out our two 150-foot lengths of climbing rope and retreated back to camp with all the rope we had fixed halfway to the gully leading up to the south summit.

We lay in our feathers that night listening to the wind buffeting the top pyramid of Everest and rocking our little square of canvas. No real doubts but nagging little thoughts of how vulnerable we were, how much we were at the mercy of the weather, how lucky we should be if our ascent even took place—and then we were off—into double boots, crampons, oversuits and harness, downing a cup of tea and away along the ropes with Jümars sliding on the icy sheets. It took only a quarter of the time to reach our high point of the day before. So much for fixed ropes—then on to the virgin slopes. Rope-length after rope-length until Dougal's lead took us to the foot of the final couloir.

Dougal Haston writes:

Crossing into it, we realized that we were in for a hard time. The snow was soft and deep and it looked much longer than we had expected. Just before the rock step my oxygen packed up and it took an hour's fiddling to fix it. Doug led on to the step and, climbing carefully and well, was up it in one and a half hours. Here we left a fixed rope. The next few hours were spent in a type of wading up steep snow (up to 60°). The leader first of all had to clear a layer of powder with his hands, pack it down until it was reasonably consolidated, then try to stand up, usually sinking up to his knees. Near the South Summit a piece of rock provided some relief. About three P.M. we pulled over the cornice and took shelter in Tibet.

Doug writes:

We considered bivouacking. There was a lot to recommend it; loose unconsolidated snow that might later firm up with the rising wind and the lateness of the hour, but then there was the feeling of getting the job

PLATE 34

Photo by Christian Bonington

Looking down the lower reaches of the left couloir. Camp V is visible left of center. Three climbers are climbing from the camp towards the couloir.

PLATE 35

Photo by Doug Scott

Dougal Haston on the col between the south and main summits of Everest. Bivouac was in shadow at his right.

done there and then while we had oxygen and strength. We decided
to have a cup of hot water (victuals were low) and have a go at the
ridge. Dougal wriggled into his bivouac sack while I tried to scoop out
a snow hole to escape the spindrift. I had not gone more than a few
feet when Dougal emerged with the hot water. Thus fortified we set
off along the ridge.

Dougal writes:

We knew that the way to the summit was not technically difficult
but also wondered about the time factor and whether the snow conditions
would be similar to those encountered on the ascent. A bivouac was
looking more and more probable. We deliberated, waiting till the sun
went off the ridge then making an attempt, but finally decided to push
on for the top in the present conditions.

At four P.M. we left the South Summit and after a rope-length on
the ridge were relieved to find that though not ideal the snow conditions
did improve. The Hillary Step was deeply masked in powder snow and
I shovelled my way up it without too much trouble. There was some
windslab avalanche danger above but by treading carefully close to the
cornice I avoided it. Soon after we were moving together in beautiful
sunset colours to the top.

This was marked by a curious metal structure with strips of red flag
attached which can only be evidence at last of a long-doubted Chinese
ascent of the old British route from the North Col. The view was as
much and more as any climber could expect who has struggled to the
top of Everest—purples, reds, blacks with the twilight shadow of our
mountain projected out on to the plains of Tibet. Down we had to go
to the not-so-inviting thought of a bivouac. Soon retracing our steps,
we were back at the South Summit, leaving a rope in place at the Hillary
Step—thinking of the second ascent and more. While I boiled some
more water, Doug started on a snow cave. Soon we were both working
on it.

Doug writes:

After another cup of hot water we both set to work on the hole. I
hacked away at the roof with the ice pick. Dougal scooped out the loose
snow with his gloved hands. At eight o'clock, just as the remaining
oxygen failed, we had our snow cave. We snuggled into the hole at
28,700 feet, Dougal in his down suit and duvet boots. For me a nylon-
fibre-pile suit and nylon oversuit and frozen boots. There was to be no
sleep that night. With the elation of Everest to sustain us for a while
we began the long ritual of rubbing and pounding our feet into luke-
warmness. We continued the effort through that long night until the

dawn, a red glow giving out as much heat as an electric fire a million miles away. The cold by this time had worried its way into our limbs and backs and was not far from the body core. Hypothermia approaching, we put on our frozen boots, gaiters and crampons and plunged down the windblown trail to Camp VI.

Bonington writes:

We had solved the problem on the Southwest Face. It wasn't the "Ultimate Challenge", that rather unfortunate title our American publishers chose for the story of our 1972 expedition. No mountain problem can be described as ultimate, since no sooner is one problem solved, than the next is discovered—this is the joy of the sport. It was, however, a complex and intriguing problem and as a result a very satisfying one. Even our best friends had given us no more than an even chance of success when we set out and quite a few put the odds against a lot higher than that. This in itself increased the attraction of the challenge for climbing is all about playing with uncertainties. We had needed a big, strong expedition to solve the problem, but even within the precision of the planning, there was plenty of room for individual discovery, not just for the members of the summit team, but for everyone who went out in front or even those who had a support role throughout the expedition. I got my own satisfaction from playing my mountain logistics games as well as from those few days in the lead below the rock band. Each one of us absorbed the sheer magnificence of that ever-expanding view of mountains from the side of Everest—and then there's the magic of Everest itself; it not only has altitude and scale, it also has an atmosphere of history that one inevitably becomes involved in. Perhaps, most important of all, we came back with a regard for each other heightened rather than lessened. The Southwest Face had been a good experience.

Summary of Statistics.

ASCENT: Mount Everest, First Ascent of the Southwest Face, September 24, 1975 (Haston, Scott); September 26 (Boardman, Pertemba and almost certainly Burke).

PERSONNEL: Christian Bonington, leader; Hamish MacInnes, deputy leader; Peter Boardman, Martin Boysen, Paul Braithwaite, Mick Burke, Michael Cheney, Charles Clarke, David Clarke, James Duff, Nick Estcourt, Allen Fyffe, Adrian Gordon, Dougal Haston, Mike Rhodes, Ronnie Richards, Doug Scott, Mike Thompson, Bob Stoodley; BBC Team: Arthur Chesterman, Ned Kelly, Chris Ralling, Ian Stuart.

PLATE 36

Aerial photo by James Wickwire

K2 from the West. Northwest Ridge on left skyline.

The Northwest Ridge of K2

JAMES WICKWIRE

O N the Pakistani-Chinese border, K2 rises as a rocky, isolated pyramid to 28,741 feet*, a scant two rope-lengths below the height of Everest. Although K2 is not as frequented by mountaineers as its higher neighbor 900 miles to the east, the six expeditions that have unsuccessfully attempted it—and the only one that succeeded—have written memorable pages in the history of Himalayan mountaineering.

Who can forget the bizarre circumstances surrounding the 1902 Eckenstein expedition on which, among other occurrences, Aleister Crowley, the notorious "Beast 666," pulled a pistol on another expedition member; the elaborate undertaking of the Duke of Abruzzi in 1909 which first thoroughly explored the mountain's defenses; the magnificent reconnaissance of 1938 when a small American team led by Dr. Charles Houston, with extremely light resources, very nearly reached the top; Fritz Wiessner's near miss in 1939 when, but for his reluctant Sherpa companion, Wiessner could have probably climbed without the aid of oxygen through the night to the summit; the remarkable return of Houston, Bob Bates, and the others from the heights in 1953 after surviving a ten-day storm and the accident in which six men were held by Pete Schoening's belay, and the tragic, but merciful loss of Art Gilkey which enabled the team to retreat to safety; and, finally, Compagnoni and Lacedelli's amazing oxygen-starved climb to the summit the day after Walter Bonatti's incredible bivouac at 26,000 feet? After all this, how could one have contemplated climbing K2 without a feeling of awe, a sense of interference with the past?

Since 1960, when a German-American expedition failed on the Abruzzi ridge, no expedition had attempted K2. With the dramatic Nixon overture to China in 1972, which had followed the U.S. "tilt" toward Pakistan in its war with India the previous year, it appeared that once again expeditions might venture to the Baltoro Glacier with its incomparable panoply of peaks—Payu, Masherbrum, Trango Towers, Muztagh Tower, the Gasherbrums, Broad Peak, and K2.

In December 1973, a team composed of Jim Whittaker (as leader), Lou Whittaker, Alex Bertulis, Rob Schaller, Leif Patterson, and myself

---

* Mr. Rajput of the Survey of India confirms 28,741 feet or 8760 meters as the newly accepted altitude of K2.

PLATE 37

Photo by James Wickwire

**Northwest Ridge of K2.
Pinnacled section is at the left.**

applied for permission to attempt the unclimbed, and only barely reconnoitered northwest ridge of K2 in the summer of 1975. Unknown to
us, a Polish team received permission for K2 in the summer of 1974 but
could not field an expedition, due to brevity of notice. Bob Bates, a
K2 veteran from 1938 and 1953, and Ad Carter, along with their
wives, trekked to the base of K2 that summer, becoming the first persons
to approach closely to K2 in fourteen years. To assist us in adding to
the meager knowledge of the mountain's west side, they probed the
Savoia Glacier toward the pass at its head which the Duke of Abruzzi
and his guides had reached in 1909. Poor weather, however, prevented
Bates and Carter from obtaining a clear view of the upper northwest
ridge, and, as it turned out, their reconnaissance could not have helped
us anyway.

On March 11, 1974, we received the electrifying news from the
Pakistani government that we had permission to climb K2! Our application received a big boost from Senator Edward Kennedy, a close friend
of Jim Whittaker and, most important, Prime Minister Zulfikar Ali
Bhutto. The ensuing year was a hectic scramble to raise the necessary
money, to choose the proper equipment, food, and other supplies (including oxygen), and to round out the team. Early on, Galen Rowell
and Fred Dunham joined the climbing team. Dianne Roberts, Jim's wife,
was to be our photographer. Later, Bertulis left the expedition and was
replaced by Fred Stanley. Finally, Steve Marts agreed to be our cinematographer, and we had a ten-person team.

At the last minute, NASA agreed to fill our experimental oxygen
bottles to a pressure of 4,000 psi, a major boost in capacity over previous systems.

The long flight to Pakistan was a relief after the pressure-packed final
stage of preparations. We now had only K2 to worry about—or so we
thought. We hoped to avoid a lengthy stay in Rawalpindi, the former
military garrison town in northern Pakistan at the foot of the Himalaya.
But poor flying weather kept us pinned down for two weeks. By the
time we boarded a Pakistani Air Force C-130 for the spectacular flight
to Skardu, virtually all of us had succumbed to one form of diarrhea or
another.

Flying past ice-festooned Nanga Parbat and the desert valley where
Skardu is located, we continued on to K2 for an aerial reconnaissance.
Approached from the west, K2 is a classic pyramid. Its ridges though
are much steeper than its Egyptian counterparts. All of us were surprised
at the amount of rock showing. Unlike the snowy southern and eastern
aspects of K2, seen from the west, the peak is a forbidding rock monolith.
Border restrictions kept us in Pakistan air space, which prevented our
seeing the lower portions of the northwest ridge where we knew good
luck would be necessary to get by some ferocious-looking gendarmes at

PLATE 38

Photo by Galen A. Rowell

**Porters at Concordia. Behind rise
Gasherbrums, Sia Kangri and Mitre.**

23,000 feet. Lou Whittaker thought he saw a snow ramp past the gendarmes on the Chinese side but couldn't be sure.

Our return to Skardu, the traditional jumping-off point for expeditions to the Baltoro, seemed anticlimactic. K2's awesomeness lingered on. We hoped to see K2 again from the ground in two weeks, but it was to be nearly a month before we walked into Concordia, that vast meeting place of glaciers from which K2 rises in its classic thrust eight miles to the north.

In the interim, we were plagued by more than our fair share of misfortune. Pakistan International Airlines off-loaded 62 boxes of our expedition gear in Rawalpindi, including most of the precious oxygen. This delayed us from leaving Skardu, making a 57-mile Jeep ride to Dasso, and beginning the 120-mile hike to K2. Once the missing equipment arrived, things went reasonably well until we reached Askole, the last permanent village in the Braldu river valley, three days' march from the snout of the Baltoro Glacier. There we learned that 200 additional porters programmed to carry atta, lentils, tea, and fuel for our 600 approach porters were not available. A late spring which kept most of the Askole men at work tilling their sparse fields prevented Major Manzoor Hussain, our liaison officer, from mustering more than 75 men. Instead of progressing toward the mountain as a single, advancing party, we now faced the discouraging prospect of load-shuttling, a game that can only mean delay.

At Payu, a couple of miles from the Baltoro, we had our first real taste of the Balti tactics that would keep the question of our ever reaching K2 unanswered to the last. Overcast skies became a pretext for a sitdown strike and the porters' demand for additional rupees not covered by the government regulations we thought we could rely upon. The regulations soon ceased to have any relevance, except, for instance, when it came to our obligation to provide medical assistance to the porters.

The remainder of the approach march, which should have been a stirring walk through perhaps the most spectacular mountain valley in the world, was instead an almost continual hassle of porter strikes and demands for higher wages. At each halt along the way, we thought the expedition might never reach its objective. With the sickness of Ghulam Rasul, the porters' sirdar, our liaison officer was unable to maintain steady movement toward the mountain. Miscalculations about the amount of porter food necessary only added to our troubles.

At Ghoro, one stage short of Concordia, we were at a complete standstill. Strong measures were called for. After over three hours of negotiations without success, we threatened to burn all the equipment and money. The next day the porters carried.

During the entire approach, Rob Schaller performed heroics in treating the sick and ailing porters and village people. Each day would find Rob engrossed for several hours in dispensing most of the 20,000 aspirin we brought with us, as well as dealing with more serious medical problems. As a result of his close contact with the porters, Rob came down with bronchitis, which he was never fully able to shake for the duration of the expedition. Worse, Leif Patterson and Galen Rowell were later burdened with the same problem, which deteriorated into pneumonia.

Base Camp was finally established on June 5 at 17,600 feet on the Savoia Glacier, about three weeks behind the schedule originally set. Within two days, Camp I was located at 19,000 feet, on the first rise above the main Savoia Glacier. Above was a steep ice face leading to Savoia Pass. The maps showed the pass elevation at 21,870 feet; we were disappointed after climbing the ice face to discover it was only 20,500 feet, leaving a much greater vertical distance to the summit. Lou Whittaker and I probed above the pass, hoping to find a passage past the pinnacles on the north side. Edging out on the cornice, I could see only a sheer drop to the glacier 6,000 feet below. Discouraged, we retreated. Three days later, another probe to the left yielded no better result. A reasonable route did not exist on the Chinese side of the ridge.

Camp II had meanwhile been established in a hollow below the crest of the pass on the north side. Wind was a constant nemesis there, even in good weather. Our only remaining choice was to try the right side of the broad slope above us, with a possibility we might turn pinnacles on that side, along the top, or perhaps on the Chinese side (but higher up than the earlier probes).

Deep avalanche-prone snow lay between Camp II and the steeper face. We worked hard plowing through but were then rewarded with our most enjoyable climbing of the trip. With support from Rob Schaller and Steve Marts (who quickly became more than cinematographer), Lou and I climbed the 45° to 50° face for several hundred feet, strenuous climbing on hard ice overlaid with unstable snow. Coming up a last steep snow gully, I emerged on the ridge at 21,500 feet. Towering above was the summit pyramid of K2, but to reach it we still had to negotiate the pinnacles. The route led left up a shallow snow gully flanked by rock outcrops, but deteriorating weather forced us down.

For five days we were pounded by high winds and driving snow. Nearly out of food and fuel, we made a dash for Base Camp as the storm petered out. Leif had made a remarkable recovery from his bout with pneumonia and was eager to go higher. He went back up to Camp II with Jim, Lou, Steve, and me. In another day of climbing above Camp II, we could push the route only another 150 feet. Another storm blew in, and we were pinned down for another five days.

PLATE 40

Photo by James Wickwire

The pinnacled ridge of K2 seen from
the top of the first pinnacle.

Jim descended to Camp I following a sober discussion among us with the inescapable conclusion that our chances for the summit were growing very slim. With Galen and Rob knocked out completely with pneumonia and bronchitis, and the two Freds suffering from minor ailments, our climbing strength was greatly reduced. The high-altitude porters had not performed well; only three of them made it as far as Camp II, forcing us to rely on a winch system to get loads up the ice face. It was now July, and the storms and resultant delays left us a long way from the summit.

In any event, we decided to push the route farther, hoping for a breakthrough which would negate our pessimistic assessment. On July 3, the storm blown out, Lou, Leif, and I climbed back up the fixed ropes. Steve followed to film. I was able to finish the steep gully with a couple of hard moves on the near-vertical rock at its top. Above the difficulties, I could see from a narrow ridge of snow that climbing or circumventing the pinnacles was out of the question. First Lou, then Leif, came up. Each of us recognized the inevitable: the expedition was at an end. Ahead, the pinnacles were silhouetted against the mass of K2. The slopes on either side were in excess of 70° for several thousand feet. At 22,000 feet, perched on the narrow top of the first pinnacle, we could go no higher. There was not sufficient time to withdraw and start anew on the west-southwest ridge, which splits the west face of K2.

The return trip was pleasantly uneventful, except for two medical emergencies. Our best high-altitude porter, Akbar Ali, became gravely ill from round-worm infestation. His intestine became perforated, and only Rob's round-the-clock efforts kept him alive. We evacuated Akbar to Concordia, where a requested military helicopter was to pick him up. It never came, but the sick porter gradually recovered his strength. Later, just beyond Dokass, one of the 80 porters who carried out our loads became deathly sick from a perforated ulcer. Again, Rob was successful in keeping him alive. Most remarkably, the helicopter that had been requested for Akbar came to Payu just when the newly sick porter reached there. He was flown out to Skardu and survived.

*   *   *   *   *

All of us believe that the northwest ridge of K2 is not a feasible route to the summit. The only possible alternative to the pinnacled ridge would be a dangerous face climb and traverse to reach the ridge above the pinnacles. On the mountain's west side, the best route, given our experience with the northwest ridge, is the west-southwest ridge. It is no easy proposition, with some very difficult climbing in the last 3000 feet to the summit.

Northeast Ridge of M-6

TALBOT BIELEFELDT

W E began by finding that the road over
Rohtang Pass to Keylang was closed by record snowfall, thus adding a
week of trekking to the expedition. Then, the first day out of Manali,
we ran into a police officer who said he had already climbed M-6. It
seems that in September, 1974, the India-Tibet Border Police had attempted the northeast ridge of the mountain. Backing off, the Indians
walked around the north side of the peak to the southwest ridge, which
they climbed to the top for the first ascent.

We cabled the Ministry of Defense from Keylang for permission to
attempt an unclimbed peak inside the restricted Inner Defense Line.
Receiving provisional approval, we moved ahead, only to be hauled out
by the police three days later. Lute Jerstad, Vijay Devasher, and liaison
officer Lieutenant Dey returned to Keylang to make amends to the
Deputy Commissioner of Lahoul, while the rest of us headed back for
M-6.

Two obvious unclimbed routes remained: the attempted northeast
ridge, and the direct north face—the latter a 2000-foot, 50° ice slope.
It took us two days to retrace our steps and two more to ascend the
Milang Nala and Mulkila Glacier to Base Camp at 14,100 feet. At the
snout of the glacier we paid off the muleteers and made the last carry
with porters hired from local villages.

Our planned three-day approach was now into day 13. An impressive effort by Wangyal, James O'Neill, Tom Ettinger, and Tony
Case put Camp I at 16,400 feet and Camp II at 18,375 feet, during three
days of intermittant storm. Lute, Vijay, and Lieutenant Dey rejoined
us during this period, and after a snowbound rest day, the group moved
up in strength on June 13. Deep snow made for slow going and decided us in favor of M-6's northeast ridge (the one attempted by the
Border Police) rather than the north face. (As it turned out, the north
face seems to have a relatively stable line up a rocky rib. It remains an
attractive potential route.)

Camp III (19,350 feet) was cut into the crest of the sharp ridge connecting M-6 and Mulkila (M-4). Over 500 feet of rope were fixed between the bergschrund and the crest. We occupied the camp that same
day, breaking the acclimatization rule of "carry high, sleep low." We
paid for our haste, with three of the four scheduled to climb on June
15 being ill. (Eventually two strong members of the expedition—Trevor
Pelling and Guy Rainsford—would lose their chance at the summit be-

cause of altitude sickness). I came up from Camp II to join Tony Case that afternoon, and we began the ascent of the ridge.

Worried both about the cornice collapsing on the south side of the crest and avalanche danger on the opposite slope, we plowed through deep snow across the top of the north face. We had been slow in getting ropes and snow anchors up to the higher camps and ran out of pickets and line short of the steep rock band that seemed the main obstacle on the route. Descending to Camp II on the 16th, we left the lead to Jerstad and Ettinger.

James O'Neill and Gene Howard joined Lute and Tom on the ridge on the 17th with additional equipment. Reaching the cliff band, the four encountered unstable rock and ice-filled cracks. Scratching over a couple of F6 moves in crampons, they reached the top of the cliff late in the afternoon, finally turning back near sunset at a false summit on the upper ridge. Darkness, icy ropes and slipping Jümars hampered the descent, and it was 10:30 P.M. before Sherpa Gyalgen could serve dinner at High Camp.

With a predawn start from Camp II, Bob O'Loughlin, Tony Case, Jim Bright, Namgyal, Wangyal, and I climbed to Camp III on the 18th. We were joined by Gyalgen, and the seven of us reached the false summit by ten o'clock. The remainder of the route was another deep-snow ordeal, and it was afternoon before the mountain was climbed.

The descent and march out were uneventful, aided considerably by cleared roads and by a series of truck rides arranged by Lieutenant Dey.

Western climbers may be put off by some of the conditions of Indian mountaineering, including the scarcity of maps and abundance of bureaucracy. Perseverance and a sense of humor help here, as do people such as our Ladakhi high-altitude porters and Nepali Sherpas. These did a magnificent job of herding their employers safely through the hazards of government cartography and village merchants.

Summary of Statistics:

AREA: Western Himalaya, District Lahoul, Himachal Pradesh, India.

NEW ROUTE AND SECOND ASCENT: The northeast ridge of M-6, 20,600 feet, from the Mulkila Glacier. Ropes fixed through the crux above Camp III on June 17, 1975. Summit June 18.

PERSONNEL: Talbot Bielefeldt, Jim Bright, Tony Case, Everett Howard, Lute Jerstad (leader), Robert O'Loughlin, James O'Neill, Trevor Pelling, Guy Rainsford—*United States*; Vijay Devasher, Lieutenant Sumasher Dey (liaison officer)—*India*; Karm Chand, Namgyal Chering, Wangyal, Zorba—Ladakhi high-altitude porters; Dawa* (sirdar), Gyalgen*—Sherpas.

---

* Both men are named Dawa Gyalgen.

References:

John Millar: "A Himalaya Summer" (conclusion); *Austrian Alpine Club Newsletter*, XXXIX, Summer, 1973.

Fritz Kolb: *Himalaya Venture*; Lutterworth Press, London, 1959.

L. Krenek: "The Mountains of Central Lahul"; *Himalaya Journal*, XIII, 1946.

A.A.J., 1973, pages 489-90.

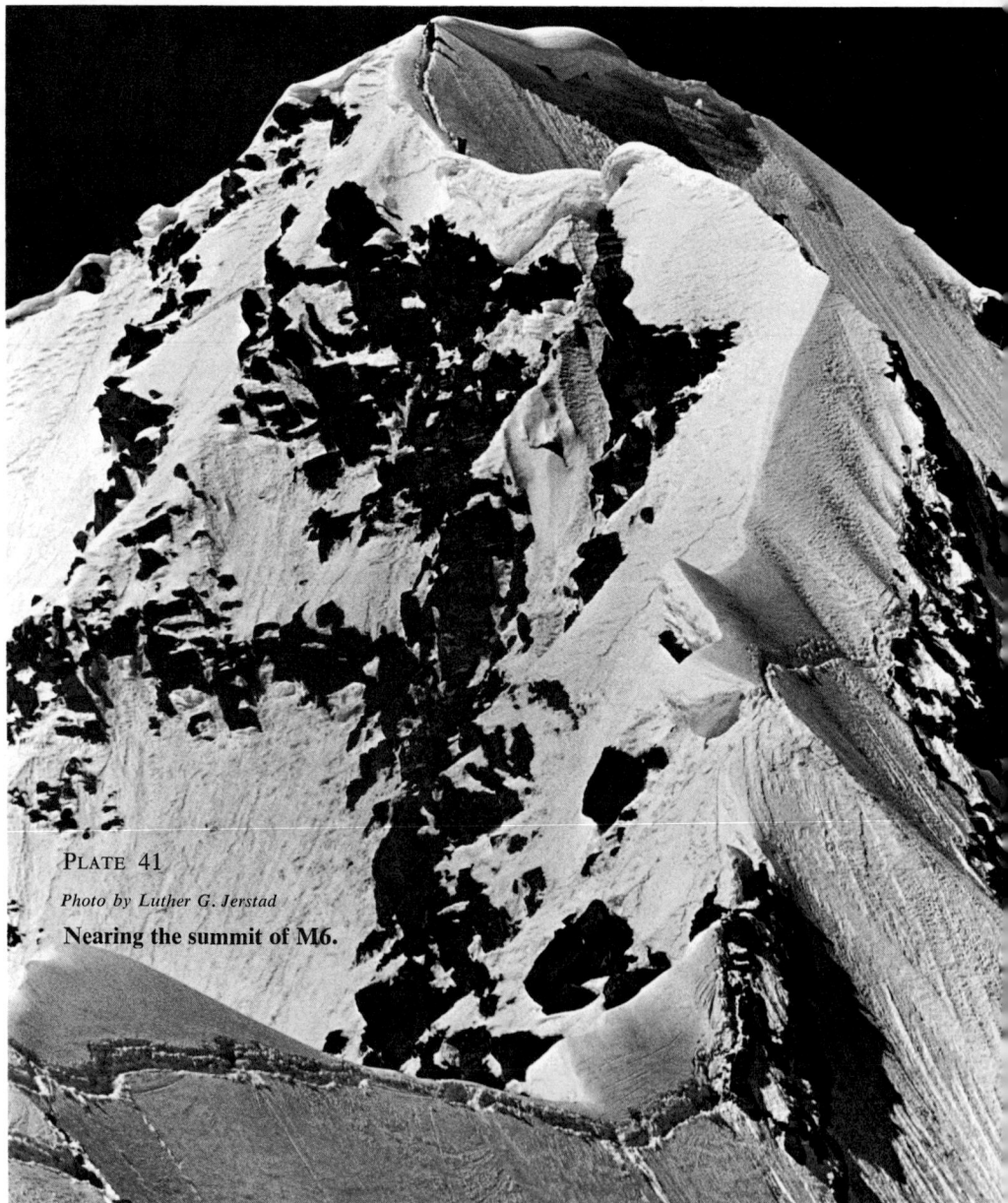

PLATE 41

Photo by Luther G. Jerstad

Nearing the summit of M6.

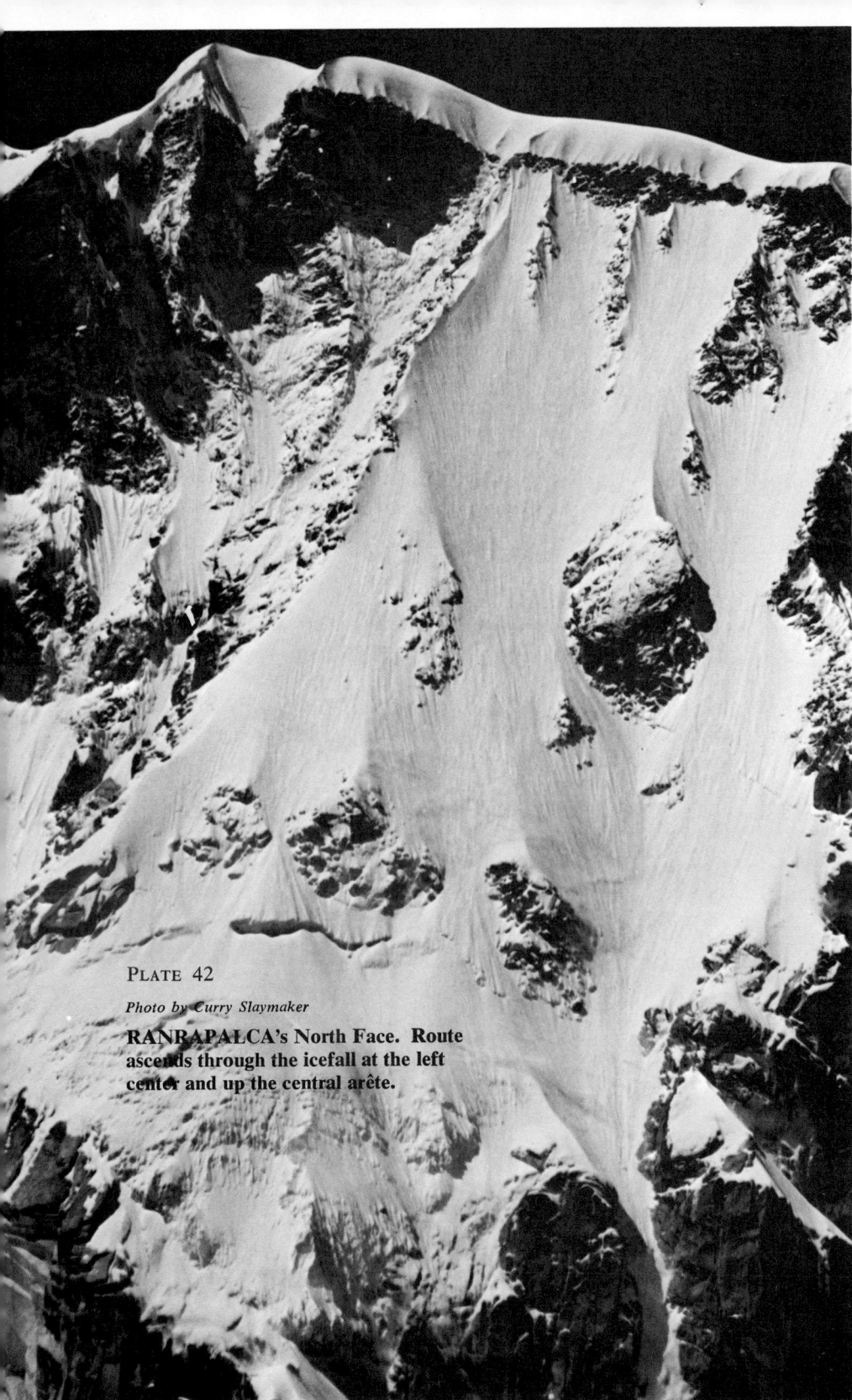

PLATE 42

Photo by Curry Slaymaker

RANRAPALCA's North Face. Route ascends through the icefall at the left center and up the central arête.

Ranrapalca's North Face, Cordillera Blanca

MICHAEL J. ROURKE

A DMITTEDLY, ours is an enviable position. Few visitors to the Cordillera Blanca have had the opportunity to stay as long as they would have liked; for Curry Slaymaker, Murray Johns, and myself it is our *campo de trabajo*. Nevertheless, we were beginning to feel like tethered animals just beyond the reach of a late summer garden's ripe produce. For Curry and me, employees of the Peruvian Ministry of Agriculture and administrators of Parque Nacional Huascarán, the frustration was a bit less. We could at least program extended weekend trips to the mountains which corresponded with our work. But Murray, who had interested us in the north face last year after studying it from various communications stations in the Cordillera Negra, had sold his soul to G.T.E. and had been unable to get away even for a walk in the *campo* in the last eleven months. By mid-August, however, we finally agreed that the weather would soon be changing and that a few of our responsibilities could be attended later and so on the 16th we left for Collón and the Quebrada Ishinka.

One learns a great deal facilitating climbers' movement to and from the mountains, so that I felt I had pretty well mastered the *campesino*'s understanding of time. Needless-to-say, we all were very surprised when Modesto Sánchez, our arriero from Collón, presented himself promptly at six A.M. with three exceptionally fit animals just as he promised the previous evening. I still wonder what his thoughts must have been as he patiently waited an hour and a half for three people who had taken about that much time the day before underlining the importance of his punctuality.

Ishinka's quiñual forests are the most extensive in the western Cordillera Blanca and the valley itself must be considered one of the most exceptional in the Callejón de Huaylas. Murray paused more than once during the hike in to point to a possible line on various rock spires, imagining himself in North Wales. He was soaring after his long absence from the mountains.

We established an acclimatization camp at 14,500 feet in Yanarajupampa just below Laguna Ishinka with a breathtaking panorama of Nevados Urus, Tokllaraju, and Palcaraju. The following two days were used shuttling equipment to the base of the north face where we established our Base Camp at 16,150 feet. I had made a reconnaissance of this area a month earlier and had been extolling its views since then. Neither Curry nor Murray felt I had exaggerated. At that time I judged that we would gain access to the face via a 250-foot, nearly vertical couloir a bit to the west of the face itself, bypassing what appeared to me a very complicated icefall which crossed the face at about 17,400 feet. By our August arrival, however, the ice in the couloir had disappeared and it was evident that it was not the most feasible way up. Murray estimated that the most direct line followed a 650-foot snow ramp to and through the icefall, which we agreed to try. We had brought 1200 feet of additional line which we intended to fix if necessary in order to finish the final 2000 feet above the icefall in a single day. Curry and I used the next two days preparing a route up the ramp and through the icefall which presented challenging gymnastic exercises in ice chimneys and labyrinthine chutes. Our fixed rope led us just below a bergschrund 80 feet above the icefall. Remembering that we had brought two climbing ropes for rappelling during the descent, Murray suggested we gain a bit more time for our summit attempt and fixed our climbing rope across a delicate bridge above the 'schrund.

According to a preliminary climbing schedule prepared before departing Huaraz and designed to facilitate Murray's acclimatization, we were to rest the next day. However, our spirits were high and we all felt strong so we decided to get an early start the following morning and go for the summit.

For some reason the best laid plans the night before never seem to be realized the morning after. Our "early start" resulted in an 8:45 A.M. departure. However, the night had been clear and we were confident that our efforts during the previous two days would assure our success. We ascended the fixed ropes in good time, but the weather began to deteriorate as we crossed the bergschrund. Murray and I leapfrogged leads up the face securing our progress with pickets and screws, confident of Curry's weighty belay in the center of the rope. Our progress was slowed by the most unusual snow and ice conditions I have yet experienced in the Cordillera Blanca. The best description I can give is a surface of sawtoothed waves, the crests of which had to be knocked away so as to advance to the next level, and this on slopes averaging 55-60°. By 6:15 P.M., Murray had in 55 minutes completed the final pitch of the face up 60° ice capped with an unstable rock mantle. By the time I reached his anchor the sun had set and visibility was nearly zero.

Our only disappointment while planning this climb was knowing that the face did not lead directly to Ranrapalca's 20,237-foot summit. In fact, we didn't exactly know where we would be after completing the face. From Huaraz it appeared that the summit was set back toward the southeast. Indeed it is, about half a mile, as we discovered the next morning after a moderately frightful bivouac. We spent a short while scouting a possible descent down the northeast ridge, dismissed it, then entrusted the dubious leading honors to Curry, who magnanimously broke steps across the crusted pampa to the final summit pyramid where we exchanged one-at-a-time ascents up the final 100 feet to the summit.

The seven-hour descent involved laborious down-climbing, carefully probing each footstep through our frozen ocean. The decision to leave for the summit a day earlier than planned proved a wise one as it began to snow heavily upon our return to Base Camp and continued during the following three days as we cleaned the mountain and departed the valley.

Summary of Statistics:

AREA: Cordillera Blanca, Perú.

NEW ROUTE: Ranrapalca, 6,168 meters (20,237 feet), North Face, August 22, 1975.

PERSONNEL: Murray Johns, Australia; Curry Slaymaker and Michael Rourke, United States.

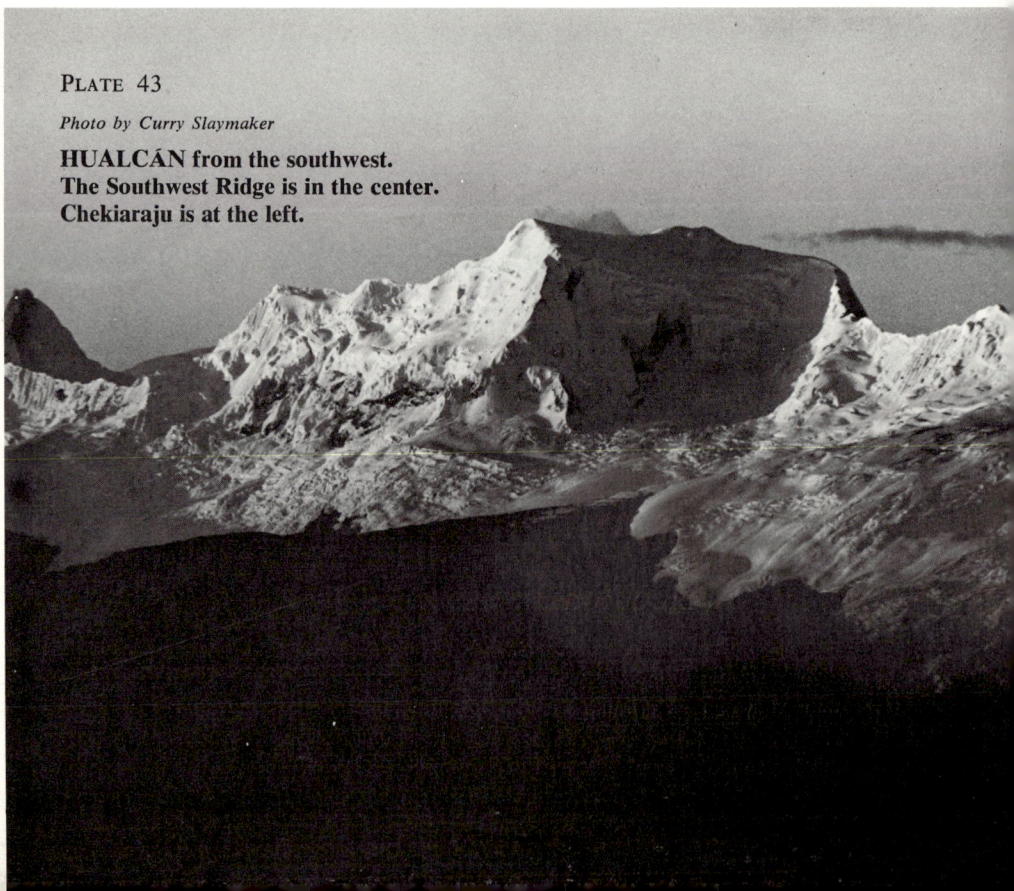

PLATE 43

Photo by Curry Slaymaker

**HUALCÁN from the southwest.
The Southwest Ridge is in the center.
Chekiaraju is at the left.**

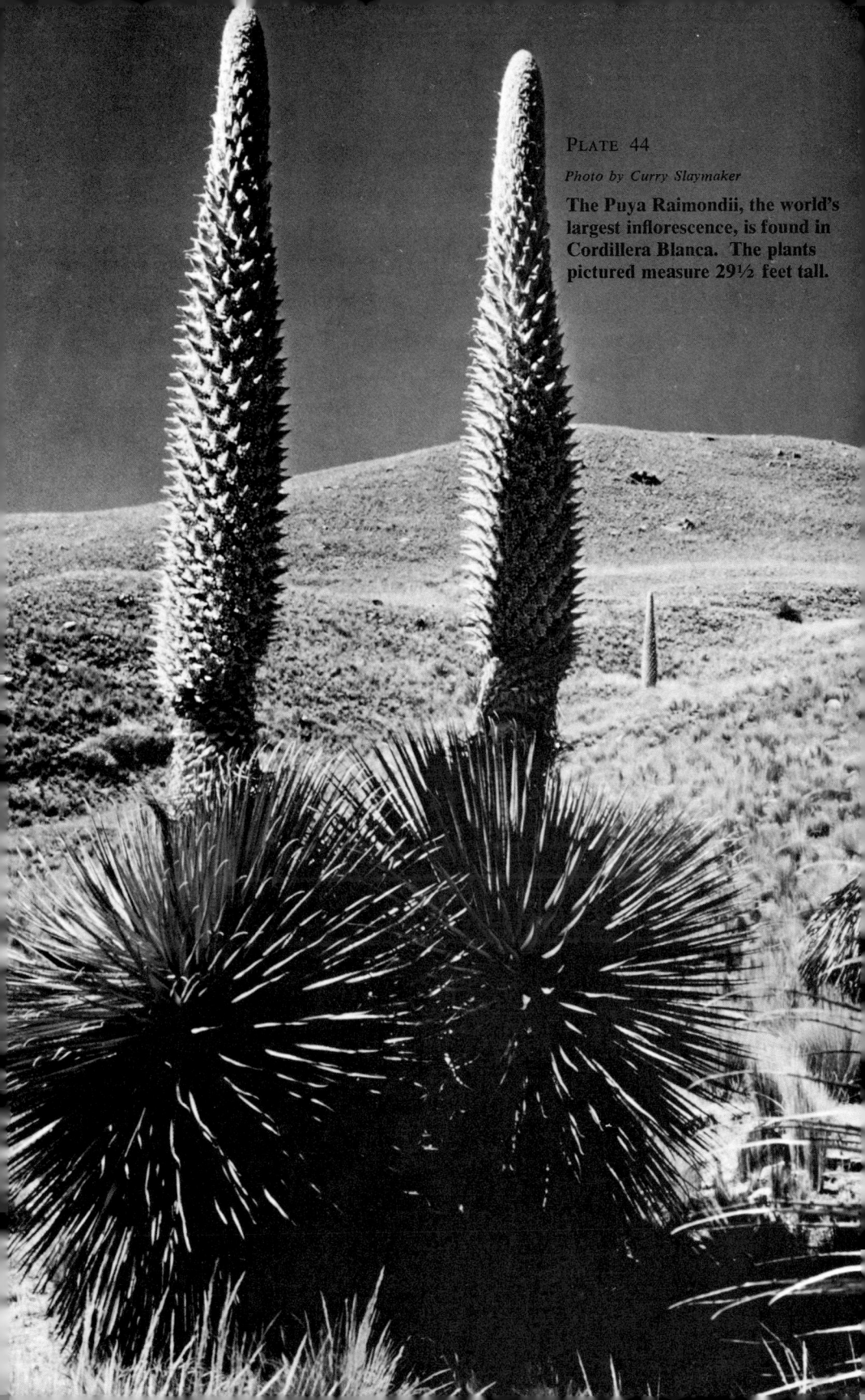

PLATE 44

Photo by Curry Slaymaker

The Puya Raimondii, the world's largest inflorescence, is found in Cordillera Blanca. The plants pictured measure 29½ feet tall.

Parque Nacional Huascarán, Cordillera Blanca, Peru

MICHAEL J. ROURKE

THE Parque Nacional Huascarán, situated in the northern Peruvian Andes approximately 400 kilometers (240 miles) north of Lima, embraces the entire Cordillera Blanca (with the exception of the northern-most Champará massif). Of the twenty odd mountain ranges in Perú, the Cordillera Blanca is the most frequented by mountaineers and hikers and one of the most accessible. The remotest peaks are only a day and a half from the central highway which services the Callejones (Valleys) of Huaylas and Conchucos. The range includes twenty-seven *nevados* of over 6,000 meters (19,686 feet) above sea level. The highest of these is Nevado Huascarán, 6,768 meters (22,206 feet), Peru's highest peak and the fourth highest in the Western Hemisphere. Eighteen major trails cross the park from altitudes of 2,500 to 4,980 meters (8,203 to 16,339 feet).

Historically, the Callejón de Huaylas is the central area affected by the Peruvian earthquake of May 31, 1970, which claimed the lives of an estimated 67,000 persons. (*A.A.J.*, 1971, pp. 241-260). In accordance with the reconstruction of this region and with Perú's increasing concern to conserve her natural resources, the Cordillera Blanca was finally officially reserved as "Parque Nacional Huascarán" on July 1, 1975.

In 1972, John Curry Slaymaker returned to the Cordillera Blanca where he had worked as a Peace Corps volunteer with the national park project several years earlier. His intentions were innocent: a visit with old friends and a couple of months tramping in the mountains. What followed is a classic example of being in the right place at the right moment. At that time, ORDEZA, a post-earthquake governmental organization founded to rebuild the destroyed area, had budgeted $70,000.00 for the national park project but had no one to administer it. The peg and the hole corresponded and in March, 1973, Slaymaker was appointed director. I joined forces with him in February of 1974, following two years in Huaraz as a volunteer teacher with the Benedictine Fathers in Los Pinos. Several others joined us, but our project was often dismissed as "the gringo operation" and given little importance. The Peace Corps program in Perú was discontinued, resulting in the discharge of two of our fine volunteers. Not long after, Curry and I also received curt letters of dismissal. We felt crushed and promptly began an appeal. By April of 1975, our case had been reconsidered and we both were reinstated. Our personal futures as Peruvian government employees are uncertain, but the park's foundation is at least secured.

Parque Nacional Huascarán consists of 340,000 hectares (840,000 acres) in the northern Andean sierra of Ancash, including portions of the provinces of Recuay, Huaraz, Carhuaz, Yungay, Huaylas, Pomabamba, Mariscal Luzuriaga, Huari, Sihuas, and Bolognesi. It is 152 kilometers (92 miles) long, stretching from the Quebrada Quitaraksa (Huallanca) in the north to Nevado Rajutuna (Aquia) in the south and averages 30 kilometers (18 miles) in width. Its eastern and western borders average 4,000 meters (13,124 feet) in elevation.

Varieties of flora extend from orchids, lupines, and agave near the valley entrances to forests of quishuar and quinual, which at 4,750 meters (15,585 feet) rank among the highest in the world. Perhaps the park's most famous species is the Puya raymondii, or as it is known locally, "kunco." Little scientific information has been documented concerning bromeliaceous; however it is considered the world's largest inflorescence and is only found in isolated regions of Perú and Bolivia.

The fauna of the Cordillera Blanca is equally extensive, although not as easily observed as in our North American national parks. Aquatic birds, huachuas (geese) and various species of ducks, populate many of the park's 200 lakes. Terrestrial birds, partridges, humming birds, woodpeckers, hawks, and condors, among others, are frequently seen in the valleys. Among the mammals are found the puma, spectacled bear, red and gray fox, deer, vizcacha, and the vicuña, whose wool is the most valued in the world. Many of these animals appear on the World Wildlife Foundation's endangered species list.

Archaeological ruins dating from the Chavín period are scattered throughout the Cordillera Blanca. *Chullpas,* round or rectangular towerlike structures used as burial places for important persons, *huancas,* large rock pillars occasionally displaying petroglyphs, and agricultural terraces are the most commonly found. The term "Chavín" itself refers to the style, period, and site at Chavín de Huantar located east of the Cordillera Blanca in the Callejón de Conchucos on the Mosna River. This culture is considered the matrix of the Peruvian-Bolivian civilizations.

The Central Park Office, located in Huaraz on Avenida Centenario No 912, in the Dirección Regional del Ministerio de Agricultura, is the center for all climbing and hiking information in the park. For visitor protection, registration is required for all backpacking and climbing activity. Party leaders are required to register their party members prior to each outing and complete a visit summary upon returning. While this may appear a troublesome requirement, it has proven an invaluable orientation to numerous climbing and trekking parties.

At this time, it is impossible to provide a timely rescue service in the Cordillera Blanca. Climbers climb at their own risk and in the event

PLATE 45

Photo by Curry Slaymaker

Vicuña in Andean Sierra. Along with the guanaco, the vicuña is on the verge of extinction.

of an accident must be prepared to evacuate injured party members without outside assistance. Therefore, it is strongly recommended that each climbing party have four members. All should have considerable experience climbing on rock, snow, and ice, and be familiar with mountain rescue techniques.

Easy access to the Cordillera Blanca presents the special danger of pulmonary edema during or after rapid ascent into the mountains without proper acclimatization. Every climber must be knowledgeable of the symptoms and treatment of edema conditions. (*A.A.J.*, 1961, pp. 420-422 and *A.A.J.*, 1972, pp. 83-92). Three other medical problems are also prevalent: frostbite, dysentery, and hepatitis. The danger of frostbite can be great at high altitudes. Above 6,000 meters (19,686 feet) temperatures are often below $-23°$ C. ($0°$ F.) and freezing temperatures occur at 4,000 meters (13,124 feet). The new alpine approach on difficult routes often includes several bivouacs. Frostbite is becoming more of a hazard as a result. (*A.A.J.*, 1962, pp. 1-26). To avoid dysentery and hepatitis, all doubtful water should be boiled or treated with tincture of iodine. Be selective in choosing locally prepared foods. Consult your physician concerning medications and possible inoculations before travelling.

Finally, I would recommend that all visitors to the Cordillera Blanca request information prior to departing. The following references might be useful:

Maps: 1. Carta Nacional del Perú, 1:100,000; Hojas: 19 h Carhuaz, 19 i Huari, 20 i Recuay, 18 h Corongo, 21 i Chiquián
These maps are distributed exclusively by: Instituto Geográfico Militar, Avda. Andrés Aramburú, No 1198, Apartado 2038, Lima 34, Perú.
2. Cordillera Blanca (Perú), Parte Sur, 1:100,000, 1939, German Alpine Club (copies available).
3. Cordillera Blanca (Perú), Parte Norte, 1932, 1:100,000, German Alpine Club, (Out of print).
4. Nevado Huascarán, Cordillera Blanca, Perú, 1:25,000, 1964, Instituto cartográfico Freytag-Berndt y Artaria, Vienna.
5. Map of the Northern Cordillera Blanca, Perú; Alpamayo region, Ricker and Holdsworth, *A.A.J.*, 1971, pp. 263-265.

Literature: *Cordillera Blanca,* H. Kinzl and E. Schneider, Innsbruck, Austria, 1950. 168 pages.
Revista Peruana de Andinismo y Glaciología, César Morales Arnao, Director, Redacción Calle Hernando de Soto 250, Salamanca de Monterrico, Lima 3, Perú.

Institutions: Parque Nacional Huascarán, Ministerio de Agricultura, Sub-Zona Agraria III, Huaraz, Ancash, Perú.
Instituto Nacional de Recreación, Sección de Andinismo, Estadio Nacional, Lima, Perú.
Presidente, Club Andinista Cordillera Blanca, 582 Guzman Barrón, Huaraz, Ancash, Perú.

Sea-Going Climbers in Southern Chile

JACK MILLER

IN mid-November, 1974, the four of us, William Rodarmor, Peter Bruchhausen, myself, and our inflatable boat Huap Huap,* more affectionately known as Fat Martha, arrived at Otway Sound, 80 kilometers north of South America's southern tip. Our starting point on this inland sea was the same as for our 1966 explorations (see *A.A.J.*, 1976, 15:2, pp. 326-333) to Isla Santa Inés, where we discovered several new fjords and climbed various peaks. During storm-bound days there, with little to do but stare at the charts, we discovered the route of this year's travels, a sea voyage that would carry us right through the most unknown mountains of Fuegia-Patagonia.

The Otway Water was a full week in calming down to the point where we could load our 900 kilograms between Martha's sleek neoprene flanks, crank up the Evinrude, and set out. Seizing the moment of good weather, we traveled 95 km. in 13 hours, arriving just at dark near the head of Condor Fjord, a large opening off the Otway where water pours out through Jerómino Channel into the Strait of Magellen.

Here began our first series of portages, four of them connecting inland lakes with the sullen Gulf of Xaultegua. This passage was surely investigated by seamen of sail, as an alternative to the tempestuous Strait, but the terrain is difficult enough to make us doubt that any earlier party carried a boat across.

Golfo Xaultegua, by nature of its inaccessibility and the continual storms lashing its steep-sided fjord walls, was threatening—at the same time extremely intriguing to us. We had gotten ourselves into one of Fuegia's hidden corners and were fully aware of being cut off from the rest of the world should anything happen to Martha. The Gulf offered access to the north slopes of Mount Wyndham, sister to Mount Wharton across the Strait that we climbed in 1966, but we opted to use a rare period of calm to sail rather than climb, mindful that the prevailing west wind could keep us locked in indefinitely. As it was, rough seas caught us crossing Xaultegua, but Peter's astute handling of the boat (backed up by the happy quality of inflatable boats of being unsinkable when full of water) got us through then, as always. The potential horrors of Xaul-

---

* Fuegian for "Outback"

tegua were never actualized for us; indeed, the gulf presented us with a wondrous variety of wildlife—albatross, penguins, terns, petrels, condors, ducks, geese and seal.

We entered the mysterious Canal Gajardo, a long, narrow sea channel that some incredible accident of nature, or perhaps scouring glaciers, laid right through the mountains for us. The largest peak, Gran Campo Nevado, was our primary goal. This great mesa-like mountain with its icecap of 230 km² was one that did exist on a map, and probably the largest untravelled ice mass remaining in Patagonia.*

Climbing above the narrows of the Gajardo, we worked out an intricate route, involving a high camp and a pitch of direct-aid ice climbing right onto the ice plateau. Now, as ants on the banquet table, we had to decide whether the salt shaker, the sugar bowl, or the coffee cup was the true summit. The triple summit we chose was as high as any, although it meant more than 10 km. of flat icecap walking to reach it.

The view from "Triad," as we three called it, was revealing. Our exceptionally clear day showed up peaks in all directions, peaks that are indicated only vaguely, when at all, on the rough maps that exist for this part of the world. We saw as far as the Paine Towers, and we learned that they are by no means the only spectacular rock towers in the region. Nor is Eric Shipton's Mount Burney (*A.A.J.*, 1974, pages 129-130) the most noteworthy summit: lying near the shipping lanes it is simply the most obvious. Mountains bearing the name "Molar" (Muela) and "Watchtower" (Atalaya), as well as many of the unnamed and the unmapped ones, would each be worth an expedition. We had come expecting Gran Campo to be the last prize and learned it was only one of several.

We were nearly swept away by a spectacular event. Warm weather and almost continual calving of the ice sheet had filled the fjords adjoining the narrows with icebergs. The tide, surging twice a day through this channel only 60 meters wide to fill 1400 km² Skyring Sound, was carrying a load of churning icebergs. We had nearly driven the inflated and vulnerable boat into it all, unwittingly. As we watched from the banks, the giant grinding mill slowed, stopped, and began running the other way, dramatically depicting the exact moment of the turn of the tide.

Foul weather prevented further climbing of our newly discovered plums, but allowed us to pass through Skyring Waters and over "Shipton's Portage" and two others into Obstruction Sound (it is rumored that Indians have made these portages) and into a new system of canals. Tchaikovsky could not have written a finer finale, as, during the last days,

* British, led by John Ridgeway did approach the edges of this glacier in 1973 but accomplished little on it.

PLATES 46 and 47

Photos by William Rodarmor

"Fat Martha" in the Seno Otway, Patagonia.

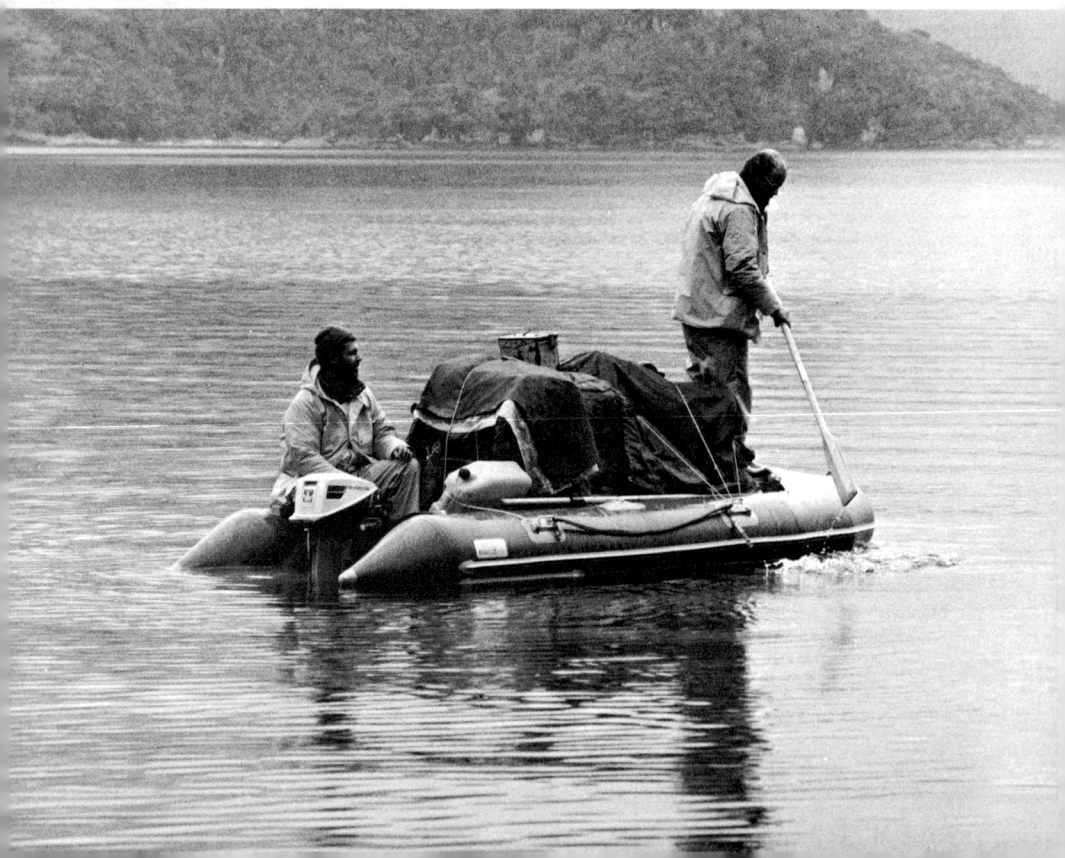

we sailed through a ballet of black-neck swans and dolphins which gracefully guided us into more known waters, and at last to the frontier port of Natales.

Our trip, with its seven portages and 583 km in the canals was, if nothing else, a prolific testimonial to Shipton's 1962 demonstration that a climbing team can operate without reliance on outside help in these wild canals. His recent use of naval ships and a helicopter to climb Mount Burney casts a few doubts; we are relieved to find that in fact a determined, self-reliant party can climb wherever it wants, in Fuegia. That is, with the aid of gracious ladies, like Fat Martha.

PLATE 48

Photo by Peter Bruchhausen

**On the GRAN CAMPO NEVADO,
Patagonia.**

Mount Kenya's Diamond Couloir

MICHAEL COVINGTON

AFRICA was about the last place I ever expected to find myself. Not because it lacks interest, but just to see all those elephants and tigers running around loose! I had heard of Mount Kenya and Kilimanjaro but neither of them had the lure of the Himalaya or even the Alps. One afternoon in the early fall of 1974 I received a phone call from Roger Brown and Barry Corbet of Summit Films in Denver. They asked me to join them and Yvon Chouinard in Yosemite on the making of a semi-documentary film. This led to an invitation from Summit Films to accompany the group to East Africa where we could attempt the Diamond Couloir on Mount Kenya. A superb 200-foot ice headwall was still virgin. Tom Frost, who was to do the high-angle photography, was also part of the group.

When we arrived in Kenya just about everything that could go wrong did. Our equipment was scattered all over the world; there were complications getting permission to film even though Roger had informed the local officials of our intentions months in advance. Making the best of it, my friend Greta, the lead actress, and I played tourist. Greta could have gone on like that for weeks but Yvon and I were anxious to get going. After four days in Nairobi most of the lost equipment arrived and some of us headed for the mountain.

It was a new and exciting experience hiking up through the various climate zones and listening to the strange sounds coming from the jungles along side the trail. The hike to Base Camp was long and grueling but the novelty made it interesting. Day after day passed and the porters brought everything but our climbing equipment.

After several "strolls" to fight off frustration we finally decided to try the third ascent of the Point John Couloir. We scrounged a few tie-offs, runners, and carabiners. We had our crampons, axes and a rope, and so started up. The ice was terrific and after a couple of hours of jury-rigging and long run-outs we were up.

The strolls were getting us into condition. The lead actor came down with pulmonary edema after one day at Base Camp and had to leave the mountain for a while. The upset gave us a couple of extra days and so we made plans to try the Diamond Couloir now rather than wait until we were through filming. Though I wasn't in favor of an early attempt, Yvon and I left camp late one afternoon and hiked up to bivouac nearer to the climb. When it came time to go the next morning, I couldn't be budged, but rolled over and lapsed into peaceful sleep. A few hours later I was awakened by yells from Brown, who was on his way up to take pictures from the Darwin Glacier. Although the Diamond Couloir had nothing to do with the film at this point, he wanted to film it anyway. After watching him climb the moraine to his camera position, I decided to see where Yvon had gone.

When I reached the glacier, I looked around not quite ready to admit that Yvon was nearing the end of the first pitch of the Diamond Couloir. I sat down, put my crampons on and raced up the glacier towards the base of the climb. The thin air soon reduced my run to a slower more rhythmical pace. I glanced across to the ravaged figure of a monkey frozen onto the ice. Hm, only in Africa! When I reached the base I yelled to Yvon to throw the rope down. I tied in and started climbing.

The first pitch was about 120 feet and tilted to about 75°. For the most part the ice was pretty good, but there were sections which were not. "Just a stroll, eh? I should have guessed." "Hey, all right man! Glad you changed your mind. I never could have made it on my own, but I know we can do it." It was a good meeting. Now we were both pretty fired up and ready to go.

Above us the couloir leaned back to around 50° for several pitches. It was warm and friendly, almost too warm, too warm to be nosing about in couloirs. The clouds were gathering. It was spacy watching them rise from the rain forests into the Teleki valley below us. Eventually they get all stacked up there and then consume everything in mist. In the middle of the fifth pitch the angle rose sharply. We were nearing the end of the easy stuff.

Except for the first pitch we had been climbing on the left side of the couloir which seemed to offer protection from the obvious fall-line. Now the route lay to the right and so I led across to a sloping rock stance with a fixed pin to belay from. Just as I reached the stance, I heard a rumble from above. Terror raced through me. In the worst possible place and 75 feet above my protection, I looped a finger through the pin as a rock avalanche poured down the chute. It went on for ages. The whole summit seemed to be caving in. I could hardly believe I was still there. I yelled down to Yvon. He too had survived the pelting. Had the heat caused the slide? Then I remembered that Tom Frost and Roger Gossick were paralleling us via the Ice Window route, hoping to get some tight shots of the final bit. I yelled up and sure enough Tom replied. "Sorry about that. Are you guys OK?" My swearing would have raised the dead. Calmly he replied, "I knew you guys would be OK. You're the champs. We won't drop anything more." Just then, another much larger slide broke off. In all the excitement I had forgotten to

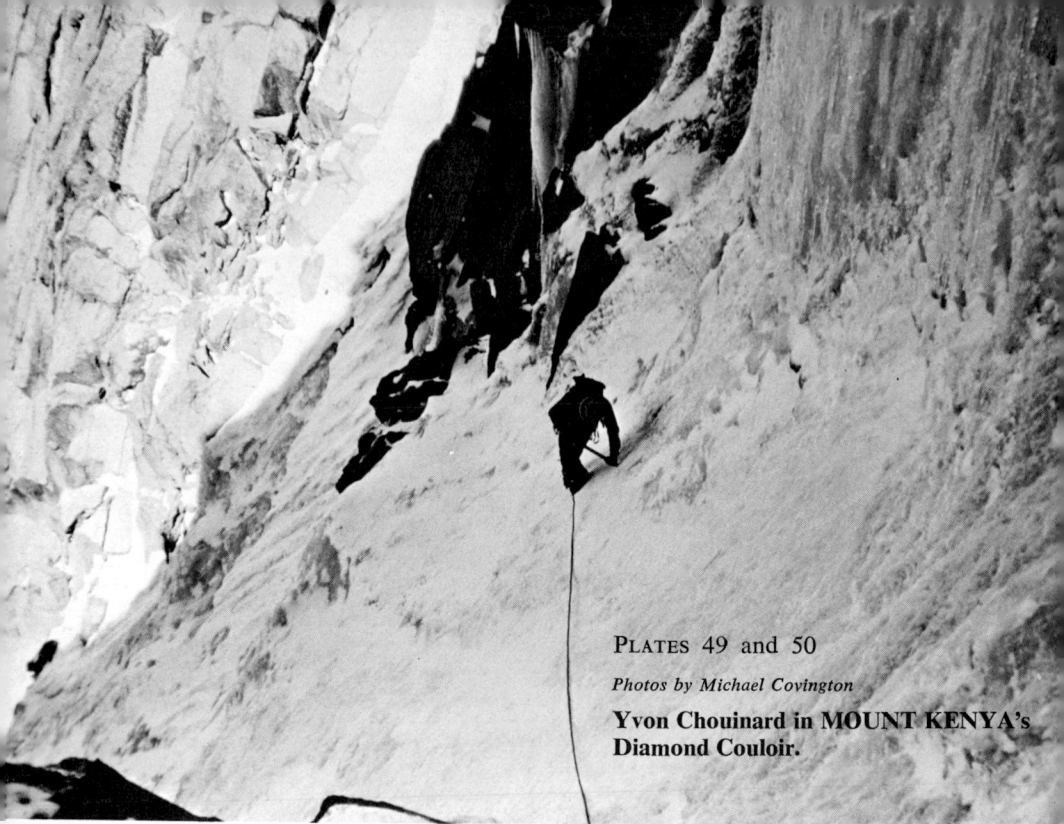

PLATES 49 and 50

Photos by Michael Covington

Yvon Chouinard in MOUNT KENYA's Diamond Couloir.

PLATE 51

Photo by Michael Covington

MOUNT KENYA's Diamond Couloir.

clip in and so again I looped a finger in the pin, and again the slide passed over.

After reaching me, Yvon led an interesting pitch of mixed climbing. Although the headwall seemed to loom just above, I climbed almost a full pitch past his belay before getting to the base of the fragile obstacle. We were in the clouds now and the setting had changed drastically from a warm and friendly environment into a safer but more eery one. The climbing was steep and the visibility was usually less than a pitch. An occasional icicle fell or running water dripped from ledge to ledge. Otherwise the silence was all consuming. Peaceful, but spooky.

The final headwall looked uninviting. The right was barred by threatening thin sheets of transparent ice which tapered into a "Jaws" type setting of elongated icicles. The center had a short 40-foot rock outcrop surrounded with thin ice. The left had the best ice but it rose into the mist at an intimidating angle. We decided on the center.

Putting his tools in their holsters, Yvon climbed up, using handjams between the ice and the rock, to a small cave at the top of the outcrop. A thin sheet of ice separated him in his bomb-bay cave from the final difficulties. "Hang on!" he shouted, "I'm going to have to chop my way out of here." It took little to disengage the curtain. Two or three whacks and it departed the face, exploded onto the ramp near me, and then fired off down the couloir in the mist below. Spooky spooky! How to get back out onto the smooth, nearly vertical sheet of ice above? First he placed his hammer up inside the cave and then leaned out as if trying to reach over a roof. One swing with the axe and it was buried in the ice above. Then he removed his hammer and placed it up alongside the axe. Both tools gave off a precarious dull thunk. Although the curtain was not entirely gone, Yvon was too committed to come down now. I tensed, expecting a fall as he leaned way out and engaged a crampon inches above the lip of the curtain. Slowly he moved up onto the ice and then removed a tool and swung again. This time the axe found good ice and Yvon let out a welcome "Wha hoo!" There were still 20 feet of nearly vertical ice before the angle eased, but it was in the bag now. The ice was super, almost too good. It was harder to get the tools unstuck than make them stick.

It was a fantastic pitch to watch. Tom and Roger who were filming from a nearby shelf were impressed. I climbed up and joined Yvon. We just sat there and enjoyed the view which had improved while I was climbing. There was still a short vertical section to climb before we could really call it a day, but for now we were content just sitting there.

Eventually we pulled ourselves together to finish it off. I picked up my tools to start up. Even though the ice was still good, I had a hard time with it. I'd reached a ramp leading off to the right, which I followed until I was standing in the middle of the Diamond Glacier. Yvon climbed up and we watched Frost and Roger exit via the spectacular Ice Window. Then they too joined us. Tom was anxious to do some more filming in a giant ice cave just above us and so asked if we intended to continue on up into the Gate of The Mist.

Yvon went to help Tom in the cave while Roger and I started looking for a way down. In all the excitement no one had bothered to find out the easiest way off this thing. Again I picked up my tools and headed off across the Diamond Glacier aiming for a rock outcrop barely visible in the mist.

Summary of Statistics:

ASCENT: First direct finish of the Diamond Couloir, Mount Kenya, Kenya, East Africa, January, 1975 (Yvon Chouinard, Michael Covington). Nine Pitches; 5½ hours.

Rock Climbing in Australia

HENRY BARBER made a six-week visit to Australia in the southern autumn of 1975. He climbed in six states, refusing to use aid on any climb. Before his arrival in March, there were no climbs rated above 21 which did not require aid. By the time he left, he and others had done 19 climbs of grade 22 or better. The following photographs were taken of him on some of these routes.

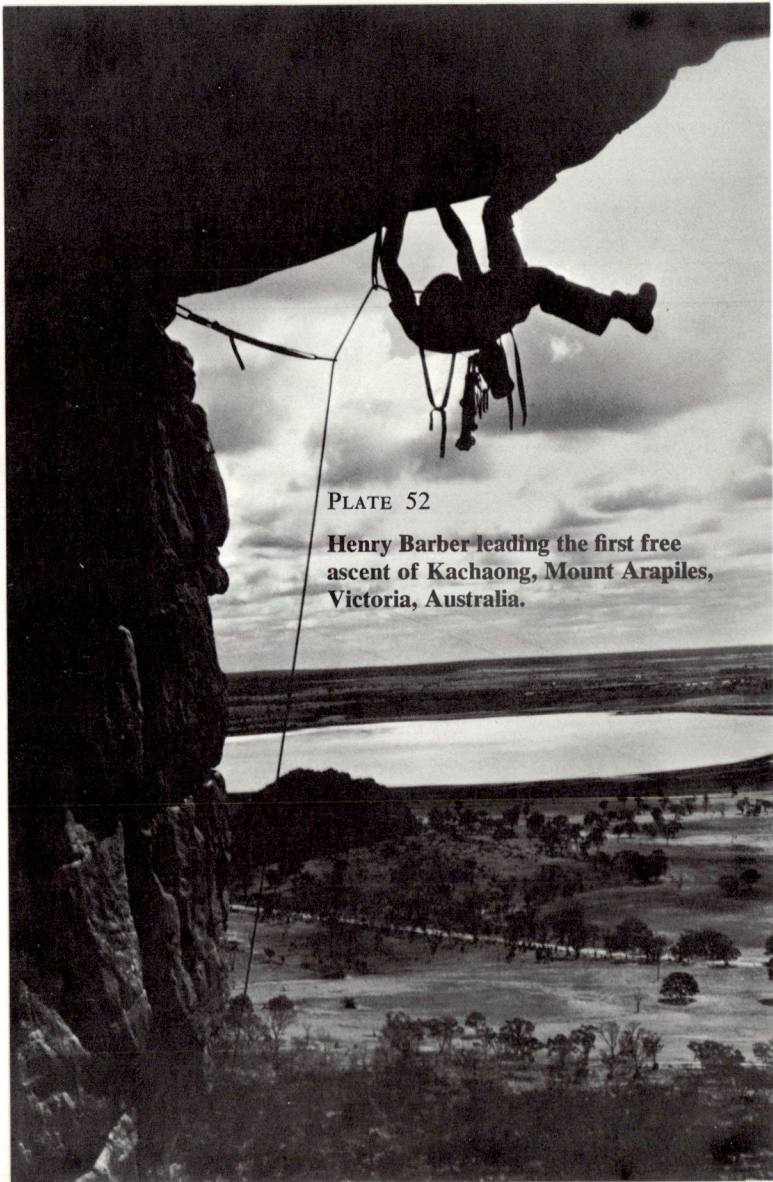

PLATE 52

Henry Barber leading the first free ascent of Kachaong, Mount Arapiles, Victoria, Australia.

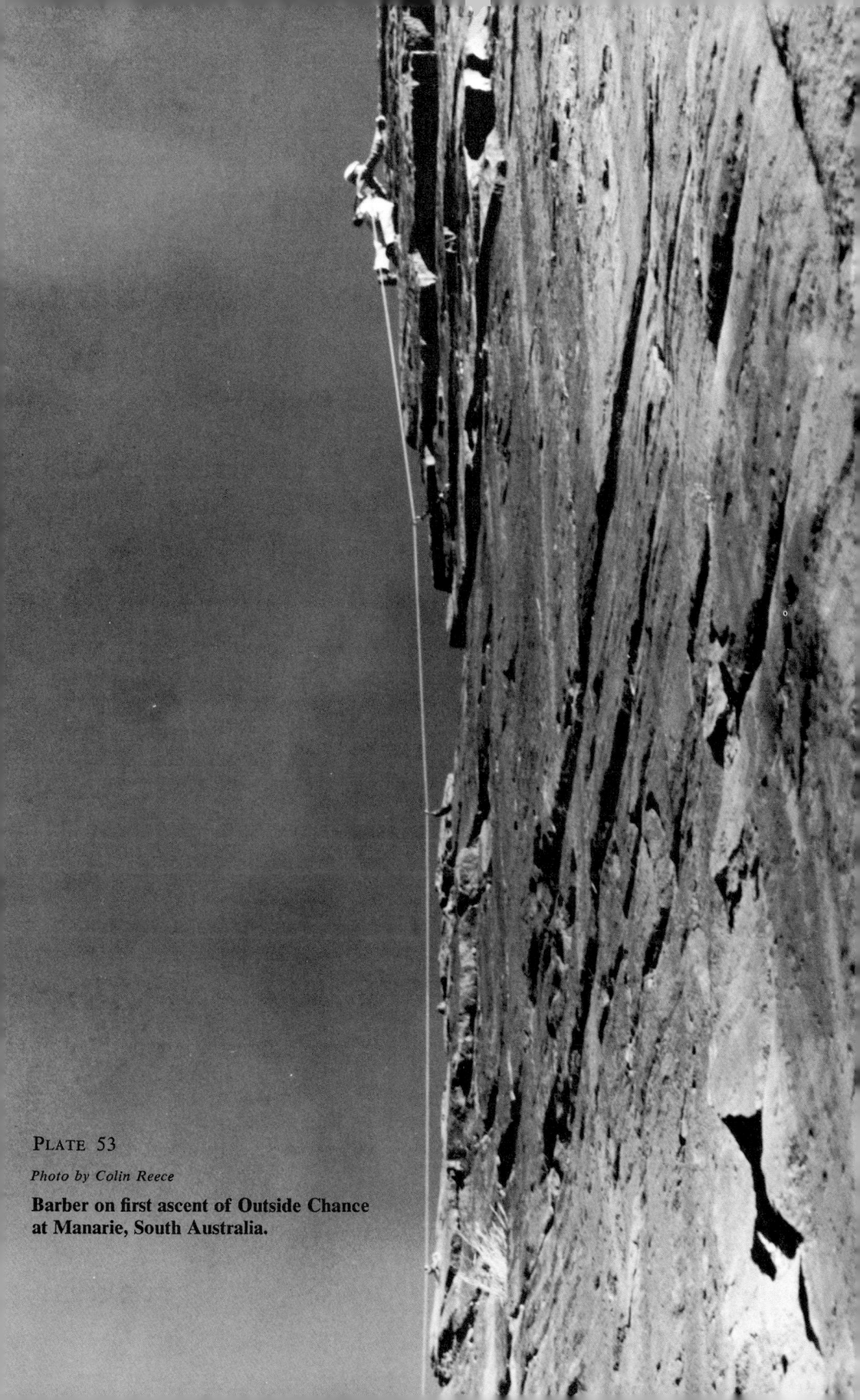

PLATE 53

Photo by Colin Reece

**Barber on first ascent of Outside Chance
at Manarie, South Australia.**

PLATE 54

Photo by John Chapin

Barber leading the first free ascent of
Taste of Honey (Grade 23 to 24),
Mount Arapiles, Victoria.

PLATE 55

Photo by Ian Sedgeman

Barber on Manic Depressive, Bundaleer, Australia's hardest climb to date (Grade 25).

PLATE 56

First ascent of Gullible Trench,
Devil's Gullet, Tasmania.

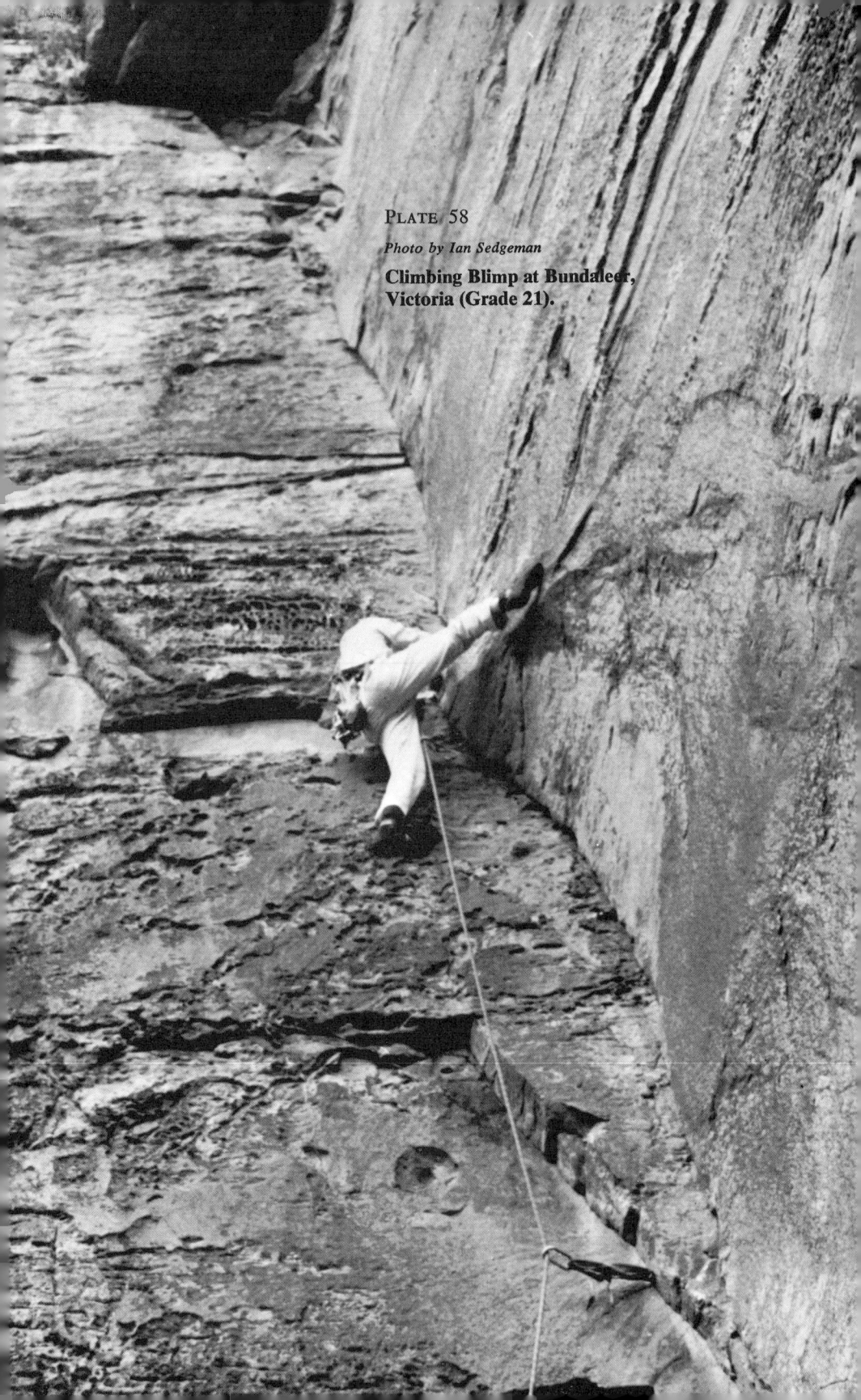

PLATE 58

Photo by Ian Sedgeman

**Climbing Blimp at Bundaleer,
Victoria (Grade 21).**

Man of the Trail

FRED STEPHENS

What would one not give to be young again, riding with a packtrain through the Canadian forests? To emerge from the jackpine shadow on to gravel flats beside a sparkling river. To pass through a kaleidoscopic symphony of fireweed and paint-brush, while, through rifts in the clouds, gleaming peaks burst out in their upward soaring. Scarcely differing from scenes be-held by explorers of long ago, the cayuses enter the rushing ford, led, as if by a centaur: The Man of the Trail.

—J. MONROE THORINGTON

FRED STEPHENS was born in Michigan in 1869 and spent his early days wandering from the lumber camps through Montana, where he endured hardships that were his lot throughout life. As cowpuncher and trapper he enlarged his experience by hunting, trapping, prospecting and logging, eventually crossing into Canada and reaching the rivers and forests which became the route of the Canadian Pacific, the last spike of which had been driven in 1885, scarcely a dozen years before his arrival. This, and the country of the watershed northward, would be the territory of his adventurous life. He was fortunate in arriving at a time when exploring tourists were attempting to penetrate and clarify the complex geography of the Canadian Rockies and who, as employers, could be guided by this re-markable woodsman.

Walter D. Wilcox (1869-1949) was the first to undertake an ex-tended journey under his guidance. In 1896, when Stephens was working for Tom Wilson, Wilcox and his companion, R.L. Barrett, went with him by way of the north fork of the Saskatchewan, over the divide now known as Wilcox Pass, and down the Sunwapta, failing to see the Columbia Icefield on their way. They searched in vain for Mount Brown and Mount Hooker, whose exaggerated altitudes ascribed to them by the Scots botanist, David Douglas in 1827, perplexed climbers through most of the century. At Fortress Lake:

"It was absolutely essential for us to reach the other end of that body of water. One side of the lake was an impassable down-fall of timber. The other side was a steep slope covered with snow-bent alders and willow. Just the same Stephens got us across the lake. In two days,

397

with Barrett's help, he built a raft that would hold four men and a lot of equipment. There were roughly hewn oars and a mast, to which we could attach a pack-cover for a sail. With two men rowing constantly we reached the far end of the lake in four and a half hours."

From this point they retraced their route.

The German explorer, Habel, set out from Field on July 15, 1897, accompanied by Fred Stephens and Ralph Edwards, two of Tom Wilson's packers, and Frank Wellman, cook. These three were mounted, and there were four pack-horses, but Habel did not take a saddle-horse, "as the nature of the valley seemed too unfavorable for equestrian exercise." On July 17, via Emerald Lake, they gained Yoho Pass and discovered the great waterfall, for which Sir William Van Horne soon afterward suggested the name "Takakkaw," a Cree word meaning "It is magnificient." On the 22nd they descended to the foot of the fall, and on the 25th made their sixth camp near the ice cave of Yoho Glacier. On the 27th they ascended the tongue, roped and climbed to an elevation of 8840 feet on the snowfield. A further excursion on the 28th took them to the eastern side of the valley, where "Hidden Peak" was completely visible. On this occasion Habel named Trolltinder, and they continued to 9370 feet on the highest point of the ridge bordering the southern part of the glacial basin on Mount Balfour. The Appalachian Club later bestowed the name Mount Habel on Hidden Peak. (App. viii, 327; ix, 21; CAJ. xxx, 58.)

This was also the year in which the noted war-correspondent, Stanley Washburn, met Stephens, and thus began a lasting friendship.

"Fred was sitting on a bunk, about three feet deep in blankets, with legs crossed and eyes on ceiling, his entire attention going to a banjo, on which he was producing some excellent jig music. With the sweet absorption of a babe, he strummed away for five minutes and then, uncrossing his long legs, came across and met us with the grace of an emperor. He stood six feet and one inch in his stockinged feet, twenty-nine years old, with the shoulders and muscles of an athlete, and soft blue eyes that drifted back and forth. Big hands, big feet, and a big soul."

On their first trip, August, 1897, Fred rode while Washburn and a companion walked. Washburn used a steamer trunk which made one side-pack, while the grub pile formed the other and the tent filled in the top. Their journey began at Laggan, up the Bow River and returned by the Pipestone.

The war with Cuba was ended by 1898 and Washburn and two companions were again on the trail. They went by train from Calgary to Lacombe, where Fred had settled and now had an outfit of fourteen

PLATE 59

FRED STEPHENS (1869-1928).

horses and a cook. They followed the Saskatchewan to Rocky Mountain House, but bad weather soon caused their return.

Norman Collie, the British climber, who had already been in the Canadian Rockies and discovered the Columbia Icefield from the summit of Mount Athabasca in 1898, came again in 1900, taking Stephens with him on the first ascent of Mount Edith at Banff. This was before their unlucky venture in attempting to reach high peaks by way of Bush River. Despite his skill, Fred had a difficult time with rafts in the torrential water; but the expedition was really beaten by the impenetrable British Columbia forests.

Washburn was on the trail for the third time, with Stephens, in July, 1901, the outfit including 15 horses and two men, F. Hippach, packer, and John Scales, an English photographer, as cook. Nine days of travel from Laggan took them over Bow Pass to the Saskatchewan Forks. They ran out of grub, crossed the river on a raft and shot five sheep on Wilcox Mountain, thence returning by way of Rocky Mountain House to Laggan.

Collie's journey in 1902 was far more successful. He wrote to Fred, asking for an estimate on a trip of seven or eight weeks. Fred replied, suggesting the quantity of flour, bacon, etc., and Collie wrote back, nearly doubling the amount. With H.E.M. Stutfield, H. Woolley and G.M. Weed, they joined their party with that of J. Outram, who brought the Swiss Kaufmann brothers as guides. After accounting for Mount Freshfield they went to Glacier Lake, and so it came about that Jim Simpson, who was with Outram's outfit, met Fred.* Stephens and Simpson cut trail along the canyon leading to the base of Mount Forbes. The climbing party delayed in returning from their conquest of this great peak and Fred, armed with a spare ice-axe, was about to start out at the head of a search party, expressing himself strongly on the subject of climbing a mountain for mere amusement.

Ever persistent, Washburn tried again with Stephens in 1903, two additional tourists being Dr. August Eggers (1862-1936) and Professor Herschel Parker (1867-1944), who held the chair of physics at Columbia. Eggers and Parker, later in the summer, made the first ascent of Delta-form Mountain, and Parker in 1912 with Belmore Brown just missed completing the first ascent of Mount McKinley. Eggers had a delightful personality, but Washburn did not take to Parker, perhaps because as Washburn admitted "I had climbed mountains and always despised it cordially." The party was not a happy one and soon turned back.

Six years later Washburn left on his most extensive expedition, June, 1909. This time they would follow the advancing line of the Grand Trunk

---

* Jim Simpson's vivid memories of Stephens were recorded in the *American Alpine Journal, 1974,* on pages 46 and 47.

Pacific from Edmonton to Prince Rupert, taking four months. Starting from Lacombe with 22 horses, the party, led by Stephens, included Fred's brother, Nick, and Sawyer, a civil engineer. Nick Stephens was a great hand at making a "happy home" at every camp. With an axe and an old horn-handled knife he could do everything from chopping down trees to building a cabin and furniture. They went by way of Rocky Mountain House, where there was now a ferry, and down the Sunwapta to eventually reach Yellowhead Pass.

They had been fifty days on the way when they arrived at Lewis Swift's place, a landmark on the Edmonton trail two-and-a-quarter miles below Maligne River on the west side of the Athabaska, Stephens and Washburn crossing the river on a small raft to reach it. In the early seventies Lewis Swift was a young man in Buffalo selling lightning rods. He drifted to the Black Hills, took part in a gold rush, and for a time was a driver on the stage line from Bismarck, N.D., to Deadwood. In the nineties he sold out a claim in southern British Columbia, bought a pack outfit and started for the head of Fraser River. With 17 horses he went from Kamloops up the North Thompson and after nearly three months emerged on the flat at the junction of the McLennon and the Fraser at the west end of Yellowhead Pass. This was the head of canoe transportation on the Fraser and had long been known as Tête Jaune Cache. Swift arrived there in August, 1891, crossed the pass and reached the Athabasca, living there for twenty years until engineers for the Grand Trunk Pacific arrived and he was made general store-keeper. He married and had four children.

Washburn, Stephens and others made a canoe trip down the Fraser from Tête Jaune to Fort George, whence autos went over the Cariboo Trail to the Canadian Pacific. Fred still played his banjo and sometimes added a favorite song with refrain ending:

"Once I was happy, but look at me now,
Ten years in States Prison for stealing a cow."

He was always carefree and cheerful. "Life is too short" he wrote, "to worry about money. If I lose all I have tomorrow, I can get a couple of bear traps and by next spring I'll be on my feet again. The mountains are always here and I know where there's a bunch of bear and a colony of beaver, and I can get along here and live like a prince, while Morgan, Rockefeller, and those other poor millionaires are lying awake nights, lest someone come and steal their money." As to fishing he said: "I don't want any of your new-fangled tinkle-tankle. Give me a tepee-pole with a few feet of clothes line, a bent nail and a piece of bacon and when I get a bite, you'll soon see a fish in the frying pan. If there's a bush in the way, that'll come too, and we can sort the fish after."

When A.L. Mumm returned to London with the report on the new mountaineering area opened up by the approach of the Grand Trunk

Pacific Railroad, Collie decided to try his hand once more at a Canadian venture. Collie, Mumm and guide Inderbinen were the climbers; Fred Stephens was in charge of the outfit, John Yates, who was very familiar with this north country, Allan McConachie and George Swain making up the trail crew. They set out from Wolf Creek, near present-day Edson, on July 17, 1910. The party of six that made the first ascent of Mount Phillips included Fred who, although in 1902 strongly against climbing for mere pleasure, was becoming more tolerant of mountaineer's vagaries.

In 1913 Geoffrey Howard of the British Alpine Club arranged with Stephens to take him and a party which included Mumm and Inderbinen from Jasper up the Whirlpool to Athabasca Pass, where they ascended Mount Brown.

Conrad Kain, the Austrian guide, recorded his memories of Stephens: "At the time when the railroad was finished as far as Calgary, a rich English lord arrived to make an exploring journey in the mountains. He engaged two packers [Tom Wilson and Stephens] and eight horses. On the very same day they made a long trip to Kananaskis, stopping there for the night. The first packer got supper ready, while Stephens fixed up the sleeping tent for the lord. When the meal was ready Fred called the lord to eat: 'Supper is ready, don't wait, it gets cold.' The lord came out of the tent and saw, to his great astonishment, that the two had already started in. So he shouted in his London dialect; 'By Jove, don't you know, I am not accustomed to eating with my servants.' 'Goddam,' said Fred, 'If you are not, then just wait!'

"It went worse with a Spanish prince, who was on a bear hunt. The party had a strenuous day in pouring rain through bush and windfalls and, as the packer was very tired, the cook made what is called a 'quick lunch,' consisting of tea, bacon, green peas, bread and butter. The prince's servant brought the food into the tent, but came right back with the news that His Royal Highness wanted scrambled eggs. 'So,' said Fred, 'he wants scrambled eggs does he? Get along and tell that fellow that if he doesn't eat lunch he doesn't get anything! If it is good enough for us after all our hard work, it's going to be good enough for His Royal Highness!'

"It went roughly with a German officer during a trip. One morning, after breakfast, the officer took a map and an ice-axe, stood on a rock and gave orders for the day. The free Canadians knew no discipline and thought that the man had gone crazy during the night. When the preaching and commanding came to an end and the people realized they were not dealing with a lunatic, Fred Stephens interrupted with the words: 'Are you all through, you god-damned silly fool? If not, I'm going to knock you clear off the place you are standing on! Do you think you have soldiers or slaves in front of you? We know what to do and how to bring you quick and safe to the place you're going to. But don't give us any more of your German sauerkraut stories.' "

Here follow extracts from Stephens' letters to Washburn during 1912-22:

1912. "I got the boy [Jesse Stephens was born in 1899] with me now at Lacombe, and he gets on fine. Haven't any more double harness scrapes lately and things don't look too bad. Well, am busy making cinches and pack saddles so goodbye for now.

"Now here is what I have to say in regards to a trip. North of Mt. Robson there lies a great Mountain [Mt. Sir Alexander] never explored by White Men and not named. Collie has seen it, I have seen it; he thinks it is higher than Robson. Phillips thinks it is higher and here is a chance to get some good material for riting. I believe you could get there quite easy and make a great Hit. Of course I know how you look at that climbing stunt, just the same as I, but that would not be necessary. We could explore around its Base and so on. Guess you could scare up someone else to entertain Mrs. Stanley."

Centralia, Washington, February 14, 1914. "I am here at the same old stand with Jesse; he goes to school and does fine in Music. I wanted to get book on conjuring for him. I hear Conan Doyle* is going to make a trip in the Yellowhead country this coming summer. . . .

". . . .the regular rates is $10 a day when you deal with the aristocrats, say Collie or Stutfield or any climbing party, but the Idea is to keep to work. If you don't get so much the price is just about double what it used to be.

"I will try to get Jesse [aet. 19] to the coast soon. He is just able to walk a little, but it don't count for much as he is up and down for the last 60 days. No one can do anything for him only let him rest and grow stronger. He had the same thing 4 years ago and was knocked out for 4 months; leakage of the heart with rheumatism. I was all ready to go to the north end of Vancouver Island to trap this winter, but Jess getting sick upset all my plans.

"Furs have never been so high. Beaver 16 and 18 dollars; muskrats $1.00 to 1.50; mink 6 & 7; weasel 1.50-2.00; Kyotes $16, 18 and 20. Any trapper can make good money now.

"Well, as for a mountain trip the best place to go that no one knows much about is north of Kamloops into the Cariboo range; one main trail leads north to the head of Goat River, but the new unexplored country

---

* Conan Doyle visited Canada in June 1914, having come to New York on May 27. He went up to Montreal first to see the country he had written about in *The Refugees;* then on to Edmonton and Jasper Park and just over the border into British Columbia. Chapter xxv of his book deals with this, and there is a brief account in J. Dickson Carr's biography of Conan Doyle, pp. 284-8. Doyle went back to England in July, 1914, just in time for the war. (Information supplied by T.S. Blakeney, A.C.)

would be east of that, between it and the Head of Canoe River. Another trip would be from Jasper north to the Peace, or start from the Peace and come to Jasper."

July, 1919. Jesse J. Stephens died, aged 20. Teacher of violin and piano. "Jess grew up to be a fine boy, absolutely Honest, very bright in school and a musical genius. I am safe in saying that he surpassed any-one in Canada at his age. I would like to know what he could have accomplished in another 10 years. It is all over now, but if old St. Peter had a better job for him I had no way out of it only let him go, so there is the only trail I had to follow. I look on this life as a joke, one of these jokes nobody gets interested in after you tell or act it out.

"Any way while Jess was here we had a lot of good times together and I used to go to Edmonton to see him perform. I was very glad I gave him the chance I did and was very proud of him. So after all I got a lot of comfort out of life while it lasted, but it was like the trapper that comes to his shack on fire; the pine logs snapped, cartridges exploding and flames jumping up in the dark. He said it was fine while it lasted, but a damn inhospitable place after it was over.

"I have a government job in sight, building a trail up the Brazeau over Poboktan Pass and down to the Athabasca. About $6000 if I land it, but I don't give a cent what I do just so I keep contented and get outdoor life.

"The North Smoky, Sheep Creek country, would be a good place as this has never anything written on it. Just had a letter from Dr. Collie. He said the same thing and wants to go there."

December 16, 1920. Washburn to Stephens: "What I want mainly is to get out in a wild untravelled country where we would not see a human being for all the time we were gone. The more I see of pack horses the less I think of the human race."

Xmas, 1920. Stephens to Washburn: "Before Frank [Hippach] left he brought your saddle to me. I never used it myself but let a lady here in town use it and she keeps it in the house, it is better for it. Last Spring I gave it a good coat of oil and it is the same as when you last used it. It is 35° below now. The country I mentioned lies one Hundred miles north of Jasper, fearfull rugged, lots of game only known by a few trappers. Donald Phillips goes there with Hunting parties once in a while. I have seen a part of it. Dr. Collie is quite ready to go there and wants to get a Geographical Idea of it if he ever gets the time to spare. Now I mean to touch the upper waters of the big Smoky, cross at the head of the Fraser-Beaver river which is the divide between B.C. and Alberta. This touches the head of Sheep creek and tributary of the big Smoky, then works north."

May 3, 1921. Stephens to Washburn, while the latter was a patient in Roosevelt Hospital: "Never say quit; don't give up. Just make yourself think you are going to help me eat that mallard duck I am going to kill for you this week. Be thankful you aren't under a spruce tree for a Hospital up in this cold country. Don't give up like the Irishmen. They were emigrants to California; one said 'No Mike we don't want to go to Imperial Valley, it gets 125 in the shade there.' 'Yes,' said Mike, 'but we won't have to stay in the shade all the time.' "

"A man emigrated to Peace River 40 years ago by the name of Clark with his wife and 5 boys. Another man followed with 5 girls by the name of Johnson. 15 years later the Clark boys married the Johnson girls and they made a little settlement of their own 100 miles from the nearest Postoffice. An old friend of Clark's heard where he had gone and wanted to go see him. He was a Baptist preacher. He thought it would be great to go in a new country and build the first church and convert the Pioneers, and his name would go down in History as the first minister in the Grizzly Bear settlement. He travelled 300 miles by boat. Hired an Indian to take Him the other 100 miles. On the 4th day they came to a cabin belonging to the old friend's daughter. After supper he asked Her if there was any Baptists in the settlement. She thought a moment, looked at the old Preacher and replied: 'Well, I don't know. My husband is a trapper, the skins are all nailed up in the woodshed. You can go and see for yourself.' Now, Stanley, if this doesn't help you a little you are mighty sick. I could tell it better around the campfire."

"I just came in last night and have been chased so much by the Mounted Police and game wardens for poaching beaver I almost wish I was in Roosevelt Hospital myself, but I made a Hundred a week while I was out, besides the fun."

Kalispell, Montana, January 11, 1922. Stephens to Washburn: "As for the boy [Stanley, Jr.] he should be able to go on a summer trip as I often have boys go out with me and I believe every boy ought to have a few bumps to weld him into a man. We would go up Stoney, across the big Smoky, go up 20 miles, go north, touch the head of the Beaver, go down Sheep creek 10 miles, then go north toward Pine Pass. All north of the Smoky is very out of the way country, very little is known of it only by trappers."

Kalispell, August 30, 1923. Stephens to Washburn: "With all my experience as a trapper I can't stop the depredations of that animal known as *Old Age* [F.S. was then 54]. I feel fine and yet I notice I can't dodge a Kicking Horse as I used to. I came over here to see if I can get some mink and marten alive as I think I will settle here later.

"Whenever I get into civilization I see so many crooked people, so much selfishness and so much poverty I soon want to get back to the hills. It seems five out of every ten who are entrusted with other peoples affairs are ready to sell them out. I notice a lot of unrest among the people and wonder how it will all end.

"I want to get things ready for the foxes and mink and it is a lot of work. We got 19 black silver fox and 19 mink and we hope to have some Blue fox and some marten."

This was Fred's last letter to Washburn. He went east to New York in December, 1923, to visit the family. We know nothing more. Perhaps, as he would have said, "My pipe is out."

Stephens, however, continued to write to Norman Collie, although the latter did not return to Canada after 1911. One letter, dated July 24, 1927 said: "I know Doctor you are too old [Collie was then 68: Fred 58] for any of that strenuous mountain climbing; isn't it Hell to get old when one doesn't want it?" He described his attempts at raising foxes and how a crooked partner's running off with $1500 and the death of many foxes had left him $5000 out of pocket. He protested against the rottenness of government, the wickedness of the Ku Klux Klan, the lying deceitful kyotes, and all the miserable grafters, game wardens, and fences which interfered with a man's freedom. "Now Doctor, you know when things are going the wrong way with a fellow he isn't in the right frame of mind to write a good letter, but any way I hope to change things around and then look for the good news. Any way we can ponder over the good times we have had, and I hope you stay well and write at least twice a year, and you and Washburn are two of my most prized friends."

One final letter, undated, from Fred to Collie, sums up the philosophy of this Man of the Trail:

"I know some valleys hidden away where the beaver still build lodges, where there are fish in the streams, where caribou roam and wild raspberries grow. Say, friend Norman, come, and let the whole damn world race for dollars!"

John Norman Collie died at Sligachan, Skye, early in December, 1942, aged 83.

Stanley Washburn died of coronary thrombosis on December 14, 1950, aged 72.

Fred Stephens became ill early in November, 1928 and treated himself for some time. He wrote in his diary: "Today will be my last day. Stanley will be interested in this." He died that night, prior to December 19, 1928, aged 59.

Altitude Illness— 1976 Version

CHARLES S. HOUSTON, M.D.

As more and more thousands of people easily and speedily reach high mountain ranges which previously were almost inaccessible, the incidence of high altitude illness has also increased. It is probable that somewhere between 0.5 and 5.0% of all persons going above 10,000 feet can expect symptoms, and it seems likely that between 100 and 200 persons die each year, needlessly. As Dr. Drummond Rennie put it so well, "Altitude sickness kills people, and because these are people who go up into the mountains, it kills the young, the fit, the enthusiastic, the audacious and hardworking, and it is killing them in ever increasing numbers. . . ."

Altitude illness has attracted more interest in mountaineering literature than in medical journals, where it is still considered a medical curiosity. Surprisingly few practicing doctors know anything about altitude illness—even most surprisingly, some who practice near the mountains. In contrast climbers are becoming more and more knowledgeable. Research into various aspects of altitude hypoxia has increased, and bits and pieces of data are falling together to make an emerging picture of what happens when man goes high. In this brief paper I will simply outline some of what we know about altitude illness today, along with concepts which are currently popular.

There is growing consensus that altitude illness is a single entity which can be manifest in several different forms or combinations. Until recently we spoke of acute mountain sickness (AMS), high altitude pulmonary edema (HAPE), cerebral (brain) edema (CE), and retinal hemorrhages (RH) thinking of them as separate entities although all were caused by oxygen lack. It has become clear that these rarely exist alone: the victim usually shows a great deal of one condition, and some of the others. We think today of altitude illness as a spectrum of clinical pathology rather than a set of individual diseases.

This is of much more than academic importance, because it means that an individual with pulmonary edema almost certainly has some brain edema too and often shows retinal hemorrhages as well. It is quite logical that many parts of the body should be affected, some more, some less, since oxygen cannot be stored except briefly in myoglobin—a special case —and since all living human tissues are totally dependent on oxygen for effectiveness and for their existence.

407

Start then with the realization that we are talking about different forms of a common problem: oxygen lack or hypoxia due to altitude causes altitude illness. Some prefer to speak of "altitude edema" since edema (swelling due to excess water) is an integral part of altitude illness. Although the signs and symptoms are widely known, they are worth listing briefly.

FORMS OF ALTITUDE ILLNESS

Acute Mountain Sickness (AMS)	Headache, weakness, nausea, vomiting, breathing and sleep disturbance
High Altitude Pulmonary Edema (HAPE)	Shortness of breath, weakness, cough, stupor, death
Cerebral Edema (CE)	Severe headache, vomiting, lethargy, stupor, coma, death
Retinal Hemorrhage (RH)	Rarely symptomatic; tiny hemorrhages in the back of eye

Few people know that Dr. T.H. Ravenhill clearly described these forms of altitude illness in 1913, calling them "normal puna," "cardiac puna," and "nervous puna." He was puzzled that persons with "cardiac puna"—which we call HAPE—had no evidence of heart disease. Since Ravenhill's time, many excellent case reports and review articles have appeared; some of these are shown in the appendix.

AMS is common, often beginning as low as 6000 feet in especially susceptible persons, and worsening as altitude increases. Headache, weakness, some shortness of breath, loss of appetite, vomiting, and disturbances of sleep usually begin within a few hours of arrival, are worst the next morning, and slowly improve. AMS is rarely serious although dehydration may need intravenous treatment, and usually disappears; it is very much like a bad hangover. Light activity, plenty of fluids, aspirin, time, and no upward progress are usually all that is needed. AMS should dictate slowing down or halting the climb, and the patient should be carefully watched for more serious developments, but AMS alone seldom forces descent. Like all forms of altitude illness it is minimized or prevented by taking time to go high, and its symptoms are lessened—for parties such as rescue groups which must go very high very fast—by taking Diamox in advance.

HAPE seldom occurs below 9000 feet, although a few deaths from HAPE have occurred even lower. Until recently we felt that HAPE did not begin until 24 or 72 hours after a too rapid ascent to dangerous altitude; today we feel that HAPE may begin subtly and insidiously within six or eight hours of arrival, in the form of interstitial edema (accumulation of water in the loose tissues which surround the alveolar air sacs).

The classical form of HAPE with its severe shortness of breath and weakness, the cough producing bloody sputum, and the bubbling lungs develops later, as the interstitial fluid seeps into the alveolar air sacs. The climber usually notices increasing fatigue, shortness of breath and cough; frothy then pink and often bloody sputum is coughed up. Usually there is little fever, the pulse is often fast, and vomiting or even diarrhea may occur. Curiously enough the patient may have a very severe headache or none at all. Often HAPE progresses swiftly, the climber becomes mentally confused and may even hallucinate. This suggests that CE is also present. Bubbling noises are heard in the chest, even from across the tent, and as one climber vividly described his companion, "he seemed to be drowning in his own juices." This indeed is exactly what happens.

As fluid accumulates, the oxygen becomes less effective—quite understandably because of the increasing barrier to the diffusion from alveolus to lung capillary. Once HAPE is diagnosed, or even strongly suspected, the party must start down. This is the only truly effective treatment. Rest in camp may help, but the party runs the risk of being unable to move because of weather at a time when the condition is worse. There is considerable debate about treatment: most physicians experienced in altitude believe that furosemide (Lasix) should be given by mouth or intravenously. This will squeeze fluid out of water logged tissues by causing a profuse flow of urine, and often relieves HAPE dramatically. However, no medicine, no amount of rest, no oxygen is a substitute for getting down. The party is taking a greater risk by delaying evacuation than by starting down at night or in dubious weather. Getting down even a few thousand feet is usually dramatic, unless the disease has gone too far, and then further descent to hospital care, oxygen under pressure, and more medication are necessary to save life.

HAPE can be mistaken for pneumonia and vice versa of course. However true bacterial or viral pneumonia is unusual on a climbing trip although it does occur. Think pneumonia last—get down. Other conditions have wrongly been called HAPE: pericarditis, coronary thrombosis, hyperventilation (which is quite common) or air in pleural cavity or mediastinum. These are uncommon medical problems which should be treated as HAPE is treated by descent to low altitude and competent medical care.

Brain edema (CE) has about the same time frame as HAPE although it often is slower to begin and is much less common. Full blown CE is uncommon below 12-13,000 feet. Characteristically the climber develops a severe and increasing headache, vomiting is common, he staggers like a drunk when walking, and until recently this was attributed to clumsy boots, slippery snow, uneven terrain. It is not these, the brain has accumulated water in the specific areas which control walking, and ataxia results. It is unusual for this clumsiness to affect hand or arm motions. Hallucinations begin: the climber sees weird sights such as bulldozers on the summit, he hears voices, and believes that he has other companions nearby. Behavior becomes irrational and simple tasks impossible. Lethargy leads to stupor and the patient drifts into coma and may die. Even more urgently than HAPE, CE demands immediate descent. Intravenous steroids have been used quite often and there is anecdotal evidence that they work, but they are not effective in less than four to six hours. Other medical treatments to reduce brain swelling have not been used frequently enough to permit comment. Here again, once CE is suspected—descent is mandatory at once and under almost any conditions.

Retinal hemorrhages (RH) are common at altitude, probably occurring in 20 to 30% of all persons who climb above 14,000 feet. The more strenuous the exertion the more frequent the hemorrhage we believe. The climber rarely knows that he has a retinal hemorrhage, which is probably why they have not been observed until very recently. It is our impression that retinal hemorrhages disappear in two to six months leaving no after effects. This is supported by the fact that roughly 30% of all newborn infants have retinal hemorrhages which clear rapidly without residuals. Therefore retinal hemorrhages alone are not considered by most altitude wise doctors as cause for descent, or reason to not climb again. The really important question of whether or not retinal hemorrhages are indicative of hemorrhages elsewhere—for example in the brain—has not been settled. Nor is it likely to be for some time.

As more and more cases of altitude illness are carefully described, it is more and more clear that patients with HAPE have some CE as well, and that the difference between AMS and HAPE plus CE is only a matter of degree. Indeed some experienced researchers believe that AMS is actually caused by early brain edema.

Of course the majority of people who go to altitude carefully and slowly have only minor temporary discomfort. They adapt, they acclimatize. This process is an intricate one, and does not belong in this summary paper. However it does lead us to look at the response to altitude hypoxia as divided into two stages: some immediate reactions (deeper faster breathing, rapid bounding pulse, increased hemoglobin) seem clearly intended to bring more oxygen to the tissues despite less oxygen in the air. These are the "struggle for oxygen" responses defined by Barbashova. While these are providing temporary protection against hypoxia, other slowly evolving changes take place within the cells enabling them to use oxygen more effectively. These are the true adaptations. Some take days, others weeks, others a lifetime to perfect. As the cellular adaptations mature, the "struggle responses" decrease and disappear. In the fully acclimatized individual the "struggle responses" are minimal. By contrast, the patient with altitude illness shows strong struggle responses.

Meanwhile, while the cells are adapting, trouble develops. A current concept, particularly attractive although still only an hypothesis, may explain why hypoxia causes the type of reaction which we see. This concept or hypothesis runs as follows: lack of oxygen causes a change in the delicate membranes which enclose each living cell, a change which produces an increase of sodium within the cell, while potassium moves out. The increased sodium attracts water into the cell, and the cell swells. The extent and location of swollen cells dictate what signs and symptoms will result. The membrane change is attributed to a temporary breakdown in the "sodium pump" which depends upon adenosinetriphosphate (ATP) the fuel for most living processes, which is oxygen dependent.

It may be some time before we can prove or disprove this hypothesis, even though we know that most of the signs and symptoms of altitude illness are due to abnormal shifts of water and electrolytes.

There are obviously many other concurrent changes: certain hormones are increased while others decrease, the number of tiny capillaries increases, and the mass of a special form of hemoglobin (myoglobin) increases, enabling oxygen to be "temporarily stored." Circulating hemoglobin, after an immediate rise and fall again slowly rises; certain portions of the Krebs Cycle of metabolism within the cells change to enable more metabolism to occur without oxygen. Possibly the most significant change of all is a considerable increase in mitochondria—the tiny granules—which are called the true powerhouses of the cell.

In summary what do we know for sure? *First:* All forms of altitude illness are increasing in frequency and perhaps in severity, most probably because more people are going too high too fast. *Second:* Evidence is increasing to show that what we have until recently considered as separate diseases are in fact all part of a continuum of one disease, a disturbance of water and salt. *Third:* As yet there is no reliable way of predicting who will and who will not be taken with altitude illness, or which individuals, smitten once, may be smitten again. *Fourth:* No medicine is a proven preventive, although Diamox does help somewhat. *Fifth:* We do have a proven treatment: immediate rapid descent to safe altitude. Other treatment such as oxygen, steroids, aspirin, may help but is less and less valuable the longer the condition persists. *Sixth:* We cannot say for sure whether a person with one attack is more or less likely to have another. We cannot say for sure whether or not persons well acclimatized to high altitude, going down for a few days or weeks have a greater risk of altitude illness when they return to altitude, than do those going high for the first time.

We can say with a moderate degree of confidence that taking one day to climb each thousand feet will protect most people, but today we would start this slow rate of ascent at 7000 feet rather than 10,000 feet as was recommended earlier. A number of near fatal cases and deaths have occurred within a day of reaching 9500 feet from sea level.

Finally, we can say with great confidence that almost any one with altitude illness who starts down early in the disease will recover rapidly and completely. As should be the case in all of medicine, prevention is the most important aspect in the management of altitude illness.

Selected Papers on High Altitude Illness

This is in no sense a complete bibliography, but a selection of some of the better, more authoritative publications of recent years on the subject of altitude illness in its various forms, and a few of the basic papers which give background. From references in most of the papers cited can be found almost all of the major publications in the field.

Some Experiences of Mountain Sickness in the Andes, Ravenhill, T.H., Jour Trop Med and Hyg, 20, 313, Oct 15, 1913.
This appears to be the first definite description of acute mountain sickness, pulmonary edema, and cerebral edema due to altitude. The author describes his personal observations of numerous cases, and his puzzlement that some altitude residents do, while others do not, become ill on reascent to altitude after a brief stay at sea level. No references; a classic paper.

An Annotated Bibliography of Acute Mountain Sickness, Hall, W.H., U.S. Army Research Institute of Environmental Medicine, June 1964.
Twenty-two papers, selected from publications in the last seventy years, are carefully described. Only acute mountain sickness is included. Most of the classical reports are included.

Acute Mountain Sickness, Singh, I., Khanna, P.K., Srivastava, M.C., Lal, M., Roy, S.B., Subramanyan, C.S.V., New Engl Jour Med, 280, 175, 1969.
Clinical observations on 1925 individuals with various forms of acute mountain sickness in the Himalayan Sino-Indian war. Relationships between acute mountain sickness, cerebral and pulmonary edema and antidiuresis are discussed. Various treatments are evaluated.

Effect of Acetazolamide on Acute Mountain Sickness, Forward, S.A., Lansdowne, M., Follansbee, J.N., and Hansen, J.E., New Engl Jour Med, 279, 839, 1968.
In a double blind study, either placebo or acetazolamide was given to forty-three subjects rapidly transported to 12,800 feet for five days. Significant reductions were observed in the most prominent symptoms of acute mountain sickness, but the mechanism of action was not identified.

A Hypothesis Regarding the Pathophysiology of Acute Mountain Sickness, Hansen, J.E., and Evans, W.O., Arch Env Health, 21, 666, 1970.
Acute mountain sickness is a syndrome of unknown etiology which occurs, after a time lag, following abrupt exposure to oxygen lack and which includes a characteristic spectrum of symptoms. The authors collected evidence to suggest that brain compression causes the symptoms of acute mountain sickness.

Acute Mountain Sickness: Increased Severity in Eucapnic Hypoxia, Maher, J.T., Cymerman, A., Reeves, J.T., Cruz, J.C., Denniston, J.C. and Grover, R.F., Aviation Space and Env Med, 826, June 1975.
In carefully controlled studies in the low-pressure chamber, arterial carbon dioxide levels were held constant by increasing carbon dioxide in ambient air at a simulated altitude of 4000 meters for four days, with ambient barometric pressure adjusted to maintain the same alveolar oxygen levels in both groups.

The benefits previously attributed to carbon dioxide are shown to be due to the hyperventilation which raised alveolar oxygen; in fact, when alveolar oxygen is the same, added carbon dioxide appears to aggravate symptoms.

Acute Pulmonary Edema of High Altitude, Houston, C.S., New Engl Jour Med, 263, 478, 1960.
A case of acute pulmonary edema occurring in a healthy skier at 12,000 feet is reported with brief reviews of four similar but less well documented cases among mountaineers. Though the mechanism was unknown, the combined effects of anoxia, cold, and exertion were suspected as causative. This early case report stimulated further studies.

High Altitude Pulmonary Edema, Hultgren, H.N., Spickard, W.B., Hellriegel, K., and Houston, C.S., Medicine, 40, 289, September 1961.
This early article reports eighteen patients with pulmonary edema at 12,000 feet in the Andes and thirteen suggestive cases occurring in mountaineers. The literature is reviewed and mechanisms examined. Fifteen of the eighteen persons studied in the Andes developed the condition after re-entry to altitude to which they were fully acclimatized, raising the possibility that such persons are more vulnerable.

High Altitude Pulmonary Edema, Singh, I., Kapila, C.C., Khanna, P.K., Nanda, R.B., and Rao, B.D.P., Lancet, 229, Jan 30, 1965.
Three hundred thirty-two Indian soldiers developed pulmonary edema at altitudes above 11,000 feet following rapid ascent. The condition occurred in 15.5% of persons reaching altitude for the first time, and in 13.0% of those returning after a stay at low altitude. Pulmonary edema, cerebral edema and acute mountain sickness are suggested to be various reactions to the same underlying physiologic response to hypoxia, and mechanisms are proposed. Treatment with aminophylline, atropine, morphine and digoxin is discussed; the latter apparently ineffective. Failure of oxygen to relieve hemoglobin desaturation is noted.

High Altitude Pulmonary Edema, Menon, N.D., New Engl Jour Med, 273, 66, July 8, 1965.
One hundred and one patients with proven high-altitude pulmonary edema were treated while still at 11,500 feet; digitalis and oxygen appeared to be more effective than either alone. Among troops taken rapidly to altitude the incidence appeared to be 5%

The Preterminal Arterioles in the Pulmonary Circulation of High Altitude Natives, Recavarren, S., Circulation 33, 177, February 1966.
Quoting the work of others, the author speculates that increased pulmonary artery muscularization correlates, in individuals fully acclimatized by long residence at altitude, with the susceptibility to pulmonary edema by increased capillary hydrostatic pressure, increased capillary permeability, and points out that normal lung capillary pressures have been observed after edema has appeared.

Pulmonary Edema of High Altitude, Viswanathan, R., Jain, S.K., and Subramanian, S., Amer Rev. of Resp Dis, 100, 342, 1969.
In a series of three reviews the authors examine the production of edema in animals, the clinical and hemodynamic features, and the pathogenesis, and conclude that the condition is due to an abnormal hypoxic response in susceptible individuals who manifest a genetically determined condition by greater than normal pre-capillary vascular resistance in lungs, leading to pulmonary artery hypertension. The mechanism whereby edema results is not explained.

Water Metabolism in Humans During Acute High Altitude Exposure,
Krzywicki, H.J., Consolazio, F., Johnson, H.L., Nielsen, W.C., and Barnhart, R.A., Jour Appl Physiol, 30, 806, 1971.
Two groups of six men were studied before and after six days at 14,000 feet. Total body water was significantly decreased; extra-cellular water increased; and intra-cellular water decreased. Heavy physical exertion was performed before and during the altitude exposure; hypo-hydration and diuresis occurred, suggesting that water loss may have been an adaptive mechanism to acute altitude exposure. This report disagrees with the work of some others.

Hormonal and Electrolyte Response to Exposure to 17,500 Feet, Frayser, R., Rennie, I.D.B., Gray, G.W., and Houston, C.S., Jour Appl Physiol, 38, 636, April 1975.
Changes in cortisols, renin and aldosterone were found at day three after ascent to 17,500 feet, returning to normal on the fifth day. Sodium and potassium excretion was decreased. The changes observed are believed due to the stress and alkalosis of acute hypoxia, and return to normal as the body adapts. References and discussion of varying findings by other observers are included.

"State of the Art Review": Pathogenesis of Pulmonary Edema, Staub, N.C., Amer Rev Resp Dis, 109, 358, 1974.
A careful review of the development and pathology of various types of interstitial and alveolar edema, with extensive references and illustration of the various causes, including hypoxia.

Cerebral Form of High Altitude Illness, Houston, C.S., and Dickinson, J., The Lancet, 785, Oct 18, 1975.
Twelve cases of severe altitude illness in which neurological signs and symptoms dominated the clinical pictures are described. Two patients died and autopsy confirmed the presence of cerebral and pulmonary edema; other pathology was identified in several of the patients. The importance of early descent is emphasized.

Brain Edema, Fishman, R.A., New Engl Jour Med, 293, 706, Oct 2, 1975.
A brief, tightly written review of the various causes and pathophysiology of brain edema from various causes; management is discussed.

Acute High-Altitude Illness in Mountaineers and Problems of Rescue, Wilson, R., Annals of Internal Med, 78, 3, 421, March 1973.
Syndromes of acute mountain sickness share hypoxia as a cause, but expression of the illness varies. Cerebral edema causes headache, selective neurologic defect and coma and perhaps even pulmonary edema, although microthrombi in pulmonary capillaries are often seen and may be causal. Retinal hemorrhages frequently occur at high altitude. Acute mountain sickness is difficult to treat on a mountain, even with oxygen. Drugs are of uncertain usefulness; therefore immediate descent is important.

Adaptation to High Altitude, Lenfant, C., and Sullivan K., New Engl Jour Med, 284, 1298, June 10, 1971.
A concise and careful review of the process of acclimatization. Major emphasis is placed on changes in the oxygen transport mechanisms in response to altitude hypoxia. Many references.

Physiological Adjustments to Altitude Changes, Dill, D.B., Jour Am Med Assoc, 205, 123, Sept 9, 1968.
Physiological adaptation to high altitude involves rapid responses in respira-

tion and slower responses in nervous, muscular, and cardiovascular systems. An excellent criterion of adaptation is measurement of the capacity for supplying oxygen to tissues: the oxygen consumption (V_{o_2} maximum). Such measurements reveal four stages of response. At 10,000 feet stage 1 is reached in minutes; V_{o_2} max declines 10%. In one to three days, (stage 2), it declines another 10%; this is the stage of unpleasant subjective responses. In a few weeks, stage 3, performance approaches the level of stage 1. Red blood cell volume increases in stage 4, reaching its maximum after a year or more. Performance improves pari passu: eventually sea-level performance can be achieved at 13,200. Above 17,500 feet there is deterioration rather than adaptation.

Cellular Level of Adaptation, Barbashova, Z.I., Handbook of Physiology: Adaptation to Environment, Section 4, pp 37-54, 1964.
The writer suggests that two levels of adaptation to hypoxia occur: the immediate or "struggle for oxygen" responses of hyperventilation, increased cardiac output, increased hemoglobin, and slower adaptation of intracellular enzymes. As the latter mature, the former diminish. Acclimatized man shows few "struggle responses" and highly developed cellular adaptation.

Altitude, Migration, and Fertility in the Andes, Abelson, A.E., Baker, T.S., and Baker, P.T., Population Biology, 21(1), 12, 1974.
Using anthropological and sociological techniques Andean populations were examined to determine the impact upon fertility, live births, and infant mortality by altitude hypoxia and by migration from high to low or low to high altitude. Despite the complexity of such studies, evidence suggests that altitude decreases fertility, increases neonatal mortality and increases the probability of birth defects.

Retinal Hemorrhage at High Altitude, Frayser, R. Houston, C.S., Gray, G., Bryan, A.C., New Engl Jour Med, 282, 1183, 1970.
Nine out of twenty-five individuals taken to 17,500 feet were found to have retinal hemorrhage. Of seventeen of these persons who went up rapidly six had hemorrhage; of eight who climbed slowly to altitude, three showed hemorrhage. Incidence of retinal hemorrhage was unrelated to other symptoms of altitude sickness, but seemed to be reduced in the nine individuals premedicated with acetazolamide. This is the first report of retinal hemorrhage in healthy individuals exposed to high altitude hypoxia.

The Response of the Retinal Circulation to Altitude, Frayser, R., Houston, C.S., Gray, G., Bryan, A.C., and Rennie, I.D.B., Arch Int. Med, 127, 708, 1971.
Individuals taken rapidly or slowly to 17,500 feet showed increases in retinal blood flow of 89% over control values within two hours, and by 128% over control after four days. Retinal blood flow increased by 105% over control values in acclimatized subjects. Both arterioles and venules show increased diameter and tortuosity beginning a few hours after arrival at altitude.

Ocular Changes in Pulmonary Insufficiency, Spalter, H.F., and Bruce, G.M., Tr Am Acad Ophthal and Otol, 661, July 1964.
Changes in the ocular fundi in patients with hypoxia due to chronic pulmonary disease are described. The retinopathy (which included increased diameter and tortuosity of vessels, papilledema and hemorrhages) was attributed to carbon dioxide retention and resulting acidosis. Literature is reviewed and photographs presented.

HAPS

The Arctic Institute High Altitude Physiology Study on Mount Logan

CHARLES S. HOUSTON, M.D.

THE small group of scientists who met in New York that fall day in 1966 were intrigued by the invitation "To talk about the feasibility of establishing a permanent laboratory at 18,000 feet to study the effects of high altitude on man." The project had been proposed as a logical next step for the Icefield Ranges Research Program (IRRP) which the Arctic Institute of North America was conducting among several other programs in the Arctic. The Kluane Lake Base had been summer home since 1961 to scores of scientists studying the rocks and glaciers, the flora and fauna, weather, lakes and rivers in the wild and unspoiled southwestern tip of the Canadian Yukon, and a program in human physiology would be a natural addition. Kluane Lake is surrounded on the northeast and northwest by thousands of square miles of rolling hills, eroded valleys and lakes and tundra—almost untouched. To the southeast and southwest lie vast snowfields and glaciers studded with hundreds of great mountains which culminate in Mount Logan and Mount St. Elias.

Logan seemed ready-made for such a project. Its several summits surround three sides of an enormous bowl-shaped plateau some fifteen miles long and six miles wide, which slopes smoothly and gently from 19,000 to 11,000 feet before plunging over a precipice to glaciers six thousand feet below. We thought the plateau might be partially sheltered from very high winds by these surrounding peaks; it offered ample landing space for the STOL aircraft equipped with wheels and skis, and it appeared to be almost completely free of crevasses except for the lower two or three miles. We could select a site at an appropriate altitude, climbing to it along the usual route up Logan, and supplying it by air with the Helio-courier which was already working on other AINA projects. And our pilot already had more high-mountain flying experience than any one in the country.

Kluane Lake (altitude 2500 feet) was about 80 air miles southeast of Logan; Kluane had a gravel airstrip and a number of buildings, relics for the most part from the construction of the Alaska Highway which ran a hundred yards from the camp. Whitehorse, nearest town of any size, was 150 rough miles to the east, but excellent telephone service, an erratic bus, and twice weekly mail made it much less remote than it had been when Walter Wood (who had established IRRP and was now proposing the altitude study) first visited the area in 1934 by pack train from Whitehorse. It would be easy to set up an adequate base laboratory; the question was could we build and maintain a respectable laboratory in the high, hostile climate on the Logan Plateau?

There were other unanswered questions: Would weather allow us to fly up and back as needed? Would snow on the plateau be safe for landing—not too soft, nor yet storm-piled into compact hard drifts? Could we fly enough missions to supply the large amount of food, fuel, and material needed for a productive study? What studies would be most significant—and at the same time feasible under such field conditions? Above all—could we make the project safe—at least as safe as a climbing expedition?

There had of course been many other studies of man at altitude. On Monte Rosa and the Jungfrau in the Alps, on Pikes Peak, Mount Evans and White Mountain in the Rockies, and at several stations in the Andes. Bert, Mosso, Haldane, Barcroft, Dill and many others had done meticulous work in many areas, ever since the latter part of the nineteenth century. One of the finest and most comprehensive studies was carried on by Pugh during the winter of 1961 when a group of British and American scientists lived in a specially constructed hut at 19,000 feet in the Himalayas. What could we add—or do better? Most work had been done at 14-15,000 feet; we would be several thousand feet higher—and 17,500 feet is considered by some as the highest altitude where man can acclimatize more rapidly than he deteriorates. We would supplement the 1961 study by bringing into play some modern techniques.

That fall day in 1966 we were stimulated by two other considerations. First was the rather startling increase in the number and severity of cases of altitude illness among mountaineers, presumably because of the speed and ease with which more and more people were able to reach high mountainous country. Some rather horrible episodes had already occurred; more were inevitable. What could we learn that might help identify susceptibles (if there are such) or to decrease severity and the risk of death? Could we find out why a person might be ill on one climb and not on another? A similar consideration was the desire of the military for more information about the impact of high altitude on troops. In the 1962 Indo-Chinese border war, large numbers of Indians had been flown hastily from the plains high into the mountains; predictably, large numbers were disabled by altitude illness, whereas the Chinese, acclimatized by months of residence on the high Tibetan plateaux had little altitude difficulty. The Indian physicians had published many thought-provoking papers on the subject, opening new areas for study.

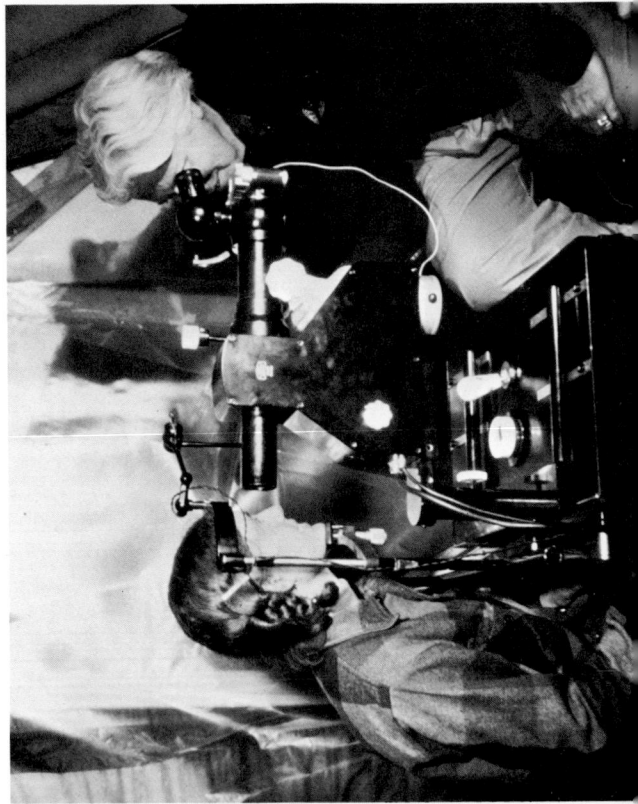

Logan High Laboratory and living quarters, 17,500 feet, in 1971.

Dr. Regina Frayser taking photographs of the retina blood vessels in a member of the support team at Logan High.

From the beginning there was a second, perhaps major stimulus. In addition to the mountaineers who voluntarily expose themselves to altitude, there are millions of patients with heart or lung disease who are short of oxygen even at sea level. Could we learn from the reactions of healthy man, in the abnormally low oxygen environment of altitude, lessons which would help the sick person in the normal atmosphere of sea level? This might turn out to be the most significant contribution we could make and would more than justify our efforts.

This then was the background against which Walter Wood (climber, geographer, scientist) and Bob Raylor (Director of the Washington office of the Arctic Institute) did the planning; Drs. Charles Bryan and John Cocker would represent the Canadian Forces Institute for Environmental Medicine, Dr. Lowell Becker had been engaged in altitude work in the Andes, Barry Bishop was a geographer mountaineer—one of the few then to have climbed Everest, and I had been actively interested in altitude during Himalayan expeditions and during World War II.

THE EARLY YEARS: Bob Faylor and Dick Ragle did the planning for the first year, enabling 15 doctors, students and technicians, to assemble at Kluane Lake Base in July 1967. The Canadian Forces flew enormous cases of scientific supplies and equipment, to Burwash Landing 35 miles away, and these "Paul Bunyans" were trucked to Kluane, though only a fraction of the equipment would go any higher. The indomitable Barry Bishop led a party of eight from a snow landing at 10,000 feet in the Trench between King Peak and Logan up a long laborious route to the Logan Plateau, reporting by radio that there was ample space for building and no crevasses. Faylor had designed a plywood laboratory; pre-cut to fit the small Helio-courier cabin it was flown up in pieces and christened "Faylor's Folly" quite unjustly as it turned out. Phil Upton made 25 uneventful trips to the Logan "landing strip" during the eighteen days when weather permitted, and we came to respect weather as a potentially serious obstacle. We learned many lessons that summer, some of which would affect all subsequent operations.

The first episode occurred almost at once. As Bishop's party climbed in early July, they encountered deep new snow and frequent storms. Two individuals were unable to continue and were left, together with a stong climber in a well-stocked camp at 16,000 feet, planning either to continue after a few days' rest or to descend to 10,000 feet for evacuation. But the weather deteriorated. One man apparently grew sicker, and his condition as described by radio sounded more and more alarming over the next few days; finally the speaker reported that his tentmate was "gradually losing consciousness." Their location was inaccessible to fixed wing aircraft, and the only available helicopter was chartered by the Yukon Centennial party. On July 13th, told that the sick man was critically ill, we rudely commandeered the helicopter, and although the pilot had never landed that high before, in two trips he plucked the party of three from their 16,000-foot camp and brought them to base. We were astonished: the "sick man" was apparently well except for some difficulty in walking which we would later recognize as characteristic of altitude ataxia. By contrast, the one who had called so urgently and persistently for help had pulmonary edema, could scarcely walk and seemed not fully rational—a condition we would come to know as indicative of altitude brain edema. The third climber, from whom we had heard nothing, was fine. Two apparently unaffected individuals had listened while a third broadcast emergency calls for help— for one of them. The correct decisions were made, at the right time, but for the wrong person! This taught us that we must listen not only to the words, but to the tone, the mood, the unspoken vibrations which came over the air from the mountain. One of the insidious effects of altitude is blunting of intellect, judgment and perception. In later years each evening broadcast would be heard on two levels; the spoken word and the unspoken intuitive messages.

There were other lessons too. During one storm a tent was almost completely buried and the three occupants developed shortness of breath and headache before realizing that carbon dioxide from their breathing and carbon monoxide from their stove were building up to danger levels in the sealed tent—another example of intellectual blunting. Such experiences are not uncommon and should have been recognized. No one who was at Kluane that year will forget their return: staggering like drunks because of altitude ataxia, relieved at returning safely from the hostile environment, "intoxicated" by the comforts of Base, one of them, a natural comic, convulsed the entire camp with laughter for most of one night.

At Logan High construction went on. Bishop's determined crew completed the insulated building, although they were living in marginal conditions: two bedraggled tents with broken zippers, miserable cooking equipment and haphazard meals. But the laboratory was completed, sealed, and marked with a tall pole against winter snow cover. The first stage was accomplished successfully!

We concluded from that first year that we could sustain a laboratory at 17,500 feet on Mount Logan, although storm and poor snow conditions might make landings impossible for several days at a time. We had appreciated how subtle and tricky the effects of altitude might be. Much more careful advance planning of food and equipment would be needed. Though we did not yet know whether we could do good scientific work under such conditions, we thought it possible. In the fall of 1967 the planning group decided to go ahead for a second year.

Accordingly in June 1968 a strong climbing party was landed at 10,000 feet in the Trench and climbed laboriously to Logan High. Once again the Canadian Forces sent equipment and supplies to Kluane, where a smaller scientific party with more modest ambitions assembled in early July. Once again the altitude taught us lessons which would influence our future programs.

For example: one member of the support party climbing up from 10,000 feet became exhausted, and at 18,000 feet was irrational and unable to help himself. He was half carried to a tent near the site of the buried laboratory, but storm delayed his evacuation. Some 30 hours after reaching Logan High he was flown to Whitehorse, recovering remarkably on the way, though still unable to walk on arrival. He was found to have pulmonary edema, but recovered rapidly and within a few days was back at Kluane asking to return to Logan High! A curious, unexplained finding was the presence of small hemorrhages in the retinae of both eyes!

Then one of the scientists with little mountain experience was flown to Logan High after two days at 8500 feet. At Logan High his headache was severe and persistent, though he felt able to climb several hundred feet above camp. He had an irregular heart action from time to time, became short of breath, and felt that he had trouble with his eyes. He was soon brought down and at Kluane he too was found to have unexplained retinal hemorrhages.

Another scientist flew directly to Logan High where he was quite well for five days. He flew back to Kluane for consultation, returning to Logan High 36 hours later where he became mentally confused and short of breath. He was immediately returned to Kluane and found to have pulmonary edema which cleared almost immediately. This seemed to re-enforce the belief that acclimatized persons, re-ascending after a stay at low altitude, might be especially vulnerable.

During the second year ten individuals were flown from Kluane to Logan High, and about 100 blood studies completed with acceptable accuracy. In July, 19 flights were made to Logan High during the 25 flyable days, and almost as many more were made in June before the scientific work began.

The climbing party had twice been struck by altitude sickness, which we had not expected. Living in tents at Logan High for any extended time would be unpleasant and sapping, and larger quarters would be needed; these would have to be well marked to be easily found. Quite likely new buildings would be needed every few years as the old ones slowly sank in the snow! We recognized the possible risks of flying people directly from

Kluane to Logan High, even though this would provide cases of altitude illness for study.

But the project was clearly successful. We were confident that the dangers could be minimized and reliable data obtained, and with these reassurances the planning group met in the fall of 1968 to lay long-range plans. Ongoing funds were given by the Fleischmann and the Kresge Foundations, by the Defense Research Board of Canada, and later by the National Institutes of Health. The Canadian Forces increased their support. Word got around, and curious climbers applied to be members of the support team. The scientists came to know each other better, and administration smoothed out.

The scientific protocol planned for the third year included studies of retinal circulation, because following our observations, others too had found hemorrhages, and we began to wonder just how common—and how serious—they might be. A prominent part of the plan for 1969 included photographs and measurement of the retinal circulation.

The general format was much the same: climbers would leave Kluane Lake in late May, fly to Trench, and slowly move up to Logan High. There, hopefully, they would easily find the marker over the cache, although the original laboratory would undoubtedly have sunk too deeply into the snow to be usable. A new kind of building would be used: the Versadome, made of double nylon coverings stretched on an intricate framework of tubular steel. The floor of plywood is on trusses laid on heavy plastic, providing a dead airspace which gives some insulation from the cold. The design has several advantages: it can easily be transported in the Helio-courier, can be erected by a small crew in a few days, and is quite resistant to very strong winds. The double nylon walls make these buildings reasonably warm since space heaters are used. Versadomes and variants have been used each year since.

Scientific studies were designed to examine the changes in the distribution of water and electrolytes which take place during oxygen lack, thus contributing to altitude edema. Measurements of fluid intake and urine output along with daily physical examinations would give estimates of water balance, and perhaps give early warning of altitude sickness. A new scientist with experience in retinal photography would join us, because the unexplained observation of retinal hemorrhages had opened up a new, intriguing and unexplored field. We would still adhere to the plan of flying experimental subjects directly from Kluane Lake to Logan High, expecting them to be ill and thus more suited to the acute studies which we were planning. Scientists too would fly directly from low to high altitude, but in advance of the subjects to allow time for them to adjust. We felt, then though not today, that this would be safe, given proper safeguards. We anticipated that the month of July should enable us to study eight subjects, each of whom would spend five to ten days at Logan High.

We were able to charter a Beaver, a single engine cargo aircraft with a payload of over 1000 pounds to transport supplies and people to 10,000 feet—close to its service ceiling, but only the Helio-courier could supply Logan High—placing heavy responsibility on our pilot. However, in 1968 we had shown that the Jet Ranger helicopter was capable of landing and taking off with a payload of 300 pounds at Logan High; since several of these helicopters were based in Whitehorse, we felt that emergency flights could be made if necessary if our plane were out of service. Weather, though not exactly ideal, seldom caused more than two or three days without flying in succession. Radios were marginally effective: the costly crystal sets which formed the backbone of our communication system frequently gave trouble, maintenance and repair were sloppy, and on several occasions sets were returned by the maker after servicing with the wrong crystal frequency, a faulty crystal oven, or other poor workmanship. Had we been able to afford them, we would have bought more elaborate and more costly radios elsewhere. Military radios on loan from the Canadian Forces, in contrast, operated flawlessly throughout the summer. We had occasional radio blackouts when no transmissions could be sent or received for up to six or eight hours at a time, due to weather.

Things went well in 1969, although one episode might have ended disastrously. One of the subjects, a very fit Canadian Forces officer, flown to Logan High became lethargic on the first day, and within 30 hours of arrival could not be roused. Despite oxygen and other treatment, emergency evacuation was called for and accomplished near midnight 36 hours after he had arrived; at Kluane Lake he recovered in eight hours, and in five or six days was his normal self. We recognized this to be a severe case of brain edema.

During the third program year we also realized more than ever that scientists working at Logan High, flown directly up from Kluane Lake were themselves affected by the very phenomena they were studying, and —more significantly—their radioed observations could not be considered totally reliable. It became clear that an experienced physician had to be at Kluane Lake at all times during the project, listening with the inner ear to spoken and unspoken communications, and making hard decisions whenever these were necessary. The evening radio contact—soon to be known as "the hour of charm" was given to conversational exchanges between Kluane and Logan High, during which observers at Kluane tried to estimate just what the condition of the various people might be. This chit-chat became very helpful, but it was disconcerting to find that people in Whitehorse were also listening avidly to our news!

THE MIDDLE YEARS: By the end of the summer of 1969 HAPS was well established. The logistic patterns were set, reasonably safe and comfortable living was possible, and the flying risks acceptable—providing we had an excellent pilot and aircraft. We accepted the risks taken by flying directly to 17,500 feet, feeling that these could be mitigated by taking acetazolamide in advance, though this did alter our findings. The HAPS group was more than 30 strong including scientists, subjects, support team, pilot and staff. The problem of supplying Logan High was partially resolved when the Canadian Forces agreed to parachute loads at Logan High, thus providing ample oxygen, propane, lumber and food, and excellent real-life practice for the crew. Best of all a respectable amount of scientific information had been accumulated and was being published, though we still had a long way to go before a long-range master plan of research was developed. The group was working as a team: young climbers were eager to join, and we had more applicants than we could use. The scientists were excited about the work, time-consuming and demanding though it was. Canadian Forces support was increasing, and as experience had grown, our confidence in our ability to handle the likely situations had increased.

In 1971 much the same program was followed: ten experimental subjects volunteered from the Canadian Forces and were taken to Logan High in two groups for testing. Five scientists, two technicians, and nine mountaineers made up the party, and despite unusually bad weather (a phrase which seems to have recurred annually!) about three-quarters of the ambitious scientific plan was completed. There were several instructive episodes. One member of the support team, after climbing for one day above the landing at 10,000 feet, became weak and lethargic and unable to continue. Properly conservative, the team leader called for helicopter evacuation; on arrival at Kluane the climber was found in good health. Two weeks later he asked and was permitted to return to 10,000 feet, to be flown to Logan High with the scientists acclimatizing there. Once again he felt unwell, behaved inappropriately, and was returned to Base. Once again he was found well, but as we added together all the pieces it became clear that his "illness" was emotional rather than physical. In retrospect the party agreed that he should not have been taken.

A young member of a mountain expedition attempting the regular route to the summit became ill around 13,000 feet, grew rapidly worse, and with difficulty was brought down to our 10,000-foot camp at Trench, where by good fortune one of the HAPS physicians had just arrived. The climber had severe pulmonary edema, and was treated for 24 hours without improvement before a dramatic night-time helicopter rescue brought him to Base where he recovered completely in a few days. The worst feature of 1971 was the down time of the aircraft. First one thing then another grounded our only plane for 16 of the 31 project days. Had we not been able to charter a helicopter at crucial times, the project might not only have failed but people might have been endangered. We were convinced that two aircraft, and hopefully two pilots, were essential to our effectiveness, and even to safety.

As the 1971 field season ended the scientists agreed that we needed a breathing space to review the data, write papers and to look ahead— planning for a long-term grant application which would give more stability to the program. We also agreed that the risks of flying people directly to Logan High were not justified by the additional data; a staging camp was needed.

Accordingly, no formal HAPS program took place in 1972. Some of the scientists and climbers did go to Kluane under different auspices, looking for an intermediate camp roughly half-way from Kluane to Logan High, through which we could stage scientists and subjects before exposing them to the acute stress of Logan High. An ideal location was found on the Badham-Donjek plateau at 9500 feet and christened Eclipse.

THE LATER YEARS: Both 1973 and 1974 were good years. The Canadian Forces provided air transportation for the party from western Canada to Kluane Lake and most of the supplies and equipment. Fifteen volunteers from the Canadian Forces were briefed about the program and took enthusiastic part. They were taught snow and ice climbing by trained instructors at the intermediate camp—Eclipse—and more elaborate and sophisticated studies were accomplished. The generosity of the Kresge Foundation enabled us to buy a back-up airplane, though it was grounded by one thing or another during most of the project. The most welcome event was award of a five-year grant from the National Institutes of Health, sufficient to provide most of the cash needs of the program. The Canadian donation of flying time, food, supplies and equipment and volunteer subjects together with some funds from Defense Research Board more than matched this dollar award. The program had become truly bi-national, half of the scientists coming from Canadian universities. Though the weather was often "unusually severe," and the scientific program more ambitious each year, we were able to accomplish most of what we planned. The staging camp at 9500 feet decreased the severity of altitude sickness in subjects and scientists—not an unmixed blessing because we were less able to study the acute illness—but an additional safeguard.

The ninth season—1975 was the most ambitious and least successful. Before the project started, our back-up aircraft was damaged while landing at the intermediate camp, and although it was daringly flown out, structural damage kept it out of commission for the rest of the summer. The faithful original aircraft developed an oil leak, causing a forced landing and ruining an engine; replacement was accomplished but the plane was not fully serviceable for most of the time. The weather was "unusually unfavorable" and for the first time in nine years none of the experimental subjects reached Logan High. Instead, scientists who had been fretfully acclimatizing for ten days at Eclipse, flew to Logan High and conducted a full schedule of studies on six of the acclimatized support team who three months later would have baseline studies done at sea level. Only about 20% of what we hoped to do was actually accomplished, but some new directions and concepts evolved.

So much for the bare bones chronicle. What has been accomplished?

SCIENTIFIC PUBLICATIONS: Rightly or wrongly, accomplishment in science is often measured in numbers of papers published, although quality and impeccability of data are important. HAPS personnel has published some 30 papers, mostly in refereed journals where peer review is a prerequisite. Other papers have been given to mountaineering journals, various audiences, and to the Armed Forces. It seems to us important to broadcast information about altitude illness, which is occurring more and more frequently as more people have easier access to high altitudes. The observation of retinal hemorrhages in 1968 led the team to a detailed study of retinal circulation, the first time this phenomenon had been described at altitude. (Singh noted a few "vitreous hemorrhages" in the eyes of several of his 2000 cases of acute altitude illness seen during the Indo-Chinese border conflict.)

Other investigators have confirmed the HAPS observations: between 20 and 30% of all persons climbing above 14,000 feet are likely to have retinal hemorrhage, although very few will be aware of them. We believe that they disappear completely leaving no scars and that they are not cause for descent. We also believe that they are increased by exertion. Whether or not these tiny bleeding points in the back of the eye are typical of bleeding areas elsewhere, for example in the brain, no one can say at present; there is no hard evidence that high-altitude climbing causes lasting damage.

The HAPS investigations have confirmed the findings of other groups that some shifts of body water and electrolytes occur at altitude; the evidence suggests that these changes in water distribution are primarily responsible for the signs and symptoms of altitude illness. The HAPS team has begun to study a number of hormones which may be involved in acclimatization, by mediating water and electrolyte distribution. These studies are only beginning, and the data are not always in complete agreement with those of others. New theories of a contributing factor in pulmonary edema are evolving from studies of platelets made by HAPS scientists. Maldistribution of pulmonary ventilation is being studied as are certain promising leads towards prediction of persons more likely than others to be sick at altitude. The condition now known as brain edema has been defined and is accepted as one of various manifestations of altitude illness.

The protective value of acetazolamide taken before ascent has been demonstrated by others; the HAPS group has confirmed these observations, and believes that acetazolamide does give modest protection against acute altitude illness.

Studies of the brain waves, by electroencephalograms taken at rest, during sleep, and after over-breathing and oxygen administration have begun; we have shown that these can be measured at altitude, but whether they will give significant information remains to be seen.

Responsible scientists who are spending other people's money, whether from federal institutes or private foundations, have an obligation to ask "What have we done?" and "What does it all mean?" HAPS has added appreciably to the fund of knowledge of how man adjusts to altitude. We have observed and publicized previously undescribed aspects of altitude illness, and called attention to the possibility that retinal hemorrhages, reported by others to be present in 30% of newborn infants, may possibly be due to the same mechanism and somehow related to oxygen lack.

As to relevance, we have warned a large number of mountaineers about the risks of rapid ascent, advising them on prevention and management of altitude illness. Whether this campaign will be any more effective than those urging use of seat belts or warning against cigarettes is unclear. Most climbers feel that "it can't happen to me"—until it does. We are beginning to identify definite similarities between the responses of healthy individuals to high altitude and those of persons with chronic heart or lung disease at sea level. Indeed spin-off projects stimulated by HAPS are now studying chronic pulmonary patients at the modest altitudes to which jet aircraft are pressurized, or to which they would be exposed during a visit to the Rockies. We have little doubt that responses of such chronically hypoxic patients are similar to those of mountain climbers, and may be amenable to the same identifying, predictive, and management techniques.

SAFETY: From the beginning safety has been paramount—safety to the scientists, safety to the climb-up party, and safety to the experimental subjects. Every one of the scientists has undergone—many times—all of the procedures. Subjects are carefully briefed in advance, and sign informed consent papers in compliance with the regulations for National Institutes of Health grants. We take no risks with any subject that we have not many times taken with ourselves. After several seasons we were convinced that flying directly from Kluane Lake to Logan High was unacceptable, and introduced the staging camp. We have seen more cases and more serious cases of altitude illness among other parties on Mount Logan than in our own group.

THE FUTURE: Each of us has somewhat different ideas about future directions. To some, Logan High offers a setting in which to pursue "targets of opportunity"—special research studies which are made tempting by new discoveries in allied fields. To others there is a pressing need to develop a strategic plan for a five-year project, into which new tactics can be fitted each year. The pace with which science is advancing is accelerating with great speed; investigative techniques are constantly being refined; new bits of data and new concepts emerge continually. Some of us feel the need to coordinate, to try to make some order out of knowledge, and especially today perhaps, to show how relevant basic science can be to clinical problems. Some feel that neat packets of information, carefully verified and published for others to learn from, are not enough to justify costly research in today's world. On Logan High, should we not be developing over-view concepts of altitude illness, acclimatization and basic changes? And should we not be trying to relate these findings to the problems caused by oxygen lack in patients at low altitude?

Logan High is admirably suited for certain types of work—studies which involve active persons engaged in normal daily activities, with ample space to move about, and with living conditions near "normal." Most workers are satisfied that low pressure chambers, however well equipped, are too artificial to simulate real life, although many sophisticated studies can be best done in such chambers, or while breathing low-oxygen mixtures. But the type of work which interests us can be done in an unfettered setting where, despite cold, and storm, and isolation, more natural activities are possible. Yet we are not interested only in mountaineers. What we are seeking is—and should be—related to the problems of oxygen lack from many different causes. Logan High seems ideal for such studies, high enough, well tested, reasonably safe, reasonably accessible, despite logistic interruptions due to weather.

Climbs and Expeditions

We are well aware that this section could not exist without the help of many other than the Editorial Board. We are very grateful to all those who have assisted us. It is impossible to mention all who have done so much, but we do wish to thank especially Dr. Adolf Diemberger, Michael Cheney, Kamal K. Guha, Soli S. Mehta, Ichiro Yoshizawa, José Paytubi, César Morales Arnao, Ken Wilson, Vojslav Arko, Mario Fantin, Bernard Amy, Marek Brniak and many others.

UNITED STATES

Alaska

Mount McKinley. Some forty-five expeditions composed of 362 climbers attempted to climb Mount McKinley. Of these, 177 people from 27 expeditions reached the summit. Some are reported elsewhere. The following reached the main summit by the West Buttress: Joe Horiskey, Bill Westbrook, Dan Boyd, Alan Ewert, May 20; Roy Magnuson, Maynard Bradsma, Thomas Cardina, George Hubbard, Douglas Mantle, Boris Savic, Carl Stude, John McKinley, Mark Goebel, July 7; Norio Ohkubo, Somikiko Chinju, Kengo Nogaki, Kagunori Yamanoue, Naohisa Matsuda, Kenji Moritada, Japanese, July 17; Mike Dunn, Mark Fields, July 26; Leonard Cook, George Smith, August 2; Charles Campbell, Jonathan Gross, Bill Glinkman, Charles Potter, August 3; Koichi Takaoka, Akira Takasaki, Naomi Ihara, Takanori Sasaki, Kazutomo Kimura, Akira Konno, Japanese, August 2. Akio Shoji, Masaaki Hatakeyama and Teruzo Nakamura climbed from the 14,000-foot basin on the West Buttress route directly via the western rib to the summit on August 8. The following climbed by the Muldrow: Earl Redman, Ola Royrvik, Dan Solie, Bjarne Holm, David Hawley, Stephen Clautice, Monte Plumlee (descent via West Buttress), April 21; Alois Infanger, Michael Allison, Chris Goethe, Eric Huggard, Ralph Jordan, Peter Kirn, Rick Lynsky, John Robinson, Lucy Smith, Miriam Stone, July 3; Scott Danielson, Jeff King, Brad Fisher, July 8; John Jenkins, Frederick Smith, Bern Hinckley, Timothy Wheeler, August 9.

Mount McKinley, South Buttress-Thayer Basin-West Buttress Traverse. Jim Carpenter, Greg Kallio, Bill Laxson, Steve Lyford, Jim Miller, Dick Morse, Jeff Thomas and I began on June 18, traveling up the Kahiltna's East Fork. After a few avalanche scares on the South Buttress, we attained its crest on July 3. From igloos at the col we pro-

---

NOTE: All dates in this section refer to 1975 unless otherwise stated.

ceeded down a ramp into Thayer Basin. Here we followed Thayer's route up to the junction of Karstens Ridge, where near the top of P 17,425 we chopped out a large ice cave. At our cave we were plagued with four days of storms, making carries to the upper Harper very arduous. On the 16th we established our 18,000-foot high camp in igloos in the Harper Basin. The next evening all eight reached the summit of the South Peak, descending in a storm. Bad weather persisted until a break on the 20th when we attempted the North Peak but we were turned back in the upper plateau. We descended the mountain over Denali Pass and down the West Buttress in three days.

ROGER ROBINSON

Mount Foraker, First Winter Ascent, Southeast Ridge. A Mountaineering Club of Alaska party was flown to the Kahiltna Glacier on February 13. It consisted of Steve and Gary Tandy, Don and Dave Pahlke, Larry Tedrick, Brian Miskil and Gaylan McCord. They attempted the unclimbed south ridge which rises from the west fork of the Kahiltna. Poor snow conditions and a 180-foot fall (fortunately causing only a broken rib) persuaded them to give up the attempt there. The Tandy brothers alone remained, the others flying out on March 6. The Tandys shifted to the second-ascent route, the southeast ridge. From the 6500-foot base of the ridge, they climbed to place Camp I at 8500 feet. Camp II was placed at 10,800 feet in a snow cave on the face on March 9. They rested the next day as it stormed. On the 11th they reached the main crest of the southeast ridge but found it better to climb below rather than on the sharp, icy ridge. They set up camp at 13,200 feet on March 12. On March 13 they had a narrow corniced ridge from 13,300 to 14,000 feet but above there found few climbing difficulties before reaching the summit.

Mount Foraker. A group of four led by Steve van Meter climbed Foraker by its southeast ridge, which was first climbed in 1963, reaching the summit on July 14. At the same time a Japanese group, K. Sonehara, M. Inukai, Y. Abe, T. Momose and K. Yaguchi, climbed the northeast ridge directly from the Kahiltna (not going over Mount Crosson). They also reached the summit on July 14. Further details are lacking.

Mount Hunter, East Ridge. The Eihokai-Osaka Expedition was composed of Kazuteru Jo, leader, Katsuyuki Jo, Yasuyuki Yamashita, Shintaro Sekizuka and Hideki Nakai. They were flown by Cliff Hudson to the Tokositna Glacier on May 25. Base Camp, 10 miles up the north fork of the glacier, was established on the 28th. They attacked the snow wall to reach the east ridge. Camp I was placed directly under the col on June 1. A 65-foot cornice collapsed on the ridge on June 2; Katsuyuki Jo narrowly escaped, but they lost precious equipment. The route along the knife edge to Camp II was difficult. Camp II was placed just beyond the second peak on the ridge on June 5. Beyond the end of the knife edge and below a 35-foot ice wall, they found a 1000-foot-long flat ridge. Camp III was placed there in a snow cave on June 7. More knife edge required fixed rope. On June 10 Katsuyuki Jo and Sekizuka left Camp III just after midnight. They passed a roof-like peak and a small rock peak. A snow and ice wall took three hours to climb. After 15 hours they dug a snow cave near the junction with the northeast ridge. They left again just after midnight on June 11, crossed the snowfield, climbed a snow wall on the east side and followed the ridge to the top (14,470 feet), where they arrived at 5:30 A.M. Yamashita and Nakai reached the summit that same day at eight A.M.

ICHIRO YOSHIZAWA, *A.A.C.* and *Japanese Alpine Club*

West Face of Mount Huntington, Alpine-Style. Since the climb would be a second ascent, following the Harvard route, one should up the ante: do it alpine-style. Jeff Bevan, Randy McGregor, Bruce Wehman and I flew to the Tokositna Glacier on June 25, spent the next week hauling loads to the base of the mountain, climbed and fixed ropes on the "Stegosaur." On the afternoon of June 30 Jeff and Randy informed us that they were spooked and depressed and were giving up. Bruce and I decided to go it alone. We fixed a 600-foot rope off the north side of the Stegosaur from the Harvard party's "Alley" camp. On July 4 we got a fair-weather forecast over the radio. On July 5 we were off and soon arrived at the base of the ice gully. Two and a half pitches took us to the 600-foot rappel rope. The Alley pitch was snow with ice so far below the surface that it was not worth digging for. After three more pitches we hit the face proper. The rock was covered with verglas. Pitches up to F8 took us up the chimney, now at 7:30 P.M. a natural funnel. We made the best of the ledge for a bivouac, both half-sitting with our feet dangling. We were off again at three A.M. The first lead of the Bastion had a few F5 walls but the next part went fast since there was enough ice to avoid all the rock. Another quick lead and the Nose appeared, a classic Yosemite-type aid pitch. Finally falling ice again told us it was time to call it a day and move right to a second bivouac. The next morning we started out with three easy pitches with great expectations of an easy day to the Harvard bivouac site. Then, after a couple of false leads, I started up on a tongue of ice which did not have enough support to allow completion; I moved left and found a traverse which went. We were well to the right of the Harvard route on the bottom half of the wall on an easier ledge-crack system, but the first belay was only halfway up what was supposed to be a one-pitch wall. All the cracks were filled with ice ahead and Bruce did some A2 for 30 feet. The next crack system was running water; I had to use more aid before a few free moves took me to the top of the rock. Two more leads brought me to a rock from which the bivouac site was obvious, but it was nine P.M. before we reached it. We did not get started until seven A.M. After one fifth-class lead, Bruce and I alternated fourth-class leads to the north ridge. An unbelayed stroll led us to the last difficulties: three successively harder bergschrunds. I went around the first two. The third one gave in only after real effort and a short fall. Bruce led up an easy snow pitch and a few more feet took us to the summit shortly after noon on July 8. We completed the descent in two and a half more days, beleaguered by falling rocks and ice and, on the lower slopes, early-morning avalanches.

DEAN F. SMITH

Moose's Tooth, East Face Attempt. In early June Lou Dawson, Tom Merrill, Bob Sullivan and I made an attempt on the east face of the Moose's Tooth. Cliff Hudson flew us to the Buckskin Glacier a half-mile from the base of the climb. Sullivan and I fixed ropes over the bergschrund and on the first pitch that same day. The weather soon closed in. On the third day it cleared and we started up, climbing 900 feet in 20 hours. By far, the hardest task was the hauling of our twelve days of food and bivouac gear. Both while climbing and in bivouacs, all of us were hit by falling ice and rocks knocked off by the leaders. Merrill decided the climb was too dangerous and started down. We made 300 feet on the second day and bivouacked below the arches that bar access to the large ledges 1700 feet up, the high point of two previous attempts. The weather then deteriorated. The next three pitches were the hardest, with several short pendulums, A4 nailing and a long tension traverse. Dawson reported that he was only 200 feet of easy climbing below large ledges at 1700 feet. Sullivan was halfway up the pitch, cleaning on Jümars, and I was still at the bivouac when a huge avalanche swept down, repeatedly hitting me with basketball-sized chunks of ice; our attempt was over. The slide missed the other two, except for bouncing pieces. Ice ripped through a bivouac tent, a sleeping bag and a hammock, broke stays in my pack and pulled one of the belay bolts (a ⅜-inch self-drive) half out. We beat a hasty and disappointed retreat.

MICHAEL KENNEDY, *Elk Mountain Climbing Club*

Mount Tatum, Northeast Ridge. On July 7 to 10, my brother Steve Hackett and I climbed Mount Tatum (11,140 feet). We left Wonder Lake early on the 7th and spent the whole day walking to McGonagall Pass. The next day, after a late start, we ascended the northeast ridge of Tatum, reaching the summit late in the evening. The ridge was a long, 3½-mile snow trudge with some fairly exposed cornices in its upper reaches.

JAMES HACKETT, *Mountaineering Club of Alaska*

Mount Brooks. On June 14 Mark Bondurant, Reinhold Seyde and I reached the summit of Mount Brooks (11,940 feet). On June 11 we left Oastler Pass, crossed the Muldrow Glacier and climbed up the north ridge on loose rock and snow to 7000 feet. After sitting out a storm on the 12th and part of the 13th, we left for the summit at three P.M. and got to the summit at 4:15 A.M. We had extremely deep snow.

Douglas Migden, *Unaffiliated*

Mount Silverthrone Traverse. On April 2 and 3 four of us flew to the Ruth Amphitheater with Cliff Hudson, where we met our fifth member, who had skied in with two companions. We were Jim Bergdahl, Garret Brown, Roger Fuiten, Sandy Mapes and I. Our route led up the north fork of the Ruth Glacier, where we spent days hauling loads up the large icefall between 7000 and 9000 feet. By April 17 we had surmounted the icefall and proceeded to a small cwm formed by the two southern spurs of Silverthrone, where we put our high camp at 11,300 feet. After placing a cache at 12,300 feet on April 20, on the 22nd we carried a second load to the summit (13,220 feet), relayed the 12,300-foot cache to the top and carried the combined load down to a camp on Silverthrone's northeast flank at 12,200 feet. Though the climbing was not difficult, the exposure was great in places. Views of Denali, eight miles away, were superb. We proceeded down to Silverthrone col and established Camp at 10,650 feet. We had originally hoped to traverse the whole Tripyramid ridge but balked at carrying 80-pound packs over the three summits. We therefore decided to attempt to traverse the three peaks in a day and return to the col. On April 24, in continuing good weather, we climbed West Tripyramid and traversed southward to the central peak, where we saw the ridge to the east peak, steep and heavily corniced. After another flawless day, in which we rested, the weather finally turned bad and we descended the Brooks Glacier all the way to the Muldrow. After another fierce storm, we parted company with Fuiten, who skied over McGonagall Pass to the road. The rest of us skied down the Muldrow and over Anderson Pass, where a cache had been placed a month before. Three more days of skiing on the middle fork of the Chulitna River finally brought us on April 30 to the Anchorage-Fairbanks highway.

A. Reynolds, *Kadota Climbing Club*

Tokosha Mountains. The Teton-like Tokosha Mountains, named in 1906 by Belmore Browne and meaning "the place where there are no trees" in Tanaina, lie between the termini of the Ruth and Tokositna Glaciers. This granite-cored, compact uplift was a mecca for first ascents during the past year. In mid-winter Dirk Bodnar, Mark Fouts,

Brian Okonek and I climbed the following summits in unsettled weather: P 4930, P 4969 and P 4955 on December 30, 1974 and P 5019 on January 1. The three earthquakes we experienced were exciting, but more memorable was the exhausting, 18-mile slog out at −39° F. It was like sunny Chamonix when Okonek and I returned to bag the high peaks in March: mornings on coarse granite peaks, afternoon slaloms through boulder gates on the glacier. We climbed Tokosha Peak (6148 feet), the highpoint of the massif, on March 3. We were joined by Michel Flouret on P 5950 and P 5793 on March 5. Summer found Flouret, Felice Pache and Parry Rich battling the typical Chulitna monsoon, mosquitoes and mazes of alders on the approach to traverse P 4842 from east to west and P 5705 from west to east on July 30.

DAVID JOHNSTON, *Mountaineering Club of Alaska*

Mount Deborah, North Face Attempt; P 9400 and P 9830. Our party consisted of Don Brooks*, Dave Huntley, Eric Reynolds and me*. Cliff Hudson flew us to the north side of Deborah, where we established Base Camp on the Gillam Glacier. The next five days were spent fixing ropes, ferrying loads and establishing a high camp on the prominent cleaver which merges into the face proper some 4000 feet from the summit. Our plan was for an alpine-style push from this point. Several storms with 100-mph winds which flattened our tents, broke the poles and in which we lost crampons and climbing gear, our lack of fixed rope and rock pitons and the problem of descent off a rather inaccessible summit caused us to abandon the project and turn our attention during the second week of May to surrounding peaks. At the end of Deborah's west ridge lies P 9400, which was climbed by Brooks and Huntley via the northeast ridge. Descent was by the northwest face. Several miles northwest of this peak lies P 9830. It has a long east-west ridge separating it from a smaller summit on the eastern end. Reynolds and I climbed the north face of this smaller peak, a 2100-foot ice face, and did a traverse of the ridge to the main peak. Descent was via a couloir on the southeast face.

· DAVID E. DAVIS, *Unaffiliated*

South Peak of Mount Hayes Attempt. We failed to reach the south peak of Mount Hayes because a huge crevasse lay at right angles to our climbing route 50 feet below the summit. We had only two snow pickets left, which we needed for the descent. In another attempt we shall bring a ladder. The lower part of the south face of the south peak, across which we traversed to reach the south ridge, has great avalanche danger. The south ridge is not difficult except for some steep, snow-covered

---

*Recipient of a grant from the Boyd N. Everett Climbing Fellowship.

ice and some unstable hard snow in the form of lobster tails near the summit, which is guarded by several séracs. We used four days and nights for the attempt including reconnaissance and load-carrying.

TOSHIRO MATSUNAGA, *A.A.C.* and *Japanese Alpine Club*

Kichatna Spires. During the month of July a group of Alaska climbers, Clancy Crawford, Charlie Hostetler, Paul Denkewalter, Peter Sennhauser and I, climbed, skied and explored a small portion of the Cathedral Spires. Al Curtis flew us under the clouds and onto the Tatina Glacier on July 2. Base Camp was set up at the head of Tatina Glacier. On July 4 Paul, Peter and I climbed a spire just west of camp (7400 feet; "Pollak Spire"). The climb involved a 1000-foot snow gully, five rock pitches (one F8), and lots of wet weather. On July 6 Clancy and Charlie climbed the three summit spires of a peak west of Mount Jeffers (6800 feet; "Three-O-Spire"). Their climb involved a nasty icefall and some good 5th-class climbing. On July 10 Clancy, Charlie and I climbed a spire just north of Mount Nevermore (7800 feet; "Mount Neveragain"). After 1500 feet of steep snow and ice climbing followed by five gratifying rock-climbing pitches, we arrived on this superb summit with its rewards: view of everywhere. On the same day Peter and Paul did some 5th-class rock climbing on the slabs of Mount Jeffers. After several days of being stuck in our tents by the typical Spires weather (rain, snow, high winds and white-out), Paul and I ventured out and up a peak. We left camp to climb a magnificent snow spire east of camp (7600 feet; "Whiteout Spire"). The almost zero visibility made the climb through the icefall thrilling, especially the crevasses I fell into. Five pitches of front-pointing and snow-climbing brought us to the summit. After another long spell of bad weather it cleared. And on July 18, Charlie, Paul and I skied down glacier to climb Sunshine Couloir (7000 feet). We climbed its fantastic 1500-foot ice gully and 40-foot rock pitch to its summit. The ice was 60° to 70° and in almost perfect condition. One of the best climbs of the expedition. Ice conditions in late July are great.

GARY BOCARDE

Eekayruk, Falsoola, Brooks Range. Starting from the pipeline road on August 17, our group crossed the Dietrich River and followed Kuyuktuvuk and Trembley Creeks, then crossed into the Hammond River valley. After hiking over Kinnorutin Pass we climbed Doonerak (7457 feet) by its south ridge from St. Patricks Creek on August 22. Records of two previous ascents were found on the summit. Snow kept us in our tents for several days and on August 27 we started hiking back the same way as we wanted to avoid more snow on the passes. However the weather improved and on August 31 we climbed Eekayruk Mountain (6490 feet) via a snow couloir on its north face. After we reached the summit, we saw a higher point on the northwest ridge of the mountain (approximately 6530 feet) which we also climbed and where we placed the summit register. Next day we climbed Falsoola Mountain (6320 feet) by a couloir leading from the south fork of the Trembley Creek valley to the southeast ridge, and from there to the summit. Both Falsoola and Eekayruk have not, to our knowledge, been climbed previously. We hiked out the same day we climbed Falsoola (September 1). The weather in the late summer was mixed, occasionally very beautiful, with one severe multi-day snowstorm, and we saw no mosquitos or people, only a few planes overhead and a mysterious footprint along the Hammond River. All climbs were made by all party members: Irene and Colin Miller, Skip Walker, Fred Rowley, and Vera Komarkova. The last three party members were associated with the Institute of Arctic and Alpine Re-search, University of Colorado, Boulder, Colorado.

IRENE MILLER

Romanzof Mountains, Brooks Range. During three weeks of June, Geoff Radford and I climbed around the Okpilak River drainage in the eastern Brooks Range. The area is of interest as it contains the highest and most heavily glaciated peaks of the Brooks Range. In addition, we were attracted by a large intrusion of granite in the predominately sedimentary landscape, which had not been fully explored for climbing possibilities. From a glacier camp about two miles southeast of Mount Michelson, we climbed Michelson (8855 feet) and Tugak Peak (8500+ feet), and made first ascents of three prominent rock pinnacles south of camp (8300+, 7900+, and 7900+ feet). These are all granite and offer enjoyable fourth- and mid-fifth-class rock routes; we saw no extended faces comparable to the granite of the Arrigetch. Access to the ridges often involved steep ice gullies. We then moved further south to the sedimentary peaks near the headwaters of the Okpilak, making a first ascent of Peak 8760 and the second ascent of Mount Isto (9050 feet), the highest peak in the Brooks Range. This had first been climbed by Post, Mason, and Keeler in 1958. Our last climb was back on the granite of Mount Hubley (8915 feet), climbed in near white-out condi-tions via the Bravo Glacier, from a camp on the Okpilak River. The next week was spent hiking north amid caribou, wolves, fox, and plenti-ful birdlife, to an airfield on the Arctic Ocean. Our timing was re-warded by a total absence of mosquitos throughout the trip.

GORDON BENNER

Mount Michelson, Brooks Range. Tom Elliott and I climbed Mount Michelson (8855 feet) and Tugak Peak (approx. 8600 feet) on August 3 and 4, 1974, respectively. We reached the Michelson area during the second week of a three-week hike which began at the southern boundary of the Arctic National Wildlife Range on the East Fork of the Chandalar River. We followed the Hulahula River through the Romanzof Mountains, spent four days around Michelson and completed our trip at Barter Island. Both climbs were done in good weather from a camp at 6900 feet on the north side of Esetuk Glacier. We ascended Michelson by the southeast face after a slow but fairly easy snow and rock climb of a south ridge one half mile east of the summit. Our route up Tugak was a direct climb of the north ridge.

RICK NOTLING, *Unaffiliated*

Mount Hill, Northern Boundary Range. On August 12, 1974, while working for the U.S. Geological Survey, I climbed this peak (Boundary Peak 78). I ascended the southeast ridge from the col between it and a smaller peak just across the Canadian border. The ascent of the rounded ridge took an hour and a half and involved mixed 3rd- and 4th-class rock and steep wet snow. There was no evidence of prior climbers in the summit rocks; the International Boundary Commission Reports indicate that this peak was not occupied by the survey party which passed through the area in 1909.

WALTER VENNUM

Marcus Baker, Chugach Mountains. In August, Kate Allen, John Wittmayer, Randall Jones and I spent twelve days relaying equipment up to the headwall of the Matanuska Glacier to our Base Camp. During this time we made two superb first ascents. From the base of the Matanuska tributary feeding from the great ice wall on the southeast shoulder of Mount Sergeant Robinson a solo climber ascended the mountain-sheep pastures to the east ridge of P 8380 and followed this ridge above the glacier. Traversing the snow subsummit, he climbed the glacial east face of the 600-foot summit pyramid. On the east side of the Matanuska Glacier, a few miles below the main headwall, stands a group of four sublime alpine spires. The fine 9000-foot northernmost horn was climbed by two of the party by the north arm of its cascading glacier above the steep icefall and over the firn shoulders to and up the west ridge. From Base Camp we worked our way up the northeast ridge of Marcus Baker, two members reaching the summit at dusk on the sixth day. The remainder of the party joined them on top the following day.

DENNIS SCHMITT, *Unaffiliated*

Marcus Baker, North Summit. Mark Fouts, Ward Warren and I approached by the winding, 30-mile Matanuska Glacier. On June 11 we placed Base Camp at the bottom of Marcus Baker's north ridge. The next three days were spent threading our way up the north ridge to the north summit (12,360 feet). The route was technically not difficult. The main south summit is 800 feet higher and three miles further along the ridge. Our retreat to civilization was made by ascending to the 9000-foot pass between the Matanuska and Marcus Baker Glaciers and skiing down the latter to Grasshopper valley, where we were picked up and flown back to Anchorage.

CHARLES R. HAMMOND, *Mountaineering Club of Alaska*

Mount Sanford, Wrangell Range. On August 8 Randy Hargesheimer, Rich Swenson, Jean Borrett and I crossed the Copper River by raft and began the hike to Mount Sanford (16,237 feet). Our route followed Boulder Creek and Sheep Glacier to a point on the north side at 10,750 feet, where we received an airdrop. After several short storms we reached the summit on August 17.

ANDREW KNAPP, *Minnesota Rovers Outing Club*

Blackburn. Teruo Takeda and Yoshiaki Fujii of the Sado Alpine Club were landed on May 23 on the Nabesna Glacier at 6500 feet. They placed Camp I in the west col at 10,000 feet on the 25th. Camp II was placed on May 28 at 13,125 feet. They climbed to the summit (16,530 feet) on May 29.

ICHIRO YOSHIZAWA, *A.A.C.* and *Japanese Alpine Club*

Mount Jette, St. Elias Mountains. On July 6, R.A. Bindschadler, W.D. Harrison, C.F. Raymond and I made what we believe to be the first ascent of Mount Jette (8460 feet), boundary peak 177 in the St. Elias range between Alaska and the northwestern tip of British Columbia. The peak is named after Sir Louis Jetté, who was one of the boundary arbitrators. Our base was the University of Alaska-Washington camp on Variegated Glacier, where we and other glaciologists are investigating causes of the surge behavior of this glacier. A six-hour ascent was made after a bivouac on the pass between Variegated and Butler Glaciers. About a mile of scrambling along a ridge and several easy but dangerous pitches on rotten rock, gave access to steep but easy snow slopes leading to the summit. Near disaster struck on the descent when one of the party was virtually carried off the ridge as it disintegrated around him. Luckily he was held uninjured by the few surviving strands of the rope.

PETER H. WEICKMANN, *Unaffiliated*

Mount Wilbur, Fairweather Group. Ken Loken flew David Jones, Clark Gerhardt, Craig McKibben and me from Juneau to Lituya Bay on May 19. We disembarked on a rocky beach near the snout of the North Crillon Glacier. A few hours of unpleasant toil through brush and over moraine got us onto a pressure ridge, which we climbed to its end and on up the glacier. The next morning we continued traveling in a miserable, wet snowfall. By that night we had Base Camp in a basin below Mounts Wilbur (10,821 feet) and Orville (10,495 feet). Wilbur was almost 6500 feet above us. Its south ridge snaked down from the summit in a series of cornices until it was blocked by an enormous monolithic gendarme. Below, the ridge broadened for a few thousand feet. The lower part of the route almost resembled a face. Orville did not look at all promising. The 21st was an inside-the-tent day. The morning of May 22 was cold; the sky was an intense blue and no clouds were in sight. While Clark, Craig and I organized food and gear for a five-day push, Dave snowshoed over to the head of the basin and, to our surprise, up the slope next to the icefall to check out a glacial plateau 1500 feet above camp. That afternoon we waded through deep snow past the icefall to the top of the plateau, where we camped. Early the next morning we were off. Each successive pitch became steeper. Some unprotected mixed climbing took us to a narrow gully, which led to the second plateau. Above, the route ascended for 1000 feet up a rock-studded face to the huge gendarme. We passed the gendarme on its southwest side, a delicate maneuver because of the thin, unstable mantle of ice and snow. We continued up along the narrow, knife-edged ridge on hard ice and deep snow. There was absolutely no place to stop and so we kept moving up the ridge, sometimes over, sometimes around the cornices. Finally I surmounted a hump of snow to find Craig and Dave on a section of cornice large enough for all of us to stand on. We scooped out a platform for a bivouac. The morning of May 23 was cold and breezy. Two quick pitches got us around the last cornice and onto easier ground to the summit. The descent was interrupted by my unroped 100-foot fall into a crevasse, from which I escaped luckily unhurt.

GREGORY C. MARKOV

P 12,606, Fairweather Range. On April 24 Bill Sumner, Mike Heath and I reached Base Camp at 6500 feet on the Fairweather Glacier, hoping to climb either Mount Salisbury (12,170 feet), P 12,606 or both. Continual bad weather pinned us down for the next two weeks. Finally, on May 9, the weather improved and we climbed 2000 feet up Salisbury's northwest face, which rises 5000 feet at a sustained 50° to 55°, before a violent, warm storm forced a retreat. In the short remaining time we decided to gamble on a quick alpine push to reach P 12,606. Steep snow couloirs on the south side provided access to the high plateau between Mount Quincy Adams and the final 2000 feet of the north ridge of P 12,606. We climbed the second couloir from the right, unroped, up 45° to 50° snow for 2000 feet. Near its exit to the plateau, the couloir became increasingly difficult and we had several hard leads to finish it.

Ahead there were no more technical difficulties, but the weather again worsened. Lightweight snowshoes helped us through the basin's deep snow to reach the north ridge. After 14 hours of climbing we reached the summit. On the descent we bivouacked at the top of the couloir. The next morning we abseiled several hundred feet to reach the easier snow. During three weeks we had only four marginal climbing days. We are proposing to the authorities the name of "Mount Tlingit" in honor of the native people who first inhabited this magnificent area.

DUSAN JAGERSKY

Mount Lituya. After many a rainy night in Juneau, Larry McGee of Channel Flying landed our trio at Cape Fairweather on a glacial lake above the beach. My wife Diana is quite feminine, Jim Nelson young and thin and I overweight and so our pilot was a bit skeptical when we told him to pick us up after three weeks. Five days later we were at the base of the north ridge of Mount Lituya, 6000 feet below the summit, exhausted and sunburned. The next day, July 10, was a rest day with beautiful weather. Friends had told us that if we moved fast we should do the whole ridge and descend in a day. They also told us that snow flukes would be good and ice screws useless, and so, going light, we had three flukes and one screw. We carried everything from the beach in a single push, over 25 miles. After another rest day, forced on us by bad weather, we started up the ridge; candy in our pockets, terrordactyls on our hips and down parkas in two packs. We also had two freeze-dried dinners and a stove, "just in case." My diary says: "Hairy—steep ice, no belays. Jim does a good job step-kicking. Bivy in a whiteout in 'Ice Palace Schrund' near the top of the ridge. Cold! Day 2: Cloudy morning. Lead off on 50° ice. No belays with only one ice screw. Company policy: nobody falls. Many leads to the summit. Off route on the way down and back to the summit. Down the south ridge with double cornices and much exposure. Last pitch on south ridge spectacular over ice mushrooms. Another bivy above the icefall at two A.M. Whiteout. Day 3: Up at 5:45; cloudy. Down icefall and back to camp."

DAVID DAILEY, *Unaffiliated*

Ice Climbing in Alaska. There is a growing interest in ice climbing in Alaska. Two areas have been getting most of the attention: Portage glacier and Thunderbird Falls. Terry Becker, Jim Hale, Gary Bocarde, Paul Denkewalter, and Peter Sennhauser have been putting up the majority of the routes. In the Portage glacier area there are numerous frozen waterfalls. The Hand, with its five fingers is the most popular, with climbs ranging from 100 to 350 feet of steep water ice (90° sections). Thunderbird Falls area has several challenging climbs, the most difficult being Ripple Falls. Three pitches of climbing: two very steep and sustained.

GARY BOCARDE

Mendenhall Towers, Juneau Icefields. Craig McKibben, Brian Cox, my wife Sharon and I left the Mendenhall Loop Road on July 5 and walked 15 miles up to the base of the Mendenhall Towers in 1½ days. On July 7 Brian, Craig and I climbed the southeast ridge of the second tower (of the seven, numbered west to east) and returned to camp in 18 hours. On July 9 we climbed the south ridge of the third tower and returned in 20 hours. The descent of the southwest face was a vertical horror of loose blocks, in semi-darkness with a thunder storm approaching. Both routes were of 14 pitches of varied climbing on good rock in a magnificent alpine setting. The hardest climbing was F9. Craig and Brian did most of the leading.

MALCOLM MOORE

Washington—Cascade Mountains

Mount Adams, Stormy Monday Couloir. Craig Reininger and I made an ascent of a spectacular snow and ice finger on the north side of Mount Adams on July 6 and 7. Starting from the lower Adams Glacier we ascended a snow finger to its left until we came up against a rock band at the top. We then traversed left two leads across loose fourth-class rock in crampons until we reached a sickle-shaped 50° ice gully. This was followed to the top of the west face of the north ridge and onto the summit plateau. A brewing electrical storm made our equipment buzz and shocked us through the wet rope as we literally ran down the north ridge. Moderate rockfall. NCCS II or III.

ERIC SIMONSON

Mount Rainier, Nisqually Ice Cliff. Jerry Hasfjord and I made the first winter ascent of the Nisqually Ice Cliff after several previous attempts on March 3 and 4. Since we were afraid of encroaching bad weather, we went light and fast. This enabled us to make the summit round-trip from Paradise in 30 hours nonstop. We encountered deep snow, disappearing snow bridges and extremely cold temperatures during the all-night climb. Descending via Gibraltar Ledge we were back to Tacoma by dinner after one of the most exhausing efforts either of us had done. NCCS II.

ERIC SIMONSON

Dragontail Peak, Sundown Route. Keith Boyer and I climbed this new route, which begins to the right of the northwest face route (Davis-

Beckey, 1962) and is separated from it by a prominent black ridge which leads directly to the summit. The first two pitches out of the moat lean to the north and become steep immediately. These are followed by a series of ledges (easy class five), then the wall steepens again. After a mid-day start, we bivouacked after eight pitches. Sunday morning found us continuing up the final five pitches. The crux was in this section: a long pillar with a jam-crack in a corner, laybacking off jams to friction up to a mediocre belay. Beyond this, the climbing improved steadily until we stepped through the notch just southwest of the summit. July 26 and 27. NCCS IV, F8, 13 pitches.

C. M. HOLT

Mount Adams, Lava Glacier Headwall. On June 21, Craig Eihlers, Clint Crocker, Matt Kerns, and I hiked the Killen Creek Trail #113 to Mountaineers Camp for our base. On June 22, we climbed to approximately 8500 feet by crossing over the lower portion of the north ridge. The ascent began by crossing the lowest and first of three schrunds of the extreme right or west side of the Lava Glacier beneath the north ridge. We ascended diagonally across the headwall using rock outcroppings for protection from continual rockfall. So far this route had been just right of the west portion route shown on page 63 of Fred Beckey's *Cascade Alpine Guide.* We then crossed the west portion route just beneath rock cliffs and entered an obvious chute slightly above mid-center of the headwall itself and between the east and west portion routes. Referring to page 63, this chute is located immediately above "ea" in "Headwall." We then ascended directly upward joining the east and west portion junction on the upper portion of the north ridge route. From here, follow the route to the summit. We descended by way of the north ridge.

DAVID E. ROWLAND

Cathedral Rock. Randy Johnson, Terri Van Hollebeke and I did a new route on this peak on July 1, 1973. It begins in an obvious chimney on the southeast face; the first lead ascends a mossy dihedral out of a cave and ends at a tree. Two leads of class three and one of class four bring one to the summit ridge, from which it is a scramble to the summit. NCCS I, F6.

C. M. HOLT

Mount Maude, Central Couloir, On July 19, Tim Boyer, his brother Keith, and I climbed the couloir in one day from the car. Apart from a short rock pitch to gain the snow above the bergschrund, the climb was uneventful 45°-50° snow (at the steepest places). I'm not sure if this would hold enough snow to form a good ice climb by September. This is, at any rate, the easiest of the north face routes. NCCS II, F6.

C. M. HOLT

California—Sierra Nevada

Peak 12,160+, Peaklet Wall. This peak appears to be a smaller image of Mount Humphreys when viewed from the east. In August, Jay Jensen, Gordon Wiltsie, Helmut Kiene, and I climbed the 1800-foot northeast face, locally referred to as "Peaklet Wall." It proved to be much easier than it looked, with long sections of broken cliff that could be climbed unroped (F3 to F5). Overall, the climb was slightly longer and more difficult than the east face of Mount Whitney. The crux was a 200-foot vertical dihedral with a bulge at the top. NCCS III, F7.

GALEN A. ROWELL

Wheeler Crest, Big Gray Pinnacle. In November, I joined a visiting French climber, David Belden, in making the first ascent of this 1000-foot tower by a prominent dihedral on the east face. The climbing was mostly in cracks and chimneys with a F10 crux past a 20-foot ceiling via face moves on the righthand wall after the only crack ends. The tower is the most obvious free-standing pinnacle about two miles north of the Smokestack. NCCS IV, F10.

GALEN A. ROWELL

Mount Humphreys, South Pillar of Southeast Face. On December 30, Jay Jensen and I made a one-day new route up this 1500-foot pillar. At five A.M. we left the valley floor in unusually mild winter conditions, using four-wheel drive to reach a roadhead at 9000 feet. By the time we began technical climbing at over 12,000 feet, a cold front had moved in rapidly, causing a 25° mid-day temperature drop in nearby cities. In the valley, 70 mph winds blew down trees and power lines. At nearly 14,000 feet on Mount Humphreys, even stronger winds threatened to blow us off our stances. On difficult climbing we could only remove our hands from gloves for a few moves before wind chill dictated thrusting them under our belts. We climbed unroped up to F7 and belayed only three pitches. Although ledges and low angle areas were snowbound, we found the steeper rock surprisingly free of snow. Urged on by the cold and the fine high-country granite, we reached the 13,986-foot summit at two P.M., traversing the mountain via a descent of the F4 northeast ridge. We reached our vehicle just at dark as snowflakes began to fall. The round trip took eleven hours and the pillar itself is rated NCCS III, F8.

GALEN A. ROWELL

Peak 11,440+. Spring Lake Wall, "That's a Sheer Cliff" Route. The north face of Peak 11,440+ in the Mineral King region drops sheerly into Spring Lake. Unknown to Vern Clevenger and me, Fred Beckey had climbed the right side of the face earlier in 1975. As we veered from the unofficial trail to approach the face, a backpacker began yelling at us excitedly, "Come back! Come back! That's a sheer cliff!" We decided that his quote would be a fitting name if we could climb the wall. The center of the face had several dihedrals rising vertically nearly 1000 feet. Rashly, Vern and I began the climb at two P.M. after our approach from the roadhead. We thought if all the climbing was free, then we could finish the climb by dark. Late in the day we had climbed only two F9 pitches, one of them poorly protected and devious. We descended and returned the next morning, climbing two more F9 pitches up cracks, chimneys, and bulges before the route eased back into lower angle F7 and F8. By noon we reached the summit. NCCS IV, F9.

GALEN A. ROWELL

Middle Palisade, East Face. On August 31, Tim Ryan and I climbed a new route on the east face of Middle Palisade (14,040 feet). We cramponed up to the highest point of the glacier. Tim led the first pitch, the most difficult of the climb; this delicate traverse went directly up from the bergschrund, then descended to the left. The next pitch traversed an easy 60-foot ledge, then went up a very loose chimney. The following pitch traversed left on the face, then led up to a belay beneath an overhang. After another pitch upward, the route traversed left around a corner into a broad chute that led up to the first notch south of Middle Palisade. From this col, we traversed to the right for one pitch before ascending to the summit ridge. NCCS III, F5.

JOHN D. MENDENHALL

Mount Sill. On July 15 Woody Stark and I climbed Mount Sill by a new route that starts from Lake 11,672 in the Glacier Creek drainage. We started toward the glacier routes, but instead of turning left toward the glacier, we climbed the headwall seen from the lake. Once on the ridge, we traversed to the summit. One rappel was used to avoid aid.

RICHARD H. WEBSTER

The Needles, South Face of Wizard. In mid-April, Dave Black, Fred Beckey, and I did a new seven-pitch route on Wizard. Visible from the road, and on the approach from the southeast, is a prominent crack system. We followed the system for five pitches of jamming and chimneying to a large ledge beneath the massive summit block. We then traversed far to the left to a hidden crack system. (The hidden crack may be seen in "Summit"—February 1974, page 3.) We named the route "Spellbound." NCCS III, F9.

ROBB DELLINGER, *Buff Mountaineers*

Kettle Dome, West Face. Fred Beckey, Phil Warrender and I made the first ascent of this route on October 20, 1974; the first technical climb to be established on this small but attractive dome. A long poorly protected crack led us into the center of a shallow bowl in the middle of the face. Two pitches of enjoyable friction ended below a vertical headwall. Here we traversed right 100 feet to a flared corner and climbed this to the crest of the southwest ridge. After one moderate pitch along the ridge we scrambled the last 200 feet to the seldom visited summit. NCCS II, F6.

WALTER VENNUM

Fresno Dome, Torn and Frayed. This short, four-pitch climb was done by Jack Forsythe and me in June. It lies on the right side of a prominent pillar a few hundred feet right of the Beckey-Stuart route. Three obvious pitches lead to a huge ledge from where easy face-climbing leads right, then up to the unroping spot. NCCS II, F8.

SIMON KING, *Unaffiliated*

Fresno Dome, Blue Connection. This one-pitch route starts 50 feet to the right of Torn and Frayed and involves an easy ramp followed by a tricky face move and ending with an unprotected water groove. Jack Forsythe and I made the first ascent in June. NCCS I, F8.

SIMON KING, *Unaffiliated*

Tuttle Creek, Goin' Nuts. In August 1974, Elliot Dubreuil and I climbed the red wall just west of Stonehouse Buttress on the south face of Lone Pine Peak. I believe that it was the first time this wall had been climbed, the other south face routes being much farther west. Starting about 150 feet right of the large left-facing dihedral that forms the west side of the face, we climbed up past two small trees and continued straight up. Fourteen full pitches of fifth-class climbing over excellent pink granite led to the top. We did the climb clean and hammerless.

STEVE EDDY, *Unaffiliated*

Tuttle Creek, Keyhole Wall. On May 18, Jack Roberts and I climbed a classic six-pitch new route on this spectacular wall; we called it the

"Locksmith Route". The route climbs the smooth central and highest portion of the face, and can be identified by the first two pitches which are a whitish right-facing open-book. The route is quite continuous in finger-jams and cracks, as well as face-climbing problems. NCCS III, F8 or F9. On January 15, 1976, Alan Bartlett and I climbed a slightly shorter open-book route about 100 yards to the east. We dubbed this the "Pass Key"; the route is one continuous crack and chimney system. NCCS II, F7.

FRED BECKEY

Lone Pine Peak, South Face. On June 14, Chuck Sink and I put up a new route on Lone Pine's south face. The route begins above the start of the giant couloir cutting the face diagonally. It is nearly all free and follows cracks just right of a prominent right facing dihedral. Other than some minor bushwhacking while searching for the face, we enjoyed excellent climbing on sound rock.

ALAN J. KEARNEY

Banner Peak, East Face. On August 9 and 10, Arne Myrabo and I climbed what we believe to be a new route on the east face of Banner Peak. No evidence of a previous ascent was discovered. The route starts about 200 feet to the right of the east-face-direct route on a rib which continues up and slightly right to about 200 feet below the summit crest and about 800 feet north of the actual summit. The climb begins on the left side of the rib in left-facing books which continue for about 200 feet. We climbed the rib for about ten pitches of class 4 and class 5. From this point, 200 feet short of the summit crest, we traversed up and left two easy pitches to a stance slightly left of some white water stains on overhanging rock. A short difficult pitch straight up leads to the crest. Easy climbing leads 800 feet north to the summit. One bivouac was required on the face because we started the first day from Agnew Meadows. We climbed clean. NCCS III, F8.

KIM GRANDFIELD, *Unaffiliated*

Mount Whitney, East Face Direct. In August 1974, Gary Colliver and I completed a new route on the east face of Mount Whitney. We started climbing in a crack system which starts to the left of the wash-board. After seven pitches of F8 to F9 climbing and 300 feet of 3rd class we gained the top of the washboard. Two crack systems take off from here. We chose the straight-in crack to the right. Two pitches of F8 and two of F9 end 400 feet directly below the summit. We climbed clean. NCCS IV, F9.

CHRIS VANDIVER, *Unaffiliated*

Crowley Buttress, Eagle Eyes. In July 1973, Mark Gaynor, Ken Boche, and I climbed a new route up the west face of Crowley Buttress in the Nelson Lake area. The climb began in a chimney on the right. After 100 feet we exited from the chimney to the left and climbed a F9 jam-crack for another 100 feet. We proceeded up and left for 600 feet of F7 to F9 to the summit. NCCS IV, F9.

CHRIS VANDIVER, *Unaffiliated*

Mount Conness, West Face, Rosy Crown Route. In June 1974, Gary Colliver and I put up a new route starting 300 feet to the right of the Harding route. We climbed free for a full 150 feet. The second pitch went free until the crack became shallow. We passed a roof with aid and then climbed free to a loose-looking flake. From here the path of least resistance (F9) and 8 more pitches led to the summit. NCCS IV, F9, A2.

CHRIS VANDIVER, *Unaffiliated*

Bubbs Creek Wall was climbed on June 8 and 9, 1974 by Mark Losleben, Mike McGoey, Reed Cundiff, and Fred Beckey by a new route.

Fuller Butte, Northeast face, White Dike Route. This very enjoyable four-pitch free climb was done April 21 by Dave Black, Jim Black and Fred Beckey. The dike makes the polished granite possible; the climbing is continuously interesting. Bolts were placed at several belay spots and also several times to protect long run-outs. NCCS II, F9.

Wells Peak, East Face. This face, north of The Smokestack and Adams Rib, resembles Mount Whitney in miniature. Reconnaissance located a good start and some very continuous face climbing. The final ascent was made on February 23 and 24, 1974, by Jack Roberts, Allen Bartlett, and Fred Beckey. Except for a few moves of aid on the second pitch, the entire climb is free, and on generally good rock. Three consecutive steep pitches led from a bivouac at the foot of the wall to a broken terrace. Higher, a long crack system leads to the apex of a pillar. (A weird mantling traverse and an overhanging free problem are the key areas.) Rock directly above proved unyielding, so the party made a short rappel to the gully south of it, then continued several more pitches to the summit. Descent was by a snow gully on the north. NCCS IV, F8, A1.

Sunrise Wall. This is the prominent east-facing granite wall just above the trail to Nelson Lake, across the divide from Tuolomne Meadows. Karl Kaiyala, Reed Cundiff, and I made the first climb of the wall on

October 13, 1974 after fixing the first pitch the evening before. The route follows a continuous crack system (a right-facing dihedral) which is very obvious from the trail. The first three pitches are free, with some strenuous sections; most of the fourth pitch is aid, with some bottoming crack problems. Grade III; F8, A3.

FRED BECKEY

Witch Tower, The Needles, West Face. The first route on the impressive west face was done November 17, 1974 by Dave Black, Steve Eddy, and me; the beginning is from a short pillar over 100 yards south of the divide notch. The climb is superb, and would be a classic anywhere. Four of six pitches are F9, with not a loose stone on the climb, which is largely small face holds or thin jams—continuous all the way to the summit ridge south of the pointed tip. The first pitch goes straight up a crack ending in hard fingertip jams; one continues up until convolution moves spread one across left under an overhang (F9); bubbly small holds continue over a pitch, where awkward jamming takes one under a blocking overhang. The left side is possible after much probing (F9), with not much to work on; finally an improbable traverse to the right takes one to a layback heading for the summit spine. Grade III, F9.

FRED BECKEY

Four Gables, North Peak via East Face. This was a new route, done June 15, 1974 with Mike Levine, following the buttress on the face seen plainly from the highway north of Bishop. Once on the buttress, reasonably sound granite led the climbing to a sharp crest about 500 feet below the summit. Very shattered rock forced a traverse left into a steep snow gully, which was taken to the summit ridge. NCCS II, F6.

FRED BECKEY

Spring Lake Wall. A color photo in a packer's brochure shows this face to good advantage. The north-facing wall is about 700 feet high, rises above Spring Lake (Middle Fork Kaweah drainage), and is reached by an uphill grind from Mineral King. Robb Dellinger, Debbie Winters and I placed the first route on this attractive face July 14, 1974, following essentially a direct crack and dihedral system to the summit. The rock is very good and the climbing continuously excellent. NCCS III, F6.

FRED BECKEY

Mount Russell, South Ridge to East Peak. This very prominent crest is really a continuation of the main divide from the Whitney-Russell col. (It is the left profile as seen from Upper Boy Scout Lake.) Greg Thomsen, Ed Ehrenfeldt, and I made the climb on September 15, 1974. The climbing over and around a serrate crest of granite teeth is quite spectacular and provides a number of short problems. The nearness of the summit-route gully to the west offers escapes, and is therefore a detraction to any claim of boldness. NCCS II, F7.

FRED BECKEY

Kettle Dome, West Face. The first climb of this face was done on October 20, 1974 by Walt Vennum, Phil Warrender, and me; the route is on the right side (long side) of the face, near where it corners to the south. The route is all face climbing, much on small holds, with a shortage of protection opportunity, especially on the first pitch. About 6 pitches. NCCS II; F7.

FRED BECKEY

Clyde Palisade, Primrose Ridge. This prominent crest adorns the north face of Clyde Palisade to end on the west summit. It is very visible from Glacier Lodge and usually divides the light from shadow. Dave Black, Mike Graber, and I made the first climb in late July, taking most of the day from a high camp at about 12,000 feet where a rock outcrop breaks the glacier. Icy snow led to the lowest portion of the very thin crest (this is just west of the spur that continues north). From here 13 demanding pitches took us to the summit, with each pitch religiously staying on the crest; 3 of the pitches were a minimum of F9. NCCS IV, F9; all chocks.

FRED BECKEY

"Hair-raiser Buttress," Granite Basin. Vern Clevenger and I climbed this route in June. The route ascends the only prominent, pitted buttress in the middle of the Granite Basin group. We started off some boulders slightly uphill from the low point and center of the buttress and then took the central line for three pitches to the top, always following the area most solution-pocked. The final pitch is the crux, some F9 and considerable F8, all protected by bolts. NCSS II, F9.

THOMAS HIGGINS

Sugarloaf Dome, Southwest Face. This face was climbed in June by Fred Beckey and me. Sugarloaf is the prominent formation across the Merced River from Bonnell Point in Little Yosemite Valley. Leave the trail at a point where you walk next to a cascade and gain a bushy ledge below the southwest face. Starting just left of the left-most tree on the ledge, climb several difficult free pitches to a point where you nail a short crack to a tree. Climb up and right for a pitch and nail a small short arch

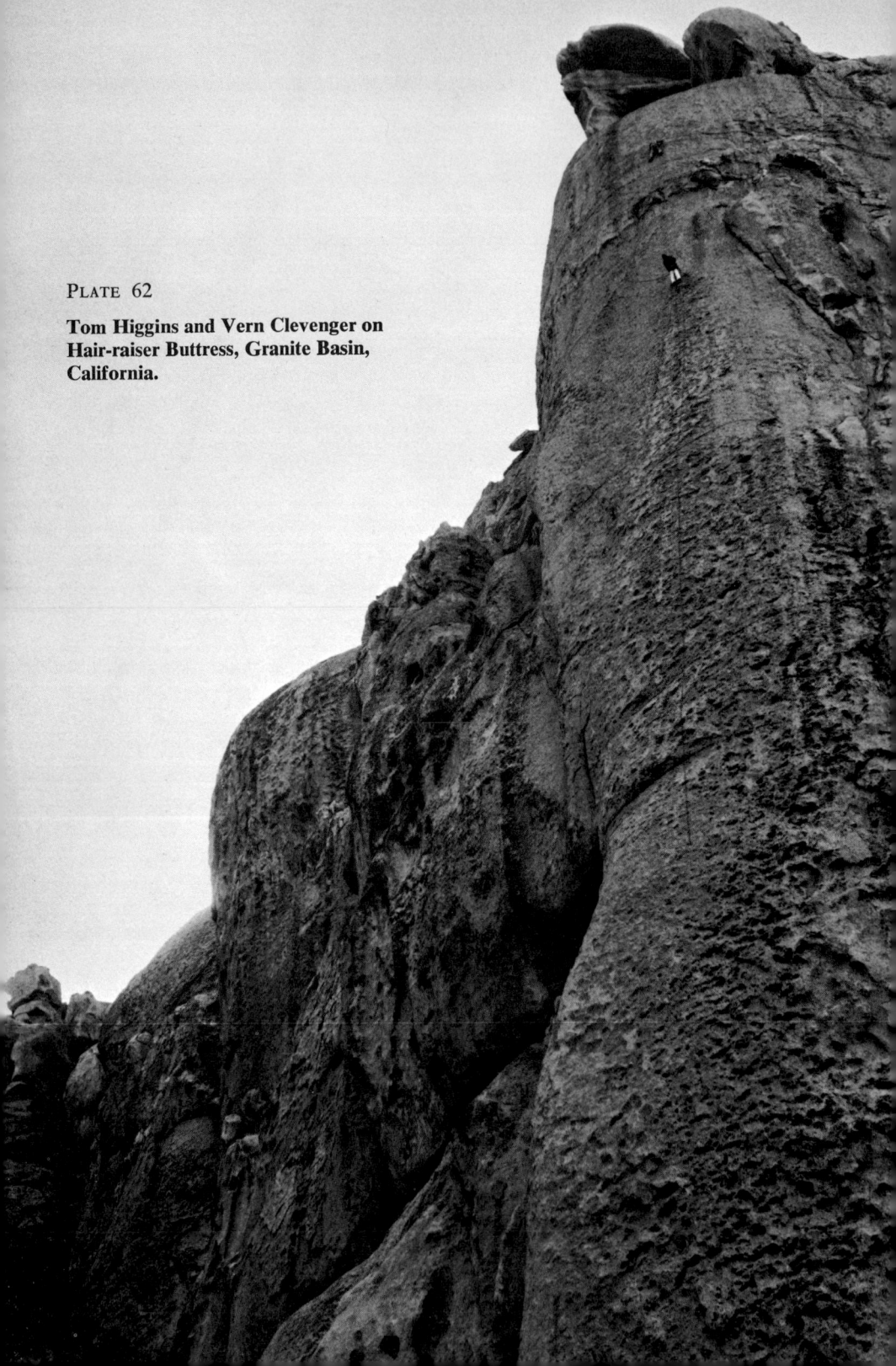

PLATE 62

Tom Higgins and Vern Clevenger on Hair-raiser Buttress, Granite Basin, California.

PLATE 63

Photo by Nancy Wyrick

Rappelling off the TOTEM POLE.

PLATE 64

Photo by Ken Wyrick

Eric Bjørnstad on the TOTEM POLE.

to a large ledge. From the left end of the ledge, join the Salathé route and climb up and right for two pitches more to the summit.

MICHAEL WARBURTON

Nevada

Rainbow Mountain (Mount Charleston), Solar Plexus Route. The route keeps well east of the great arch on the south face of the Solar Wall, south-facing and often warm in the desert sun. It was virtually all face-climbing, much on small holds on solid sandstone. The blankest portion of the climb just barely works out, with the key traverse possible only because of the soundness of the mini-holds. The climb was done on March 3 by Alan Bartlett, Stan Molenski and me. NCCS III, F8.

FRED BECKEY

Utah

Bootleg Tower, Day Canyon, Moab. Day Canyon is one of dozens of pristine canyons, rarely visited, only a few miles from Moab. Though few have towers, Day Canyon, home of an early bootlegger, has several challenging ones. In 1974 Terry McKenna and I made the first ascent of sandstone Bootleg Tower. NCCS I, F8, A2.

ERIC BJØRNSTAD

Echo Rock, Window Route. Echo Rock, a few miles southwest of the Moab airstrip, was first climbed six years ago. In 1974 Ken Wyrick, Terry McKenna and I made a new route, the north edge, on this 275-foot sandstone citadel. We started on the east flank, a lead below an eight-by-ten-foot square tunnel which runs completely through the rock. Once within this phenomenally square passage, it is apparent that the window is the product of eons of wind, rain and frost erosion. The second lead took us through the window from east to west. With a shoulder-stand we climbed a high-angle jam-crack, using chocks and pitons for aid. Near the top of the pitch, the crack split the wall in two. The tower thins and gives an engaging view to the exposed other side. A short traverse to the right from beneath the summit overhangs put us on the top of the most amazing tower structure I had ever seen. Since our ascent, the Window Route has been reclimbed four times. NCCS III, F7, A2.

ERIC BJØRNSTAD

Valley of the Gods, Southeast Utah. Driving south from Mexican Hat, you get fleeting glimpses of thin sandstone towers to the west before the highway bends its way toward the Arizona border. An arrow on a wooden sign points down a dusty road to the "Valley of the Gods." Ron Wiggle and I spent a few days in 1974 exploring this isolated valley and reconnoitering its numerous climbing possibilities. We climbed the highest and northernmost free-standing monolith in the area by an obvious direct line on its northeast side. Routine aid took us to a sloping bench near the midpoint. The balance of the route was up and into a dihedral of chunky, decaying white and red rock with only marginal safety. The final few feet were climbed on denser rock, partly free, with sound chocks for protection. Our only difficulty was an increasing wind pummeling hot sand into our eyes. We rappelled our ascent line, carefully dislodging much of the threatening loose rock on our way. NCCS III, F7, A3.

ERIC BJØRNSTAD

Sewing Machine Needle, Southern Canyonlands, Lake Powell. In May, dressed for the early desert summer, Fred Beckey, Reid Cunduff, Lou Dawson and I turned onto a dusty road between the bridges over the Dirt Devil and Colorado Rivers. Twenty-five jarring miles later, we were belaying my car down an arroyo as we rebuilt an old mining road that took us a few miles nearer to the thin 300-foot Sewing Machine Needle. The next day we carried loads up the talus slope and belayed Dawson up 150 feet of steep rubble to a belay stance. It snowed and we retreated. The following morning we regained our lines and exchanged duties above. In the recurring freezing rain Lou Dawson elected to lead and reached the summit a few hours later. NCCS III, F8, A2.

ERIC BJØRNSTAD

Arizona

Totem Pole, Monument Valley. Ken Wyrick and I were hired by Universal Studios to "put the rope up" for the filming of the desert part of the movie *Eiger Sanction.* We spent 14 days on the Totem Pole and its nearby walls. Our duties were primarily to work with Clint Eastwood, stuntmen and the climber-cinephotographers, Pete White, Mike Hoover and Peter Pilafian. Our ascent was the fifth. At the end we cleaned the Totem Pole of its bolts and pitons as requested by the Navajo Council. Thus ended an era of climbing on what is surely the thinnest, tallest sandstone tower in the world. All climbing is prohibited within the tribal park and the law is energetically enforced by the Navajo police.

ERIC BJØRNSTAD

Earth Angel, Long Canyon. In the spring of 1974 Ross Hardwick and I found and climbed the largest of the sandstone towers yet ascended in the Sedona-Oak Creek area. Earth Angel is a lofty 800-foot beauty poised against a secluded canyon wall several miles north of Sedona. The eight-pitch route follows obvious cracks and chimneys up the tower's front. The sixth pitch is noteworthy, as here one is faced with a layback or with tunneling behind a gigantic pillar ominously late for its date with the forces of gravity. Either alternative leads one to a secure ledge above the pillar. Descent was via five rappels down the north side. NCCS IV, F10.

SCOTT BAXTER, *Sindicato Granítico*

Idaho

Mount Leatherman and Other Winter Ascents, Big Lost River Range. Rick Albano and I made the following climbs, which we believe were the first winter ascents: Mount Leatherman, up the west ridge and down east ridge, on March 19, Class V; P 11,899 (west of Leatherman) via south ridge, on March 18, Class IV; P 12,023 (southeast of Leatherman) via west face and south ridge, on March 21, Class V. The Class V climbs both had pitches of F5, loose rock and high avalanche danger. Despite these factors, the range offers reasonable scope for winter climbing, especially for long ridge traverses.

WILLIAM MARCH, *Idaho State University Outdoor Program*

Huddleson's Bluff, South Fork of the Clearwater River. On October 19, 1973, we crossed the cold river and hiked downstream to the wall. In the morning we crossed the sometimes very exposed ledge at the base of the main wall to where Dave had left a fixed rope from his previous solo attempt. The second pitch leads through the two most obvious roofs on the Wall near two large patches of white rock. The rope drag became so great that Dave ended the second pitch just above the corner of the second roof. From here he nailed up a right-leaning, slightly overhanging crack until it petered out. He then traversed left on skyhooks until he got to the chicken heads that lead up to the partially dead belay tree. The fourth pitch ascends the rock to the left of the dirt-filled crack, wandering back and forth until a ledge 20 feet below the top is reached. From the tree up, the climbing was all moderate and free. The aid climbing was strenuous and difficult. It took us a day and a half to complete the climb. NCCS III, F7, A4.

C. MICHAEL HOLT

Little Roman Nose, Southern Selkirks. Mark Guthrie and I did the first ascent of the north face on September 27. We climbed the obvious dihedral that can be seen from the lake below it in four pitches of mixed free and aid climbing; the climbing was predominantly free. The first pitch is easy class five; the second goes around a tree to the left and up around a small overhang onto a slab, then up a steep crack to another tree. The third goes out onto the edge of the dihedral, and then works back into the corner to a grassy ledge. The fourth pitch traverses off the ledge (crux) and up and out onto the face to a ramp. This ramp is traversed left back into the dihedral which is followed to the top. There are many possible routes on this fine face. The route was done with nuts only, and no hammer. NCCS II, F8, A2.

C. MICHAEL HOLT

The Elephant's Perch, Northwest Face, Sawtooth Range. On September 6 Bill March and I climbed the northwest face of the Elephant's Perch. There is a prominent, left-facing curving corner starting about halfway up the face. The climb follows this feature and the principal difficulties are to gain the base of this crack. Start several hundred feet left of the corner and scramble for two pitches up a shallow gully chimney until level with the base of a prominent curving orange crack. At this point, traverse right on a large ledge and descend 15 feet onto a ledge and tree. Above is a wide crack with a dead tree jammed in the upper part. Climb this for 100 feet. F9, A2. Make a skyhook move for aid to gain a ledge at the right. Above is a superb, V-shaped chimney. Climb the wall on the right and gain the chimney at 20 feet. Continue up the chimney for 120 feet. Pitch 3: Traverse up and right to large detached flake, tension traverse right to gain the foot of the prominent corner which is climbed to a ledge, and belay below a bush. Pitch 4: (100 feet) Use two points of aid to gain crack on the left and climb this free to a small belay stance. Pitch 5: (120 feet) Continue up the crack using some aid. Pitch 6: (150 feet) Climb an awkward chimney crack and continue more easily to summit. NCCS III, F9, A2.

JEFF SPLITTGERBER, *Idaho State University Outdoor Program*

Montana

Lost Pinnacle. Between the chain of lakes and Sunlight Basin lies a small area of granite faces and pinnacles. On a warm weekend in August I hiked into the area and crossed wobbly boulders, raging creeks, and fought my way through vicious thorned bushes to an obscure and lonely pinnacle above Sunlight Basin. I climbed the short north ridge to a notch and then ascended a thirty-foot corner to the top. NCCS I, F3. A variation in an off-width crack provided the second ascent, both made on August 30. NCCS I, F7.

ALAN J. KEARNEY

Shoshone Spire, Bitterroot Range. About three miles up Blodgett Canyon is this triangular rock of solid granite. The upper face is reached by climbing three pitches to the large ledge system at the base of the face. The following two routes, done by Elliott Dubreuil and me, start from this ledge. *South Face*. From the ledge climb the right side of the overhang on the left side of the face. Second pitch ends in a hanging belay in a bottomless cave. Climb the roof of the cave on the right and continue straight up. The fourth pitch ends at the top. If done clean, this route has some long runouts. Although it was June 27, it snowed on us while we were climbing the last two pitches. F8. *In Memoriam*. July 9. This climb goes up the middle of the south face starting from the large ledge. The first pitch goes up a crack where a long lost-arrow is needed for protection. Climb up to a bolt (F9) and up 25 feet to an unprotected mantle (F9), then left to a crack. The next three pitches are all F10. Continue up the crack to a difficult smooth dihedral and a belay on top of a pedestal. Climb up the crescent crack, traverse right on the horizontal dike and climb the overhang. Last pitch ascends crack to the summit with a difficult thin section near the top. F10.

STEVEN EDDY

Wyoming—Wind River Range

Temple Peak. On August 12, Woody Stark and I climbed Temple Peak by a new route that starts from Temple Pass. We climbed up talus to the base of the spire between Silver Saddle and the Class-4 route, around its right side and then up to the saddle above it. From here three chutes go up the northeast headwall between the summit of Temple and the class-4 chute. Our route went up the left chute with the window at the top. Care should be taken with ice and rotten rock high in the chute. NCCS II, F7.

RICHARD H. WEBSTER

Spider Peak, Northeast Buttress. Spider Peak is a remarkable remnant of the high-level erosion plateau of the northern portion of the Wind River Mountains. Brian Leo, Steve Jackson and I made an interesting new climb on August 31, following slabs and cracks on the steep minor buttress on the east part of the very ice-polished north face. NCCS III, F8.

FRED BECKEY

Arrowhead Mountain, North Face. The rather hidden north face of this peak is one of the many surprises in the northern part of the Wind Rivers. The central and western portion of the face is glacier polished. From a camp below the peak on September 5 Andy Carson and I vetoed getting stuck on what appeared to be poor cracks systems there and followed the line of a prominent rib on the face which ends just east of the summit. NCCS II or III, F7.

FRED BECKEY

Sulphur Peak and "Cutthroat Spire", North Faces, Wind River Range. In September, 1974, Lou Dawson and I made two new routes near Peak Lake above the upper Green River. We climbed a really fine mixed route of some difficulty on the north face of Sulphur Peak. We followed a steep ice gully for six 150-foot pitches, then climbed six pitches up a series of chimneys and cracks in the center of the face. This route is similar to the one described by William March in *A.A.J.*, 1975, page 137, but takes a more direct line. We found a piton in place shortly after leaving the ice, probably left by March for his tension traverse. NCCS III, F9, 55° to 60° ice, no aid, 6 hours, 1600 feet. The following day we climbed the north face of the prominent gendarme right (west) of Sulphur Peak, which we tentatively named "Cutthroat Spire." We found no trace of previous parties. The route consisted of three easy pitches on the lower rock band, five up a moderate icefield and six up the final tower. Three of the pitches on the tower involved extensive and difficult aid climbing. NCCS IV, F9, A-4, 45° ice, 1600 feet.

MICHAEL KENNEDY, *Elk Mountain Climbing Club*

Colorado

Climbs in Rocky Mountain National Park, 1975. Ever since David Rearick and Bob Kamps in 1960 first climbed the Longs Peak Diamond, the impressive alpine wall has been appreciated both as a test piece and for its esthetic qualities. Other firsts since then, besides 15 new routes and variations, include a winter climb by a new route by Layton Kor and Wayne Goss and a partially new route solo by Bill Forrest. The 1970s ushered in a new era of free climbing standards and techniques; with it came attempts to climb the Diamond free and clean. Most attempts concentrated on the Diamond-7 route on the left side of the precipice, where the rock is more climbable. Bit by bit skepticism gave way to reality and finally in early 1975 two Boulder climbers, Wayne Goss and Jim Logan, climbed the Diamond all free and clean. They followed the first four pitches of Diamond-7 and then traversed to the Black Dagger Chimney. Finding this too wet, they continued right to Forrest's Finish, which they followed until it was possible to traverse back left to the top of the Black Dagger Chimney. There one final pitch separated them from success; spurred on by approaching darkness, Goss led up a nearly blank wall in a slight rain to finish the climb at Table Rock. On this all-free climb there was no yo-yoing on leads, resting on protection, pitons or Jümars. The ascent took 12 hours. Shortly afterwards, there was another first for the Diamond: Stephanie Alwood, Molly Higgins and Laurie Manson completed the first all-woman ascent via Diamond-7. They had one hanging bivouac after a first night on Broadway. In mid-July James Dunn and Kris Wood climbed the Yellow

PLATE 65

Photo by Ken Williams

North Faces of Sulphur Peak (left) and Cutthroat Spire, Upper Peak Lake Area, Wind River Range, Wyoming.

Wall route all free. They climbed to Broadway in poor weather, did 4½ pitches to join Forrest's Finish and eventually completed the climb as Goss and Logan had. The pitch above the Black Dagger Chimney was the crux for both. The Yellow Wall start involved several days of climbing due to persistent rain, but they did the route all free and clean. Two new routes were done on the Diamond between the Obelisk and Curving Vine routes. Bob Dodds, Ron Olevsky and Paul Kasputts climbed the first crack left of the Curving Vine to Obelisk Ledge; they traversed a short way right and finished the climb at Table Ledge. The climb took over a week (NCCS V, F8, A2). A few days later George Hurley and Bob Bliss put up a second new route a few feet left of the previous one, all clean with two pitches of aid. Hurley said it was easier than Diamond-7 and may prove an alternative to that crowded route. They took a single day (NCCS V, F8, A2). In late August Tobin Sorenson and Bruce Adams rappelled to Broadway from Chasm View and repeated the Dodds-Olevsky-Kasputts route with several important variations; they mention one F10 pitch. They did the climb free and clean in a single day. Other impressive firsts in the park included the second and first all-free ascent of the northwest face of Chiefs' Heads. The route, first done in the early 1960s by Layton Kor and Bob Culp, had defied numerous later attempts. In July Bill Westbay and Dan McClure did the climb, eliminating the aid with two F8 pitches. On Lumpy Ridge, a low-lying rock-climbing area also in the park, two women distinguished themselves by being the first women to complete F10 climbs; they both swung leads with their partners. Diane Russell climbed the notorious Crack of Fear on Twin Owls, leading pitches one and three. Molly Higgins did the Turn Korner route on Sundance. Near Twin Owls, John Bachar did the first free solo of the difficult Gollums Arch, a strenuous F10 finger crack. James Dunn did another impressive first on the Twin Owls, Peaches and Cream (F11). The summer was tragically marred by the death of Diana Hunter, who slipped while soloing above a climb which she and her partner had just completed on Cathedral Wall in the Loch Vale of the park.

MICHAEL COVINGTON

Taylor Peak, East Face. The east face of Taylor Peak is situated above Sky Pond in the Loch Vale region of Rocky Mountain National Park. Early in April Doug Scott, Doug Snively, and I established a new route there in semi-winter conditions. The route ascends a right-leaning snow ramp which begins about 60 meters left of the prominent prow which dominates the center of the east face. We followed these two pitches to the base of a large prominent snowfield which we climbed unbelayed for 300 meters to steeper, safer territory. Using the steep band of snow and rock for protection we climbed up and left for three pitches to a spectacular snow bench. One more pitch up and right got us to the top, which we reached in the early afternoon. The climbing although not difficult was a little precarious due to snow and ice balconies which periodically swept the route. The major problem was to keep from being hit by the tombstone locomotives.

MICHAEL COVINGTON

Notchtop. In late April Doug Snively and I completed a new route up the steep snow-plastered north face of Notch Top. The climb began from a bivouac situated above the Grace Falls where we followed a snow and rock ramp which led up and right to the base of a large snowfield. In low-angle snow we skirted the first rock band on the right and climbed up steepening slopes to the second rock band. The first pitch led up and left to a belay above the notch on the main wall just across from a prominent spire. From here we diagonaled up and left for 7 pitches on 45° and 50° snow to finish in a col between the Notch Top ridge and Continental Divide. The crux was a long unprotected snow pitch which averaged 50°. Eight hours.

MICHAEL COVINGTON

Ptarmigan Towers, East Side. Tower 2: To the right of the bottom of the 2-4 gully is a deep, wet chimney/gully. On the vertical wall to its right is a prominent and attractive jam-crack, which diagonals up and left for about 300 feet before joining the more broken rock of the "Sunshine Ledges" route. Tom Gries and I climbed the jam-crack (the "Tundra Turkey Crack") in August, encountering three leads of good climbing and even difficulty. NCCS II, F8. *Tower 4:* Just below and right of the top of Tower 4, as seen from Lake Nanita, are two deep, overhanging 200-foot chimneys. We established a route that followed the indistinct northeast corner of this tower, mostly in clean dihedrals a bit to its left, and finishing in the rightmost of the two aforementioned chimneys. The rock was generally good until the crux summit pitch, which involved a very wide, overhanging chimney of crumbling granite. NCCS III, F8 or F9. Both routes were climbed hammerless.

LAWRENCE HAMILTON, *Unaffiliated*

Arrowhead Peak, South Face. Two new routes were established on this appealing face in July. "Artemis" ascends the large, prominent dihedral about 100 feet to the right of the low point of the McHenrys-Arrowhead Ridge. Moderate slabs lead to a ledge at the base of the main corner, which is followed for two leads, past several overhangs, to the top. Tom Gries and I did the first ascent. NCCS II, F9. To the east of this lies "Warhead", which climbs the face near its highest part. John Byrd, Tom Gries, and I began this route from a huge flake lying on a ledge at the slabby base of the wall. Wet and tricky friction was encountered on the second pitch, and the third pitch surmounted the major left-curving arch that blocks access to the upper face by laybacking up a black flake. Above this, very clean and enjoyable climbing followed the left-facing dihedral formed by a higher arch, and continuing cracks and corners beyond. Seven pitches were done, all on excellent granite. NCCS III, F9. Both routes were done clean.

LAWRENCE HAMILTON, *Unaffiliated*

New Route, Glenwood Canyon. In August, Harvey Carter and I completed *The Internationale*, the longest and most sustained route in Glenwood Canyon to date. It consisted of 18 pitches of climbing; many of these were 5.8 or 5.9, and there is one 60-foot section of aid. The climb connects two granite buttresses and a limestone one; we climbed the granite and a third of the limestone on our first attempt, during which we made one bivouac. On the successful climb, we traversed into the limestone band (avoiding the first 10 pitches) reclimbed to our high point and finished in good order the same day. The route awaits a continuous ascent, and might be possible in a day to a fast and strong party. NCCS V, F9, A-2 (2000 feet).

MICHAEL KENNEDY, *Elk Mountain Climbing Club*

Notchtop Mountain, East Face, Religion. Australian Keith Bell and I established this long excellent free climb on the highest part of the face in late August, 1973. We began (with a jump) in the left-most of three prominent roofed right-facing dihedrals on the lower east face, well to the left of *Optimismus*. This first pitch was fairly sustained and ended on a ledge to the left of the dihedral's roof. A pitch higher easy climbing was encountered, as *Religion* was crossed by the *Spiral* route's meadows. The steep upper wall was attacked on the fifth pitch, with a long diagonal traverse up and to the left. The sixth pitch then diagonaled for a rope-length back right, in one of the exposed maneuvers so characteristic of the harder Notchtop routes. Climbing continued more or less up the center of the face to a prominent vertical gully that ended a few feet from the summit of the Notch Spire. The last pitch and a half contained several old pins; evidently we had joined the finish of the *South Ridge* route at this point, which went free with one section of very solid F8. Except for the vicinity of the *Spiral* meadows, the climbing on this route was very consistent and worthwhile, comparable to the *Culp-Bossier* route on Hallets. At least four of the pitches involved F8 difficulties. NCCS III, F8.

LAWRENCE HAMILTON, *Unaffiliated*

CANADA

Yukon Territory

Mount Vancouver, Northeast Ridge. The 1975 M.I.T. Outing Club Expedition assembled in mid-June at Haines Junction. We consisted of Cliff Cantor*, Bob Dangel, Paul Ledoux, Rob Milne*, Hal Murray, Bob Walker, John Yates and me as leader. We conversed briefly with a Japanese party that had just completed an ascent of the north side of Mount Vancouver, a route we had considered as a possible alternative if we found the northeast ridge impractical. On June 16 in the evening, we were transported in three helicopter loads to a strikingly beautiful location near the base of the northeast ridge at 4800 feet on the Hubbard Glacier. The ridge above us rose in a series of steps to a snow-covered peak at 10,600 feet, above which it widened and became easier, merging with the main summit mass at 11,500 feet. We planned a high camp just beyond P 10,600, from which we felt we might push to the summit in one day. Climbing at night to obtain better snow conditions, we explored route possibilities and established Camp I above an active icefall which guarded a large, amphitheater-like basin on the south side of the ridge. From here, we were able to reach the 8200-foot plateau on the ridge with relative ease, occupying Camp II on June 22. We fixed 1100 feet of rope below the plateau to facilitate load carrying. Above the plateau, the ridge rose in three steps to P 10,600, the first step being the most difficult. This was a triangular-shaped face of rock and snow with sharp edges and steep, snow-filled gullies. On the night of June 24, Murray and I climbed up the right side of the face and on to the corniced, knife-edged ridge beyond while Ledoux, Milne, Walker, and Cantor fixed 1600 feet of rope up the central gully. On the night of June 26, following a snowstorm, Murray, Yates, and Cantor fixed 500 feet of rope along the knife-edged ridge, while Walker, Milne, and I fixed another 1000 feet up the central gully of the second step and climbed on over easier terrain to the summit of P 10,600. On the night of June 27, all of us packed loads to Camp III just beyond P 10,600, the rapid progress made possible by virtue of the fixed rope. The night of June 28 was clear and calm. Carrying only bivouac gear, we passed one final ice pitch on the ridge, then intersected the main summit mass up which we climbed with ease. We reached the north summit (15,825 feet), the highest, at about nine A.M. on June 29. The descent was tiresome and slow, but we finally reached Camp III after 17 hours of climbing. By the morning of July 3, we were all back in Base Camp, having removed our fixed ropes and equipment. Dangel and Milne flew back to Haines Junction with most of the climbing gear on July 5, while the rest of us donned skis and shouldered packs for an overland

---

*Recipients of American Alpine Club Climbing Fellowship grants.

return via the Hubbard and Kaskawulsh Glaciers. We covered 68 miles of spectacular glacial terrain during the next seven days, arriving back at Kluane Lake on July 11.

BARTON DEWOLF

Mount Vancouver, North Buttress. A Japanese expedition made the first ascent of the north buttress of Mount Vancouver from the Hubbard Glacier. The first-ascent route (*AAJ*, 1950, p. 367) went up what might better be called the northwest ridge, though they called it the north ridge. The earlier route started from the Seward Glacier side. The two routes are completely distinct and meet only on the summit. Details are lacking.

St. Elias Ski Traverse. From April 12 to May 13 Craig Patterson, Steve Darrow and I traversed the St. Elias Range. Our route followed the Tana Glacier onto the Bagley Icefield to the Seward Glacier, which flows between Mounts St. Elias and Logan. We continued around Mount King George on the Hubbard, then north to the Kaskawulsh Glacier, finally ending at Kluane Lake on the Alaska Highway. The highest elevation we were forced to ski to was only 6700 feet, making it an ideal sled trip. Total mileage was 220 miles. We were unsupported by food caches or airdrops. The loaded sleds weighed 180 pounds when we started. Poor weather prevented climbing more than one 8500-foot crag near Mount Queen Mary.

TED GILLETTE, *Yosemite Climbing School*

Mount Logan. A few parties climbed Mount Logan, all by the King Trench route. A Japanese group led by Seiichiro Takai, was on the mountain from June 25 to July 9. A Kluane National Park Warden Service expedition of four members was led by me. Ron Chambers and I reached the west and north peaks. We were on the mountain from June 28 to July 22. On July 2 Gerald Holdsworth and party left for the King Trench route to continue his glaciology project. The guides Peter Schlunegger and Jacob Wyss reached the summit of the west peak and descended with us. The Arctic Institute of North America's support team were led to the Mount Logan High Plateau by Jürg Hofer to continue their annual High-Altitude Physiological Research Project. Some of their members climbed the north and west peaks.

HANS FUHRER, *Kluane National Park*

Weisshorn, Southeast Ridge Attempt. The southeast ridge of the Weisshorn was attempted by the Kluane National Park Warden Service, led by Jürg Hofer and me. The ridge presented more difficulties than we had estimated. A very dangerous double cornice caused our retreat on the first day. Fixed ropes would have been necessary to tackle the difficult by-pass. The next day the weather deteriorated; storms held us tight in a snow cave for ten days until we got airlifted to Kluane on May 5.

HANS FUHRER, *Kluane National Park*

Mount Gibson. A basic climbing and rescue school, directed by me, was held from April 14 to 19 on the Steele and Foster Glaciers. Mount Gibson was climbed at the end of the school.

HANS FUHRER, *Kluane National Park*

P 12,200, Lowell Glacier, St. Elias Mountains. In August, 1974 Mike Price, Randy Hargesheimer, Dave Lawrence, Matt Kerr, Cheryl Soshnik and I left the Alaska Highway and spent ten days trekking up Slims River and the Kaskawulsh Glacier. We climbed P 12,200, whose summit forms a triple divide for the Kaskawulsh, Lowell and Hubbard Glaciers, nine miles northwest of Alverstone. (First ascent by Victor Josendahl, Irena and John Meulemans, Robert Booher and Leigh Clark, 1961.— *Editor.*) Our route followed the ridge on the north-northeast side of the mountain from camp in the valley to the east.

ANDREW KNAPP, *Minnesota Rovers Outing Club*

Mount Steele, East Ridge. The Kajika party, Kunio Asaoka, Takashi Nakamura, Koichi Takeuchi, Miss Tokiko Michioka, Shigo Ito and I established Base Camp below the east ridge on April 19. Camp I was established at 10,300 feet on the 21st. Above 11,600 feet we fixed seven ropes on a snow wall before placing Camp II at 12,700 feet on April 27. We fixed three more ropes to 14,000 feet. On the 28th Asaoka, Nakamura and Takeuchi passed the knife edge and continued up the 30° slope to the top of Steele (16,440 feet). A second attempt by the other three of us failed in high winds.

TETSUO MORI, *Kajika Alpine Club, Japan*

Mount Steele, East Ridge. In early July, a party of six Canadians, Bruce Fairley, Neil Humphrey, Heidi Piltz, Eric White, Ellen Wood and I, helicoptered to 7500 feet on the Steele Glacier below the east ridge, which we climbed over the next couple of weeks, spending a total of nine nights in snow caves. We hiked out down the Steele Glacier and the Donjek River in seven days.

ROLAND BURTON, *Alpine Club of Canada*

Tombstone Range. Lured by a note in the *Canadian Alpine Journal* promising "Bugaboo-style granite," at least two parties visited the Tombstone Range, thirty miles north of Dawson in the central Yukon, in the summer of 1975. In early June Mark Fagan, Jon Krakauer, and I double-packed three weeks' supplies to the head of the Klondike River from the Dempster Highway on skis. We were disappointed to find very bad rock everywhere and a dearth of natural lines on the impressive-looking peaks. Krakauer and I failed on the 1000-foot east face of "Little Tombstone" only about thirty feet below the top when the cracks we were climbing with aid petered out. Krakauer took a 45-foot leader fall with no protection above a hanging-belay anchor when a hold broke as he was attempting to free-climb the last moves. With Fagan, Krakauer and I later made an easy first ascent. In the middle of June a party of six (Bob Cuthbert, Eric White, Robin Mounsey, Fred Thiessen, Alan Denis, and Neil Humphries) helicoptered in to the upper Chandindu valley. They, too, were greatly disappointed with the slabs of "Graham-cracker rock," loose flakes, and poor lines. During three days of bad weather, Denis and Mounsey managed to get up a difficult rib on the north face of the eastern satellite of Tombstone Mountain. After nasty bivouacs and some A4 nailing, they had a miserable descent in a rain storm. Later the party did a 1500-foot wide mixed route on the peak just north of Monolith Peak, as well as other first ascents in the range. Monolith itself, apparently still unclimbed, is the prize of the range.

DAVID ROBERTS

North West Territories

The Cirque of the Unclimbables, Logan Mountains. Jamie Farrar and I repeated Buckingham's 1960 routes with minor variations on Terrace Tower, Crescent Spire, and Sir James MacBrien. After abandoning one attempt on the south face of Phenocryst Spires, we returned to climb a large dihedral which splits the face between Phenocryst and the high point between it and Huey's Spire. Nine long pitches of primarily crack climbing led to a gap on the narrow ridge between Huey's and Phenocryst. The final pitch to the ridge was an appealing variety of jams, laybacks, and face-climbing. Four pitches along the ridge led to the high point which we had seen from below. Here we discovered a cairn built by a previous party. Nine rappels, utilizing fixed pins, and 500 feet of down-climbing brought us to the moraine above the glacier. One afternoon Bill Putnam and I climbed a snow couloir which led to the ridge joining Harrison-Smith and West Cathedral Peak. This is a finger-like slope near the upper end of the first cirque, separated by a broad rock rib from What-Notch. Averaging 45° at the bottom, the slope steepened to about 60° near the top. Climbing on glacial ice or ice mantled with a couple of inches of snow, we moved continuously the entire way, except near the top where we belayed from inside several crevasses. We attained the ridge and a nearby high point in three hours of climbing. Upon later inspection we believe this to be the summit of the fourth Pentadactyl Spire, previously unclimbed. The precipitous nature of the surrounding terrain forced us to down-climb our ascent route. Using our three ice screws judiciously, we descended 18 pitches without mishap in just over three hours. Later in August (we were there from the 10th to the 26th), Mark Kremen and I repeated Buckingham's route on Meringue. On our final day of climbing, Farrar and I did the second ascent of the southeast ridge of Sir James MacBrien, a spectacularly situated climb, requiring one pitch of aid and offering some superb crack and slab climbing.

DOUG BURBANK

Logan Mountains. Hans Ueli Brunner, Paul Muggli and I left Switzerland in early June for the Logan Mountains. On June 19 to 21 climbed the Frost route on Lotus Flower Tower with much snow, though the conditions on the face were good. We climbed the south ridge of Proboscis on June 24 in a single day, again with much snow and some dangerous cornices. On June 27 we made the first ascent of the west peak of Huey's Spire by its south face. Buckingham climbed the middle and east peaks. This was our most difficult climb. Two other Swiss, Edgar Oberson and Maurice Cochand, came in on the plane which flew us out on July 2. They climbed the Lotus Flower Tower but were weathered off other climbs.

RUEDI HOMBERGER, *Schweizer Alpen Club*

Baffin Island

Tirokwa, West Face. We were a small expedition, two people, Jill Lawrence and I. Our objective was the west face of Mount Thor, but after hearing of the Japanese team's bolting epic and subsequent failure, we turned to the west face of Tirokwa. This face abuts the unnamed westerly satellite peak and is a 4000-foot triangular cliff with a prominent central spur. The route takes a ramp cutting the lower face of the spur for 10 rope-lengths, then follows the crest of the spur for four pitches before traversing left onto the north flank of the spur for two pitches and climbing the centre of the north flank by a prominent crack system for 10 pitches to reach a saddle. We then followed the ridge of the spur for five pitches until it abuts the upper face and then climbed diagonally to the right for three pitches and finally for four pitches up easier rock to the summit. The route is on steep rock throughout, rather loose on the first four pitches. It is remarkably sustained at F6 to F8 with three pitches of F9 and three of fourth class. We used two pins for anchors and 2 nuts for direct aid to start the third pitch after the ramp. All other belays were from nuts. Climbing time was 15 hours. We descended the southwest ridge with two rappels in three hours.

PETER LIVESEY, *Alpine Club*

Mount Asgard, Northwest Face, Cumberland Peninsula, Baffin Island.
In mid-July Pat Padden, Shary McVoy, Rick Sylvester, and I* were
finally on our way to the unclimbed northwest face of Mount Asgard.
Upon our arrival at the Eskimo village of Pangnirtung, we were met by
Charlie Porter, who had similar ambitions to ours. After a week of
waiting in Pangnirtung for a helicopter, we were eventually standing at
the base of the 2000-foot northwest face of the twin summits of Mount
Asgard. We had chosen an obvious dihedral slanting up to the left, the
same line that had been attempted in 1972 by Doug Scott and party.
After 250 feet of mixed free and aid climbing we placed a few bolts up
to the left to another crack system. Deteriorating weather forced us
down to Base Camp on Turner Glacier, where we spent the next five days
in our tents as the storm raged outside. Pat and I were now out of
time and food and so hiked out to Pangnirtung while Rick and Shary
stayed on. Charlie Porter now showed up and joined Rick and Shary.
By starting 80 feet to the right of the original start, they moved up,
eventually penduluming into the main dihedral higher up, thus placing
only 1 bolt. After getting two-thirds of the way, a bad snow storm forced
them to retreat. By now Rick and Shary were going hungry from lack
of food and had to hike out to Pangnirtung for more. Charlie elected
to go up on the climb, completing the climb in stormy weather from
September 1-10. Winter had now arrived in full force by dumping four
feet of fresh snow on the mountains.

CRAIG MARTINSON, *North Star Mountaineers*

Cumberland Peninsula, Baffin Island. Maurice Dupont-Roc and his
wife Andrée, Mme Martine Salembier, Mlle Martine Regnault, Charles
Russignaga, Noël Humbert, Bernard Constantin, Patrice Bruner, the Swiss
Hans Peter Duttle and I as leader spent 25 days on Cumberland Peninsula. We walked 120 miles, crossed countless swamps, rivers, sand and
moraines. M. and Mme Dupont-Roc, Mme Salembier and Russignaga
climbed Tête Blanche (7074 feet), the highest point on the island, from
Camp III on an unnamed glacier between Turner and Highway Glaciers.
This was a second ascent and the first female ascent. The approach and
return were made by paddling up Summit and Glacier Lakes. Bruner,
Duttle, Mlle Regnault, Constantin, Humbert and I from Summit Lake
made the 8th ascent of Asgard, which measured 2070 meters (6792 feet)
on my altimeter. Tirokwa Peak (c. 5900 feet) was given its 4th ascent
by Constantin, Bruner, Russignaga, Humbert, M. and Mme Dupont-Roc,
Mme Salembier and me. By a new route Bruner, Duttle, Constantin,
Mme Salembier, Humbert, Mlle Regnault and I made the 4th ascent of
Thor Peak (c. 5575 feet). In the course of a reconnaissance of the Merag

*Recipient of a grant from the A.A.C. Climbing Fellowship Fund.

Glacier, Mlle Regnault, Russignaga, M. Dupont-Roc and I made the 4th ascent of Moljnir. The twin summits of c. 5575-foot Munin and Hugin were climbed from Boot Col for the second time with a first descent from Hugin directly to the Fork Beard Glacier. Russignaga, Mlle Regnault, M. Dupont-Roc and I in 18 hours traversed the entire ridge from the Aiguille du Couchant to Munin, making the 8th ascent of the former, the 4th of Sleipnir and the 3rd of Munin. Duttle and Mme Salembier made the first ascent of a peak at the head of the Fork Beard Glacier.

JACQUES DURVILLE, *Club Alpin Français*

Peaks in Pangnirtung Pass Area. The Northumbria Baffin Island Expedition was composed of climbers from the northeast of England: Dave McDonald, Ken Rawlinson, Len Wilson, Dennis Lee, Steve Blake, Kevin McLane, George Simms and me. We arrived in Pangnirtung on June 20. The fjord was still blocked with broken ice and it was not until June 23 that we were able to travel up in two canoes. Base Camp was established near the foot of Mount Ulu. On June 24 McDonald, McLane, Rawlinson and Lee began an attempt on the 2500-foot-high north face of Ulu, taking a line to the left of the centre aiming for a prominent corner that appeared to lead to the summit. Both pairs reached about half-height over increasingly loose rock before the crack system faded out. Resolved not to use bolts for aid, they retreated. On June 27 McLane and Lee made the first ascent of the southeast ridge of the west summit of Turnweather, some 2500 feet of Grade IV climbing. McDonald and Simms made the first ascent of a peak three miles northeast of Turnweather, a straightforward climb on rock followed by a snow slope and a traverse between the twin peaks of the mountain. It is hoped to give this peak the Inuit name for Sentinel. Rawlinson and Blake made the first ascent of the central pillar of Overlord, a 42-pitch Grade VI route with two bivouacs. The pillar ended in a 300-foot snow slope leading to the summit. We took 11 days to carry food and equipment some 25 miles up the valley via Windy Lake to Summit Lake. The weather was consistently bad and we were weather-bound several days. On July 15 McDonald and McLane left for a large peak opposite Mount Thor on the west side of the Weasel Glacier. They reached the summit of their peak via a 3500-foot ice couloir. Climbing was consistently hard and the weather very bad. Unable to find an easy way off, they abseiled down the gully. We have applied to the Canadian government to name this mountain "Mount Northumbria." Other climbs were halted by bad weather.

RICHARD GODFREY, *England*

Canadian Rockies

Mount Queen Mary, Northeast Face. In the Royal Group of the Canadian Rockies, south of Assiniboine, Mount Queen Mary has a spectacular long ice face on its unnamed northeast hanging glacier. The face was climbed this fall for the first time and apparently it was the second time the mountain had been climbed since the original ascent 53 years ago. After being chased out of the Palliser Pass area by a snowstorm, Doug McCarty, Jim Kanzler, and I drove to Canal Flat for an entry via the Kootenay and Albert drainages, where a new logging road put a British Columbia approach into a different perspective. A day of elk trails and open forest took us to a spectacular camp spot under the face, close to the ice. September 21 was as perfect as the previous two days had been, and the crampon climb up the 2600-foot face went well. The low sun angle of the season kept the surface temperature low, and therefore ice screws bit beautifully. A final summit pitch up the rock castle, plastered with fresh snow, was best done with crampons on. It was so warm on the summit (10,600 feet) that we nearly fell asleep for an hour before beginning the descent by the same route; the original route was plastered with new snow, and in any event appeared loose, distasteful and not at all easy. Climbers in search of new areas to visit will find the Royal Group has some rewarding possibilities.

FRED BECKEY

South Twin, King Edward and Sundial. In July and August I spent 18 days alone around the headwaters of the Athabasca River. Seeing the view from the top of Wooley Shoulder, I hoped to climb the regular route on Mount Alberta. Two days later in a storm, with 800 feet of terrifying rotten rock below me and 1000 feet more above, I reconsidered. The next day I traversed the wide ledge that runs along the base of the Twins at 7500 feet. From a camp on the ledge I climbed South Twin via a long couloir leading to the false (west) summit. This route might offer a better descent from North Twin than going over Stutfield Peak, being easier to find in a storm (the top of the couloir is obvious just west of the minor summit) and having the tedious but safe ledge. In the couloir I had the choice of steep, slushy snow or rotten rock. That night it began to rain, bringing to an end the longest stretch (two days) of good weather on the trip. There were several short breaks in the drizzle that week in which I climbed the northwest ridge of Mount King Edward, another crumbling classic, and the north face of Sundial, a 500-foot snow and ice face with a beautiful shape. An attempt on the north face-northwest ridge of Mount Dais forced me farther and farther to the right until I ended up finishing the climb by the regular south-face route. I believe the South Twin, King Edward and Sundial climbs are new routes.

DANE WATERMAN

Mount Noyes. In late July, Jack Cade, Hugh Johnston, Pierre Le-Mieux and I met much of Clan Gmoser at the height of land near the extreme head of Porcupine Creek in the Murchison Group. We had spent the previous five days in the headwaters area of that stream making some new ascents. One of these was an unnamed peak, 10,300 feet, which had previously been ascended only by the Dominion Survey. Our route was via the talus, scree and cliffs of the west buttress, descending by the much easier south ridge. Within a few feet of the very summit of this peak, an extensive deposit of frozen ground moraine covers the glacially polished bedrock to a depth of more than 20 feet. We exposed the polish at a fringe and noted that the direction of glacier movement was almost exactly parallel to the main line of the Canadian Rockies in this area. Hans Gmoser, with his father, brother and nephew, none of whom share his avocation or ability to speak English, joined us for a late lunch on the 25th after which we proceeded down the initially very steep valley of Noyes Creek into the teeth of an exceedingly stiff northwest wind and snow squalls. Hugh, Pierre and I set out early the next morning to ascend the north peak of Mount Noyes, hitherto unclimbed. Our route caused us to return to that height of land and the pass between the north fork of Silverhorn Creek and Noyes Creek. Thence, we ascended diagonally across the upper part of the glacier on the east side of the summits to the final rock cliffs. These were very easily scaled, and within four hours of leaving our camp we were rewarded with a fine view and diminishing winds.

WILLIAM L. PUTNAM

Tumbling Glacier, Kootenay Park. On September 6 Greg Spohr and I pitched a tent on the meadows just south of the glacier. To avoid crevasses, the next morning we skirted around the south side of the glacier, then traversed underneath the rock wall to arrive at the start of the prominent ice couloir. The too-warm weather caused a steady fall of ice chunks up to fist size. After deliberation we ran out a hasty pitch to a stance on the left side of the couloir under protecting rocks. From here a rapid traverse to the right brought us to safer ground and we now began to enjoy the climb. In fact, climbing conditions were better than expected thanks to the snow cover left by miserable August weather. We progressed rapidly through the middle section leading to the great ice bulge. Here a narrow gully to the left led up for three pitches, after which the angle eased. We soon arrived on a snowy platform for lunch. Another 40 minutes of easy climbing brought us to the summit of P 10,240 with a storm rapidly closing in. We descended a long snow gully leading down to the southwest, from where an excellent goat trail led back over the pass between P 10,240 and its southerly neighbor P 10,020. After a long descent followed by steep, strenuous bushwhacking, we finally reached in the last light the trail down by Numa Creek.

PETER ZVENGROWSKI, *Calgary Mountain Club*

Interior Ranges

Peaks near Mount Lunn, Northern Cariboos. After Wayne Misener,

Bill Robinson, Warren Thompson and I had driven in deteriorating weather to McBride, we drove along a well-maintained logging road 25 miles up Castle Creek to the road end at 3500 feet. From there we proceeded up the northwest fork of the creek through nearly impenetrable brush and insatiable mosquitoes for 3½ hours to the terminal moraine at the base of the icefields below Mount Lunn. From the north side of the moraine, despite rain, we ascended northwest up steep scree through more brush to timberline and Base Camp in a meadow at 7500 feet. After another rainy day we started in the fog at 9:30 A.M. traversing the glacier toward Mount Lunn, ascending a conspicuous knoll (Peak 1), a mile north of Lunn; Lunn is a 9280-foot rock easily visible from the valley. From Peak 1 we continued along the ridge over the snow-covered 9500-foot peak (Peak 2) behind and east of Lunn. From there we dropped down to Mount Lunn, where we erected a cairn and installed a register. We hoped to go on to P 8621 but got off route in the fog and ended up on the narrow rock and corniced ice ridge joining Lunn to P 9275. As it was too late to make a bid for the summit, we retraced our steps, seeing on the way that a 250-foot ice cliff separates the western ridge of Lunn from P 8621. On the second climbing day the weather was beautiful. We climbed the ridge west of Base Camp to the top of the closest peak (Peak 3; 2½ miles north of Lunn; 9020 feet). We continued to the southwest, dropping 100 feet and then ascending 40° ice to Peak 4 at 9200 feet. In a sweeping traverse we kept on west on the ridge 1½ miles to 9030-foot Peak 5. From there we traversed back dropping onto an adjacent glacier and another ridge some 2½ miles northeasterly. The ridge contained two small peaks, the larger of which was 8400 feet high.

RICHARD MITCHELL, *Mountaineers*

Leaning Towers Group, Southern Selkirks. Chuck Sink and I spent from July 16 to 25 near the Leaning Towers, east of Kootenay Lake. We were ferried across the lake to the outlet of Campbell Creek and the beginning of a 14-mile trek comprised mainly of brush, talus and snow slopes. Two days of tramping up Campbell Creek over and through these obstacles brought us to a pass southwest of the towers; we traversed around the headwaters of Pinnacle Creek and crossed a second pass south of the towers. From there we dropped down and traversed northeast to a dazzling blue-green lake nestled in a small cirque. We then ascended two ridges lying perpendicular to the Leaning Towers. These ridges were mainly gneiss and schist and afforded no major problems aside from the hazard of very loose talus on several of the six peaks climbed. These were Turok, Andar, P 9160, Heather, P 9500 and Mount Michael, all NCCS I, F3. Turning our efforts to the southwest, we ascended the spectacular northeast ridges of two granite peaks which required rope, chocks and free-climbing skill. (P 8600, NCCS II, F7; and P 8900, NCCS II, F9 via the east face to the crest of the northeast ridge and climbing left of a huge gendarme before again regaining the crest.) We moved camp back to the headwaters of Pinnacle Creek and climbed a third sound granite peak of 8900 feet via snow up the northwest side to the west ridge. From the false summit we made a short rappel and climbed to the true summit in one more lead. NCCS II, F5. There were no cairns or evidence of ascents on any of these nine peaks although we could make out large cairns on the summits of the Leaning Towers.

ALAN J. KEARNEY

Snowpatch Spire, East Face, Deus ex Machina Route, Bugaboos. On August 4 to 6, 1974 Mike Jefferson, Dennis Saunders and I did this new route, beginning in an F9 off-width crack a few hundred feet north of the Chouinard route and directly below the north summit. We ascended the left side of a Yosemite-style exfoliation "pinnacle" for two pitches and then up the left of two parallel thin cracks (A3 and F8) to a hanging bivouac below the Ceilings. Two pitches later on some excellent large ledges we traversed left some 30 feet to cracks which led up to another good bivouac ledge. We stopped four hours before dark and watched gathering clouds, which later rained and hailed on us all night. Two more pitches of mixed climbing led to a black, dirty overhanging (140°) slot (A2, A3) followed by a fist-jam crack and another easy pitch to the summit. NCCS VI, F9, A2.

JOHN SHERVAIS

Mount Carmarthen, Southeast Buttress of Welsh Wall, North Star Area, Purcell Range. On July 3, William S. Nicolai, Patricia Johnson and I climbed this buttress from camp in the Welsh Lakes. The climb is accessible via the Centaurus Glacier in an hour and a half. It was five pitches on good Bugaboo granite. NCCS II, F7.

BRIAN L. BERRY

Mount Nelson, East Ridge, Southern Purcells. The east ridge of Mount Nelson is the most direct route to the summit starting from Paradise Mine. On June 23 Hans Gyr and I left the mine, followed the ridge and traversed along the southern slopes of Mount Trafalgar to gain the Trafalgar-Nelson col. From here mainly 3rd and 4th-class climbing on decomposed rock, with a short 5th-class pitch on a band of solid conglomerate rock near the top, led to the summit. The climb could conveniently be combined with a traverse of Trafalgar.

PETER ZVENGROWSKI, *Calgary Mountain Club*

Coast Range

P 8815 and P 8798, Niut Range. On January 29 Kreig McBride and I made the first winter ascents of P 8815 and P 8798. The latter lies east of the former and both are due west of Tatlayoko's northern end. We climbed from an igloo camp in the basin immediately north, culminating a three-day snowshoe approach. We ascended a 1000-foot couloir and boulder-hopped to the col between the peaks. The east peak was climbed via snow gullies and ridges on the southwest side and the west peak by its eastern ridge. Both peaks had been previously ascended from the col by helicopter-borne survey parties and from the lake by McBride and David Shannon in the summer of 1971.

DAVID TUCKER, *Larrabee Domino Club*

Mount Waddington from the North. From July 18 to August 3, Mike Warburton and I traversed the Coast Range from east to west via the Tiedemann and Franklin Glaciers and climbed the north ridge of Mount Waddington by a new route. We approached the range by plane from Campbell River. While on our way in to Ephemeron Lake, we air-dropped some of our supplies at Rainy Knob. It then took us one and a half days to reach Rainy Knob via Nabob Pass and the Tiedemann Glacier. In one day from Rainy Knob we took most of our food up to the Waddington-Combatant Col via the right side of the upper Tiedemann Glacier and returned. In the next seven days there were three days of good climbing weather and four days of storm, but it was enough for us to ascend the Bravo Icefall and headwall to Bravo Col, thence to the bergschrund under the main rock tower. On July 27 from our snow cave under the main rock tower, we ascended the northeast face to the first big notch on the north ridge. We bypassed the large overhanging ice bulge by traversing up and left on the face and then followed the north ridge to the summit across the gap the Steck party encountered in 1950. We descended via the regular southeast chimney rappel route and arrived back at our snow cave in darkness. It had been an exciting long day. On July 28 we returned to the Waddington-Combatant Col by following a direct northeast line on snow. A hanging glacier near the bottom of this route presented unexpected difficulties. In retrospect we were lucky to get down to the col this way. On July 29, to get off the col, we down-climbed the rock buttress which splits the upper Scimitar Glacier. Some rappels and uneasy moments near the bottom of the icefall made for a memorable day. That night we camped near the sharp bend in the Scimitar underneath Fury Gap. The weather worsened as we ascended the far west side of the glacier up to Fury Gap and then shifted over to the east side of the gap to descend on to the upper Franklin. A three-day storm then pounded us as we struggled along the Franklin Glacier to reach its snout and then along the north side of the Franklin River to the logging camp at Knight Inlet. Alec Dalgleish's memorial cairn at Icefall Point and an encounter with a grizzly along the abandoned (washed out) logging road to Knight Inlet highlighted this part of our trip.

R.D. CAUGHRON

Mount Waddington, New Route. During July Dave Mention and I climbed Mount Waddington by a new variation. Other party members were Tim Riordan, Jack Tackle and Dave Brunk. We approached the mountain by the Franklin Glacier, with Base Camp on the Dias Glacier. Tim and Jack attempted the south face. Rockfall and an oncoming storm forced retreat. Upon their return, Dave and I packed to climb. Our route ascended a couloir, just left of the south face, to the northwest ridge. Then via the Angel Glacier we climbed the false summit and descended to a point where we traversed the main pinnacle along its northern base. The main pinnacle was climbed in storm via the southeast chimney. Deep snow with white-out conditions made our descent down the southeast ridge and over the col south of Spearman Peak difficult. Our traverse of Mount Waddington took 6½ days from Base Camp.

JEFF JONES, *unaffiliated*

GREENLAND

Ketil and Other Peaks, Tasermiut Fjord. During August a group of French climbers led by F. Guillot explored peaks around Koromint valley (Kimukât on the 250,000 map). We arrived at Narsarssuaq airport on July 23, helicoptered to Nanortalik and traveled by fishing boat to Koromint. Base Camp was on the shore of the fjord. Until April 17, when the boat returned, the climbers M. Agier, B. and M.F. Amy, P. Chapoutot, B. Domenech, B. Gorgeon, F. Guillot, J.F. and C. Lemoine, Cl. Laurendeau, M. Perrotet, J. Ratti and J. Walter made several reconnaissances and nine new routes, all alpine-style. We made the following climbs: Pointe de la RDVN (P 1500; 4922 feet) by west ridge, 1650 feet of TD sup; Nalumasortok (2051 meters; 6729 feet) by south col and east ridge; Nalumasortok by south face, 3300 feet of TD; Suikagssuak East (The Horn; 1880 meters; 6168 feet) by north couloir and west ridge, 2625 feet of D sup; Suikagssuak North (1830 meters; 6004 feet) by east couloir and ridge, 3300 feet of D; Ketil, P 2010 of the three Pingasut; 6595 feet) by direct south face, 3300 feet of TD sup, new route, 2nd ascent of the mountain on August 5 and 6, descent by different route; Pingasut Central (1640 meters; 5380 feet) by east ridge, AD; Itikiklik Dome (1945 meters; 6382 feet) by west side, D; P 1680 (5512 feet) by west slope. The rock was generally good, except for spots where frost or lichen had disintegrated the granite. The weather was good with short rainy periods; it changes so slowly that it does not cause precipitous retreats. There are still many other excellent groups of mountains to be explored.

BERNARD AMY, *Club Alpin Français*

Apostelens Tommel Finger and Ketil, West Face, South Greenland. A French expedition led by Maurice Barrard accomplished two extremely difficult ascents just north of Kap Farvel. From July 22 to 29 Barrard, Pierre-Henri Feuillet, Yves Payrau, Michel Pellé, Dominique Marchal, Georges Narbaud and Gérard Vellay made the first ascent of the sharp Apostelens Tommel Finger above Lindenows Fjord. They climbed the 5100-foot wall, finding good rock on all but five leads, where the rock was frost-shattered. Descent by the same route took two days. They then moved to Tasermiut Fjord. From August 7 to 11, Barrard, Marchal, Narbaud, Payrau and Vellay made the first ascent of the west face of Ketil, a 5000-foot climb of sustained great difficulty for all but the last 1000 feet. This route had been attempted in 1974 by a party led by Barrard; they were able to use some of the pitons placed a year before. The first ascent of Ketil was made in July of 1974 by Austrians from Lienz who climbed the couloir on the northwest and traversed to the south face.

Upernivik Island, West Greenland. The expedition of the Lidau Section of the German Alpine Club was a complete success. We climbed from August 9 to 27 in the mountains of Upernivik Island at 72° N. We were Volker Stelzer, Klaus, Gustav and Susi Harder, Joe and Waltraut Eggert, Grit Doleschel, Wolfgang Ruhland, Werner Scharl, Otto Schäfler, Franz Neubauer, Willi Eggert, Rolf Haas, Thomas Hummler, Dieter Trapmann and I as leader. We made 18 ascents, including three new routes and one first ascent. The new routes were as follows: "Eisschaufel" (Snow Shovel; 1820 meters or 5971 feet) via east ridge by Haas, Schäfler and via north face by Scharl, Ruhland and "Piacco" (2040 meters or 6693 feet) via northeast face by J. Eggert, Hagg, Stelzer. The first ascent was Cathedral on Qioqe (1920 meters or 6300 feet) via west face by Ruhland, Schäfler, Haas, Scharl.

HEINZ HAGG, *Deutscher Alpenverein*

Karrat Isfjord, West Greenland. An expedition of the Deggendorf Section of the German Alpine Club, led by Georg Leitl, climbed north of Umanak from June 29 to July 31 and made 12 first ascents.

Scottish Expedition to South Greenland. A University of St. Andrews party visited the mountains between Tasermiut and Ilua fjords at 60° N. During a period of eight weeks a total of 45 peaks were either climbed or attempted, 40 first ascents were made, and our canoes logged over 200 miles in pack ice conditions. Our party was composed of John Cant, Norman MacKenzie, Richard Henderson, Peter Hunt, Colin Matheson, Douglas Brown, Ray Sharples, Peter Aldred and me as leader. We flew from Glasgow via Iceland to Narsarssuaq and went by the weekly coastal boat to Nanortalik. We chartered a boat to our Base Camp by Stordalens Havn at the eastern end of a big transverse valley that links the two fjords. Our main objective was to enter the "Land of the Towers" south of the valley, but it was only at the sixth and the most westerly of the glaciers that our access was finally made through the mountain rampart. One group operated there and climbed some of the high-grade towers by stylish and demanding routes, while the other group climbed from a hidden loch, ringed by attractive peaks, north of the valley and intermingled with the mountains visited by the 1971 St. Andrews expedition (*A.A.J.*, 1972. 18:1, p. 156). At the halfway stage we regrouped for new objectives in the side valleys close to Base Camp, while for the final efforts we placed another party by canoe amongst the most easterly of the smooth and sheer pinnacles of the "Land of the Towers," while another canoe party voyaged east to climb on the islands of Pamiagdluk and Quvernit. Weather conditions were excellent throughout the summer: most climbs were done on windless and sunny days and bivouacs were seldom contemplated by the parties abseiling down in the night gloom. Two mountains may illustrate the nature of the routes: Angiartarfik (1845 meters or 6053 feet; Grade III), a complex massive peak above Base Camp, was ascended by front-pointing in crampons up 2300 feet of frozen high-angled snow and then descended on the same slope in soft thawing slush: this, the easiest route on the peak, became impracticable by mid-July when the snow melted off to expose a crevassed slope of green ice; Twin Pillars of Pamiagdluk (1373 meters or 4505 feet; Grade V), a welded pair of abrupt pinnacles comprising the highest peak on this island, was climbed in a three-day sortie by traversing on to its steep slabby east wall and following a thin 300-metre line to the summit crest. The gradings for the mountains climbed were 5-Is, 15-IIs, 12-IIIs, 6-IVs, 6-Vs. We returned to Scotland at the end of August by the same route after a twelve-week stay. There were no accidents, illness, hunger, thirst, discomfort and drama; good fortune with a small dash of efficient organisation made this one of the most successful of our University expeditions to Greenland.

PHILIP GRIBBON, *Scottish Mountaineering Club*

Staunings Alper, Complete North-South Traverse. The very rugged mountains, the Staunings Alper, which lie at 72° north latitude, were traversed for the first time along their entire length between July 28 and August 30, from Kap Petersen to Syd Kap, a distance of 170 miles, and then another 100 miles back to Mesters Vig, another 100 miles. The Cambridge University party was led by Keith J. Miller and further composed of James Bishop, Christopher Padfield and John Thorogood. Though they climbed to no summits, they crossed numerous high passes and explored a considerable amount of virgin glacial country.

MEXICO

Baja California

Gran Trono Blanco. The Libro Abierto route on the north face follows a continuous right-facing dihedral for six pitches. There was a little aid on the first three pitches, but these went largely free. The steep route is delightful, mostly cracks and jam chimneys. Except for part of the third pitch, the rock is very solid. The dihedral is just west of two routes done in 1974. It was climbed on March 24 by Alan Bartlett, Mike Graber and me. NCCS IV, F9, A2.

FRED BECKEY

Gran Trono Blanco, South Wall, Sierra Juárez. On November 9, 10 and 11, John Vawter, Dick Savidge and I completed a new route on the south face of El Gran Trono Blanco. It consists of 11 pitches, 7 completely free and 4 mixed (these involving only a few aid moves or a tension traverse). The route takes the only available crack system left of the previously done route, "Happy Hooker" (*A.A.J.*, 1975, p. 154), recognized by the huge right-facing chimney in the center of the south face. The climb starts just past the left-end of an obvious large roof and continues for four pitches to the "Hotel," a very spacious but sloping ledge on which we spent two nights. The crux is the next two pitches, involving delicate and varying mixed climbing. The climbing above the "Hotel" is superb and continually challenging, with an intimidating amount of exposure. We used only three pin placements (2 knifeblades, 1 lost-arrow); emphasis was on wired stoppers with a variety of sky-hooks. NCCS V, F9, A3.

WERNER R. LANDRY

SOUTH AMERICA

Venezuela

Pico Vértigo, Sierra Nevada de Mérida. A Venezuelan party led by T. Viscarret made in January the second ascent of Pico Vértigo (c. 16,000 feet), a sharp rock peak which local climbers call the "Petit Dru of Venezuela." The first ascent had been made in 1962 by a joint British-Venezuelan group (*A.A.J.*, 1963, 13:2, pp. 503-4).

EVELIO ECHEVARRÍA

Colombia

Traverse of the Sierra Nevada de Santa Marta; Pico Simmons. Tom Simpson and I entered the range from above Ciénaga Magdalena (San Pedro de la Sierra), went into the *paramo* by Cuchilla Cimarona, and continued along the western spine of the Viscungue valley and up this valley to the base of Pico Simmons, which we climbed. The two of us kept on around the "Horqueta" by a southern route, down past Noboba (lake), down the Donachui and on over to Atanquez. This I believe is the first complete traverse of the Sierra. We were there from December 29 to January 12, 1976.

PHILIP DE GRUYTER

Sierra Nevada de Santa Marta Western peaks. Ours was the third University of Vermont climbing and spider-collecting expedition to this range. Since Arhuaco Indians had apparently sealed off the sierra to all outsiders, we chose this time the western approach. Entering from San Pedro, we reached the highland after five days of ridge crossing and reconnaissances. Tom Buechner, John Kochalka and I climbed Mission Peak (14,300 feet), highest of the Donan Chucua ridge on March 7. Kochalka also ascended several other peaks around 14,000 feet, some for the first time. On March 14, all three climbers mentioned plus Dave Vreeland climbed Nevado Tesoro (5250 meters, 17,225 feet) and on the 15th, Pico Simmons (5660 meters, 18,570 feet) via the west glacier. We returned in five days to San Pedro, in which area Kochalka then did spider-collecting.

PIETER CROW, *Green Mountain Club*

Huila, Tolima and Cocuy peaks. "Andes-75," a Polish expedition from Gdansk composed of seven speleologists and climbers led by Walenty Fiut, explored the main caves of central Colombia and also did some mountaineering in the Cordillera Central and in the Sierra Nevada del Cocuy in the eastern part of the country. In the former, the Poles made the first ascent of the unnamed (southern) peak of the Huila massif (c. 5150 meters, 16,897 feet) in late December; they have asked the Colombian government to name this peak "Pico Polonia." With the German H. Frank and the Colombians H. González and J. Curzio they also made the third ascent of Pico Mayor del Huila (c. 5350 meters, 17,553 feet). On January 3, 1976, two expedition members ascended Nevado del Tolima (5215 meters, 17,112 feet). In the Cocuy range, W. Fiut, H. Frank, G. Goeggel, S. Gaviria and D. Otero climbed on January 19 and 20 Nevado Pan de Azúcar (Nevado del Púlpito, 5210 meters, 17,093 feet) and "Toti," locally known as Nevado Paloblanco (5074 meters, 16,646 feet). Fiut alone also climbed Púlpito del Diablo ("Devil's Pulpit"), a rock block about 16,000 feet, rising in the middle of the west glacier of Nevado Pan de Azúcar, probably a third ascent.

EVELIO ECHEVARRÍA

Nevado de Cocuy. Six Colombian students, Santiago Pérez, Pancho and Sergio Gaviria, Juan Manuel Diaz, Andrés Uribe and Pepe Luis Moreno, climbed Ritacuba Blanco (17,926 feet) on March 25. Moreno and S. Gaviria also made the first Colombian ascent of Ritacuba Negro (17,681 feet) the next day. A crevasse on the latter, where some equipment was found, appears to be the spot where Ian Harverson and Peter Jennings were lost in December 1973 (*A.A.J.*, 1974, p. 123).

Ecuador

Spanish Climbs in 1974. In August 1974 a Spanish expedition from Granada not only climbed Chimborazo, Cotopaxi and Illiniza Norte by the normal routes, but also ascended the Italian route on Obispo (17,451 feet) and Illiniza Sur (17,277 feet) by a new route, the northeast face. The climbers were R. Pinilla, leader, J. Conde, A. Muñoz, E. Sánchez, J. Sáez and A. Tinaut.

Ecuadorian ascents. Marco Cruz and the Frenchman Joseph Bergé made in October 1974 the first ascent of the north face of Quilindaña, the "Matterhorn of Ecuador" (4898 meters, 16,070 feet), the last 1000 feet being on a near vertical rock wall of not very good quality. Climbers of San Gabriel Institute, Quito, ascended Nevado Cayambe (5789 meters, 18,993 feet) by way of its west side, beginning at the Espinoza Glacier and then reaching the last part of the mountain by a detour to the east, a new route (late 1974). Also in late 1974 climbers of the National Poly-technical School made the second ascent of Fraile Grande, Altar group (5200 meters, 17,060 feet), which had been ascended, with difficulty, by the Italian Tremonti party in November 1972. In May 1975, another party from the Polytechnical climbed El Sangay, which according to surveys by this expedition is only 5160 meters (16,929 feet) high. (Information obtained through Patricio Torres, of *El Comercio*, Quito.)

EVELIO ECHEVARRÍA

Sara Urco. Nevado Sara Urco (4676 meters, 15,343 feet) had re-mained a mysterious mountain. Since Whymper's ascent in 1880 it had been climbed only once, in 1955, by twelve members of the Club Nuevos Horizontes, who experienced poor visibility during the ascent and could not study the mountain itself and its surroundings. On December 6, six climbers of the Escuela Politécnica of Quito reached the top and again, on December 20, B. Chiriboga and M. Cruz climbed it, both parties having better luck with the weather. These two 1975 groups ascertained that the mountain has fairly large glaciers on its north, northeast and south sides, did not find proof of volcanic activity and discovered no less than 25 lakes on its northwest slopes.

EVELIO ECHEVARRÍA

Peru—Cordillera Blanca

Huascarán. Generally this was a disappointing year for climbers in the Cordillera Blanca. The weather never completely stabilized, a condi-tion which has grown progressively worse in the last four years. Twenty-four groups composed of 134 climbers attempted the Garganta route to Huascarán south and north peaks in 1975, 58 reaching one or the other summit; three lost their lives. On June 11 German Peter Götz died at

18,000 feet, six hours after manifesting symptoms of pulmonary and cerebral edema. His companions were not familiar with the illness. On July 24 Reinhard Siegl and Heinrich Gentner departed from their Garganta camp towards the north summit in forceful winds; they did not return. Ascents follow: *South Peak:* Vincent Dubeń, Ivan Gálfy, Ivan Fiala, Taras Pacák, Czechs, May 20; Georg Brosig, Heinrich Schön, Germans, June 12; Wayne Cates, Dave Hansen, Peter Herwick, USA, June 13; Robert Broughton, Kenneth Groff, USA, June 24; Dan Langmade, David Ciochetti, USA, June 30; Walter and Barbara Pschorr, Germans, July 18; Tomás Gross, Czech, Felipe Mautino, Peruvian, July 23; Jon Jones, Canadian, John Leader, English, July 24; Tim Schuld, Mark Fried, Dennie Black, Joseph A. Vance, George Stransky, R.H. Seaper, Stephen Yeagle, Bruce Schneider, Rick Droker, USA, July 26; Pat Weidman and an Argentine companion, July 27; Adam Lewandowski, Kasimier Rosiak, Jan Wozniak, Polish, August 30. *North Peak:* Arthur Mudge, Sheldon Moomaw, Kesler Teter, Fred Lang, USA, July 25; María Elena Flores, Sofía Medina, Dolores Novia, Eliura Paredes, Mexicans, July 26; Michiko Abiko, Akie Toyama, Mosako Kokubu, Miwako Majima, Japanese women, August 10; Honorato Caldúa, Joaquim Vargas, Fortunato Lliuya, Marcelino Morales, Peruvians, July 26; Ferdinand Pfordte, Franz Bauer, Germans, July 29; Władysław Barowier, Ryszard Koziol, Andrzej Skirczynski, Polish, August 28. John Hawley, John Otter, Bud Ford and Dave Campbell, USA, climbed Huascarán Norte on July 12 and Huascarán Sur on July 15.

MICHAEL J. ROURKE, *Parque Nacional Huascarán*

Climbing in the Cordillera Blanca. Netherlanders M.A. Bonhomme, M.A. Briet, K.E.J. Dijk, P. Dekker, R. Staaftjes, J.K. Richert, H. Tollenaar and A.C.A. van Helbergen climbed the south (higher) summit of *Alpamayo* by the north ridge and over the north summit in early June. Mexican, German and French parties failed in their attempts on Alpamayo. In the southern part of the range, on August 20 New Zealanders John Atkinson and John Black climbed the east face of *Pucaraju* by its southern rib, mostly on rock. The final climb took six hours. A Spanish expedition led by Jordi Pons reached about 19,100 feet on *Chopicalqui*'s southwest ridge before being turned back by bad weather. An attempt by a different Spanish expedition, led by Juan Hugas, to climb *Pucahirca Central* by the 1961 Italian route up the southeast ridge failed 150 feet from the summit, where a bergschrund halted progress. Michael Cohen, USA and Tony Parlane, New Zealand, climbed *Pucaranra* via the west face from the Quebrada Cojup on July 4. An Italian expedition failed on the north face of the same peak. Robert Boyd, Brock Wagstaff, Karl Gerdes and Paul Tamm, USA, climbed *Chinchey* by its west face on June 26. There were numerous ascents of *Pisco,* especially by European trekking tours. The Base Camp area there has become a disgraceful mess! Various ascents were also made of *Copa*, whose southern summit is 6188 meters or 20,303 feet high; this peak is gaining attention by climbers whose one ambition is to "get high." Unfortunately, like Huascarán, it is mistakenly considered a "walk-up" and far too many ill-prepared climbers are attempting it. *Yanapaccha Norte* was climbed by members of the Club Andinista Cordillera Blanca: Gloria Cáceres, Alcides Ames, Curry Slaymaker, Dan Langmade, David Ciochetti, Joachim Packa, Pat Weidman and me.

MICHAEL J. ROURKE, *Parque Nacional Huascarán*

Correction: On page 156 of *A.A.J.*, 1975, it stated that Romano had climbed Huascarán, but he did not reach the top. However, from the expedition on which he took part Alberto Miori, Argentine, and William Smith, English, did get to the summit.

Nevado Santa Cruz. We four, Jean Baehler, Claude Guinans, Serge Claudet and I, started our approach from Colcas, an hacienda above Caraz with one porter and ten donkeys. We took three days to go past the lake, Cullicocha, between 14,100- and 15,100-foot passes, then to go by the village of Alpamayo and to reach Base Camp on July 11 at 14,775 feet on the northeast side of the Nevado Santa Cruz. Camp I was placed at 17,725 feet at the foot of the great northeast face, where the first ascent of the mountain had been made in 1948 by Swiss. We had hoped to climb the north ridge and began to fix ropes on the lower part, despite snowy weather. We gave up the route in favor of the 1948 route. Camp II was placed on the north ridge where we emerged from the face at 19,700 feet. On July 21 Baehler, Guinans and Claudet reached the summit (20,535 feet). The descent was made *en rappel* down the great face.

JEAN-JACQUES ASPER, *Club Montagnard de l'Androsace, Switzerland*

Alpamayo, Southwest Face. A very strong team of Italians, led by Casimiro Ferrari and composed of Angelo Zoia, Danilo Borgonovo, Pino Negri, Pinuccio Castelnovo and Dr. Sandro Liati supported by the industrialist Franco Busnelli, made the first ascent of the southwest face of Alpamayo. They placed Base Camp at 12,625 feet in the Quebrada Santa Cruz. Camp I was at 15,700 feet at the foot of the glacier on the southeast slope of the Quebrada. They fixed some 650 feet of rope to reach the pass (17,400 feet) at the south end of the south ridge of Alpamayo. Camp II was some 150 feet lower in full view of the southwest face. On June 16, 17 and 18 they fixed ropes to within 650 feet of the top of the 3000-foot-high, ice-fluted face, climbing almost always in the shade. On June 20 all six climbers reached the summit.

Alpamayo and Neighboring Peaks. Mike Yokell, Matt Wells, Dan Manning, Steve Kentz, Carol Harden, Sue Giller, Jane Bunin and I established Base Camp at 15,000 feet at Pucacocha, northeast of Alpamayo. We made alpine-style ascents, using no fixed ropes or established camps. We were hampered by snow or rain almost half the days. Ascents were *Alpamayo* (19,510 feet) via the complete north ridge from the lowest point on the ridge between Alpamayo and Jancarurish by Yokell and me. (Climbing the lower part of the ridge added a day of technical climbing on a corniced ridge.); via the north ridge by Wells, Manning and Kentz, who joined Yokell and me at the col before the steep rise in the ridge, all continuing on to the north and lower summit on July 10. (On the descent we removed 1000 feet of unnecessary fixed rope, deadmen and pickets.); via the east ridge by Manning and me, a second ascent. (Using a 270-foot rope, we belayed 25 pitches along this mile-long, heavily corniced ridge and descended the north ridge. We were hampered by heavy snowfall every day during the four we spent on the climb, from July 15 to 18); *Quitaraju* west summit (c. 19,800 feet) by Wells, Kentz, Harden, Giller and Bunin on July 18 (Lack of time prevented climbing to the slightly higher east summit); *Pucarashta* (c. 18,200 feet) via the north side by Wells, Manning, Harden and Giller on July 23, a third ascent; *Jancarurish* (18,377 feet) via the southeast face by Wells, Kentz and me with Netherlander Frans Visser, a new route on this short, snow-and-ice face, just left of the east rock buttress on July 26; *Tayampampa* (18,618 feet) via the south ridge, approached by a prominent east buttress, on the next day by the same party. We spent our rest days around Base Camp flattening cans, burning trash and carrying out garbage. In addition we cleaned campsites and retrieved fixed rope high on Alpamayo. We hope future expeditions will have more respect for the area. It was clean when we left.

BRUCE A. CARSON

Hualcán, Southwest ridge. J. Curry Slaymaker and David Ciochetti made the first ascent of the southwest ridge of Hualcán (20,096 feet) on July 7. A camp was established at 17,000 feet above Laguna Cochca, where a third member of the group, Dan Langmade, stayed weak with dysentery. The two needed seven hours to complete the 50° to 60° ridge on stable snow. They then passed from the west to the slightly higher east summit. They bivouacked at 19,000 feet on the descent.

MICHAEL ROURKE

Climbs in Quebrada Ulta, 1974. My wife Jennifer, Chip Morgan, Rick Wilcox and I climbed in the Quebrada Ulta for about ten days. On July 2, 1974 we climbed P 5375 (17,634 feet), the highest point between the Nevado Ulta and the Punta Shilla (incorrectly marked on the Austrian map as the *Pasaje de Ulta*). On July 4 we climbed P 5490 (18,012 feet), the southernmost of the Contrahierbas group. Later Rick, Chip and I climbed Tullparaju, which lies above the lower end of the quebrada, opposite Huascarán.

THOMAS G. LYMAN, JR.

Huandoy Oeste, West Ridge. A French expedition completed the first ascent of the west ridge of Huandoy Oeste (20,853 feet) on August 6, 1974. The climbers were J.-L. Guyonneau, J.-L. Joubert, V. Lant, G. Lemoine and A. Zagdoun. They ascended the Rajururi but then climbed to the left out of the valley to reach the ridge, which lies to the left of the south buttress route done by the Poles in 1973. This long and difficult snow and ice ridge was defended at the base by a 350-foot rock wall and ended with a 800-foot rock step. They placed some 4000 feet of fixed rope and established three high camps.

Huandoy Group. On July 14 an Italian expedition led by Carlo Zonta with Francesco Santon as deputy set up Base Camp at the Llanganuco Lakes at 12,300 feet. The next day they placed Camp I at 15,750 feet at the foot of the south face of Huandoy Sur. By July 24 they had a camp on the top of a buttress at 18,150 feet but realized the dangers were too great. They divided, some attempting the southeast spur of Chacraraju and others on the eastern side of the Huandoy group. Those who went to Chacraraju gave up that attempt after a couple of days because of falling ice. All turned to the Huandoy climbs. On August 3 Pisco was climbed by Franco Piana, Sergio Martini, Renato Casarotto and Eugenio Battaglia, on August 4 by Lorenzo Pomodoro and Alviano Baldan, and on August 8 by Toni Gnoato and Pierino Radin. From the Pisco-Huandoy Este col on August 4 Piana, Casarotto and Martini climbed the northeast ridge of Huandoy Este (19,898 feet) and returned to the col. On August 6 the same trio started up the east ridge of the same peak, a new route, and bivouacked 650 feet from the top. On the 7th they climbed over the summit and bivouacked in the col between the east and north peaks, before descending to Parón Lake. On August 5 Gnoato and Radin climbed towards Huandoy Norte (20,980 feet; the highest summit) through the Garganta; Gnoato had to quit some 650 feet from the top but Radin went on alone. The climb was repeated on August 6 by Franco Gessi, Renato Tessarolo, Dr. Walter De Stavola and Francesco Santon. On August 15 Gnoato and Radin made the first ascent of P 5455 (17,897 feet) by its south spur. It lies some two miles south of the main peak.

Huandoy. In early July Germans Heinrich Gentner and Reinhard Siegl climbed Huandoy Norte and Sur via the eastern couloir (Garganta) route from the Cook Glacier; they established camp in the central basin. They reported technical ice conditions in the couloir complicated by avalanche hazard. These two later disappeared while climbing Huascarán. Bill Smith and Steve Belk, English, members of a Peruvian expedition, climbed Huandoy Norte by the same route on July 24.

MICHAEL ROURKE

Artesonraju. During July and August 1974, an Argentinian expedition of the Centro Andino Buenos Aires was active in the Cordillera Blanca. Bad weather defeated several attempts to climb Alpamayo by both the north and south ridges. An attempt on Artesonraju (6025 meters, 19,766 feet) was, however, successful. The peak was climbed in mid-August. Climbers were R. Alvarez, H. Cuiñas, F. Olaechea, A. Perazzo, M. Serrano, G. Varoli and G. Vieiro (leader).

EVELIO ECHEVARRÍA

Polish Climbs in the Cordillera Blanca, 1973. A party of the Polish Mountaineering Club was led by Ryszard Szafirski, accompanied by his wife Aleksandra, Walenty Fiut, Piotr Malinowski, Waclaw Otreba, Marian Pawlak, Krzysztof Szafranski and Bogdan Urganowicz. They were later joined by Richard Guzzy of Chicago, an American climber of Polish descent. They were four-and-a-half months in Peru. After caving activities, the first mountains they climbed in were the Cordillera Blanca. They later went to the Vilcabamba and Huaytapallana. (See below.) Base Camp was at 13,300 feet in the Llanganuco. On May 23 Fiut, Malinowski, Otreba, Mrs. Szafirska and Szafirski reached the summit of Huandoy Norte (20,980 feet) via the plateau. On May 26 Piut, Malinowski and Szafranski climbed Pisco. On the 28th Fiut and Otreba attempted the first ascent of the east ridge of Huandoy Sur but after three days had to retreat due to risky snow conditions. Also on May 28 Malinowski and Guzzy climbed the northwest ridge of Chopicalqui (20,998 feet) while Szafranski soloed the west ridge of Yanapaccha Sur (16,733 feet). On the 30th Szafirski soloed the west face of Yanapaccha Norte (17,651 feet). Using the Garganta route on June 9 Guzzy, Malinowski, Mrs. Szafirska and Szafirski climbed Huascarán Sur while Fiut, Otreba and Szafranski ascended Huascarán Norte. A new Base Camp was placed in the Quebrada Tayapampa. On June 16 they put up a high camp on the plateau at 17,400 feet, below Jancarurish. On June 17 Malinowski and Szafranski climbed the north ridge of Alpamayo and Otreba, Pawlak and Mrs. Szafirska reached the summit of Tayapampa (18,618 feet) by its southeast ridge. The following day Fiut and Malinowski ascended the southeast face of Jancarurish (18,377 feet).

MAREK BRNIAK, *Klub Wysokogórski, Poland*

Polish Climbers in the Cordillera Blanca. The Polish Earth Sciences Society Expedition carried out glaciological studies on the Broggi Glacier. They made the following ascents: Yanapaccha Oeste, Pisco, Huandoy Norte (via east couloir), Huasacarán Norte and Sur, Tocllaraju, Copa and Aquilpo. Expedition members were Wladyslaw Borowiec, Jerzy Dobrzynski, Jan Gyurczak, Ryszard Kosiol, Roman Krasowski, Andrzej Lenda, Adam Lewandowski, Jarek Moszinski, Jerzy Niewodniczanski, Andrzej Paulo, Kazimier Rosiak, Andrzej Skwiczynski and Jan Wozniak.

MICHAEL ROURKE

Chacraraju, East Ridge Attempt. A Yugoslavian expedition of the Akademsko Planinsko Drustvo of Ljubljana was led by Aleksander Blazina. On July 4 Igor Golli died after falling 1300 feet down the south face of Chacraraju when he was pulled from his belay near the rock band on the east ridge. Later other members of the expedition unsuccessfully attempted Huascarán and climbed the southwest ridge of Chopicalqui on July 18.

MICHAEL ROURKE

Peaks Above Quebrada Honda. Our group all reached Base Camp on Viñollapampa at 13,775 feet in the Quebrada Honda on July 5. Despite bad weather we placed Camp I at 15,750 feet and Camp II at 18,000 feet up the Chinchey Glacier. Bad snow conditions prevented our reaching higher than 19,700 feet on Chinchey. On July 19 Salvador Boix, Enrique Font and I tried the south ridge and on the 20th Francisco Viñeta and Angel del Pozo attempted the northwest ridge. On July 23 Viñeta and del Pozo with the porter Humberto Henostroza climbed P 5300 (17,389 feet) in the Copap group and Font, José Fabre and Pedro Planas climbed Chaco (17,389 feet).

EMILIO BUSQUETS, *Unión Excursionista de Cataluña, Gerona*

Chinchey, Chaco. Our expedition, composed of Giacomo Casartelli, Luciano Gilardoni, Riccardo Soresini, Enrico Tettamanti, Marco Zappa and me as leader, climbed in the Quebrada Honda. Base Camp was on a lake at 14,600 feet. We placed Camp I up the icefall that heads the valley at 16,000 feet and Camp II at 18,000 feet on the Quilcayhuanca-Honda divide. Our attempts on Chinchey's north and south ridges were stopped by séracs but we put our main effort into a direct route on the west face. Our first attempt was halted by the weather but after a bivouac at 19,200 feet, Soresini, Tettamanti, Zappa, Casartelli and I climbed to the summit of Chinchey (20,413 feet) on August 18. Also on August 18 Gilardoni with the Peruvian Emilio Angeles climbed Chaco (17,454 feet) by its east face.

RINO ZOCCHI, *Club Alpino Italiano*

Climbs above Quebrada Ishinca. The following summits were reached by members of the Iowa Mountaineers: Tocllaraju (19,790 feet) from Ishinca by Donnie Black, Norman Benton, Tim Schuld, Bruce Schneider, Cleveland Bell, Rick Droker on July 15; Sven Olof Swartling, William Hagan, Stuart Jones, Bruce Hamilton, Susan Cochrane, on July 24; Urus Este (17,783 feet) by Schuld, Mark Freed, Arthur Mudge, Bell, Schneider, Jones, Harold Goodro, Benton on July 9; John Ebert, Jim Ebert, Howard Higley, Joe Vance, Fred Lang, Richard Soaper on July 10; D. Black, George Stransky, Steven Yeagle, Droker, Hamilton, Joe Gross on July 11; Les Harms, Stan Engle on July 12; Swartling, Cochran, Hagan, Mudge on July 13; Kim and Nancy Malville, Reed Loefgren on July 15; Urus Oeste (17,881 feet) by Kesler Teter, Sheldon Moomaw, K. and N. Malville, Mudge, William Reenstra on July 10; Engle, Harms, Don Warte, John Reilly, Soaper, Loefgren on July 11; Swartling, Hagan, Cochran, Benton, Dave Broemel, Hamilton on July 12; Sam Black, Hudson, Millie Rose, Schuld, Hamilton, Jones, Bell, Tom Reilly on July 13; Goodro, Loefgren, Jim Ebert on July 14; Ishinca (18,143 feet) by Hamilton, Yeagle, Droker, Broemel, Swartling, Cochran, Hagan, J. Reilly on July 10; Goodro, Lang, Jones, Schneider, Schuld, Bell on June 11; Vance, Moomaw, S. Black, Higley on July 21; Teter, K. and N. Malville, Reenstra, Soaper, Stransky on July 13; Engle, Harms, Jon Lawyer, Yeagle, Hudson, S. Black, J. Reilly on June 14.

S. JOHN EBERT

Palcaraju Oeste. Our expedition was composed of Josep Piera, leader, Albert Altet, Lluís Ambròs, Eduard Ballbè, Esteva Cardellach and me. With the veteran porter Eustaquio Henostroza, we set up Base Camp in the Quebrada Ishinca at 14,400 feet on July 29, Camp I at 16,250 feet and Camp III on the Palcaraju Glacier at 17,400 feet. The first summit attempt failed at a great crevasse at 19,500 feet, but on August 12 Piera and I reached the top of Palcaraju Oeste (20,046 feet) via the southwest ridge and west face. We two had climbed Ishinca (18,143 feet) the day before. Urus Este (17,782 feet) was climbed on August 4 by Cardellach and Piera and on August 6 by Altet and Ballbè.

JOAQUIM PRUNÉS, *Grup d'Iniciatives de Muntanya, Terrassa, Spain*

Climbs in the Cordillera Blanca. Our party consisted of Ernest and Richard Hildner, Ernest Kuncl, and me. During a brief trip into Quebrada Ishinca we ascended two peaks, Ishinca (18,143 feet) on July 20, and Urus Este (18,012 feet) on July 23. A subsequent attempt on Huascarán by the Hildners and E. Kuncl was abandoned just short of the Garganta in order to render emergency medical treatment and evacuate two injured members of a Japanese women's expedition. On

August 1 Burl Mostul, Alberto Miori, Steve Belk, and I reached the summit of Vallunaraju (18,655 feet), starting from Laguna Llaca. Although excellent weather prevailed for all of our climbs, snow on south slopes was frequently knee to hip deep, the result of unseasonal snowfall during early July.

THOMAS BOWEN, *California State University, Fresno*

Spanish Climbs in 1974. An expedition from Tarrasa made the following climbs: Urus Este (17,782 feet) on August 4, 1974 by Esteban Cardellach and José Piera and on August 6 by Alberto Altet and Eduardo Ballbe; Ishinca (18,143 feet) on August 11 by Piera and Joaquín Prunes; and Palcaraju Oeste (19,686 feet) on August 12 by Piera and Prunes. In July, 1974 Jaime Fabrés Amoros and his wife Rosa joined ten French climbers led by Patrice de Bellefont and climbed Jancarurish (18,377 feet) and Tayapampa (18,618 feet).

Jangyaraju and Vallunaraju Group*. On June 20, 28 members and friends of the Club Andinista Cordillera Blanca left Huaraz for the Quebrada Llaca as a weekend family affair. On June 21 the climbing members established camp at the base of the eastern glacier of Vallunaraju Sur directly below the south-ridge col. That afternoon Curry Slaymaker, Dan Langmade, David Ciochetti and I prepared a route through the soft crusted snow to the col. The following day three routes were made to the summit (18,389 feet) of Vallunaraju Sur: Mauro Arias, Pat Miller, César Aguirre and Joachim Packa via the central col and north ridge, Langmade and Slaymaker via the northwest face and north ridge and Ciochetti via the west face and south ridge. On August 1 Slaymaker and Ciochetti established camp at 16,400 feet in the Jangyaraju glacial basin. From there they climbed Jangyaraju Oeste (17,881 feet) via the west ridge and Vallunaraju Norte (18,675 feet) via the north ridge on August 2 and Jangyaraju Este (18,675 feet) via the northwest ridge and Jangyaraju Central (18,471 feet) via the southeast ridge.

MICHAEL ROURKE

---

* There has been confusion about these peaks in the past. They may be seen but not always named as such in the German Alpine Club map 1:100,000, 1939. Three Jangyaraju peaks are given there, from west to east, with the following altitudes: Jangyaraju Oeste (5450m), Jangyaraju Central (5630m) and Jangyaraju Este (5675m). In Evelio Echevarría's "Survey of Andean Ascents," *A.A.J.*, 1973, 18:2, pages 356, 354 and 353, they appear as Bolívar, San Martín and P 5675 respectively. The Vallunaraju peaks appear with altitudes of 5688m for the northern and 5605m for the southern one. They lie south of Jangyaraju Central and northwest of Laguna Llaca.—*Editor.*

Uruashraju. On July 27 Joachim Packa, David Ciochetti, Dan Langmade, Curry Slaymaker and I made the second ascent of Uruashraju
via the unclimbed south ridge. Domingos Giobbi describes the peak in
A.A.J., 1967, pp. 386 as "tent-shaped with west, north, northeast and
southeast ridges." Actually the peak displays west, north, east and
south (slightly southwest) ridges. On July 26 we placed camp at 17,000
feet above the Quebrada Pumahuacanca about 300 feet below the lowest
point on the south ridge. The following day we climbed the ridge and
followed it to the south buttress. A crest as described by Giobbi in
his 1965 and 1967 accounts connects this point to the summit. The
crest was heavily corniced to the west but we found adequate opportunity to protect our progress by going out on the southeast wall.

MICHAEL ROURKE

Ango. Felix Golling, German, Tom Hardy, American, Keith Woodford, Australian, and I approached Ango (16,811 feet) from the Quebrada
Pajush and climbed the snow slopes on the northwest shoulder to reach
its summit on August 13, 1974, ascending from the Ango-Chúcaro col.
The next day we climbed Chúcaro.

JOHN RICKER

Peru—Cordillera Huayhuash

Sarapo, Southwest Ridge, 1974. The members of our expedition to
Sarapo were Giovanni Albertelli, Italo Bazzani, Pietro Favalli, Erminio
Guerrini, Alfredo Rocca, Guido Rocco, Francesco Veclani, Franco
Aliprandi and I as leader. From Cajatambo we crossed the San Cristóbal
Pass to Pumarinri valley, which we descended to the river junctions, ascended and went up the Huallapa valley to where it branches, the right
going to Lake Jurau. We kept left up a very steep section which opened
into the broad Quebrada Sarapococha, at the end of which we placed
Base Camp at 14,100 feet. On July 18 we went past Sarapococha (lake)
and climbed moraine to reach the Siulá Glacier. We placed Camp I
up the glacier at 15,850 feet. From Camp I we headed east and then
south when wide crevasses prevented progress, skirting under the enormous walls of Siulá Chico and Siulá Grande. Camp II was at 16,925
feet. It was 200 yards south to the base of the center of the northwest
face of Sarapo. On July 29 Bazzini and Rocco set out, supported by
Guerrini and Veclani. The upper lip of the bergschrund overhung and
had to be crossed on the right side of a small hanging sérac. The face
was 1300 feet high and presented difficulties because of its 70° angle
and unstable snow and ice. When they reached the southwest ridge at
18,475 feet, they had to climb the crest for 800 feet with great difficulty
because of unstable snow and vertical steps. They dug out a bivouac at

18,900 feet on the ridge. On July 30 they climbed the rest of the ridge to reach a great funnel in the south face. They climbed the funnel straight up until they veered right up an ice spur which led to a steep, dangerous couloir that ended on the summit (20,155 feet).

TULLIO CORBELLINI, *Club Alpino Italiano*

Puscanturpa Norte, Northwest Face. An Italian expedition led by Graziano Bianchi and composed of Felice Boselli, Giuseppe Buizza, Giuseppe Caneva, Agostino Da Polenza, Carlo Milani, Gino Mora and Edoardo Pozzoli returned to Puscanturpa Norte, which they had unsuccessfully attempted in 1974 (*A.A.J.*, 1975, 20:1, p. 165; photo p. 167). They traveled by truck through Oyón to Surasaca Lake (14,450 feet). The approach took them two days from there via Viconga Lake and Cuyoc Pass to arrive on July 27 at Base Camp at 15,250 feet. Reconnaissance and ferrying loads went on immediately. They found they could use some but not all of the rope fixed the year before. On July 29 they were already at the 1974 high point at 17,000 feet. Camp I was set up near there on July 30, a veritable eagle's nest. The difficulties were continuous, extreme and comparable to those of the Dolomites, first on rock and then on mixed terrain. Finally on August 4 they placed a camp on a little saddle below the last 500-foot rock pitch. Bianchi and Da Polenza found a route to the right of the overhangs. They prepared the route on August 5 and nearly reached the summit snow ridge. On the 6th they climbed the last 250 feet of rock to reach the snow-covered ice of the final ridge, which they followed to the summit (18,541 feet) of this precipitous and difficult peak. (Compiled from information graciously sent by Signor Bianchi.)

Yerupajá Sur, 1974. Spaniards Alfonso Arias, Miguel and Luis López, Eduardo Barroso, André Fernández, Emilio Torrico and Emilio García climbed Yerupajá Sur in late July, 1974.

Yanacaico or Mitopunta, Southern Cordillera Huayhuash. On June 20 David Isles, Harry Eldridge, Elliott Fisher, Nan Cochran, Charles (Chip) Morgan, Hall Hutchison and I headed over the small pass north of Cajatambo and dropped into the Pumarinri valley, which we ascended towards the east until we were below the Quebrada Yanacaico. We then climbed steeply to the north into that valley to place Base Camp at 14,500 feet at the edge of vegetation. Camp I was established on June 24 at the upper end of the valley at 16,000 feet above two lovely glacial lakes on the left lateral moraine. The next day all except for Nan Cochran climbed a couloir above camp to the col between what the local shepherds call Yanacaico (but which appears on the Instituto Geográfico Militar *Yanahuanca* map as "Mitopunta") and Yanacaico Norte (c.

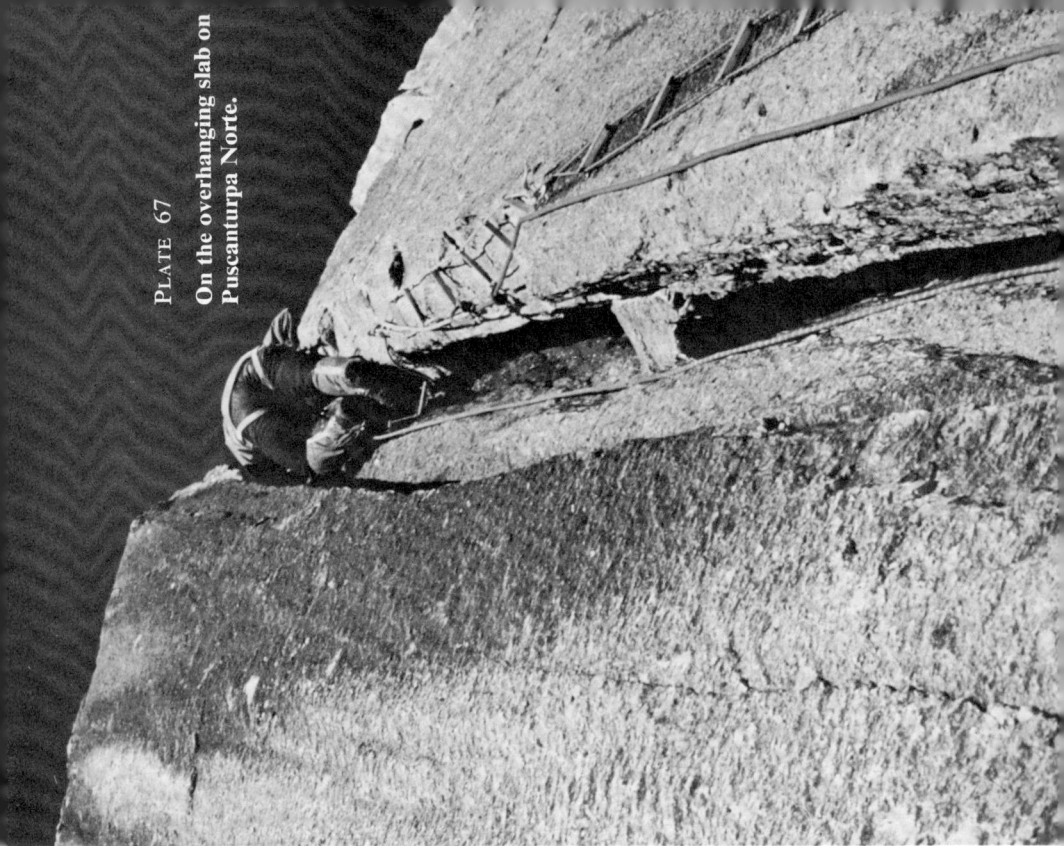

PLATE 67

On the overhanging slab on Puscanturpa Norte.

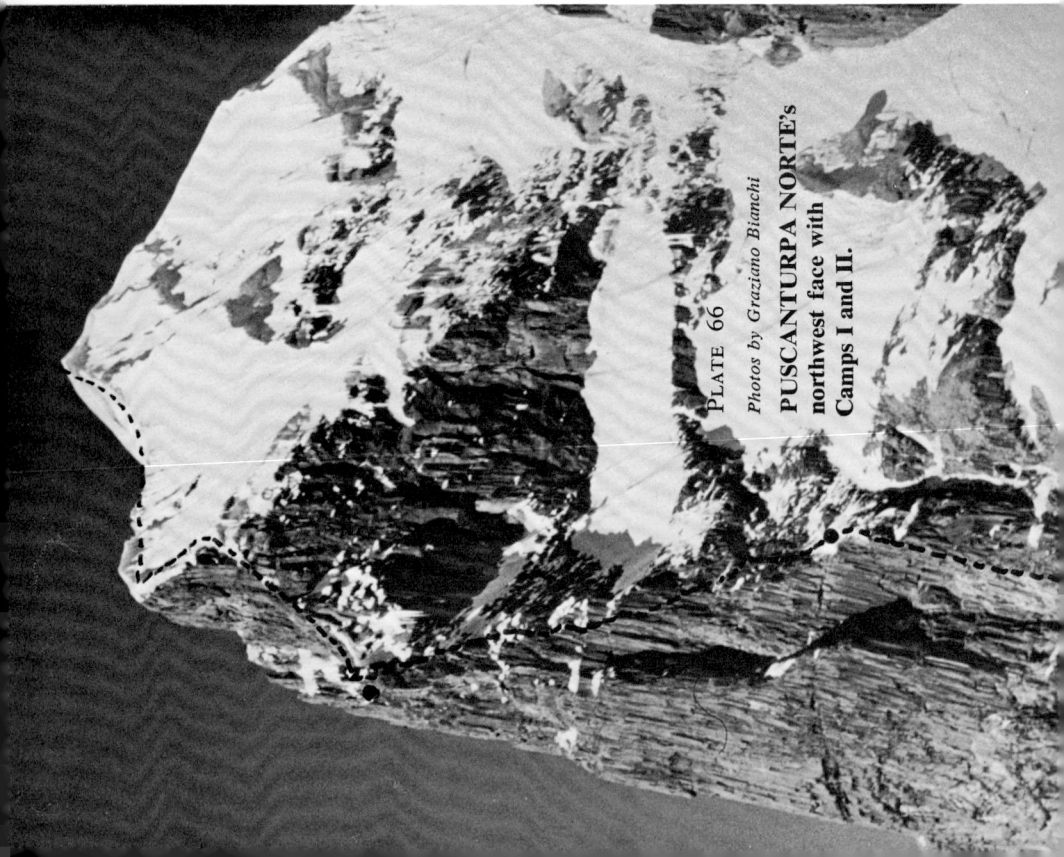

PLATE 66

Photos by Graziano Bianchi

PUSCANTURPA NORTE's northwest face with Camps I and II.

18,000 feet). We climbed to the summit of Yanacaico Norte, only the last rope-length being really steep. Fisher, Nan Cochran and I made the second ascent two days later. Most of the party continued on north along the western side of the ridge, hoping to climb the next peak to the north, P 5572, but a blank wall of perpendicular, smooth rock interrupted progress. On June 29, all but Nan and I again climbed the couloir and headed south along the ridge of Yanacaico (18,278 feet). They passed two false summits, climbed steep and corniced sections and finally reached the summit, a huge cornice which hung out to the west. We traveled for four days along the whole eastern flank of the Cordillera Huayhuash to emerge at Chiquián in our return to civilization.

H. Adams Carter

Notes on Names of Peaks in the Cordillera Huayhuash. The Quechua of different regions of Peru differs considerably. On the eastern slope of the Cordillera Huayhuash it is quite different from that of the Cordillera Blanca. For that reason and because my investigations were limited to a few days, these findings are somewhat tentative. The maps of the Instituto Geográfico Militar of Peru seem to be excellent topographically but the nomenclature is hopelessly inaccurate; for instance the pampa on the southwestern shore of Lago Viconga is really Matipaqui (broken gourd) but it appears as Matiraqui on the map. Some of the names which appear on the map are completely unknown locally; on the southern rim of the range the peak which appears on the map as "Mitopunta" is actually called Yanacaico (black corral from *yana* (black) + *caico* (corral)), getting its name from the enclosed valley of the same name above which it rises. Jirishanca comes from *jirish* (hummingbird) + *janca* or *shanca* (cold place or snow mountain); there is no mention of the hummingbird's bill, usually given as part of the meaning of the name, though this may be implied because of the shape of the peak. Ninashanca comes from *nina* (fire) + *janca* or *shanca*, possibly getting its name from red rock. *Siulá* means cold. *Rasac* means toad. *Puscanturpa* means distaff. (The first part should be pronounced *putskan,* which signifies spinning.) *Tsacra* is an animal lair and *Puyoc* means rotten or moth-eaten. One informant told me that *Sarapo* means funnel, but this I could not confirm.

H. Adams Carter

Nudo Millpo, 1974. On our expedition from Italy, I was accompanied by my wife Maria, Giuseppe Cazzaniga, Italo Valmaggia, Giancarlo Del Zotto and Celso Salvetti. From July 28 to August 22, 1974 we were in the mountains, which lie just south of the Huayhuash and west of the Raura. We explored the Pumarinri valley up to Laguna Viconga. Above and east of the Quebrada Alpayacu, all of us on August

3, 1974 climbed P 5190 (17,028 feet), the first peak on the ridge which runs southwest from Millpo Grande to Cerro Piruyapunta, and P 5160 (16,929 feet). On the 6th Cazzaniga and Valmaggia climbed Millpo Chico (17,323 feet) along its southwest ridge. On the 8th Cazzaniga, Valmaggia and Del Zotto ascended Jancacuta (17,684 feet) while Maria and I climbed P 5120 (16,962 feet), which lies 1¼ miles south of Millpo Chico and east of Jancacuta.

FABIO MASCIADRI, *Club Alpino Italiano*

Millpo Grande. The Millpo group lies south of the Huayhuash and separated from it by the Pumarinri valley and west of the Raura and separated from it by the Surasaca valley. After the 1974 Italian expedition, the eastern side of the group remained to be explored and the highest point to be climbed. Those who took part in the expedition were Celso Salvetti, leader, Fabio Masciadri, Vittorio Meroni, Italo Valmaggia and I. Leaving Lima on July 29, we set up camp in the Champahuay-pampa valley at 15,500 feet on August 1 and a high camp in the col between Millpo Grande and Millpo Chico on August 3. On the following day, Meroni and I climbed the ice-covered south face and overcoming difficulties with ice pitons, reached the summit of Millpo Grande (18,400 feet)*. On August 6 all members reached the summit of Millpo Norte (17,700 feet), climbing the east face alternately on rock and snow. During the following days we climbed three other minor peaks of about 16,500 feet.

LODOVICO GAETANI, *Club Alpino Italiano*

Huacshash, Southern Cordillera Huayhuash. After our Bolivian climbs (see that section), we went through Cajatambo and ascended the Quebrada Ularagra to establish Base Camp a mile northeast of Huacshash at 16,400 feet on the slopes of P 5295 (17,372 feet; "Cerro Amistad"). On April 6 Jaskuła, Lisiecki, my wife and I made a new route on the latter, the great chimney in the northeast ridge. On April 10 Wawrzyniak, Gutowski and Zimny made another new route on the peak, the west buttress. On April 8 Wawrzyniak, my wife and I made the second ascent of P 5265[1] (17,273 feet; 1 mile north-northeast of Huacshash) by its northeast ridge; this climb was repeated on April 13 by Chrzan and Lisiecki and on April 14 by Zimny and Jaskuła. On April 9 Wawrzyniak, my wife and I made the second ascent of Copan[1] (18,061 feet) by its

---

* This altitude seems too high from personal observations and from the Peruvian I.G.M. maps. Possibly 5500 meters or 18,045 feet would be a more accurate height.—*Editor.*

[1] First ascent by P. Malinowski and W. Jedliñski in 1974.

southwest ridge, a climb repeated on April 14 by Jaskula and Zimny. On April 8 to 10 Chrzan, Jaskula made the second ascent of Huacshash[2] (18,517 feet) by a new route, the northwest ridge. On April 11 and 12 Wawrzyniak, my wife and I, followed by Zimny and Gutowski, made another new route, the center of the southwest glacier. On April 13 and 14 Chrzan, Lisiecki, Wawrzyniak, my wife and I made the second ascent of P 5495[1] (18,028 feet; northeast of P 5265) by its southwest ridge. We suffered from bad conditions as we were there in the rainy season.

MARIUSZ GREBIENIOW, *Akademicka Wyprawa Górska, Poland*

Central Peru

Huagaruncho, Northeast Ridge. The Workers' Mountain Club of Takamatsu Expedition was composed of Hideaki Naoi, leader, Akira Yamada, Hiroshi Kuriyama, Tomomi Akiyama (female), Yoshiki Mitsumoto (female), Kazuhiro Oka and Masao Hashimoto. Leaving Huachón on June 10, they packed over three passes to the Quebrada Huagaruncho and on June 11 over another pass to place Base Camp at 14,000 feet on a terrace near a lake up in Río Huarancayo. They decided on the unclimbed northeast ridge. Camp I was placed on June 17 at 15,950 feet on the col south of Peak 29. They prepared the route in the next days, reaching a minor summit at 17,925 feet on June 28. On the 29th they prepared the route to the col in the northeast ridge at 17,625 feet beyond the minor peak. They placed Camp II in the col on July 1. The route was then prepared to 18,000 feet on the 3rd. On July 4 Hashimoto, Yamada and Oka reached the summit (18,799 feet), followed on July 6 by Akiyama, Mitsumoto, Oka and Naoi.

ICHIRO YOSHIZAWA, *A.A.C.* and *Japanese Alpine Club*

Lasontay, Cordillera Huaytapallana, 1973. Having already climbed in the Cordilleras Blanca and Vilcabamba (see above), on August 6, 1973 Fiut, Guzzy and Malinowski made the first ascent of the west ridge of Lasontay Sur or Yuracrumi (18,230 feet) and Fiut and Malinowski went on to make the first ascent of the east ridge of Lasontay Norte (18,045 feet). On August 8 they climbed the south ridge of Huaytapallana (c. 16,400 feet).

MAREK BRNIAK, *Klub Wysokogórski, Poland*

Rajuntay, South Ridge, Cordillera Central. An experienced Italian group traveled to the Italian Alpine Club hut in the Santa Eulalia valley.

---

[1] First ascent by P. Malinowski and W. Jedliñski in 1974.

[2] First ascent by three members of the Club Andino Oyen, Máximo Luna, Sergio Zúñiga and Abel Lozano, in 1957.

On August 2 they moved to a 14,775-foot base in the valley opposite the one where the hut was. Camp I was placed at 16,750 feet below the south ridge. On August 6 Mario Conti, Carlo Dell'Oro and Luigino Airoldi fixed rope on the lower part of the ridge. These three, joined by Giancarlo Riva and Emilio Valsecchi, climbed the ridge on the 7th. They placed six snow pickets and ten rock pitons on the two rock steps. Thanks to the fixed ropes and good snow conditions they reached the top at two P.M.

Llongote Central, Cordillera Yauyos. Seven members of the High Mountain Club of Lódź took part in the expedition: Wojciech Jedliński, Bogdan Mac, Piotr Malinowski, Marek Rozniecki, Jerzy Star, Grzegorz Wasiak and I as leader. On May 29, 1974 we placed Base Camp on Huascacocha. On June 2 and 3, Mac, Rozniecki, Star, Wasiak and I climbed by its west ridge P 5280 (17,323 feet), which lies between Cotoní (or Ticlla) and Huaynacutuni. On June 4 and 5 Jedliński and Malinowski ascended from the northern side the three peaks of Nevado Huamalla, P 5297 (17,397 feet) and to the west of the main peak, P 5080 and P 5210 (16,667 and 17,093 feet). On June 6 and 7 Star and I made the ascent of Llongote Central (18,406 feet) by its north face. On June 9 and 10 Jedliński, Mac, Malinowski and I climbed Acopalca (17,866 feet) and P 5420 (17,782 feet) just east of it. On June 11, I soloed P 5057 (16,591 feet; 2 miles north of the western end of Huascacocha). For our Bolivian climbs, see that section.

JERZY MICHAELSKI, *Lódź, Poland*

Surihuiri and Minaspata, Cordillera Chila. I was in overall charge of the Japan Inner Amazon Expedition and Ichiyo Muko was leader. Ko Hagiwara and Kohichi Miura entered the Cordillera Chila, east of Coropuna and north of Ampato, the main and longest source of the Amazon River. They drove to Quencco and walked to the head of the Quebrada Pacopampa and Base Camp at 16,400 feet on September 5. On the 7th they left at 7:45 and walked for three miles along scree at about 17,000 feet to reach a col below Minaspata at 12:45. They traversed along the steep east side of the north ridge and reached the ridge crest in its middle, which was difficult walking with many *penitentes*. They reached the summit of Minaspata (18,061 feet) at 2:35. They descended the north side of the east ridge, past more *penitentes*, to a col at 3:50 and bivouac. On the 8th at 9:15 they traversed the northwest side of the peak opposite the col and climbed the north ridge to arrive on top at 11:25. They descended to the southwest to a col. From there they climbed the long northwest ridge of Surihuiri over *penitentes*, false summits and a rock peak on the north side to reach a gentle snow ridge. They got to the summit of Surihuiri (18,064 feet) at 2:50 P.M., a wide snowfield in a thick fog. They returned by the same route to the bivouac. On the 9th they crossed along the eastern face of Minaspata to Base Camp.

ICHIRO YOSHIZAWA, *A.A.C.* and *Japanese Alpine Club*

Peru—Cordillera Vilcanota

Ritipampa del Quelccaya. A field party from the Institute of Polar Studies, The Ohio State University, Columbus, Ohio, made several ascents of the Ritipampa del Quelccaya, an ice plateau in the Cordillera Vilcanota, during the course of glaciological and geological investigations, in late June and early July, 1974. We approached the region from Sicuani, and climbed the icecap from the west. The field party was led by John Mercer, and included Cedomir Marangunic, Lonnie Thompson, and John Ricker. Our purpose was to conduct a preliminary study of the glaciology and glacial geology of the icecap and its environs to determine whether a large-scale investigation should be mounted. A snow pit was dug on the summit of the icecap to a depth of 3.8 meters and a 3-meter core was taken from the bottom of the pit. Preliminary analysis suggests an annual accumulation of about 3 meters. The icecap is probably temperate. Glacial geological studies were concentrated in the valley of the Río Huancane. The moraine belts, 1, 5, and 9 km from the present ice margin, were examined. Glaciological studies included an examination of the pit wall stratigraphy, firn temperature measurements, and laboratory analysis of snow samples for oxygen isotope and microparticle concentrations. Preliminary results have been published in the *Antarctic Journal of the United States* of January-February 1975.

JOHN RICKER, *A.A.C.* and PETER J. ANDERSON,
Institute of Polar Studies

Chicllarazo, Cordillera de la Apacheta, and other climbs. Chuquichanca (Cordillera Vilcanota) revisited. The Apacheta is the first high pass (15,436 feet, 4705 meters) on the Via de los Libertadores from Ayacucho to the coast, not far from Lircay's celebrated Tambrayco. I had been lured to the place by Clements Markham's narrative but felt that the charm has gone with the opening of the new road. I climbed Chicllarazo (16,925 feet, 5167 meters) from here on June 17 via Patahuasi and its west ridge. This is the gray glacier-hung peak seen east from the pass which on modern maps has unnecessarily been called "Nevado Portuguesa." It serves as a first order triangulation point and affords a view of the eastern Andes ranging from Huaytapallana to Salcantay, and of the mysterious obelisk of El Tambrayco, just 18 miles northwest. Late on June 22 I left Hacienda San José down the Pariahuanca for Panti where suspicious locals stopped me in the dark. Hours later I managed to escape uphill to Pucacocha and along the irrigation ditch northward into Quebrada Taulibamba and a dense *ceja* vegetation. The inner valley turns west and leads up to Illaycocha. At nine A.M. I was just in time to see the green lake before fog closed in. An icefall descends all along the south ridge of Illayrazo to its end in the lake. The lower part of the ridge is an amazingly well carved knife-edge, called Laso Tumi—glacier's knife—on Hacienda maps. I spent a night on Cerro Illaycocha (south of the lake, P 4690), quickly climbed Jatun Suni (16,010 feet, 4880 meters) and traversed into Jallalampa in almost constant fog and clouds. Jatun Suni refers to the flat-topped and southernmost glacier peak of the Huaytapallana Karu range, south-southwest of Illayrazo. A two-day excursion from Pucará, northwest of the Huarón mine, led me to the Chuchon entrance of Cordillera Callejón and up the Yuracyacu trail to a bivouac near Janchaycocha, Quebrada Ushpas, on June 27. At dawn I climbed Chururuyo (17,756 feet; P 5412 of the Miller survey) by its north side and east ridge. Locals rather seem to pronounce it Churuyoc. It provides a splendid view of all the lakes of the high puna, particularly in the morning, and of the distant Nevado Ulcumayo due east. On July 4 I passed the Cordillera Huaritanga from Huancayo to Huari, Chiquiac Pampa and the lake Yanacocha and climbed Cerro Asapara (15,879 feet, 4840 meters) the next day with excellent weather, then out to Añas and Trancapampa. A west-to-east traverse of the Acuyac ridge (16,404 feet, 5000 meters) offered a panorama of the lovely Laguna Pomacanchi (6 miles south) and the remote snow-peaks of Chumbivilcas and Coropuna. There is no water on Acuyac, the highest source found near Maychani (July 16). In the Marcapata valley, I made my way into the Chuquichanca granite area from San Isidro (see map in *A.A.J.*, 1971, p. 418) and climbed Nevado de Comercocha (3 miles north of Yungate, c. 15,584 feet, 4750 meters); Yungate (c. 16,076 feet, 4900 meters), and Ananta (halfway between Nevado de Comercocha and Kiruyoj, c. 15,748 feet, 4800 meters) on July 26 and 28 respectively. On Yungate the route was up the northwest gully and the south ridge to the north (main) summit and down the west side.

OLAF HARTMANN, *Göttingen University*

Colque Cruz Group, Cordillera Vilcanota, 1974. The British Commonwealth Andean Expedition consisted of Dr. Jeff Boyd, Howard Dengate and me, Australians; Mike Browne, Jim Jolly, Miss Jos Lang and Keith Woodford, New Zealanders; and Arthur Twomey, Canadian. With 19 horses hired from Mallma and Yanacancha, we moved to the head of the Quebrada Huiscachani de Yanacancha to establish Base Camp under the north face of Colque Cruz I at 15,750 feet. Weather and snow conditions were perfect during the whole stay. Colque Cruz had first been climbed by the Germans März, Steinmetz and Wellenkamp in 1953 from the south from the next valley parallel to ours, and again

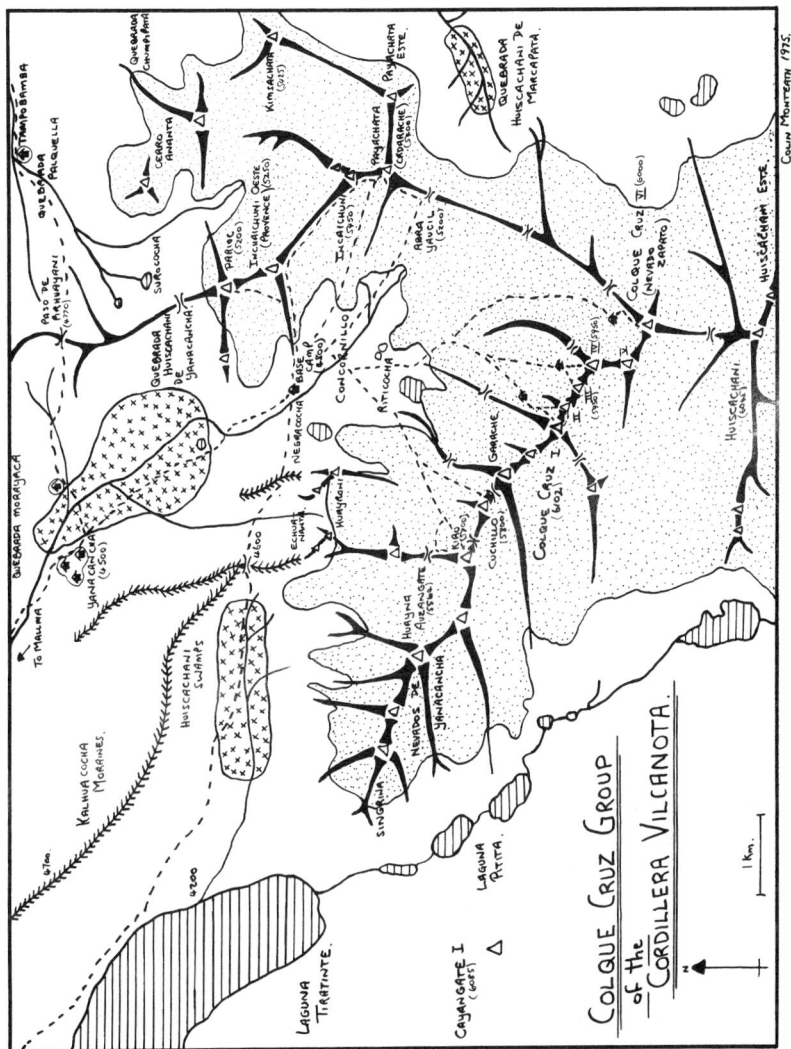

COLQUE CRUZ GROUP of the CORDILLERA VILCANOTA.

in 1965 by Japanese. Colque Cruz VI had been climbed by the Harvard Expedition in 1957. The other peaks appeared to have been virgin. No attempts had been made from our valley. During six weeks we made the following major ascents: Colque Cruz I² (20,019 feet) via north face on June 4 to 6, 1974 by Twomey, Monteath, Woodford, Browne (a really fine, though relatively straightforward snow and ice route. We were caught out on the descent by wind and darkness at 19,000 feet and bivouacked until the moon came out before descending to Camp at

17,500 feet); Colque Cruz IV[1] (19,521 feet) via north face by Wood-ford, Monteath and northeast ridge by Twomey, Jolly on June 15 and via a variation on the north face by Browne, Boyd on June 16; Colque Cruz VI[2] (c. 19,685 feet) via northeast ridge by Woodford, Jolly, Boyd, Lang, Monteath on June 23 (We decided against the complete traverse of the Colque Cruz group because of dangerous cornices.); Colque Cruz III[1] (19,521 feet) via a difficult ice route on the north face by Woodford, Jolly on June 27; Colque Cruz VI[2] via difficult northeast face by Browne, Twomey on June 27; Colque Cruz III[1] (19,685 feet) via north face by Lang, Boyd on June 26; Colque Cruz I[2] via southeast ridge by Lang, Boyd on June 30 (200 feet from the summit on this new route, Miss Lang fell 60 feet into a hidden crevasse and spent two agonizing hours prusiking and climbing out). This ascent was the ninth new route on the Colque Cruz massif; three of them led to virgin summits. Other ascents included the following: Payachata or Cadarache[2] (17,717 feet) via south ridge from Abra Yaucil by Browne, Monteath, Twomey, Woodford on May 29; Incaichuni[1] (17,881 feet) via northwest face by Browne, Mon-teath, Twomey, Woodford on May 31 and via southeast ridge by Boyd, Jolly, Lang on June 11; Parioc[1] (17,061 feet) via southwest face by Boyd, Lang on June 14 and via southwest-north traverse by Browne, Twomey on June 23; Kiru (18,767 feet) via northeast face by Jolly, Lang, Twomey, Woodford and via north ridge[2] by Boyd, Monteath, both on June 17; and Incaichuni Oeste (17,225 feet) via west ridge by Mon-teath on May 28, by Jolly, Boyd on June 9, by Monteath, Lang, Betty Heslip on June 19 and by Pauline O'Connor on June 24. After a com-plete circle around the Vilcanota range, we moved into the Auzangate area and camped under its southwest wall. From here Browne and Two-mey made on July 15 via the northeast ridge an ascent of Tacirani (17,553 feet), a fine rock and ice spire. In late July Jolly and the Australian Howard Bevan climbed the northeast ridge of Cayangate I (19,964 feet), apparently a new route.

COLIN MONTEATH, *New Zealand Alpine Club*

Peru—Cordillera Vilcabamba

Salcantay, 1973. After their climbs in the Cordillera Blanca (see that section), five of the climbers moved to the Vilcabamba, the rest having left for Poland. Base Camp was at 15,600 feet at the foot of Salcantay. On July 13, 1973 Guzzy and Pawlak climbed Chuycan (17,553 feet) and on the 15th Malinowski and Szafirski reached the summit of Salcan-tay (20,574 feet) via its north ridge.

MAREK BRNIAK, *Klub Wysokogórski, Poland*

[1] First ascent.
[2] New route.

Pumasillo, 1974. New Zealanders Alison Watkins and Howard Conway completed the west ridge on Pumasillo on June 17, 1974 after two-and-a-half days of climbing.

Bolivia

Huayna Potosí, West Face. Jim States, John Roskelley and I climbed the west face of Huayna Potosí in two days with the second bivouac on the summit. The mountain has two west faces. The left one was climbed by Janney and party in 1970. The right one is a triangle of rock and ice ending on the south summit and is 3600 feet high. It was consistently steep with several difficult pitches in thin ice gullies which we followed to get through the rock bands. To acclimatize we did the Tres Picos above the Mina Fabulosa. The southernmost and lowest (about 16,400 feet) was done by Roskelley and States. The highest and northernmost (c. 16,725 feet) and the central peaks were climbed by all. These may be the first ascents of all three. The approach was made from the Zongo valley by way of the Estancia Coscapa.

ROMAN LABA

Condoriri, Huayna Potosí, Huacaña and Other Peaks, Cordillera Real, Sajama, and Parinacota (Chile). Our Bayerische Naturfreunde (Bavarian Friends of Nature) expedition was composed of Theo Dowbenka, Alois Wolfram, Peter Rotter, Heinrich Händel, Josef Klingshirn and me as leader. We first unsuccessfully attempted a route on Condoriri (18,531 feet) from the southeast but were beaten back by the weather and new snow. On May 17 Rotter and Händel climbed by its north slope P 5328 (17,481 feet), south of Condoriri Oeste. On May 20 and 21 all of us but Rotter climbed Condoriri Oeste (18,149 feet) by its western ridge and descended the north face. Rotter climbed Estaño (16,897 feet) solo by its west face on May 22. We moved to the Huayna Potosí group, where we all climbed Huayna Potosí (19,996 feet) by its east ridge and east face. Dowbenka and Wolfram went on to the slightly lower south summit. We then traveled north to Huacaña (20,360 feet), which Dowbenka and I climbed on June 12 by its east ridge. On June 8 Dowbenka and Wolfram climbed by its southwest side P 5121 (16,801 feet), north of Lago San Francisco; Dowbenka continued solo along the ridge to the north over P 5315 and P 5329 (17,438 and 17,484 feet). On the 9th Klingshirn climbed P 5111 and P 5390 (16,768 and 17,684 feet), northeast of the lake, while Dowbenka climbed by its east side P 5380 (17,651 feet), which lies 2½ miles north of the north end of the lake. Rotter repeated this on June 11. On June 12 Händel and Wolfram climbed P 5963 (19,564 feet) by its west face; this lies a mile east of Huacaña. Also on June 12 Klingshirn soloed three peaks northwest of the lake from south to north: P 5185, P 5196 and P 5297 (17,012, 17,048, and 17,379 feet). We had to call our stay short because of nightly raids by shepherds. We then climbed to within about 250 feet of the top of Sajama but were turned back by storms. On June 27 Dowbenka and Wolfram climbed the northeast slope of Parinacota (20,768 feet), across the frontier in Chile.

HERBERT ZIEGENHARDT, *Bayerische Naturfreunde*

Condoriri, Southeast ridge. A party sent by the Federación de Andinismo de Chile tackled the southeast ridge of Condoriri (5648 meters, 18,531 feet), a shapely peak in the central district of the Cordillera Real. From Base Camp at 14,000 feet in the Tuni valley, the group climbed to 16,000 and 17,200 feet to set up high camps, which proved to be very cold. On July 21, all expedition members climbed the east face and at 18,000 feet they connected the route to the narrow southeast ridge and reached the summit with bad weather and poor visibility. Participants were C. Gálvez, R. Lamilla, M. Puig, P. Rosende and C. Sepulveda. This route appears to be a second ascent, since the Italian Agnolotti expedition had climbed the route in 1967.

HUMBERTO BARRERA, *Club Andino de Chile*

Condoriri, Wila Lloje, Jiskha Pata, Warawarani and Other Neighboring Peaks, Cordillera Real. In the first part of August a group composed of Andrea Facchetti, Melchiorre and Giovanni Foresti and me from Bergamo with Missionary Fathers Angelo Gelmi, Giuseppe Ferrari and Giuseppe Rizzi from La Paz climbed in the Cordillera Real. Because of their comparatively modest altitudes, the mountains are generally predominantly rock on the north faces and ice on the south. We made the following ascents: Condoriri (18,547 feet) via south ridge on August 3 by Gelmi, G. and M. Foresti, Calegari; Culin Thojo (17,612 feet) via west face on August 8 by Ferrari, Rizzi (3rd ascent); Jiskha Pata (18,072 feet) via southeast face (1st ascent) and Wila Jiskha Pata* (17,815 feet) via northwest ridge and down south spur (2nd ascent) both on August 9 by Calegari, M. and G. Foresti, Rizzi; Wila Lloje (18,353 feet) via north face and east ridge on August 10 by Calegari, Ferrari, Rizzi (4th ascent); Jankho Huyo (18,084 feet) via south face on August 11 by Calegari, G. Foresti, Ferrari, Rizzi (3rd ascent); Warawarani (18,182 feet) via east face on August 12 by Calegari, G. and M. Foresti, Ferrari (1st ascent).

SANTINO CALEGARI, *Club Alpino Italiano*

---

* The name of this snowy point between Jiskha Pata and Jankho Huyo means Little Jiskha Pata. It seems to be the same as WKE 27, climbed by the Germans in 1973, although we got a different altitude. The altitude does not appear on the Lago Khara Kkota 1:50,000 map.

Peaks East of Huayna Potosí, Cordillera Real. Ours was the first expedition to the Andes from Poznań. It was both scientific and mountaineering. We made biological, geological, ethnological and meteorological studies during our seven months in the field. The following participated: Krzysztof Blauth, Tomasz Chrzan, Jacek Gutowski, Andrzej Jaskuła, Andrzej Lisiecki, Leon Wawrzyniak, Zbigniew Zimny, my wife Aleksandra Grebieniow as doctor and I as leader. Our first climbing activity took place in the Cordillera Real from February 26 to March 17. Our Base Camp was on Lake Zongo at 15,785 feet, 2½ miles southeast of Huayna Potosí. We made six high camps. We made the following ascents: Khala Cruz (17,142 feet; 1 mile southwest of Lake Zonga) via north buttress on March 1 and Alhuayco (17,372 feet; east of Khala Cruz) via south ridge on March 2 by M. and A. Grebieniow, Wawrzyniak; Grincuni (16,568 feet; northeast of the former) via southeast spur by Chrzan, Lisiecki on March 1; Huiyata (16,706 feet; north of Grincuni) via south ridge by Zimny, Jaskuła, Lisiecki on March 5; Charquini Norte (17,422 feet; east of Alhuayco) via north ridge by M. and A. Grebieniow, Gutowski, Wawrzyniak on March 5. All were done in rainy weather. Alhuayco was the only first ascent. (For Peruvian climbs, see that section.)

MARIUSZ GREBIENIOW, *Akademicka Wyprawa Górska, Poland*

Illimani, Huayna Potosí, Cordillera Real. After climbing in the Cordillera Yauyos in Peru, we went to the Cordillera Real. (See full names there.) On July 8 Mac and I and on July 10 Jedlinski, Malinowski, Star and Wasiak climbed Illimani by the normal route. On July 15 Mac, Malinowski, Wasiak and I climbed the normal route on Huayna Potosí.

JERZY MICHAELSKI, *Lódz, Poland*

Northern Chile

Pasto Salado and other peaks. In different trips to the mountains located some 15 miles west of Vicuña, Coquimbo province, northern Chile, youths of the Colegio Inglés of the town of La Serena made the first recorded ascents in late 1974 of Diablos Parados (4200 meters, 13,780 feet) and El Toro (4300 meters, 14,108 feet) as training for higher summits. In November, 1974, six youths of the same school made the first ascent of Pasto Salado (4845 meters, 15,895 feet). Participants of this climb were G. Pereira, E. Rodríguez, M. Bitrán and the brothers Alberto, Hernán and Jorge Corral, all between 11 to 17.

EVELIO ECHEVARRÍA

Volcán Colorado, Puna de Atacama. In December the Volcán Colorado (18,838 feet) was climbed by Antonio Beorchia Nigris, who found ceremonial sites from pre-Columbian times.

MARIO FANTIN, *Club Alpino Italiano*

Argentina

Mercedario, East Face. An Italian expedition from Padua made the first ascent of the east face of Mercedario (21,894 feet). The leader was Toni Mastellaro and the members were Sergio Billoro, Andrea Cassutti, Dr. Pier Paolo Cago, Franco Cremonese, Almo Giambisi, Graziano Mingardo, Nino Portolan and Armando Ragana. From San Juan they traveled via Laguna Blanca to arrive at Base Camp at 13,000 feet on January 8. Two days later Camp I was placed at the foot of the face at 15,200 feet. Camps II and III were established at 16,950 and 18,050 feet on January 13 and 15. On the 16th Giambisi and Portolan left in a push for the summit, establishing Camp IV at 19,850 feet and bivouacking at 20,700 feet before reaching the summit on January 18. A second assault team had difficulties and had to be evacuated by helicopter. The first of the face was gentle (35° to 40°) and the technical difficulties came in the middle, the key being a 50° couloir between Camps III and IV which runs behind the rock rib ("Caballito") and séracs.

Tupungato. Germans Josef Heinl, leader, Peter Vogler and Georg Peter Menz made a new route on Tupungato (21,490 feet) on January 3. They approached from Santa Clara, Argentina, and placed Base Camp below the northeast ridge of Yesera. On December 25, 1974 Vogler, Menz and Wolfgang Niederacher made the first ascent of the northeast ridge of Yesera (15,730 feet). They then crossed the 15,250-foot Fraile Pass and dropped to the Tupungato Glacier. On January 1 they climbed a rib which divides the east face from the southeast-face glacier and camped at 17,000 feet. Difficult ice and rock brought them to a bivouac 1000 feet below the summit, which they finally reached up gentler snow.

Cerro Catedral, South Face. An eight-man team of the Croatian Alpine Association, the oldest in Yugoslavia, celebrated the 100th anniversary of the association with a two-month expedition to the Andes of central Argentina. After climbing the normal route on Aconcagua, they made the first ascent of the south face of Cerro Catedral (17,553 feet), near Aconcagua. On February 15, Marijan Čepelak and Vladimir Mesarič climbed the 3000-foot, 40° face.

FRANCI SAVENC, *Yugoslavia*

Correction. On page 181 of *A.A.J.*, 1975 La Mesa and Alma Negra were placed in Chile. Both peaks lie completely within the borders of the Argentine.

Chile and Argentina—Patagonia

Cerro Stanhardt Attempt. Our expedition team comprised Jim Donini and John Bragg, USA, and Brian Wyvill and me, UK, with assistance from Larry Bruce, USA, and Mick Coffey, UK. We made Base Camp at the end of the road and on the next day, November 9, 1974 started our hike through the woods to the glacier leading to the foot of Cerro Torre, Torre Egger and Cerro Stanhardt. That night we slept in a snow cave at the foot of Cerro Torre. Dawn arrived with the good weather still holding and Donini and I set off to reconnoitre a possible line on the un-climbed walls of Cerro Stanhardt, the third of the towers north of Cerro Torre. A four-hour climb across glacier and steep snowfields brought us to a col separating Stanhardt from the Bifida. Two pitches of rock climb-ing led to the overhanging, ice-encrusted north wall and, at its base, a slender snowfield leading to the great diagonal ramps slashing across the east face. By following the snowfield and ramps, we could avoid the avalanche-swept lower walls of the east face and get within striking dis-tance of the summit ridge. A nearly invisible chimney was recessed into a great corner, its walls bristling with incredible bulges of ice. As dark-ness fell, we saw that this was the line to take. We hacked out a tiny bivouac platform in the ice at the base of the chimney and left two climbing ropes for a dawn start. That night the spectacular spell of fine weather came to an end. In rapidly deteriorating weather we all left and retreated to our base in the woods. Endless storm and wind swept down for three weeks. On December 4 fine weather hurried us back up, but a malfunctioning stove prevented our staying. Two good days were wasted and the weather turned bad. This was the last good spell until December 26. On New Years Day, 1975 the weather looked fair and we were all at the previous high point. A heavy coating of ice started cascading down the chimney. The expected full storm did not arrive but we found our-selves out of position two days later when the weather became stable and sunny. On January 7 we arrived at the col again and rested on the 8th as the weather settled. January 9 was faultless. The climbing was much harder than we had anticipated because of rotten ice and loose rock. By six P.M. the four of us were gazing up through mist at the clouds over the summit ridge only 150 feet above our heads. Wet and aware of our exposed position we made a unanimous decision for down. After a wild night in our bivouac box below the north face, we made our way thank-fully off the mountain. In December during one of our retreats from the col, we spotted a boot, containing part of a leg and foot, lying on the lower reaches of the glacier coming down from Cerro Torre. Further search revealed other remnants of clothing and equipment. We concluded that these were the remains of Toni Egger, killed by an avalanche while descending with Cesare Maestri from Cerro Torre in 1959. This climb has aroused controversy and any photographic proof disappeared with Egger's body. We found parts of his rucksack, ripped to pieces, but the camera had disappeared and an intensive search over a large area of the glacier revealed nothing.

BEN CAMPBELL-KELLY, *Alpine Climbing Group, Aspirant*

Fitz Roy Group, 1974. A Polish expedition was active in various parts of the Andes from October, 1973 to September, 1974. They were Ryszard Rodziński, Henryk Cioncka, Stanislaw Jaworski, Zbigniew Kursa, Andrzej Lapinski, Antoni Panta and Zdzislaw Ryn. In February and March they climbed in Patagonia despite bad weather. They approached Fitz Roy late in the season. They attempted the American route. Two camps were established and they reached a high point 1500 feet below the summit in two attempts, on February 2 and 26. They were forced to retreat by deterioration of the weather and a minor accident from rockfall. They also made the following climbs, none first ascents: Punta Velluda (6595 feet) from the Río Blanco by Cioncka, Jaworski on February 11, 1974; Techado Negro (7130 feet) from the Río Blanco by Jaworski, Panta on February 24; Cerro Madsen (c. 6890 feet) from the Río Blanco by Panta on March 12; Cerro Solo (7375 feet) from Lago Torre by Panta, Ryn on March 15; Mojón Rojo (7297 feet) from Lago Sucio in the Río Blanco valley by Cioncka, Ryn on March 8, Cerro Eléctrico (7175 feet) from north from Río Blanco by Kursa, Panta on March 16; P 2270 (7748 feet; between Cerro Eléctrico and Aguja Guillamet) by Jaworski, Lapinski; Loma de las Pizarras (5548 feet) from Lago Sucio by Jaworski on March 14, Panta on March 21 and Cioncka, Ryn on March 24.

MAREK BRNIAK, *Klub Wysokogórski, Poland*

Fitz Roy Region, 1975. We can add a few names and details to the preliminary report given in *A.A.J.*, 1975 on page 188. The Swiss who made a one-day ascent from the col of the American route on Fitz Roy in early 1975 were Hans Peter Trachsel, Paul von Kanel and Ernst von Allmen. Trachsel and von Kanel then made the first ascent of the southern and slightly lower summit of Aguja Bífida, a needle north of Cerro Torre. They climbed to the col which separates Bífida from Cerro Stanhardt and forced their way up the southwest ridge. They did not have sufficient ice gear or rope to ascend the northern summit. The Australians who attempted the north face (northeast buttress) of Fitz Roy alpinestyle were Rick White and Bob Staszewski. After several attempts they finally climbed two-thirds of the face before bad weather drove them off for the last time.

Cerro Moyano. After six unsuccessful attempts on Cerro Moyano, our expedition reached the summit (9350 feet) on February 2, 1976. This was the last unclimbed major peak in the range between Lakes Viedma and Argentino; it is only slightly less difficult than Cerro Torre and Fitz Roy. Our expedition was composed of Dr. Luis Estevez, Guillermo Vieiro, Héctor Cuiñas, Pablo Nicola, Luciano Pera, Mario Serrano and me as leader. We flew to Río Gallegos and traveled by truck to Lago Viedma. From there we took horses to reach Base Camp at 1300 feet on January 25. We placed Camp I at 5900 feet on February 1. Cuiñas, Vieiro and I climbed the north face and northeast ridge. We started up a snow couloir to reach the 2000-foot-high face (UIAA V to VI, A1). From a little col we climbed the ridge with its towers (V to VI) to a 350-foot-high mushroom of ice. On the top of the mushroom we had to traverse 250 feet before the slope eased off to the summit. We got to the top at nine P.M. and descended after a bivouac the next day.

JORGE SKVARČA, *Club Andino Bariloche*

The Name, "Paine." The Paine peaks of Patagonia did not receive their name from some wandering Gringo. (The name is pronounced "pine-eh.") The name originated around 1886 when an Argentine traveler, trekking into southernmost Chile, saw the peak and christened it Paine because the Chilean massif has three peaks looking very much like an Argentine massif called "Paine" which was of religious importance to the Huilliches, an Argentine branch of the Araucanians of Chile. The word means "sky-blue." The Argentine writer Estanislao Zeballos has written novels about those Indians. One refers to a princess of the Paine.

EVELIO ECHEVARRÍA

Patagonian Season, 1976. As we go to press, we receive the first news of climbing in the current season from Vojslav Arko, who writes: "The expedition of the Club Andino Bariloche headed by Jorge Skvarca finally made the first ascent of Cerro Moyano on February 2, 1976. This rises between Lakes Viedma and Argentino. Jack Miller has just appeared here in Bariloche with the news that he has climbed the Cuerno Principal of Paine by a different route than the one climbed by the Chileans in 1968. New Zealanders tried Cerro Torre unsuccessfully and gave up after they lost a climber in a crevasse accident. The Americans John Bragg, Jim Donini and Jay Wilson climbed difficult Torre Egger. Italians led by Casimiro Ferrari finally succeeded in climbing the much-attempted northeast buttress of Fitz Roy. They reached the summit on February 23."

PLATE 68

Photo by Jorge Skvarča

CERRO MOYANO. The route ascends
the buttress where the sun and shade
meet.

Torre Egger. Our expedition consisted of Jim Donini, Jay Wilson and me, supported by Jane Hunter, Jane and Sherm Wilson and Maureen Donahue. We arrived in the area on December 1 and after much load carrying started the climb on December 10. Beautiful alpine free climbing on perfect granite under a brilliant sun let Jay and me fix ropes up the first 500 feet. One stormy month later, we were only 100 feet higher. When the weather finally started to improve on January 20 we found our snow cave and our equipment at the top of the glacier buried under 30 feet of fresh snow. After two hard, frustrating days, we were in our new quarters. After two more days of storm we started again. Two days of climbing took us to the top of the large snowfield almost halfway to the "Col of Conquest" between Cerros Torre and Egger. A brief storm slowed things, but after four more days we reached the col at sunset on February 4. A cold bivouac preceded descending the ropes the next day in wind and rain. February 16 saw us back at the cave and the next day we chopped a platform and pitched our box tent 2000 feet higher up the ropes. We continued fixing ropes in unsettled weather until finally, after a bad icing storm on the 21st, we three pushed the last three pitches in high winds and heavy cloud to the top on February 22, 1976. We descended to the box that night, cleaned the route the next day and were back at Base Camp on the 24th. Up to the col we were on the northeast face of Cerro Torre, following a line close to that of Maestri and Egger in 1958. From the col we were on the south face of Torre Egger. NCCS VI, F9, A4; 4500 feet of technical climbing; 4000 feet of fixed rope; ice up to 75°; 37 pitches of which 13 were on ice and 18 with substantial aid; 11 bolts, all but one for anchors.

JOHN BRAGG

EUROPE

New Routes in Chamonix: North Faces of Grands Charmoz and Grand Pilier d'Angle. During the Rassemblement International, Americans did some fine climbs in the Chamonix region. Steve Zajchowski and I were the representatives of the American Alpine Club. On July 8 with Roger Martin I did the first one-day ascent of the North Face Direct of les Droites. On the 14th I soloed the north face of the Grand Pilier d'Angle. Zajchowski did the Northeast Spur Direct on les Droites with the French climber Xavier Fourger. Zajchowski and I did the third ascent of the Couloir Nord de la Brèche des Drus in one day on July 22; previously the best time was three days. On July 28 and 29 Steve Arsenault and I did the Walker Spur. On the 30th Zajchowski soloed the Swiss route on the north face of les Courtes. On August 7 Zajchowski and I did a new route on the north face of les Grands Charmoz. *Grand Pilier d'Angle North Face:* The route follows narrow gullies in the pillar between the Fréhel-Dufour route and the Cecchinel-Nomine. It is characterized by mixed climbing in the extreme while on the actual face and by the usual sérac dangers of all the climbs in the area. The bergschrunds could present a problematic crossing. From the Col Moore, cross the plateau under the Great Couloir of the Route Major. Cross the bergschrunds below the Pear, bearing left at the level of the initial rocks of the Pear. This is most easily done at night by climbing the avalanche cone. The actual gully begins with a rock pillar to its left and at about the same level as the first rocks of the Pear. Follow this gully through difficult mixed climbing for over 1200 feet to an enclosed area with rock pillars on either side and two narrow tongues of ice descending from a vertical shield of rock. Follow the tongue on the right for several hundred feet (extremely thin ice) and traverse right onto the pillar via huge ice-encrusted flakes forming something of a chimney. At the top of the chimney is a right-leading ledge system. Follow the ledge to a slightly overhanging 10-foot corner. (The only piton of the route was used here and should still be in place.) Climb the corner and continue by easier, lower-angled slabs for 100 feet. The route here gets on the final snowfield. Follow the snowfield to the Peuterey ridge. The summit is three hours from this point in good conditions. The route is rated the same as the other routes on the face, E.D. sup. and represents a marked evolution over the Ceccinel-Nomine and the Fréhel-Dufour since it used no direct aid. An attempt on this route claimed the lives of two climbers several years ago. *Grands Charmoz North Face:* The route climbs the east side of the north face of the Grands Charmoz and finishes in the prominent couloir to the right of the Aiguille de la République. It is characterized by sustained high-quality climbing on both rock and ice and represents two ice pitches steeper than the Dru Couloir, the Couloir Chaud and the Grand Pilier d'Angle. There is considerable stonefall danger in certain sections, so the climb must be done rapidly. Approach the face from the path to the Envers des Aiguilles Hut, turning off before the path leads away from the Charmoz. Climb the left side of the Charmoz Glacier (the right bank), cross the bergschrund and start across a snowfield to a rock pillar leading to the base of the small couloir going to the Brèche de l'Aiguille de la République. Climb the pillar via an obvious chimney system, which is slightly overhanging. Two pitons were used to climb out of the bergschrund onto the pillar. Follow the chimney to the base of the small couloir (F9). Climb the couloir 600 feet to its end (stonefall) and traverse right onto the rock face for 200 feet. Go up a left-facing series of corners and continue up icy crack systems for nine pitches (F8) to easier ground. Get on the final ice slope and climb a narrowing and increasingly steep couloir for four or five pitches to an almost vertical ice wall (very steep ice, stonefall). Two pitches will overcome the headwall; two pitches more on easier ice lead to the final two or three on mixed ice and rock. The climbing here is of extreme standard and is terribly loose. Care should be taken not to dislodge huge, tottering blocks on the belays. A ridge leads to the summit. Zajchowski and I used 22 nuts or pitons for protection as well as four ice screws. We took 13 hours.

JOHN BOUCHARD

AFRICA

Nyabubuya, Northeast Gully, Ruwenzori Group. Our party included Frank Eastwood, David Higgs, Dr. Arnold Pines, Roger Reid, Alan Roberts and me. We climbed Mount Baker, Mount Speke and the four peaks of Mount Stanley. In addition, on July 21 Alan Roberts and Higgs made one new route: Nyabubuya (15,950 feet), the southeast extremity of the southern Stanley peaks. The eleven pitches took five hours. From the Elena Huts they traversed across the Elena Glacier and terraced rocks to the foot of the climb, which starts in a groove. The crux pitches occur halfway up, where overhangs barred a direct line. They climbed right on very steep, greasy slabs. A right-hand slant finally led to the summit ridge.

ERIC ROBERTS, *Alpine Club*

Mawenzi, East Face. The members of our expedition who made this climb were Dario Mozzanica, Bruno Deangeli, Giovanni Balossi and I. At dawn on February 12 we left our bivouac on the south side of Mawenzi and in 12 hours climbed five 13,000-foot ridges, dropping between to less than 11,500 feet. We bivouacked in sight of the east face at 13,800 feet. On the 13th we descended into the Gran Barranco to 10,500 feet and bivouacked on the wall of the middle spur some 350 feet higher, having placed 18 pitons. On the 14th we climbed a dihedral with 26 pitons to a bivouac some 500 feet higher. On the 15th, except for one ledge of sound rock, we struggled up the rotten edge to climb to the crest of the middle spur, where we placed our fourth bivouac at 14,000 feet. On the 16th we climbed easy friable rock to the last steep step. We climbed this up a funnel with 16 pitons. We continued up mixed rock and ice with difficulties comparable to the Major route on Mont Blanc. At seven P.M. we reached the summit of Point Brochers. We rappelled down the west face in the dark.

IVO MOZZANICA, *Club Alpino Italiano*

INDIAN OCEAN

Mont Ross, Kerguelen Island. In the Indian Ocean at about 50° S. latitude, halfway between Australia and Africa, lies storm-buffeted Kerguelen Island. Its high point, Mont Ross, is only 6070 feet high, but it

PLATE 69

Photo by Bernard (?) Washburn

North Face of the Grands Charmoz.
– · – = Bouchard-Zajchowski, 19??
······· = Welzenbach-Merkl, 19?
– ·· – = Heckmaier-Kraud, 1931.

PLATE 70

Photo by Aleš Kunaver

MAKALU, showing the Yugoslavian route. o = camp.

is heavily glaciated and where the rock is exposed, rotten. Bad weather is the rule. The fifth expedition to attempt this peak was French, led by Jean Rivolier. The group was helicoptered from their ship halfway to the mountain some four miles from the summit on the eastern side. They ran a camp up onto the southeastern side. On January 5 Jean Afanassieff and Patrick Cordier made the difficult climb to the summit in eight hours. On January 12 Patrice Bodin, Denis Ducroz and Georges Polian also climbed to the top. On the ridge running north from the main summit lies Petit Ross (5646 feet). This was climbed on January 16 by the five mentioned above and Jacques Regnard.

ASIA

Nepal

Yalungkang. A very strong team of the German and Austrian Alpine Clubs made a new route and the second ascent of Yalungkang or Kangchenjunga West (27,625 feet). The first ascent had been by the Japanese via the west ridge in 1973. (See *A.A.J.*, 1974, 19:1, pages 202-3.) The members were Siegfried Aeberli, leader, Günter Sturm, deputy, Gerhard Baur, Michael Dacher, Erich Lackner, Sepp Mayerl, Peter Vogler, Helmut Wagner, Rolf Walter, Dr. Roman Zink and Fritz Zintl. After some porter troubles during the 3½-week approach, they established Base Camp at 18,000 feet on the Yalung Glacier on April 11. They followed the route the British had used on the main peak of Kangchenjunga up to Camp III at 23,500 feet. Camp I was at 20,350 feet and Camp II at 21,650 feet. Just below Camp III there was the most difficult spot on the climb, a 50-foot vertical section of ice. Camp IV was at 25,600 feet at the foot of a 2000-foot, 45° couloir that led nearly to the summit up the south face. Although they were worried about windslab conditions, it did not avalanche with them. They used oxygen only above Camp IV. On May 9 Dacher, Lackner and Walter reached the top, on May 12 Baur, Wagner and Vogler and on May 13 Mayerl, Sturm and Zintl. Of the nine who got to the top, five were Germans and four Austrians.

Jannu. A New Zealand expedition led by Peter Farrell made an unsuccessful attempt on Jannu (25,294 feet) by a new route on the north face. On October 22 Farrell and Brian Pooley reached 24,000 feet.

KAMAL K. GUHA, *Himalayan Club*

Makalu, South Face. The sixth Yugoslav Himalayan Expedition left Dharan on August 19 and traveled through Dhankuta, Hile, Tumlingther, Khandberi, Sedus, the Kiki La to reach Base Camp at 16,250 feet on September 5. Camp I was pitched on the 7th at 19,200 feet. On the 9th we placed Camp II at 20,675 feet at the foot of the south face, first with tents and then, due to avalanche danger, in snow caves. On the 13th bad weather and avalanche danger stopped the work of fixing ropes but on the 14th we pitched the Bivouac at 21,650 feet. On September 16 Camp III was installed at 23,000 feet. When the camps were consolidated, we started to fix ropes towards Camp IV, which we established at 24,600 feet on September 23. On September 25 heavy snowfall blocked all progress. Avalanches tore Camp IV apart. All members returned to Base Camp. Camp III was reoccupied and rebuilt on October 1 and Camp IV on the 2nd. More rope was fixed and on the 4th Camp V was reached at 26,400 feet; the assault team had enough material to fix ropes to the top of the face and to proceed to the top. They completed the rock climbing and fixing of ropes on October 5. Malfunctioning oxygen apparatus forced them to continue without it. October 6 was fair. Stane Belak and Marjan Manfreda reached the top of the south face at 11:15 and proceeded along the summit ridge to reach the top at four P.M. Three more assault teams were ready. On the 8th four more set out. Cedilnik was hit on the left knee by falling ice and Robas had difficulty breathing and so they returned. Nejo Zaplotnik and Janko Ažman reached the top. While preparing for the third assault, Boris Erjavec was hit by a falling rock. He was saved from serious injury by his helmet but fell unconscious onto the fixed rope. He had to be escorted back to Base Camp. His companions, Ivč Kotnik and Viki Grošelj proceeded to the summit on October 10 in strong wind and snow. On the 11th Janez Dovžan and Zoran Brešlin started for the top. Dovžan reached the summit and returned safely, but Breslin had troubles and got only to within 35 feet. He had to spend the night out and returned to Camp V the next day.

ALEŠ KUNAVER, *Planinska Zveza Slovenije, Yugoslavia*

Nuptse Tragedy. The aim of the Joint British Army-Royal Nepalese Army Nuptse Expedition was to climb that mountain as a final work-up and testing ground for our next spring's expedition to Mount Everest. Nuptse was our second choice, the first being Cho Oyu, but this was denied us for political reasons. Nuptse (25,850 feet) had been climbed once before, by a British party in 1961 which used the central ridge of the south face. No party has attempted it since. The main difficulties had been reported to be low down. The ridge, which is narrow, steep, very rotten and exposed, is the key to the upper reaches of the peak. Above this a vertical band of rock, 1000 feet high, barred the way to the upper icefield, along which we would have to traverse for over a half-mile before climbing a 2000-foot couloir to the summit ridge. By March 28 the whole team was at the Acclimatisation Camp at Dingboche at 14,350 feet, having walked in from Kathmandu. We spent a week at that altitude, packing stores to Base Camp. In early April Base Camp was established at 17,060 feet on the west bank of the Nuptse Glacier. Following the lateral moraine and crossing the chaotic, ankle-breaking glacier boulderfield right under the vast south face of Nuptse, we established Camp I at 18,000 feet on a small snowy glacier underneath the ridge. Employing normal Himalayan tactics of "carry high, sleep low," we fought our way up the ridge. There were very few sites either large or flat enough for camps. The ridge itself was intricate and exposed. Sometimes we were on the crest, at others 60 feet below it. At times we actually had to pass through tunnels in the ridge to get to the other side to make progress. By April 27 we had established Camp IV, a kind of Advanced Base, at 21,000 feet at the end of the ridge where it abuts the south face. Camp V was made on April 30. The final obstacle, the rock band, was overcome and on May 5 Camp VI was established at 23,350 feet. On May 7 the four lead climbers made the route along the half-mile traverse and established Camp VII at 23,500 feet. The first summit attempt was made by Major G.F. Owens and Captain R.A. Summerton on May 9. They left Camp VII at 7:15 and were roughly two-thirds of the way up the summit couloir when they fell. No one saw them fall, but a team member at Camp VII was hit by stonefall on this day and so the possibility of falling rocks can not be ruled out. A later helicopter search revealed the two bodies at the bottom of the mountain at the head of the Nuptse Glacier. Despite our severe shock at the loss of two such fine and capable climbers, we determined to continue the assault. Four fresh men were at Camp VII for a bid on May 12, but the weather, which had never been good now turned much worse. On May 13 after a day of continuous snowfall and high winds, I resolved to evacuate the mountain for a spell to allow the weather to change. The withdrawal began on May 14. The night before, Camp V had been avalanched and one tent flattened by hundreds of tons of snow, fortunately without injury. It was during the withdrawal from Camps VII to VI that Lieutenant D.A.J. Brister and Rifleman Pasang Tamang fell to their deaths. They must have fallen from about two-thirds of the way along the traverse, over the rock band and onto the steep snowfield below. The helicopter search carried out later identified the bodies. Because the weather never let up, I decided to withdraw. We built a large cairn to our fallen companions at Base Camp, which we left on May 20. The other members of the team were Captains C.H. Agnew of Lochnaw the Younger, N.F. Gifford, M.T. King, E.C. Walshaw and M.H. Kefford, Lieutenant J.D.C. Peacock, Majors A.J. Muston and E.A.N. Winship, Surgeon Lieutenant Commander P.N. Dilly, Chief Technician G.P. Armstrong, Corporal M.P. Lane, and I, as leader, *British;* Lance Corporal Basantakumar Rai, Corporals Kagendrabahadur Limbu, Narbu Sherpa, Nandaraj Gurung, Angphurba Sherpa and Rifleman Kubirjang Rai, *Gurkas;* and Major Bhagirath Narsingh Rana, Sebedar Krishna Bahadur and Corporal Bishnu Bahadur, *Royal Nepalese Army,* with Sherpas Sonam Girme, Tensing and Pasang Tensing.

JONATHAN W. FLEMING, *Major, The Parachute Regiment*

Lhotse, South Face Attempt. A very strong Italian national expedition failed to climb the south face of Lhotse. The leader was Riccardo Cassin and members were Ignazio Piussi, Reinhold Messner, Franco Gugiatti, Gigi Alippi, Sereno Barbacetto, Aldo Leviti, Mario Curnis, Giuseppe Alippi, Mario Conti, Alessandro Gogna, Gianni Arcari, Fausto Lorenzi, Dr. Franco Chierego and Aldino Anghileri. Before the end of the attempt Dr. Chierego had to be evacuated with cerebral edema and Anghileri left for personal reasons. Almost immediately after arrival at their 17,400-foot Base Camp in late March, they decided against the avalanche-swept direct route and followed the route attempted by the Japanese in 1973 on the far left of the face. The route to Camp I (19,350 feet) was mixed snow and ice of not very great difficulty. From Camp I to Camp II, established on April 11 at 21,650 feet, the climbing was extraordinarily hard with vertical rock and 70° ice. The route to Camp III was somewhat easier, principally ice. This camp was established at 23,625 feet on April 16. On May 6 Barbacetto and Gogna slabbed diagonally left and reached a spot just below the southwest ridge at 24,600 feet, a site for Camp IV. This highest point reached was still more than 3300 feet short of the summit. The rest of the route would have followed just below the ridge and up the Swiss route of 1956. The expedition was plagued by bad weather and avalanches. On April 20 two avalanches partially destroyed Base Camp, injuring four Sherpas. Barbacetto and Leviti were nearly buried by an avalanche in Camp III.

Mount Everest, First Ascent by a Woman. At 12:30 P.M. on May 16 Junko Tabei, a 35-year-old mother of a three-year-old child, reached the summit of Mount Everest with Sherpa Ang Tsering. The 15-member Japanese Ladies Expedition was led by Mrs. Eiko Hisano. Base Camp was set up on March 16 at the foot of the Khumbu Icefall. Although by May 2 reconnaissance had reached close to the South Col, two days later an avalanche at Camp II nearly ended the expedition. Seven of the Japanese, including Mrs. Tabei, and six Sherpas were injured. Plans for getting three or four of the Japanese to the top had to be curtailed. On May 13 Camp V was established on the South Col and Camp VI at 27,900 feet the next day. Bad weather prevented a summit attempt on the 15th, but Junko Tabei and Ang Tsering reached their goal on May 16. We very much regret that the promised article on the expedition has not reached us by press time.

Khumbu Clean-Up by the Evergreen State College. As part of its innovative curriculum, Evergreen State College, Olympia, Washington, trained 18 students last spring in Nepali language and culture and sent them to Nepal for eleven months of individual study and research. The students were assisted in their studies by faculty member David Peterson, M.D. (Everest '71 and Dhaulagiri '73) and his wife Kathy. Individual projects range from comparative linguistics and ethnomusicology to folk tales and ornithology. Steve Valadez, Martha Stoddard, Rick Henderson, Don Weedon and Laurie Woodall joined Nick Langton on the action phase of his Khumbu clean-up project. After trekking in from Dharan, up the Arun and across the ranges of the upper Khumbu in 28 days, they joined their Sherpa team and spent three weeks on garbage patrol at Thyangboche and beyond. Nick Langton writes: "The clean-up was a success. We cleaned and built dump sites (huge holes) at Thyangboche, Pheriche, Lobuje and Gorak Shep. Base Camp was beyond our scope, but we managed to remove 1000 to 1500 pounds of trash, purely token. This Base Camp trash had to be carried down since at Base there was no ground soft enough to dig." It is hoped that this good work will be carried forward by future Khumbu trekkers.

WILLIAM F. UNSOELD

Chinese Ascent of Mount Everest. This expedition was made up of numerous Chinese and Tibetans. They arrived at the Rongbuk Monastery on March 13 near which they established Base Camp. Yaks were used up to 18,000 feet. Camp I was at 18,000 feet, Camp II at 19,700 feet and Camp III at 21,325 feet, at the foot of the North Col. The climb to the top of the col at 23,000 feet had changed a great deal and become more difficult than in 1960. Camp IV was eventually placed on the col. Camp V was established at 25,000 feet on April 27 but storms prevented further advance. On May 4 and 5, seven women and 33 men reached 26,900 feet, where Camp VI was placed. Three women and 17 men went on to 28,225 feet, where Camp VII was established but again storms prevented any advance. They descended to Base Camp. After a favorable weather report, they returned, raising Camp VI 300 feet and Camp VII 200 feet. An assault team of three women and 15 men, led by Tibetan Sodnam Norbu and the Tibetan mother-of-three, 37-year-old deputy leader Phantog, moved up on May 25. Two women and seven men were exhausted and had to withdraw. Sodnam Norbu, Darphuntso, Kunga Pasang and Tsering Tobgyal, all Tibetans, were to try for the summit on May 26; Phantog, Lotse, Samdrub, Ngopo Khyen, Tibetans, and Hou Sheng-fu, Han Chinese, were to follow the next day, but stormy weather changed their plans. The first group prepared the route over the Second Step, while the second group moved up to join them at Camp VII. On the 27th they all moved upwards. They were at the top of the Second Step by 9:30. Above there it was hard but steady work until they were some 200 feet below the top; perpendicular ice forced them to a 100-foot detour. They then climbed a rock step and finally reached the summit at 2:30 P.M. Peking time (12:30 local time). There can be no doubt about this ascent of the Chinese. They mounted a 10-foot-high, red survey pole, which was found by Dougal Haston and Doug Scott four months later; it was more deeply banked by snow and the red paint had been etched away by the wind.

Pumori, Southwest Ridge. Our expedition was composed of Philippe and Marie Odile Bernardin, Alain Boissy, Jean Clemenson, Philippe de Nuncques, Alain Robert, Gérard Siguèle, my wife Claudine and me as leader. The southwest ridge route, which compares to the Innominata route on Mont Blanc on its rock and mixed parts and to the north face of Les Courtes on its ice, was opened by the Japanese in 1974. We left Lukla on March 27 and set up Base Camp on April 3 at 17,550 feet on the moraine below Pumori. On the 6th, after climbing the moraine, we fixed ropes up an S-shaped snow couloir of 45° which led to vast snow slopes, and looked for a site for Camp I. After several days of ferrying, we established Camp I on April 11 under an overhang at 19,700 feet on the right side of a very steep couloir, 650 feet below the ridge crest. Complicated by bad weather, twelve days were needed before installing Camp II on April 23 at 21,325 feet. The first part of this section followed an almost horizontal snow-ridge traverse for 1300 feet before we gained the rock steps which constituted the continuation of the route; we then climbed a 650-foot rock wall above which a snow slope led to a tiny platform at its top, where we could pitch a single tent as Camp II. It took five days of route-preparation to establish Camp III on April 28 in a crevasse at 22,150 feet. In this section we climbed a snow wall and a rock step to gain the steep snow of the north face in order to get onto the ridge. On April 28 Claudine, de Nuncques, sirdar Mingma Tsering and I left Base Camp for the final assault. On April 30 Claudine and I left Camp II at two A.M. while de Nuncques and the sirdar left Camp III at four. Above Camp III we all climbed two difficult rock steps to gain a lacy ridge of bad snow which ended in a 1000-foot, 60° to 65° triangle of hard snow which led to the crest of the snow ridge of the south face. Finally gentler slopes led to the summit, which we reached at 1:30 P.M. While descending on May 1 between Camps II and I we met Philippe Bernardin and the Sherpa Ang Kami on the way to Camp II; they hoped to climb to the summit the next day. On May 2 we last saw the pair when at 1:30 about 500 feet from the top they were hidden by clouds. On the 3rd we searched in vain for them with strong field glasses. At four P.M. Clemenson and de Nuncques set out for Namche Bazar to request a helicopter search and made the three-day trip in 13 hours. It was bad weather on the 4th. On the 5th a thorough reconnaissance by helicopter revealed no trace of the missing climbers. Meanwhile two Sherpas had climbed on both May 3 and 4 to Camp III and told us they found no signs of our friends. Doubtless they had gone astray in the bad weather and fallen 4000 feet down the face. Further search on foot and by helicopter revealed nothing.

JEAN LESCURE, *Groupe de Haute Montagne*

Kwangde. A Nepalese expedition to the Everest region was led by Kumar Khadga Bikram Shah, President of the Nepalese Mountaineering Association. They were accompanied by a Japanese television team. They had originally hoped to climb Karyolung but called this off after establishing on that mountain Camps I and II at 16,100 and 18,700 feet on October 2 and 9; they found they would have to climb intervening peaks to reach the top. Camps I and II on Kwangde were set up at 16,400 and 18,750 feet on October 13 and 15. On October 17 Lhakpa Tenzing, Sonam Gyalzen, Shambhu Tamang and Sona Hisi reached the summit (19,997 feet) on October 17.

KAMAL K. GUHA, *Himalayan Club*

Mera. French climbers, Marcel Jolly, G. Bang, L. Honnilh, L. Limarques, with Ang Lakhpa and two other Sherpas climbed Mera (21,120 feet) in the Khumbu region on October 29, 1973. They climbed steep glacial slopes on the north. In 1953 Colonel Jimmy Roberts and a Sherpa had climbed high on the mountain but stopped just short of the summit.

Jugal Himal. Carla Maverna and Irene Affentranger climbed Jugal Himal in October.

MARIO FANTIN, *Club Alpino Italiano*

Parchamo, Rolwaling Himal. On October 14 Cosimo Zappelli, Giovanni Martinelli, Carlo Buzzi and Alberto Rauzi climbed Parchamo (20,-577 feet) above the Teshi Lapcha pass.

Manaslu. Jerónimo López Martínez, Gererdo Blázquez García and the Sherpa Soman reached the summit of Manaslu (26,760 feet) on April 27. They had made the sixth ascent of the mountain and the third from the east. The Spanish expedition, led by Jaime García Orts, had set up Camps I (16,000 feet), II (18,700 feet), III (21,325 feet), IV (23,000 feet) and V (24,600 feet) on March 31, April 1, 2, 21 and 24 respectively. On the plateau near the top the three passed a dead body, presumably that of Jäger or Schlick, lost high on the mountain in 1972. (See *A.A.J.*, 1973, 18:2, pages 484-5.) The two Spaniards froze their feet on the final climb and had to be airlifted to Kathmandu.

KAMAL K. GUHA, *Himalayan Club*

Peak 29 Attempt. The 12-man Japanese Hyogo Mountaineering Association Expedition, led by Hiroshi Maeda, tried to climb Peak 29 (25,705 feet) by its east ridge. They set up Base Camp at 14,150 feet on March 30 and Camps I (16,850 feet), II (18,850 feet), III (20,500 feet) and IV (22,475 feet) on April 6, 15, 25 and 28 respectively. When the assault team was only 2000 feet from the summit, the expedition was abandoned due to persistent bad weather.

KAMAL K. GUHA, *Himalayan Club*

Himal Chuli Attempt. A seven-man Japanese expedition from the Senshu University Alpine Club attempted the west peak (24,685 feet) of Himal Chuli by its southwest face and ridge. The expedition was led by Hidezumi Komi. Base Camp was established on March 27 at 13,125 feet. They set up Camp I (16,400 feet) on March 31 on the face, Camp II (19,850 feet) on April 12 and Camp III (21,325 feet) on April 25, both on the ridge. Their high point of 22,150 feet was reached on May 3. The expedition was given up due to unfavorable weather conditions.

KAMAL K. GUHA, *Himalayan Club*

Bauddha Attempt. A six-man expedition from the Japanese Hirosaki Overseas Climbing Club led by Shozo Kikuchi failed to climb Bauddha (21,890 feet) by its south ridge. They set up Base Camp (15,100 feet), Camp I (17,800 feet) and Camp II (19,400 feet) on March 31, April 8 and April 10 respectively. They gave up the expedition on April 21 due to continuous bad weather.

KAMAL K. GUHA, *Himalayan Club*

Annapurna I Attempt. A 9-man Austrian expedition led by Gerd Gantner attempted Annapurna I (26,545 feet) over the unclimbed "Fang." Base Camp was set up at 13,780 feet on March 24 and two days later the Sherpas quit, complaining of poor food, clothing and gear. The expedition continued without Sherpas, employing Tamang porters. Franz Tegischer was killed in his sleep at Camp II (18,050 feet) at 12:30 A.M. on April 16 when the edge of an avalanche buried the tent. His tentmate, Ernst Schwarzenländer, was able to pull himself out. At six A.M. those at Base Camp, Camp I and Camp III (20,175 feet) contacted each other by radio and so started converging on Camp II. The expedition was abandoned.

KAMAL K. GUHA, *Himalayan Club*

Annapurna South or Moditse. The Sendai Alpine Club expedition led by Yuji Sasaki in the post-monsoon season was prevented from reaching the top by bad weather and technical difficulties.

ICHIRO YOSHIZAWA, *A.A.C.* and *Japanese Alpine Club*

Dhaulagiri I Attempt. Tasashi Amamiya was leader of the 17-man Tokyo Metropolitan Mountaineering Federation expedition, which attempted the south buttress of Dhaulagiri. Base Camp was set up on March 1 at 11,350 feet, Camp I at 14,750 feet on March 6, Advanced Base at 17,225 feet on March 10, Camp II at 18,375 feet on March 18 and Camp III at 19,000 feet on March 20. Tetsu Imura, Yoshitata Numao, a local porter and Sherpas Pasang Kami, Dakiya and Dorjee were killed in their sleep at one A.M. on March 26 when an avalanche hit Camp I. Six other inmates of the camp escaped. The expedition was called off.

KAMAL K. GUHA, *Himalayan Club*

Dhaulagiri II Attempt. An 8-man expedition of the Tokyo University of Agriculture and Technology failed to climb the southwest ridge of Dhaulagiri II from the south. They claimed to have reached nearly 23,000 feet from Camp III on May 26.

MICHAEL CHENEY, *Himalayan Club*

Dhaulagiri IV. On May 9 two of the Osaka Mountaineering Federation party reached the summit of untrodden Dhaulagiri IV (25,135 feet) by its western approach, but they failed to return. They fell into the Konabon amphitheater from 24,600 feet where they seem to have bivouacked for the second night. Our 16-person expedition left Pokhara on March 15, accompanied by 70 porters and 5 Sherpas, arriving at the tongue of the Kaphe Glacier-Ghustung region in the southwest of the Dhaulagiri group. It had taken a week to cross the Budzunge Bara Pass (14,750 feet) because of heavy snowfall. A larger, heavier party would have been worse delayed. (The mountain had been attempted nine times and 14 climbers had died on the peak.—*Editor*) On April 11 Camp III was established at 18,875 feet on the north ridge of Ghustung North, where we overlooked the huge upper glacier basin surrounded by Ghustung, Gurja Himal and Dhaulagiri VI. Two more camps and a 2625-foot ice wall led us to Camp VI near the top of Junction Peak (c.

23,625 feet), which connects the ridges from Dhaulagiri IV and VI and Churen Himal. On May 2 we began chopping steps in the ice across Junction Peak and down to the west col (22,300 feet). On the 5th H. Nakamura, T. Kodama, S. Fujiwara, M. Otsu and H. Yamamoto followed fixed lines to Camp VII at 22,650 feet, carrying a week's provisions. The next day dawned clear but windy. Two left Camp VII but with little hope for the summit. The ridge was steep, sharp and icy and with unfavorable weather they gave up at eleven o'clock at 23,625 feet. From camp it was 2½ miles and 2625 feet, but they felt it feasible. However, luck was not with them. The wind rose and past midnight tore the tent in half, forcing them to abandon the site. Shiro Kawazu and Sardar Pemba Norbu came up to help them retreat to Camp V. Kawazu was in good shape and wished to make a long assault from Camp VI with young Etsuro Yasuda. After a lengthy discussion he was given permission if they did not push beyond their physical limits. May 8 was a calm, sunny day. They left Camp VI at eight A.M. to reach at 3:50 P.M. 24,000 feet, where they bivouacked. A mechanical disorder with their walkie-talkie prevented receiving, but they could send messages. On May 9 they were last seen from Camp VI by S. Kashu and Sherpa Nima Kanchha at four P.M. just below the summit before clouds covered the scene. The lower camps got an excited message from Kawazu at 7:30 reporting that they had reached the summit at 5:30 with poor visibility and strong wind and that they were forced to bivouac where they were at 24,600 feet. He talked over the radio for a last time at 8:10. The next morning Kashu and Kanchha started to meet them but the summiters were not to be seen. Finally they were found lying together beyond the bergschrund on the south face 5000 feet below. With great sorrow we abandoned further activities. The expedition leader was Tetsuya Nomura; I was climbing leader. The other members not mentioned above were N. Nishimura, F. Kimura, A Yoshimi, Miss K. Uekawa, Mrs. K. Nishimura and T. Yokoyama.

SHIRO NISHIMAE, *Mountaineering Federation of Osaka, Japan*

Dhaulagiri IV. The Kamoshika Dojin party was led by Kazuyuki Takashashi and had 11 other members including one woman. They set up Base Camp in the Myagdi Khola at 11,325 feet on September 1. The first step was to climb as far as Myagdi Matha (20,538 feet). Camps I (15,250 feet), II (17,225 feet) and III (18,850 feet) were established on the southeast ridge of that peak. Camp IV was placed on September 24 on the summit of Myagdi Matha but later moved some 200 feet lower. The second step is between Maygdi Matha and the col at 22,650 feet via the Inner Sanctuary. Camp V was in the bottom of the basin at 17,000 feet. Camps VI and VII were at 20,350 and 21,325 feet. Camp

VIII was on the col, from which the southwest ridge begins. Camp IX was on the ridge at 23,625 feet. The following reached the summit: Kazuyaki Takahashi and Yoshiteru Takahashi on October 19; Kuniaki Yagihara, Minoru Kobayashi, Tomo Negishi, Kosaku Suda, Shigehito Kogure and Yasuo Morozumi on October 20; and Tsutomu Miyazaki and Kozo Komatsu on October 21.

ICHIRO YOSHIZAWA, *A.A.C.* and *Japanese Alpine Club*

Dhaulagiri V. The success of the Okayama University Expedition was not just a lucky hit but the result of careful planning. In the 1974 pre-monsoon period three members of our expedition reconnoitered the mountain. We were able to get valuable information from two preceding Japanese expeditions. The expedition members were Eiichi Umeki, leader, Shiro Sadakane, Ken Ishihara, Genzaburo Yamasaki, Hideo Ogura, Shigeo Aoki, Hiroshi Hiratsuka, Masaru Kono, Masaaki Morioka, Norikazu Ichikawa, Haruhisa Kuroda, Hiromichi Mizohata, Dr. Yasuhiro Yumoto and I. We left Pokhara on February 16 with 230 porters and reached Temporary Base Camp on March 1 on the right side of the Myagdi Khola at 11,800 feet. After making an intermediate camp at 14,450 feet, we established Base Camp on March 14 on the Tsorabon Glacier at 16,000 feet. We made Camp I on March 22 at 17,700 feet and Camp II on April 3 at 17,350 feet on the southeast face. We fixed rope on the 50° snow and ice from Camp II to the White Peak on the end of the south ridge and up much of the narrow, icy south ridge. We placed Camp III at 21,000 feet on the south ridge on April 20 and Camp IV at 22,950 feet on April 26. On May 1 Morioka and Sherpa Pemba Tsering reached the summit.

KENJI KAWAGUCHI, *Japanese Alpine Club*

Churen Himal. Ryoten Hasegawa and Terayaki Kono reached this 24,184-foot summit via the west ridge on May 13. Nearly a month after leaving Kathmandu, the 10-man team led by Sinichi Nakajima set up Base Camp on April 7. Heavy snowfalls delayed the approach. Camps I (15,425 feet), III (21,450 feet) and IV (22,650 feet) were established on April 11, May 6 and May 12 respectively. The expedition was organized by the Meiji University Alpine Club of Japan.

KAMAL K. GUHA, *Himalayan Club*

Churen Himal. Suemitsu Ohtsuka led this six-man expedition of the Hohkei Club. On October 25 Masahiro Nagaoka and the Sherpa Parkam reached the summit from Camp IV at 22,750 feet on the west ridge. They had set up Base Camp (14,925 feet), Camps I (17,800 feet), II

(19,425 feet) and III (21,225 feet) on September 15, 22, October 5 and 12 respectively.

ICHIRO YOSHIZAWA, *A.A.C.* and *Japanese Alpine Club*

Kanjiroba. The Getsuryo Kai expedition which attempted the mountain in September and October from the north peak was led by Akira Takiguchi. The climb ended in tragedy when Seiiji Takato slipped and fell 5000 feet from 19,700 feet when he was climbing from Camp IV to Camp V.

ICHIRO YOSHIZAWA, *A.A.C.* and *Japanese Alpine Club*

India—Garhwal

Nanda Devi and Nanda Devi East. Our expedition was organized jointly by the Indian Mountaineering Foundation and eight guide-instructors of the Ecole Nationale de Ski et d'Alpinisme at Chamonix. We had as our objective to traverse from Nanda Devi (25,645 feet) to Nanda Devi East (24,391 feet) and vice versa. There were five Indians: Balwant Sandhu, Alok Chandolo, Dorjee Lathoo, Prem Chand and Dr. Devuderjit Singh; and eight Frenchmen: Yves Pollet-Villard, Walter Cecchinel, Jean Coudray, Maurice Cretton, Charles Daubas, Yvon Masino, Raymond Renaud and I. The Indians were responsible for the approach march, the recruiting of porters and Sherpas and the food for the approach and Base Camp. The French provided the equipment and food for the actual climb. The team assembled in New Delhi on April 28 but took six days to clear customs. We traveled in two days by truck to Joshimath. The approach to Base Camp took ten days. We could find only 70 porters and had to use 200 pack-goats which carried 20 pounds apiece to the Rhamani. A helicopter lifted 2½ tons to within a day of Base Camp. The 70 porters relayed supplies from the Rhamani to Base Camp. Thus precious time was lost. We had hoped for eight Sherpas but had only four good ones. Kashmiris and local porters could not be used much on the mountain. We thus lost another ten to twelve days with problems of load carrying. At a Base Camp at 16,400 feet we divided into two teams for the two peaks. On the main peak Camps I (19,000 feet), II (20,350 feet), III (22,300 feet) and IV (24,275 feet) were established on May 20, 25, June 1 and 11 respectively. On Nanda Devi East Camp I (19,350 feet), II (20,350 feet), III (21,825 feet) and IV (22,475 feet) were pitched on May 23, 26, June 6 and 13 respectively. The summit of the main peak was reached on June 14 by Coudray and Renaud and on June 16 by Balwant Sandu and Prem Chand. Pollet-Villard, Cecchinel and Dorjee Lathoo got to the top of Nanda Devi East on June 16. After preparing much of the traverse below the summits, the climbers were ready to attempt to climb the ridge linking the two peaks when the monsoon broke on June 19. It stormed for eight days, obliging us to give up.

MAURICE GICQUEL, *Club Alpin Français*

Dunagiri, Southeast Face. Our expedition consisted of two members: Joseph Trasker and me. After a two-week wait in New Delhi, the Indian Mountaineering Foundation supplied us with a liaison officer, who returned to New Delhi after completing only three days of the march-in. We climbed the southeast face of Dunagiri (23,184 feet), reaching the summit on October 8. We climbed alpine-style without porters or fixed camps. The 5000-foot-high face had in its lower half a rock ridge with snow and ice sections. The crux was at 21,000 feet where we encountered steep rock, which required some artificial aid, and difficult mixed climbing. We carried six days of food and bivouac equipment. The ascent took seven days and the descent by the same route, four more. During the descent the fingers of both my hands were frostbitten.

R.M. RENSHAW, *Alpine Club*

Dunagiri Attempt and Hanuman. The goal of our Austrian Alpine Club (ÖAK) expedition was the second ascent of 23,184-foot Dunagiri. We were originally Fräulein Hermine Müller, German, Frau Ruth Steinmann-Hess, Swiss, Dr. Erich Bosina and I, Austrians. We had difficulty in getting porters at Lata because of the ten expeditions but finally managed to get eleven porters to carry our 28 loads. On the night of May 7 Hermine Müller came down with pulmonary edema at 12,500 feet at Lata Karak and had to be evacuated. With only seven porters left, we had to relay loads to Base Camp. By chance we met the Austrian Erich Straker, who joined our team. We got to Base Camp at 15,250 feet east of Hanuman on May 13. Camp I was set up at 17,725 feet on May 16 and Camp II at 19,425 feet in the col between Dunagiri and Hanuman on the 17th. Heavy snow fell until May 22. We were back in Camp II on May 24. On the 25th we climbed the northwest ridge partially on black ice and partially in two feet of loose snow, reaching the high point of the expedition at 20,675 feet. Time was running out; above the rock step there was windslab and dangerous cornices. We settled for the third ascent of Hanuman (19,882 feet). On May 28 we placed camp at 18,500 feet and on May 29 climbed the southeast ridge, where gendarmes rise above an easy snow ridge. Frau Steinmann, Bosina, Lieutenant Jagad, the liaison officer of the Japanese Kalanka expedition, the porter Sher Singh Rana and I were on top at eleven o'clock.

ERICH VANIS, *Österreichischer Alpen Klub*

Trisul. Five Americans, Phillip Trimble, Bruce Carson, Dan Emmett, Frank Morgan, and Dutchman Hans Bruyntjes left Delhi on August 15, arriving in Lata on August 18, and at Trisul Base Camp (15,100 feet) on August 25. We moved to Camp I at 17,100 feet on August 29, to Camp II at 19,200 feet on September 1, and to Camp III at 20,800 feet on September 3. In very misty weather, the summit of Trisul (23,300 feet) was reached by the entire party on September 4 in six to seven hours from Camp III. Another snow peak a few hundred feet further along the summit ridge was observed during a partial clearing of the mist. Bruce Carson decided to walk over and investigate whether this point was higher and indeed the true summit of Trisul. Due to the heavy mist, he probably had not observed that the peak was severely corniced. When the mist cleared again in a few minutes, Bruce had disappeared, leaving only footsteps in the snow leading to the edge of the 3000-foot vertical south face of Trisul. Apparently, in the mist, he had wandered onto the huge cornice overhanging the south face and it had broken off. Carefully belayed, Hans Bruyntjes crawled over to the edge where the footsteps ended and saw only the vertical face below him. We did not have the equipment necessary to descend the face but did hope to approach it from the bottom the next day. However it snowed heavily that night and continued to storm for the next few days, making this unfeasible.

ARLENE BLUM

Trisul. The 1975 Seattle Garhwal-Himalaya Expedition was led by Michael Clarke; other members were Jan Balut, David Hambly, Ray Jewell, Carl Moore, Gordon Thomas and I. We traveled by bus through the gorges of the Alaknanda to Lata. There we met our twenty-odd porters and an untold number of sheep and goats and began the march in the footsteps of Shipton and Tilman up and into the Rishi Ganga Gorge. By May 25 Base Camp was established at 15,000 feet, somewhat higher than Longstaff's "Juniper Camp" of the 1907 first ascent. We followed Longstaff's route by the northeast shoulder. Camp I at 18,000 feet was dug out on a gentle snow slope; Camp II nestled in a splendid snow basin at 20,300 feet. On June 3, four members made an unsuccessful summit bid. Another attack was initiated and all members moved to Camp II on June 7. One day's bad weather forced inactivity, but on June 9 all but Moore and our Indian liaison officer, Flying Officer U.K. Palat, gained the summit at one P.M. The panorama was marvelous, with Nanda Devi, Changabang, Kalanka, Dunagiri and Kamet prominent. The descent and return trek were uneventful until a pagan sheep barbecue on Malatuni Pass.

P.S. MARSHALL, *Three Corner Round*

Trisul. A number of expeditions have climbed Trisul since the relaxation of the Inner Line restrictions. On May 17 Germans Martin Biock and Lothar Büttner reached the summit and skied back down. On May 20 they were followed by three climbers from the German Alpine Club led by Erich Reismüller.

Devistan. Devistan (21,910 feet) was climbed from the Trisul Glacier by the whole of the Iwate Sangaku Kyokai party on May 24, including Shozo Watanabe, leader, Yoji Kudo, Kazuo Iwabuchi, Seiichi Sawada, Kazuo Domon, Yukio Kudo and Tomo Odanaka.

ICHIRO YOSHIZAWA, *A.A.C.* and *Japanese Alpine Club*

Nanda Ghunti East. The Shinshu University Alpine Club Expedition was led by Kyoji Sugimoto. The other two members, Ichikawa and Furuzuka, climbed the East Peak (20,013 feet) on October 6.

ICHIRO YOSHIZAWA, *A.A.C.* and *Japanese Alpine Club*

P 6992, P 6911 and Bamchu. Base Camp was set up by the Japan Himalaya Mountaineering Association Expedition on a glacial lake at the end of the Changabang Glacier on August 31. After unsuccessful attempts were made on Changabang, thwarted by avalanche dangers, they moved Base Camp to the Uttar Rishi Glacier and climbed the following peaks: Bamchu (20,680 feet) on September 20 by all members; P 6992 (22,940 feet) on September 27 by Jiro Imai, Meiro Hagiwara and on September 28 by Sumi Shimizu, leader, Sadashige Inada, Mahito Nose and Hideo Tateno; and P 6911 (22,674 feet) on October 2 by Jiro Imai and Hagiwara.

ICHIRO YOSHIZAWA, *A.A.C.* and *Japanese Alpine Club*

Mrigthuni. An Indian group from Serampore climbed Mrigthuni (22,490 feet) on September 28. Nitai Roy, Sisir Ghosh, Swapan Sikdar, Rajani Rakshit, Ranjit Rit, Yadav Singh and Sher Singh reached the top.

KAMAL K. GUHA, *Himalayan Club*

Geldhung. The Durgapur Mountaineering Association went from Malari to Base Camp at Patalpani. On September 7 Sibapada Chakraborty, Amit Sinha, Dipak Pal and two Sherpas reached the summit (20,214 feet) of this virgin peak.

KAMAL K. GUHA, *Himalayan Club*

Bharat Kunta. A team from the Indo-Tibetan Border Police led by B.C. Kulbe climbed this peak in the Kedarnath massif. Kalyan Singh,

Nima Dorje, Ang Phutar, Prithvi Prasad, Kunwar Singh and Tripan Singh reached the summit (21,580 feet) on September 6.

KAMAL K. GUHA, *Himalayan Club*

P 20,240. Chanchal Mitra, Harsha Muni Nautiyal and Debi Ram claim to have climbed this virgin peak due north of Suvarna on August 9. They left for the summit from camp on the Kalindi Pass.

KAMAL K. GUHA, *Himalayan Club*

Jogin III. A ladies' expedition, organized by the Bharat Outward Bound Pioneers of Poona, set up Base Camp on the true right bank of the Kedar Ganga at 14,000 feet on May 29. Camps I, II and III were placed at 15,200, 16,100 and 17,000 feet. On June 13 Dr. Miss K.B. Sorab and Sherpa Chewang Thondup reached the summit (20,065 feet) from their 17,500-foot Camp IV.

KAMAL K. GUHA, *Himalayan Club*

Swargarohini. On October 25, 1974, Englishman Charles Clarke, Canadians Dilsher Singh Virk, Peter Fuhrman and Bruce MacKinnon and Indians Mohan Singh and Rattan Singh made the first ascent of Swargarohini's western summit from Camp IV at 17,700 feet from the west. The Indian maps give the western summit as 6247 meters (20,496 feet) and the eastern as 6252 (20,512 feet), but they claim to have reached the higher peak.

Bandar Punchh I. Seven male trainees of the Nehru Institute, led by its principal Colonel L.P. Sharma, climbed Bandar Punchh I (20,720 feet) by a new route on May 16. Five girls from the NIM climbed to the summit on June 19 by the normal route.

KAMAL K. GUHA, *Himalayan Club*

Phabrang. Keshab Mukherjee, Asit Roy, Bidhu Sarkar and Sankat Ali Mondal from Calcutta made the third ascent of Phabrang (20,250 feet) on July 19.

KAMAL K. GUHA, *Himalayan Club*

India—Himachal Pradesh

Mukerbeh. An Indian all-woman expedition climbed Mukerbeh (19,910 feet). From Camp III on May 29 six women and two Sherpas climbed to the nearby summit of Manali Peak (18,600 feet). On May 30 two of the women, Thrity Birdy and Bharati Banerjee, and three

Sherpas, Sonam Lama, Tasi Thondup and Nawang Tsering, placed Camp IV along the ridge towards Mukerbeh. On May 31 they left in doubtful weather for the summit, which they reached at 1:45. The most difficult part was a 200-foot ice step.

Tos Valley, Kulu. The North of England Expedition went from the Hindu Kush on to Kulu. In this part of the expedition were Michael Hosted, Miss Terry Funk (Swiss), John Darling, Ernest Shield, the local Sherpa Rinzing, my wife Dawn and I. We set off on September 2 to approach Base Camp at the head of the Tos valley via the Parbati valley. The monsoon ran very late and for a while we were restricted to reconnaissance with ascents of two 5000-meter peaks above Base Camp and establishing Camp I on the East Tos Glacier at 14,175 feet. In the final two weeks we made the following first ascents: Tiger Tooth (5880 meters or 19,292 feet; north above the head of the East Tos and the Tichu Glaciers) via west ridge on September 30 by P. Bean, Shield, Darling; Angdu Ri (5800 meters or 19,029 feet; north of East Tos Glacier between White Sail and P 20,495) via east ridge on September 30 by Hosted, Funk, Rinzing; and P 5880 (19,029 feet; north of East Tos Glacier between P 20,495 and Tiger Tooth) via west ridge on October 3 by Darling, Rinzing. For Tiger Tooth we had to camp first at the end of the upper East Tos Glacier and then over a 5000-meter barrier ridge on the upper Tichu Glacier.

PAUL BEAN, *Cleveland Mountaineering Club, England*

Brammah II, Kishtwar Himal. The Sapporo Alpine Club Expedition was led by Kosaku Keiryo. They set up Base Camp on August 21 on the Brammah Glacier, west of the peak up the North Nullah. On September 15 Hideo Yokoyama and Shizuo Noku reached the summit (21,080 feet).

ICHIRO YOSHIZAWA, *A.A.C.* and *Japanese Alpine Club*

Kishtwar Himal. An expedition comprising Simon and Elizabeth Brown, Pete Butler, Nicki and Jane Clough, Rob and Netti Collister and, for a short time, a liaison officer, was in the Padar region, based on Athole (Arthal), during September and October with the object of climbing Brammah II. We could not find a viable approach and failed to set foot on the mountain. A route into the Kijai Nullah from the east via the village of Ligri proved impossible. The route into and up the Kijai Nullah from the south via La was investigated at the end and found long and difficult and impracticable for loaded men unless a way was first cleared with machetes. Seen from the east the north face and ridge appear to be the only feasible route up Brammah II. The

18,375-foot col below the north face was eventually reached from the steep Donali Glacier to the north by traversing from the top of the steep Donali-Kizae col (17,060 feet) across the north face of P 5865. It is also possible to descend the snow bowl at the head of the Kijai Glacier (two abseils at the bottom; V.S. pitches in ascent) and climb an easy icefall to reach the same point. We had some lucky escapes from avalanches while descending the 17,060-foot col for more food; this led to the route being abandoned. Two of the party returned to Kishtwar via the Kiar Nullah, crossing a 16,750-foot col (first found by Fritz Kolb in 1946) between the Bhazun and Wakbal glacier systems. On the way, P 5685 (18,651 feet) was climbed. (See Fritz Kolb, "Third Choice, Adventures in the Padar Region," *Himalayan Journal,* 1947 and map by John Harriss, *Alpine Journal,* 1970.)

ROBERT COLLISTER, *Alpine Club*

Sickle Moon Tragedy. A nine-member team of the Japanese Self Defense Force was led by Lieutenant Colonel Fumio Yunoki and included two women. They reached Kishtwar on July 7, trekked through Kiyar, the last village, and set up Base Camp at the snout of the Sarbal Glacier at 12,000 feet on July 20. Camp III was established on this 21,570-foot unclimbed peak at 17,000 feet on August 2 and it took 12 days to set up Camp IV at 19,000 feet. Summit attempts which reached the northwest ridge were made on August 15 and 16 by two different groups of three each but were turned back by weather, one group only 150 feet from the top. At two A.M. on August 17 the tent of Lieutenant Satoru Takashi and Sherpa Ang Chhutar at Camp IV was hit by a falling rock. Chhutar was killed instantly and Takashi died an hour and a half later.

KAMAL K. GUHA, *Himalayan Club*

Sickle Moon. A 26-man team from the Indian Army, led by Lieutenant Colonel D.N. Thanka, commandant of the High Altitude Warfare School, left Kishtwar on August 30. Havildar Major Tsering Norbu and Naik Nim Dorje climbed this virgin peak, Sickle Moon (21,570 feet) on December 5 from Camp IV at 19,800 feet. The descent was difficult. Dorje was rescued from a crevasse by two members waiting midway between the summit and Camp IV.

KAMAL K. GUHA, *Himalayan Club*

India—Ladakh

Nun. The Nippon Himalaya Mountaineering Association expedition was led by Mitsuaki Nishigori. They were plagued by much deep snow. Camps were at 17,325, 19,000, 20,650 and 21,325 feet. From Camp

IV on the north ridge Akinori Hosaka and Aslam reached the summit ridge but were turned back by bad weather at 22,275 feet.

ICHIRO YOSHIZAWA, *A.A.C.* and *Japanese Alpine Club*

Nun. After a Japanese expedition had failed to climb Nun, the mountain was climbed by members of a 21-member Swedish team. Two reached the summit (23,410 feet) on September 16 and four more on September 20.

KAMAL K. GUHA, *Himalayan Club*

Pakistan

K6 West Peak II (P 7040). The Toyama Sanyu-kai expedition, led by Shoko Saegi, left Khapalu on June 8 and reached Base Camp at the junction of the Gondokhoro and Chogolisa Glaciers at 12,500 feet on June 14. They proceeded south to the north side of the K6 group. Camps I and II were at 14,750 and 16,400 feet. Camp III was in the col at 18,375 feet and Camp IV on the east side of the col on the south ridge of P 6800, west of P 7040 (23,097 feet). They attacked the south ridge of P 7040, but after bivouacs at 21,000 and 22,150 feet they turned back at 22,650 feet. Base Camp was evacuated on August 6.

ICHIRO YOSHIZAWA, *A.A.C.* and *Japanese Alpine Club*

K12. Yoshihiko Yamamoto led the Ichikawa Alpine Club expedition. They left Khapalu on June 17 and were at Advanced Base on the Lofomorumba Glacier at 15,000 feet when a violent snow storm caused their porters to run away. Camp I was established on July 4 at 16,750 feet, Camp II on July 10 at the end of the plateau at 17,725 feet, Camp III on July 18 at 18,700 feet under the col on the northwest ridge after crossing the plateau, Camp V on July 27 at 22,000 feet and Camp VI on August 3 at 23,300 feet. On August 4 Shigeru Kawana, Sueo Ohta and Masaru Takeyama reached the summit (24,505 feet). On the way down they bivouacked at 23,625 feet. (The summit pair of the Kyoto University party in 1974 was lost during the descent. See *A.A.J.,* 1975, 20:1, page 210. — *Editor.*)

ICHIRO YOSHIZAWA, *A.A.C.* and *Japanese Alpine Club*

K7 Reconnaissance. Bob Barton and I made a reconnaissance of K7 (22,750 feet) during the first three weeks of September. We found that K7 would be difficult from the Chogolisa Glacier and could best be attempted from the Kondus side. By climbing a 19,700-foot peak on the left side of the glacier, we were able to see that K7 has two summits, the steeper and more westerly of the two appearing to be the higher.

The right branch of the Chogolisa Glacier offers excellent unclimbed peaks around 21,000 feet and there are many fine peaks in the area with opportunities for small groups.

JONATHAN D. PROSSER, *England*

Sherpi Kangri Attempt. We did not get permission to attempt Batura Mustagh I and had to be content with unclimbed Sherpi Kangri, attempted by Japanese last year. The reason given us was that because of the construction of the Karakoram Highway the region northeast of Gilgit is out of bounds for foreigners. In Rawalpindi we had a two-week wait for a flight to Skardu. Once there we hurried to make up time lost but arrived at our 13,000-foot Base Camp with only three weeks of climbing time left. With good weather we established Camps I, II and III, the latter at 17,000 feet under the south face of Sherpi Kangri. After climbing to 19,500 feet, we realized that the difficulties were too great and the distance too far to reach the summit in six days. After establishing Camp IV at 19,500 feet, we were in a position to attempt two most attractive mountains, which lie southeast of Sherpi Kangri on the ridge to Saltoro Kangri. On August 14 John Vincent and I reached the summit of the more southeasterly and higher peak (21,300 feet) by its south ridge. Three days later, on August 17, Alan Hunt, John Cheesmond, Bob Smith and Dave Walsh climbed the other, already called "Pyramid Peak" (21,200 feet), by its east ridge. The two peaks stand 1½ and 2½ miles from Sherpi Kangri.

DAVID E. ALCOCK, *Alpine Club*

Peaks above the Biafo Glacier. After considerable trouble in getting to Skardu by air from Rawalpindi, we hired a jeep to take us and our gear to Dasso, the end of the road. We commenced the three-day walk to Askole, the last village. This section went well, the weather being good and the porters no trouble. On reaching Askole, we paid off the porters and engaged locals for the trek up the Biafo Glacier to Base Camp. Problems began there. Leaving Askole, we walked and climbed for three days up the Biafo, reaching Ho Bluk under a thin covering of snow on the third day. We issued boots and goggles as agreed. That same evening, the head porter, Ali, and the porters got in a huddle and eventually made their demands. They would go no further unless we doubled their pay and issued socks, sweaters and anoraks to everybody! We were still four days from Base Camp on the Ogre (Baintha Brakk) with only ten days left before returning home. Not being able to meet the porters' demands, we paid them off, extracting a promise to return when sent for. The following day we commenced carrying the 50- to 60-pound loads ourselves up the crevassed Biafo Glacier at 16,000 feet, but we soon saw we could not get the necessary gear to Base Camp in time for a serious attempt on the Ogre. Reluctantly we retreated to Ho Bluk on the western side of the Biafo to attempt peaks in the vicinity. Fortunately the outcome of our expedition was a moderately successful and happy one. Splitting into three pairs, we tackled three peaks in the area, alpine-style. All three climbs were successful, one pair spending three days on their mountain with two 19,000-foot bivouacs. Peter Jennings and Alan Burke made the second ascent of Razaqi (18,000 feet; west of Hu Bluk and north of P 18,290 feet on Shipton's 1950 map, *Hispar-Biafo Glacial Regions*) on June 8. My party and I had made the first ascent on June 20, 1971. Pat Fearnehough made the first ascent of "Pajo" (19,000 feet; three miles south of Ghur) on June 8. Ted Howard and I made the first ascent of "Pamshe" (c. 21,000 feet; three miles northeast of Ghur) on June 9. We were considerably higher than Ghur, our immediate neighbor. Dr. John Minors also took part.

DON MORRISON, *Yorkshire Karakoram Expedition*

Attempt on Peak above the Biafo. Delay in getting flown to Skardu prevented Doug Scott, Clive Rolands, Robert Wood and Ronnie Richards from having enough time in Baltistan to accomplish their objective. Instead the expedition turned into a reconnaissance for the Ogre in 1977. They attempted a 20,000-foot peak above the Biafo but were turned back several hundred feet below the top by difficulties of the rock.

Payu Attempt. We had bad luck on Payu (less correctly written Paiju) this year. The members were Jean François Porret, Raymond Coène, Simone Badier, Jean Bourgeois, Dr. Lucien Honnilh and I as leader. We tried to climb Payu by the route attempted by the Clinch expedition in 1974 but had to give up because of an accident of which Porret and I were the victims. While descending from Camp I at 19,350 feet, we were swept by an avalanche which fell from the snowfield above the couloir. I just managed to stop the fall in the couloir, but Porret had a very badly broken right leg. The evacuation was very difficult and we got him out of Pakistan only after 26 days. We had great porter troubles. They demanded over 50 rupees a day on the glaciers and still went on strike.

JEAN FRÉHEL, *Club Alpin Français*

Trango Tower Attempt. A British expedition gave up their attempt on the Trango Tower after Martin Boysen came close to being the victim of an unusual accident some 600 feet below the summit. On a difficult free and aid pitch, Boysen jammed his leg in a wide crack and could not remove it. His companion, Mo Anthoine, was unable to help. Finally two hours later, Boysen managed to cut his trouser leg off with a piton and freed himself. Time and food were running out and the attempt was given up. The climbers, who also included Ian McNaught-Davis, Joe Brown, Will Barker and Dave Potts, had climbed the gully south of the tower, where they placed Camp I. Above, the climbing became difficult, being either iced-up rock or mixed climbing. Camp II was a snow cave in the snowfield a third of the way up the rock tower.

Baltoro Cathedral. The Belledo section of the Italian Alpine Club climbed two routes on the Baltoro Cathedral, the southwest ridge with camps and the southeast face alpine-style. Members were Giulio Fiocchi, leader, Dr. Alberto Sironi, Giuseppe Lafranconi, Ernesto and Sergio Panzeri, Gianluigi Lanfranchi, Carlo Duchini, Amabile Valsecchi, Daniele Chiappa, Pierino Maccarinelli, Benvenuto Laritti, Giacomo Stefani and Armando Colombari. They had hoped to climb the Trango Towers but the Pakistani government instead gave them permission for the Baltoro Cathedral or Thunmo (19,246 feet). From camp at Liliwa, they cut diagonally across the Baltoro Glacier to Base Camp at 12,800 feet at the confluence of the Dunghe Glacier with the Baltoro. After three days of reconnaissance they decided on the routes. On June 23 the siege of the southwest ridge began. They had UIAA V to V+ difficulties to climb the 2500 feet on often rotten granite to Camp I. To there they fixed 3300 feet of rope. Bad weather then delayed operations. On July 3 E. Panzeri, Lafranconi, Lanfranchi and Valsecchi returned to Camp I but Panzeri fell sick and was replaced by Laritti. Despite snow, cold, fatigue and insufficient food, they pressed on. The next section presented difficult mixed climbing, particularly around 16,000 feet. They had next two rope-lengths of overhanging rock, then dangerous loose snow and nearly vertical ice. Finally from Camp IV they reached the summit at 2:30 P.M. on July 10. The attack on the 5000-foot-high southeast face began on July 3. Chiappa, Maccarinelli, Stafani, Duchini and S. Panzeri climbed 1650 feet up a gully in the east face and traversed right on a shoulder. They climbed another 1650 feet the next day to the foot of the final buttress. To there they had had UIAA III to V difficulties. Bad weather drove them back to Base Camp. Two days later, July 6, they were back at their high point. Chiappa and Maccarinelli climbed two rope-lengths where they could not place a single piton. They bivouacked at 16,400 feet. On the 7th Stefani and S. Panzeri took the lead, climbing overhanging cracks on aid and then ice, and finally more difficult and rotten cracks before returning to the bivouac. On the 8th Chiappa, Duchini and Maccarinelli left first and above the former high point climbed rotten, snow-covered flakes. Panzeri and Stefani followed. Chiappa led a vertical dihedral to get to the top of the face followed by the rest. (UIAA V, V+; A2, A3). Easier mixed climbing took them

PLATE 71

Photo by H. Adams Carter

TRANGO TOWERS. The British route ascends the center of the middle tower.

PLATE 72

Photo by H. Adams Carter

Thunmo or Baltoro Cathedral. The route to the highest summit leads up the ridge from the left. The other route ascends the face on the right.

to the top. They used 500 feet of fixed rope and 150 feet of metal ladder. A deep depression separates this high point from the summit of Thunmo.

Lopsang Peak. Like most expeditions this year in the Baltoro Glacier area, we ran into problems. The sudden opening of the region brought a flood of expeditions, overtaxing the limited facilities. The porters took full advantage of the seller's market. We therefore had troubles with the government, the local Balti people, our liaison officer and the poor weather. We passed the more exciting objectives as we moved up the Baltoro, namely the Uli Biaho Spire and the Trango group. The granitic formations deteriorated as we advanced but we made the best of what we had. The film crew caught up to us in Rawalpindi and they accompanied several members of the expedition to the summit of Karphogang (19,560 feet), a snow dome just west of the Mustagh La. On June 19 Yvon Chouinard, Dr. Joel Malta, George Lowe and Doug Tompkins reached the top. On June 18 Don Lauria, Mike Covington and I climbed Lopsang Peak (20,423 feet) via its southern couloir. Shortly after these climbs, four members left for Skardu. Lowe, Lauria and I made three attempts on P 18,700, located on the southeastern spur of Mount Biange. We reached 18,000 feet on the west arête before retreating in a storm. All the climbing was done alpine-style, which accounts for our lack of accomplishments.

DENNIS HENNEK

Broad Peak, Central Summits. A Polish expedition from Wrocław consisted of 15 climbers under the leadership of Janusz Fereński. Their Base Camp was established at 16,400 feet on the Godwin Austen Glacier on June 30. The route followed the Austrian route of 1957 with some variants, keeping more on the crest of the buttress. Camps I, II and III were at 19,000, 21,500 and 23,625 feet. On July 28 Roman Bebak, Kazimierz Głazek, Marek Kęsicki, Janusz Kuliś, Bogdan Nowaczyk and Andrzej Sirokski set off for the summit of the central peak (c. 26,300 feet) but in the afternoon Bebak withdrew while still below the col between the main and central peaks. Right above the col and near the top were two difficult rock steps. At 7:30 P.M. the five other climbers reached the summit of the central peak. After descending most of the fairly difficult ridge in the dark under worsening weather, they decided to rappel to a snow terrace on the west side, which led back to the col. Nowaczyk was lost when his rappel rope came adrift and plunged down the Chinese side. This was their only rope. During the unroped descent further on the icy slopes Kęsicki, Sikorski and Kulis slipped at different times. Kulis managed to arrest himself, but the other two fell to their deaths.

HALINA CIEPLIŃSKA-BOJARSKA, *Klub Wysokogórskiego, Poland*

Chogolisa. The Upper Austrian Karakoram Expedition was composed of Gustav Ammerer, Alois Furtner, Fred Pressl, Fritz Priesner, Christoph Pollet, Hilmar Sturm and me as leader. On August 2 and 4 members of our expedition stood on the southwest summit of Chogolisa, on the mountain where Hermann Buhl fell to his death through a cornice. Buhl and Kurt Diemberger in 1957 attacked the northeast summit of Chogolisa from the north, from the Baltoro and Chogolisa Glaciers. Because of its trapezoidal form, Chogolisa has two nearly equally high summits connected by a 3000-foot ridge. In 1958 the Japanese Fujihira and Hirai climbed to the northeast summit by the Buhl-Diemberger route. Though it was not clear which summit was higher, Eduard Sternbach and G.O. Dyhrenfurth give 25,110 feet for the southwest summit and 25,066 for the northeast. This would seem to agree with our estimates by eye. We were interested by Chogolisa's nearly completely unexplored south side and the Kaberi Glacier. We jeeped to Khapalu on June 18, crossed the Shyok River and made the 11-day approach (with two storm days) with 62 porters via the Hushe, Saltoro and Kondus valleys and the Kondus Glacier. We had to set up Base Camp just above the confluence of the Kondus and Kaberi Glaciers at 13,775 feet because the porters couldn't and wouldn't go higher in the new snow. The 12-mile distance to the foot of the south face of Chogolisa was an acute supply problem, since we had no high-altitude porters. Yet in a week we had Camps I and II at 15,425 and 16,750 feet on the Kaberi Glacier and Camp III at 18,700 feet, involving a difficult but possible route. Between Camps II and III was a giant icefall. Above the icefall and Camp III rose a 3300-foot-high, 50° ice slope to the 22,000-foot col at the foot of the 1¼-mile-long west ridge. The keys to the ascent were the icefall and the ice face. On July 7 as we were attempting to bypass the icefall on a heavily corniced ridge, I fell 100 feet with a breaking cornice, was held by Pressl, but was unhurt. Two days later we managed to bypass the icefall on the flank of the ridge with 650 feet of fixed rope. Because of bad weather and new snow, it took until July 26 to climb the ice wall, where we fixed 4250 feet of rope, and to establish Camp IV in the col. Good weather from July 29 to August 6 gave us our chance. Pressl and Ammerer left Camp IV on August 1 and postholed the long flat stretch of the west ridge and pitched their bivouac tent at 23,000 feet. Their 12-hour effort on August 2 ended on the southwest summit of Chogolisa at three P.M. Two days later Furtner and Sturm also reached the top. Camps were evacuated and we left Base Camp on August 13.

EDUARD KOBLMÜLLER, *Österreichischer Alpenverein*

Gasherbrum II, South Spur. The French Lyon Expedition was composed of Jean-Pierre Frésafond, leader, and his wife Hélène, Louis Audoubert, Frédéric Bourbousson, Marc Batard, André Chariglione, Jean

PLATE 73

Photo by H. Adams Carter

Broad Peak (left) and Gasherbrum IV from the Baltoro Glacier. The summit of Broad Peak reached by the Poles is the rock peak at the left.

PLATE 75

Photo by Fred Pressl

On the summit of CHOGOLISA. Camp IV is just visible in the col at the bottom right.

PLATE 74

Photo by Eduard Koblmüller

Camp III on CHOGOLISA. Camp IV lay in the col, 3300 feet higher.

Dupraz, Jean-Jacques Forrat, Bernard Macho, Dr. Alain Raymond, Jacques Soubis, François Valençot, Bernard Villaret de Chauvigny and me. It took us 16 days from Dasso to reach Base Camp, where we arrived on May 30. On May 31 we reconnoitered the very crevassed glacier which was to take us to Camp I, which we established on June 2. Above, a plateau led to the foot of the south face. We decided on the unclimbed south spur, which involved fixing 5000 feet of rope, starting at 20,000 and ending at 23,625 feet, the length of the spur. Camp II (22,000 feet) was established on the spur on June 9. We continued to prepare the route along the spur. On June 16 Batard, Chariglione and I got to within 500 feet of the top of the spur. On the 17th, each carrying a sleeping bag, Chariglione the food, Batard the tent and I the butane stove and walkie-talkie, we finished fixing the route and got to the top of the spur at 9:30. Chariglione was too fatigued to continue, but Batard and I kept on up to a very cold, foodless bivouac at 25,100 feet; we merely had cold water to drink. In the evening I reconnoitered to a 25,100-foot col on the southeast ridge. Next morning, June 18, at six, we left for the summit, which we reached at nine A.M. That same day Audoubert and Villaret ascended to the bivouac, which we had left set up, while Batard and I descended to Camp II. On the 19th it stormed; Audoubert and Villaret attempted to reach the summit but were forced back to the bivouac. Since it continued to storm on the 20th, they had to descend. Audoubert started down, followed by Villaret. For some inexplicable reason the latter turned around and climbed rapidly back to the bivouac. At the limit of his strength, Audoubert had to continue the descent. The storm went on, worse and worse for eight days. At the end of three, we had to descend from Camp II if we too were not to die. We could not recover Villaret's body. It took us 19 days from Base Camp to the summit. We had only two high camps. We used neither high-altitude porters nor oxygen. The expedition was chiefly financed by its members.

YANNICK SEIGNEUR, *Club Alpin Français*

Gasherbrum II and III. To mark the International Women's Year the Polish Ladies Expedition was organized under the leadership of Mrs. Wanda Rutkiewicz. For safety reasons, a men's team was added to the expedition with separate objectives. The following took part: ladies' team: Alicja Bednarz, Alison Chadwick-Onyszkiewicz, Anna Czerwinska, Halina Krüger-Syrokomska, Dr. Maria Mitkiewicz, Anna Okopinska, Krystyna Palmowska and Wanda Rutkiewicz; men's team: Leszek Cichy, Marek Janas, Andrzej Lapinski, Janusz Onyszkiewicz, deputy leader, Wladyslaw Woźniak, Marcin Zachariasiewicz, Krzysztof Zdzitowiecki and Captain Saeed Ahmed Malik, Pakistani liaison officer. The caravan started from Baha on May 29 and Base Camp was reached by the last group on June 19. Camp I was established that same day at 19,700 feet, Camp II on July 4 at 21,325 feet and Camp III at 24,125 feet six days later. Up to this point the route was on snow and ice of 40° to 50° with a few places of 60° to 70°; it required 5250 feet of fixed rope. The weather was unstable. At the end of July the weather improved and a summit bid was launched. On August 1 the men, Cichy, Onyszkiewicz and Zdzitowiecki, climbed Gasherbrum II (26,360 feet), the third ascent by a new route, the northwest face. There were 1650 feet of difficult snow and ice climbing. The next ascent of Gasherbrum II was made on August 9 also by men, Janas, Lapinski and Woźniak. They ascended the Austrian first-ascent route, the east ridge. The first ascent of Gasherbrum III (26,090 feet) was made on August 11 by members of both parties. The route followed the line of a big couloir in the center of the east face. There was difficult mixed climbing and about 350 feet of rope was fixed on the rocky traverses to ease the descent. The summit was reached at six P.M. by Wanda Rutkiewicz, Onyszkiewicz and his English wife, Alison, and Zdzitowiecki. Since 1964 this had been the highest unclimbed peak in the world. The participation of two women is a record in women's alpinism since women had not previously taken part in first ascents of peaks above 24,600 feet. The following day Halina Krüger-Syrokomska and Anna Okopinska made the first female ascent of Gasherbrum II, repeating the Austrian route. They are the first European women to have climbed an 8000-meter peak. Theirs was also the first all-female climb of an 8000er, the Japanese on Makalu and Everest and the Chinese on Everest having been made in the company of men.

POLSKI ZWIAZEK ALPINIZMU, *Poland*

Hidden Peak, Alpine-Style. After three years of trying, Reinhold Messner and Peter Habeler finally were granted permission to climb an 8000-meter peak alpine-style. They were allowed to attempt Hidden Peak (26,470 feet) by its northwest face. With twelve porters and a liaison officer they left Skardu on July 13 and reached Base Camp at 16,750 feet at the foot of Hidden Peak twelve days later. In the last days of July they climbed through two icefalls to the glacier between Gasherbrum II and Hidden Peak (Gasherbrum I). After a night at 19,350 feet they returned to Base Camp. They made a second reconnaissance, carrying supplies to be used on the final climb. They returned to their previous campsite and the next day climbed to 22,000 feet. The face was steeper than they had expected, much of it 60° bare ice but soft enough to provide good front-pointing. They again descended to Base Camp. The weather seemed to be three days bad and three days good. On August 8 it seemed favorable and they returned to the 19,350-foot camp. On the 9th they picked up their supplies and climbed, unroped and unbelayed, the 4000-foot face. In the upper part the ice gave way in part to steep ice couloirs and iced rotten rock. This part of the climb was comparable to the north face of the Matterhorn. After eight hours of very difficult climbing, at two P.M., they reached the shoulder at 23,300 feet, where, exhausted, they pitched their bivouac tent. On August 10 the first hour was easier but the slope soon steepened. About noon they traversed left onto the ridge and finally stood on top at 12:30 after six hours of climbing. They descended that night to 23,300 feet and were back in Base Camp two days later.

Urdok I and Hidden Peak. The Austrian Karakoram Expedition was made up of the German Dr. Karl Hub and Austrians Dr. Helmut Prevedel, Herbert Zefferer, Robert Schauer, my wife Leselotte and me as leader. Though we had originally headed for Baltoro Kangri we changed for the American route on Hidden Peak at the same time that Messner and Habeler were on the north face. Schauer, Zefferer and I got to the summit the day after the other party, on August 11, to complete the third ascent. After finally arriving at Skardu on July 2, we got to Base Camp at 17,000 feet on the South Gasherbrum Glacier on July 13. Camps I, II, III and IV were placed at 18,375, 21,000, 22,300 and 23,950 feet. We fixed rope on most of the ridge, which we found more difficult than we had expected. The Americans describe traversing snow bands right below the summit col at about 25,900 feet, but we had to cross bands of fairly rotten rock there. We reached the top at six P.M. On August 4, all of us except for Dr. Prevedel had made the first ascent of Urdok I (23,950 feet) from Camp III.

HANNS SCHELL, *Österreichischer Alpenklub*

Saltoro Kangri Attempt. The Hokuryo Alpine Club's expedition was composed of Shuhji Yamamoto, Kazuyu Namikawa and 12 others including two women. They arrived at Base Camp at 14,000 feet on June 3 and attempted the south ridge of Saltoro Kangri (25,400 feet). Bad conditions stopped their effort at 18,700 feet. They crossed to the main ridge to try the 1962 route of Kyoto University but this failed too, owing to the snow conditions.

ICHIRO YOSHIZAWA, *A.A.C.* and *Japanese Alpine Club*

Teram Kangri. The Shizuoka University Alpine Club expedition was led by Hajime Katayama and had 17 other members. They left Khapalu on June 1 and traveled via Goma, Ali Bransa, the Bilafond La, Lolofond and Siachen Glaciers to reach Base Camp at 16,900 feet on July 10. They used a sledge to descend the Lolofond Glacier and at the junction of the Teramsher Glacier established Advanced Base at 17,400 feet. They established Camp I (18,500 feet), II (20,350 feet), III (21,150 feet), IV (22,150 feet) and V (23,125 feet) on July 19 and 25, August 2, 7 and 9. On August 12 Kazuo Kodaka and Yasunori Kobayashi climbed over Teram Kangri II via its south ridge and on to the main summit (24,490 feet). All members reached the summit of Teram Kangri II. Base Camp was evacuated on August 19.

ICHIRO YOSHIZAWA, *A.A.C.* and *Japanese Alpine Club*

Latok I and II. Two different Japanese expeditions were in the Latok group from July to September. The Tokai section of the Japanese Alpine Club was led by Makoto Hara. Tremendous avalanches and rockfall persuaded them to give up trying Latok I (23,440 feet) and to explore the glaciers in the group. They went up the Biafo and Simgang, over the Sim La where they had to descend a 1500-foot ice wall to the Choktoi Glacier, and continued along the Panmah to the Baltoro and back to Askole. The Kyoto Climbing Club led by Noki Takada gave up their attempt on Latok II (23,320 feet) because of avalanches and rockfall.

ICHIRO YOSHIZAWA, *A.A.C.* and *Japanese Alpine Club*

Laila. The Hekiryo Alpine Club expedition was led by Yoshinora Isomura and Tomiyasu Ishikawa. They left Skardu on July 4 and went through Yuno and Arandu to Base Camp at 13,450 feet at the junction of the Chogolungma and Haramosh Glaciers on July 14. Camp I was put at 14,100 feet on the left bank of the Haramosh Glacier on July 18 and Camp II at 15,750 feet on the east ridge on July 21. It became clear that this route was impossible and they transferred efforts to the southeast face. A new Camp II was established at 16,750 feet on August 1. Camps III (18,050 feet), IV (19,200 feet) and V (21,000 feet) were established on August 2, 5 and 8. On August 9 Ryuichi Babaguchi and Kohzo Sakai reached the summit (22,921 feet) at 5:20 P.M.

ICHIRO YOSHIZAWA, *A.A.C.* and *Japanese Alpine Club*

Malubiting Central. The expedition of the Iwate Section of the Japanese Alpine Club was led by Junjiro Kasahara and Toshihiko Sato. They left Skardu and traveled through Yuno and Arandu to reach Base Camp on the Chogolungma Glacier at 14,000 feet on July 8. Camp I was placed on the upper plateau of the icefall at 16,750 feet on July 12. Camp II or Advanced Base was established at 19,150 feet on the Polan La on July 21, Camp III under the north peak at 20,675 feet on July 28 and Camp IV at 21,325 feet on the upper plateau on July 31. On August 1 Masahide Onodera, Hedeki Atsumi, Toshinori Takahashi and Kazuhiko Moro bivouacked at 23,000 feet on the west wall of the Central Peak of Malubiting. They reached the summit (23,820 feet) at nine A.M. on

August 2 after two hours of plowing through deep snow. On August 3 Hisashi Ito slipped from a fixed rope on the north ridge of the north peak and was found dead on the Barpu Glacier. On the 5th all were back in Base Camp.

ICHIRO YOSHIZAWA, *A.A.C.* and *Japanese Alpine Club*

Peaks in the Chogolungma Group. It seems incredible that neither of our expeditions to Malubiting Central in 1974 or 1975 really got to the mountain. This year we were thwarted by frightful air service from Rawalpindi to Skardu and incorrect word that the Japanese had already climbed the mountain. On receiving this information and having only 15 days left, we changed our objective and placed Base Camp at 12,150 feet two days short of Malubiting at the foot of the Kapaltang Kun group. We got there on July 18 after seven days of march through Tisar, Arandu and Khurumal with 65 porters. The expedition was composed of Dr. Achille Poluzzi, Dr. Francesco Cavazzuti, Bruno Baleotti, Oscar Bellotti, Giancarlo Calza, Paolo Cerlini, Adelmo Lunghini, Clemente Maffei, Anchise Mutti, Giovanni Pasinetti, Guido Rocco, Tullio Rocco, Massimo Sanavio, Antonietta Staffolani, Angelo Zatti and me as leader. Camp I was at 15,540 feet. On July 21 Baleotti, Calza, Maffei and Guido Rocco left Camp I, established Camp II at 16,750 feet and went on to make the first ascent of P 5350 (17,533 feet; south of Chogolungma Glacier between East Kapaltang and West Marpo Glaciers) by its northwest ridge. Various attempts on the c. 20,000-foot highest summit of Kapaltang failed. Bellotti, Lunghini, Pasinetti and Mutti moved north across the Chogolungma Glacier above Khurumal to place camps at 15,900 and 17,725 feet on P 6005 (19,701 feet). They reached the summit on August 3 by the north ridge. Meanwhile Maffei, Calza, Cavazzuti, Tullio Rocco and Sanavio had turned to the Berginsho group (south of the tongue of the Chogolungma Glacier). They placed camp at 15,000 feet and climbed P 5720 (18,767 feet), the west peak of the group, by its west ridge on August 2.

ARTURO BERGAMASCHI, *Club Alpino Italiano*

Spantik. The Kohriyama Alpine Club's expedition to Spantik (23,042 feet) was led by Yasuhiro Narita. They reached Base Camp at 14,100 feet on July 1. Avalanche danger made them change their plans and they pushed on to the Polan La and tried the west ridge of Spantik but it was not in better condition than the southeast ridge. Though they were active until July 26, they reached only 19,600 feet. They met severe difficulties at 19,150 feet.

ICHIRO YOSHIZAWA, *A.A.C.* and *Japanese Alpine Club*

Nanga Parbat Attempt. The approach of the Felix Kuen Memorial Expedition, led by Dr. Karl Maria Herrligkoffer, was considerably complicated by their not being able to go along or cross the Karakoram Highway being built by the Chinese. Although they arrived in Pakistan on May 7, it was not until May 30 that the western part of the expedition was established at Base Camp at Dhaigiri, a little above their Base Camps of 1960, 1968 and 1970. They attempted three routes. The Toni Kinshofer route ascended the southwest ridge to the Felix Kuen Icefield and then was to continue up the Diamir side over the south peak and south shoulder to the 26,660-foot summit. Four camps were established, Camps II, III and IV at 19,350, 23,000 and 24,275 feet respectively. The weather was consistently bad. There were only two cloudless, windless days in the 40 they were on the mountain. Hillmaier, Beyerlein and Margret Schnait spent a whole week stormbound in Camp III. Hillmaier and Beyerlein were finally able to establish Camp IV and after reaching a high point of 24,775 feet descended 150 feet on the traverse to the Diamir side. Weather prevented their going further. A group reconnoitered the southeast buttress to 18,375 feet. The eastern part of the expedition established three high camps, the highest at 21,000 feet, just below Rakiot Peak. Manfred and Christa Sturm with Margret Schnait and one other made the second ascent of Toshain (c. 20,000 feet; for first ascent, see *A.A.J.*, 1975, 20:1, pages 213-4. —*Editor*). (We are very grateful to Dr. Herrligkoffer for supplying this information.)

Thui Group, Hindu Raj. The Edinburgh Hindu Raj Expedition was composed of Dave Broadhead, George Gibson, Dave Page, Des Rubens and me. We traveled by jeep from Gilgit to Yasin and continued for four days through Thui and Sholtali to Base Camp at 14,000 feet on the Borumbar Glacier. Thui I has two separate tops. The higher is 6660 meters (21,654 feet) and is marked as No. 27 on Diemberger's map of the Hindu Raj (*Himalayan Journal*, 1971, XXXI, p. 320). The second higher is No. 26, P 6400 (20,998 feet), at the head of the Panarillo and Borumbar Glaciers. P 6400 was climbed on August 5 by Gibson, Rubens and me from a camp on a plateau at 20,000 feet. A previous attempt on July 31 by Broadhead and Page reached a subsidiary peak between the two summits. It would seem that the difference between the heights of the two peaks is rather less than the 260 meters given by Diemberger. To the south of the peak we climbed there are four peaks on the east side of the Borumbar Glacier. We climbed them all. The northernmost pair (c. 20,000 and 20,300 feet) were climbed by Rubens and me on August 7. The southern ones (c. 18,500 and 18,000 feet) were climbed by various separate parties between July 19 and 26. We attempted Thui III twice from the Borumbar side. On the second attempt we climbed an obvious couloir which leads up from the glacier to the main watershed and thence to a top which lies a half-mile east and a few hundred feet lower than the main summit. An attempt was also made on Thui II, crossing from the Borumbar to the Qalandar Gum Glacier. Rubens and I followed the latter to its head and traversed a subsidiary peak of 20,000 feet to a 19,800-foot col immediately north of Thui II. Bad weather foiled the final attempt, but the climb appears fairly straightforward.

GEOFFREY COHEN, *University of Edinburgh, Scotland*

Thui III. Our expedition was composed of H.P. Doswald, Dr. A. Stöckli, Frl. Dr. V. Merz, J. de Vries, H. Bumbacher, M. Dubacher, J. Huber, J. Ineichen, H. Rieder, K. Stadlin, P. Lenggenhager, and me as leader. We placed Base Camp (12,625 feet) between the Qalandar Gum and Agost Bar Glaciers. After establishing Camps I and II (14,600 and 16,400 feet) on the Qalandar Gum Glacier, Doswald, Dubacher and Huber on July 23 climbed the 3300-foot-high southwest ice wall of Thui III (20,260 feet) to make the first ascent. On July 25 Merz, Bumbacher and Stadlin and on July 28 Dubacher, de Vries and I repeated the ascent. An attempt on 20,204-foot Thui Zom was given up when the camp at 15,100 feet below the very difficult north face was destroyed by rockfall. The risk on the 7200-foot-high face was too great. We made the following first ascents: P 5160 (16,929 feet; 2 kilometers northeast of Thui An) on July 30 by Bumbacher, Stöckli; P 5160 (16,929 feet; on the south bank of the Qalandar Gum Glacier and 5 kilometers southwest of Thui III) on July 31 by Dubacher, Huber; P 4920 (16,142 feet; 3 kilometers northeast and southeast of the latter two) on July 28 by Doswald, Huber; P 4900 (16,076 feet; 1300 meters east of Thui An) on July 16 by Dubacher, Huber; P 4580 (15,026 feet; 1 kilometer northeast of Base Camp) on July 22 by Ineichen, de Vries and on August 2 by Stadlin, Stöckli; P 4398 (14,430 feet; 1½ kilometers west of Base Camp) on July 29 by Lenggenhager, Merz, de Vries.

HANS SCHIBLI, *Schweizer Alpen Club*

Langar, 1974. In *A.A.J.,* 1975 on page 216 we reported that Italians had climbed Langar but details were lacking. On August 5, 1974 Sergio De Infanti, Mario Qualizza and Aldo Scalettaris reached the summit of Wala Peak 193, which lies just north of Saraghrar North. Wala gives no altitude for this peak but the Italians give 7100* meters (23,294 feet); Wala gives a peak some two miles west of the Italian peak as Langar Main Peak at 7061 meters. The Italians established Base Camp at 13,550 feet at Totiraz Nohu alongside the Roshgol Glacier on July 17, 1974.

---

* The Hindu Kush expert, Dr. Diemberger, doubts that this peak is more than "nearly 7000 meters."

PLATE 76

Photo by Ramón Ramona Brams

**The Southwest Ridge of Saraghrar,
Hindu Kush. Bottom of ridge: 16,650
feet; Camp II: 17,450 feet; Camp III:
18,200 feet; Camp IV: 19,600 feet.**

Camps I and II were on the glacier at 15,100 and 16,825 feet. Camps III, IV, V and VI were on the steep face, where ropes were fixed, at 18,875, 19,525, 20,500 and 21,325 feet.

Buni Zom, South Face. The Bernina Alpine Club Expedition was led by Masao Okabe and had five more members. They left Chitral on July 14 and began walking at Koghozi on the 16th. They went via Birmoha, Romen, Golen Gol, Chakholi, Bokht, Phargam An to reach Base Camp on the Ghordoghan Glacier at 12,500 feet on July 25. They placed Camp I at 15,750 feet on July 26 to reconnoiter the Ghordoghan Glacier. Camp II, established on July 30, was at 17,000 feet on the east side glacier of the ridge which connects the main and south peaks. Camp III was made at 19,000 feet on August 3. The next day route preparation on the south face got up to 20,175 feet. On August 8 they reached 20,500 feet; five climbers bivouacked at 20,350 feet. On August 9 Masao Okabe, Hideo Sato and Shigeru Tabe climbed the snow face and reached the summit (21,493 feet). Base Camp was evacuated on August 16.

ICHIRO YOSHIZAWA, *A.A.C.* and *Japanese Alpine Club*

Saraghrar Attempt. The members of our expedition were Jordi Colomer, leader, Joan Claramunt, Eduard Lluis, Enric Pérez, José L. Pérez, Alfred Martínez, Francesc Sabat, Xavier Tena, Dr. Pere Xaus and I. On July 20 we placed Base Camp at Totiraz Noku (13,650 feet). Our objective was the southwest ridge of Saraghrar (24,075 feet), a steep rock wall, using tactics similar to those of Bonington on the Annapurna south face. On July 23 we placed Camp I at 16,100 feet and began the actual climb from the foot of the wall at 16,650 feet. After several days of bad weather, on the 28th we established Camp II at 17,450 feet, having fixed ropes. On August 4 we placed Camp III at 18,050 feet. Several days of bad weather followed before we climbed a very difficult part of the ridge to a height of 19,600 feet where we placed Camp IV. Bad weather came in again and obliged us to rappel to Camp I, where we spent seven days waiting for better weather. On the 22nd, in nice weather, we started back up the 5500 feet of fixed rope and on August 24 we reached 19,750 feet, but unfortunately the weather changed again. Food and time ran out and so we had to give up.

RAMÓN BRAMONA RAMS, *Club Excursionista de Gracia, Spain*

Matkash, Hindu Raj. Four climbers from Trieste, Walter Mejak, Bianca Di Beaco, Fioretta Tarlao and Fabio Benedetti climbed above Mastuj and the Yarkuhn valley. They made the difficult ascent of a peak of about 6000 meters (19,685 feet) above the Matkash Glacier, to which they gave the name of Matkash.

MARIO FANTIN, *Club Alpino Italiano*

Maharbani Sar. In *Lo Scarpone* of December 1, 1975 an account appears telling of a first ascent made by two Italians, Roberto Ive and Elio Padovan; it is not clear to the editor just where they climbed. They traveled by jeep to Munsgol and trekked to Base Camp at 11,225 feet below Peak 106 (5750 meters or 18,865 feet). They camped at 13,750 and 16,575 feet but failed 650 feet below the summit of Peak 106. They then turned to Maharbani Sar, a crystaline schist pyramid, which they climbed on August 8.

Garmush. The Austrian Hindu Kush Expedition was led by Peter Baumgartner and comprised his wife Lilo, Karl Mahrer, Dr. Franz Österreicher and Rudi Brandstötter. They flew to Gilgit, took a jeep to Yashin and donkeys to Darkot and went with 22 porters to Base Camp at 15,425 feet. After establishing a dump at 16,400 feet, they placed Camp I first at 17,000 feet and then at 17,725 feet. On August 1 Österreicher, Mahrer and Brandstötter left Camp I at five A.M., climbed the west ridge and reached the summit of Garmush (20,486 feet) at four P.M. They bivouacked on the descent.

ADOLF DIEMBERGER, *Österreichischer Alpenklub*

Kampire Dior. Led by Keiji Enda, the Hiroshima Yamano-kai expedition climbed Kampire Dior (23,436 feet). After leaving Gilgit on May 10, they traveled through Imit, Bilhanz, Bohrt and Karambar to reach on May 23 Base Camp at 13,775 feet on the lower Karambar Glacier. They established Camp I at 15,750 feet on the upper Karambar Glacier on May 27 and Camp II at 18,700 feet on the south ridge on June 2. On June 9 they traversed a peak and placed Camp III at 21,000 feet. On the 13th they traversed another peak and put Camp IV at 21,325 feet. On June 14 Kazushige Takami, Sakae Mori, Yoji Teranishi and Yasuhide Hayashi left Camp IV at three A.M. They reached the west ridge at eight o'clock, having fixed ropes on the way, and at 9:10 stood on the top.

ICHIRO YOSHIZAWA, *A.A.C.* and *Japanese Alpine Club*

Purian Sar. Shinichi Hotta led the Kyoto Karakoram Club expedition to Purian Sar, after waiting for 20 days for a flight from Rawalpindi to Gilgit. They traveled through Imit and Bilhanz, to Base Camp at Bad

Swat at 12,175 feet, which they reached on July 22. They established Temporary Camp I at 13,200 feet on July 23, Camp I at 15,425 feet on July 27, Temporary Camp II-1 at 16,475 feet on August 1, Temporary Camp II-2 at 17,000 feet on August 3, and Camp II at 17,725 feet on August 5. This was the center of a great snowfield, where they saw Purian Sar for the first time. A fist-shaped rock stands on the right side of the col on the northwest ridge, on the left side of which they placed Camp III at 18,375 feet on August 6. On August 7 Tsuyoshi Furuichi, Ryuji Hayashibara, Hiroshi Inoue and Yasunori Ito left Camp III at 5:30 A.M. and reached the top (20,647 feet) at eleven A.M. On the 8th Yoshihiro Uchida, Teruhiko Nakajima and Junichi Takahashi reached the summit. On August 10 all were back in Base Camp.

ICHIRO YOSHIZAWA, *A.A.C.* and *Japanese Alpine Club*

Tirich Mir. Of the 32 members of our group, 18 including two women reached the summit of Tirich Mir (25,290 feet by the Czech route). On July 13 we established Base Camp at 15,100 feet on the Upper Tirich Glacier. Camp I and II at 16,750 and 19,700 feet were on the glacier. Camp III was at 22,300 feet. From 21,650 to 23,625 feet we climbed a steep couloir which took us to the west shoulder. We fixed some rope in that part. Camp IV was on the shoulder. The summit was reached on July 27 and August 3. The following reached the top: Alois Strickler, Hermann Thurnbichler, Marcel Rüdi, Hans von Känel, Richard Lanzl, Hans Bäni, Hans Zebrowski, Ludwig Hösle, Heinz Bürli, Karl Fischer, Peter and Wastl Wörgötter, Gerhard and Hannelore Schmatz, Max Marti, Richard Franzl, Waldemar Schörghofer and Hanna Müller. Irg Zom (Dirgol Zom) (22,556 feet) was climbed by most to aid acclimatization.

EUGEN REISER, *Schweizer Alpen Club*

Tirich Mir via West Spur of Tirich Mir West. Our expedition again climbed alpine-style and consisted of only Gianni Calgagno and me. We first climbed Tirich Mir (25,290 feet), as a training climb, by the 1967 Czech route from the northwest col, using the fixed ropes left by the Swiss also in 1975. We bivouacked on the col and then climbed mixed ice and rock on crampons to the top on August 11. Our new Italian route ascended the west spur of Tirich Mir West to that summit and on to the main summit. The difference in altitude was 3750 feet. It was mixed climbing with difficulty of IV and two passages of V (UIAA). After some 1650 feet of difficult climbing, we bivouacked at 23,625 feet and ascended to the top on August 25.

GUIDO MACHETTO, *Club Alpino Italiano*

Tirich Mir. Jerzy Wala led a Polish party to Tirich Mir. Unfortunately they had to abandon the ascent when Jankowski died of a heart attack at over 23,000 feet.

MAREK BRNIAK, *Klub Wysokogórski, Poland*

Tirich Mir. The Iranian climber, Mischa Saleki, who lives in Germany, had the idea of traversing the Tirich Mir peaks from IV to I and then descending the unclimbed southwest ridge. His team of Germans and English seemed beset with dissension; two of the Germans left Pakistan with one expedition vehicle and much of the equipment. Plans had to be modified. Saleki, Don Whillans, Ian Nicholson and Reinhard Seifert climbed Tirich Mir by the Spanish Route and descended the same way in bad weather. Storms had washed out the jeep road and they had to walk out 80 miles.

Snow Dome, Mehrbani. In August Rob Ferguson, Dave Wilkinson and I climbed Snow Dome (16,500 feet) and Mehrbani (17,517 feet) from the Naltar valley and P 5961 (19,557 feet) from the Daintar valley. Having crossed from the Kerengi to the Sat Marao glaciers by a difficult pass, we were thwarted in an attempt on P 6885 (22,589 feet) at the head of the Kukuay Glacier by bad weather and lack of food. (See map by Trevor Braham, *Alpine Journal,* 1971).

ROBERT COLLISTER, *Alpine Club*

Afghanistan

Noshaq. We set up our Base Camp at 15,000 feet at the northwest foot of Noshaq. On July 25 the entire team, Charles Brush, James Caruthers, Robert Emrick, Jay Gingrich, Walter Hotchkiss and I climbed Korpusht-e-Yakhi (18,688 feet). On July 30 we placed Camp I at 18,000 feet and on August 3 Camp II at 20,500 feet on Noshaq's west ridge. High winds prevented our placing Camp III above 21,600 feet. On August 5 Emrick, Ginrich and I reached the Middle Peak (24,275 feet). As Emrick was unable to continue due to exhaustion, the traverse to the main peak was not attempted.

GLENN PORZAK

Noshaq. On August 22 five Spaniards climbed the west peak of Noshaq (23,786 feet), including Monserrat Jou, who thus reached a summit higher than any other Spanish woman. Javier Pérez Gil and José María Montfort bivouacked and the next day climbed to the three highest summits of Noshaq.

Asp-e-Safed III, North Face. Our French expedition made the first ascent of the north face of Asp-e-Safed III (c. 20,670 feet) in July and August. After establishing Base Camp at 15,000 feet and Camp I at

16,900 feet, we fixed rope up to 19,350 feet from July 23 to 30. The final assault was alpine style by J.L. Guyonneau, V. Lant and J. Therisod, who reached the summit on August 2 after two bivouacs, and then by M. Legrèves, G. Lemoine and me on August 4. Both groups continued along the ridge to the summit of Asp-e-Safed I (21,349 feet), making the second traverse of the ridge and descending by the north ridge to the 19,350-foot col. The four Asp-e-Safed peaks, whose north faces are from 3300 to 4000 feet high, rise above the Qazi-Deh Glacier. The climb was of sustained serious difficulty, principally on mixed terrain and ice.

ANDRÉ ZAGDOUN, *Club Alpin Français*

M6, North Face. We placed our Base Camp at 13,500 feet in the Mondaras valley off the Darya Qadzi Deh. Our High Camp was established on a rock *rognon* at 16,800 feet. Howard Lancashire and I climbed M6 (20,134 feet) by its impressive north face. In alpine-style, we crossed the bergschrund at 2:30 A.M. and climbed steep, hard ice which gave way to sugar snow overlying the ice. We gained the summit ridge at four P.M. but bivouacked at 5:30 P.M. just below the summit, which we reached the next morning. We descended the northeast ridge in six hours. M6 was first climbed in 1972 by Italians. An attempt of M5 by its west ridge failed in bad weather.

PETER HOLDEN, *Alpine Club*

Shakhaur-Nadir Shah Traverse. The Kraków Academic Alpine Club expedition ascended Shakhaur (23,347 feet) by a new route. Between July 11 and 22 we acclimatized in the Kohe Zebak group. On July 23 we reached the village of Shakhaur in the Wakhan and immediately began a five-day reconnaissance in the Shakhaur valley, in which the Kotgaz An (pass of 17,940 feet) was reached. Base Camp was established on July 31 on the Shakhaur Glacier at 12,475 feet. We decided to climb Shakhaur alpine-style from the Kotgaz An via the east ridge and to traverse along the ridge to Nadir Shah (22,356 feet) and on to the col between M3 and M4 before descending the Shakhaur Myani Glacier, making no immediate camps. On August 3 E. Chrobak, K. Liszka, J. Maczka and I climbed the Hoshk Glacier to 14,450 feet and climbed the next day to the Kotgaz An via very steep ice with penitentes. On August 5 we climbed on rock and ice, passing ice towers on the north to bivouac behind the second tower at 19,350 feet in a saddle. The next day was difficult ice and wind-drifted snow; night caught us on an ice slope at 21,325 feet. On the 7th we had to traverse 200 yards south until we could get across a crevasse with artificial aid; we reached a plateau for the third night on the ridge at 22,800 feet. On August 8 at one P.M. we climbed the last vertical pitch to the summit of Shakhaur. We found no trace of the previous ascents. That same day we descended along the easy ridge to the Nadir Shah col, where we bivouacked at 21,650 feet. By detouring around huge cornices we climbed Nadir Shah at 2:30 the next day, where we found traces of the Yugoslavs of 1968 and a bottle with the names of the Polish first-ascent party of 1962. We descended the ridge to its abrupt 1300-foot icefall, down which we made six abseils. Below was the broad M3-M4 saddle and there we spent the seventh night. The further route was marked with flags left by our support team: Z. Dudrak, W. Jedliński and A. Pawlik. The next day we descended to the col in the ridge between Nadir Shah and Shakhaur Myani Glaciers. It took three long abseils to reach the latter. Two attempts by the support team on Languta-e Barfi failed at 19,700 feet in bad weather.

MARIAN BALA, *Kraków Academic Alpine Club, Poland*

Sad Ishtragh Group, Darrah-e-Qalat. The North of England Expedition was made up of Michael Anderson, New Zealand, Miss Terry Funk, Switzerland, Michael Hosted, my wife Dawn and me. We drove to Kabul and used local transport from Kunduz to Eshkashem. We made a one-day approach march south into the Darrah-e-Qalat, which terminates in the Sad Ishtragh massif. We had bad weather at first but made the following first ascents: Kohe Nova (5200 meters or 17,061 feet; one mile north of Wala 91) via east face on July 19 by P. and D. Bean; Kohe Barabar (5050 meters or 16,568 feet; one mile northeast of Wala 91) via south couloir on July 20 by P. and D. Bean; and Kohe Akhery (5100 meters or 16,733 feet; Wala Peak 98) via north face on July 24 by Hosted, Funk. Anderson and I made the second ascent of P 4750 (15,584 feet; Wala Peak 107) on July 24. We also found and crossed an ice pass (4885 meters) connecting the Qalat and Syarpalas Glaciers and made other minor ascents.

PAUL BEAN, *Cleveland Mountaineering Club, England*

Koh-e-Bandaka. The first Rumanian Hindu Kush expedition was made up of Valentin Garner, Ionel Coman, Anton Demeter and Zoltan Kovacs. On August 26 they climbed Koh-e-Bandaka (22,451 feet).

ADOLF DIEMBERGER, *Österreichischer Alpenklub*

Restrictions on Expeditions in Afghanistan. Friedrich Weber of Mark-toberdorf, Germany informs us that the Afghan government is now collecting duty on food imported amounting to one to two dollars per kilo. Porter fees are very high; they had to pay $16 per day for each porter for the 1½-day pack from Qazi Deh to the Noshaq Base Camp.

Kohe Purwakshan, *Wakhan Pamir.* The Warsaw expedition was made up of M. Kołaczkowski, Z. Gmaj, W. Gorzko, J.S. Graczyk, M. Mikołajczyk, W. Obojski, S. Saganek, K. Sierakowski, M. Sygowski and me. Our primary object was to explore the Purwakshan valley in the central part of the Wakhan Pamir (north of Rokot and north of the Abe Panj or Oxus River). On our return we visited the region of Kohe Baba Tangi and the Urgunt-e Payan valley in the Hindu Kush. Base Camp was placed at 15,100 feet below the main glacier in the Purwakshan valley. We made the following first ascents: P 5290 (17,356 feet; west of lower valley) by Obojski, Saganek and P 5325 (17,467 feet; east of lower valley) by Mikołajczyk, Popko both on July 22; P 4922 (16,148 feet; just south of P 5290) by Gmaj, Sygowski on July 23; P 5440 (17,881 feet; northwest of P 5290) by Graczyk, Kołaczkowski, Obojski on July 24; Kohe Purwakshan (6080 meters or 19,948 feet; east of glacier) by Mikołajczyk, Popko on July 26 via southwest spur and plateau to main (east) summit; P 6110 (20,046 feet; at head of glacier) by Graczyk, Kołaczkowski, Obojski, Sierakowski on July 31 and by Mikołajczyk, Popko on August 3 via left side of south glacier; P 5544 (18,189 feet; west of glacier) by Gorzko, Saganek, Sygowski on August 1; P 5950 (19,521 feet; west of P 6110) by Popko by traversing from P 6110 on August 3.

MACIEJ POPKO, *Polski Zwiazek Alpinizmu (Poland)*

USSR

Omission from the Pamirs Article, A.A.J., 1975. On pages 77 and 78 we unfortunately omitted the name of Marty Hoey. She did reach the summit of Pik Lenin with Evans, Lev, Stanley and Carson and waited with Lev for Williamson when he made his summit attempt.

Koshtantau, Caucasus. Vera Watson led four climbers representing the American Alpine Club at the second session of the Inter-nation Camp Bezengi in August. The others were Margaret Young, Robert Summers and I. Thirty-nine climbers from six countries spent three and a half weeks at Camp Bezengi, a permanent facility located at the junction of the Mishirgi and Bezengi valleys in the central Caucasus. The camp will accommodate up to about three hundred climbers and staff (about 200 Russian climbers were there in addition to the international group); it is very well located as a base for climbing in this area. A large number of interesting and challenging climbs are available up to grade six, almost all requiring more than one day from base. All four U.S. climbers reached the summit of Koshtantau (16,900 feet) and between them reached five lesser summits.

RICHARD K. IRVIN

Club Activities

EDITED BY FREDERICK O. JOHNSON

A.A.C., Oregon Section. At its winter dinner the Oregon Section hosted the Club's officers and board members. The evening proved to be a memorable one because of the camaraderie generated between the veterans of previous K2 expeditions who were present and members of the forthcoming 1975 expedition. Galen Rowell provided the framework with his narrative presentation, "K2—Past and Present," beginning with the attempts of the Duke of the Abruzzi and concluding with the preparations of the current team. At the appropriate places in his presentation Galen deferred to Dee Molenaar, who gave a moving summary of the 1953 expedition, and to Bill Hackett, who described his 1960 attempt and who voiced the sentiments of the assembled company in wishing the expedition Godspeed.

At the spring dinner, Section members Bob Hyslop and Joe Throop told of their explorations on the west side of Mount Deborah, preparatory to a concerted summit bid by a new route this summer. At the fall dinner we returned to the Karakoram with a talk by Eric Shipton.

A committee of the Section, chaired by Jack Grauer, developed recommendations concerning proposed developments of the Timberline Lodge ski area on Mount Hood which were forwarded to the Forest Service.

The Section was saddened this year by the untimely loss of its former chairman, Carmie Dafoe, Jr.

T.C.P. ZIMMERMAN, *Chairman*

A.A.C., Sierra Nevada Section. The Section had five meetings in 1975 including our now traditional spring meeting in Yosemite and fall picnic at Raffi Bedayn's home. A major concern has been the Yosemite Master Plan being drafted by the National Park Service. R.D. Caughron chaired a Yosemite Task Force that polled members for their views on the subject, met with the Park Service, and presented two position statements of the Section's views. The task force did an excellent job of publicizing the issues being considered in Yosemite to Club members.

Programs at the meetings were given by Chris Jones on the first ascent of North Twin, Vera Watson on the 1975 International Climbers Camp in the Caucasus, and by Frank Uher on a climb of the southeast ridge of Mount Foraker. Eric Shipton was our guest at the fall picnic, after which he showed a superb series of slides of the five British Everest expeditions from 1922 to 1938.

Our Section members climbed in the Karakoram, the Himalaya, the Andes, the Caucasus, Alaska, and the Coast Range of British Columbia. We were deeply saddened by the loss of Bruce Carson, one of the Club's most promising climbers.

There are currently 146 members in the Section. Officers for 1975-1976 include Irene Miller, Chairperson; David H. Coward, Vice-Chairperson; Arlene Blum, Secretary-Treasurer.

ARLENE BLUM, *Secretary*

A.A.C., Southern California Section. This Section met in November 1975 for the first time in two years. Pete White was elected the new Chairman; Mike Sherrick was re-elected Secretary-Treasurer. The Section voted to contribute modest monetary assistance to the A.A.C., and to the San Francsico Bay area members who had assumed a financial burden in entertaining the Russian climbers in California. An enthusiastic audience of members and guests enjoyed a program by Peter Pilafian, who showed candid shots (taken in Arizona, Mexico, and Switzerland) of the filming of *The Eiger Sanction*. Both Petes had participated in making the movie. The Section also sponsored a lecture by Eric Shipton in October. Nick Clinch, former A.A.C. President, and Glen Dawson, long-time member, made the arrangements. Shipton enthralled his audience with his dry wit, old-time black and white slides, and vivid descriptions of the pioneers' personalities and routes in attempts on Everest from both north and south.

RUTH DYAR MENDENHALL

Appalachian Mountain Club. The AMC continued its program of training in rock climbing and mountaineering. However, both large chapters (Boston and New York) made efforts to limit the participants in an effort to slow the influx of people into technical climbing and to increase leader participation in the program. Both these objectives appear to have been achieved, at least in part. The reduction in the large number of beginners led to greater leader participation and a more enjoyable program for both beginners and climbers. Although about the same number of beginners had entered the climbing group by the end of the season as previously, these came from a reduced number of initial participants. No officially sponsored AMC trips were taken this year. This is to be expected with the current de-emphasis of organized group trips by the newer climbers. However, private trips were run to the Selkirks, the Needles, Tetons, Bugaboos, Wind Rivers, and the Alps in Europe.

BOB HALL, *Vice-Chairman, Inter-Chapter Mountaineering Committee*

Chicago Mountaineering Club. The club's increasing membership continues to tax the organization's leadership resources. Despite overly large climbing parties the climbing leaders provide a high grade of training to beginners and try to promote the development of advanced climbers to leadership status. The club conducted a summer outing in the Sawtooth range in Idaho. Base Camp was near the Iron Creek Campground near Stanley. The outing was attended by 44 members. The peaks climbed were Regan, Thompson, Warbonnet, McGowan, Hayburn, Grand Mogul, Williams, Packrat and Elephant Perch.

Club members climbing with the Iowa Mountaineers in Peru were Olle Swartling, Susan Cochran, Jim Hagan and Bruce Hamilton. Base Camp was in the Quebrada Ishinca and the peaks climbed were Tocllaraju, Ishinka, Eastern Urus, and Western Urus.

Sometime this year the club hopes to publish its guidebook to rock climbing at Devil's Lake. Also, we hope to publish a revised edition of the International Directory of Mountaineering Clubs this year.

Plans are being hastily prepared to promote a club-sponsored climbing expedition to Ecuador in July or August of 1976.

GEORGE POKORNY, *Librarian*

Colorado Mountain Club. Our membership is 4606, compared with 4892 a year ago. Early in the year our Los Alamos, New Mexico, group voted to disaffiliate with our club. The distance between us has never encouraged a truly close relationship, but we have nevertheless valued their friendship and counsel over the years.

The year included the usual busy schedule of hikes and climbs on a year-round basis. Our winter schedule, particularly, has grown steadily. Major outings were taken to Scotland and the Salmon River in Idaho, with two major ones in Colorado as well.

Education and conservation remain as two activities given special emphasis. The former is highlighted by group (chapter) activity in mountaineering schools and first-aid courses conducted by several of our local groups. In all, there are perhaps 500 students involved in these efforts. Conservation is still a growing concern in our state. Another trail-improvement outing was held in the summer. Our club is also a chief sponsor of efforts to expand Rocky Mountain National Park to include some other priceless alpine wilderness areas, particularly the Indian Peaks area at the south of the Park. Our effort has an interesting historical parallel in that the formation of this Park involved people who were also involved in the founding of the club.

Our future activities will undoubtedly include, to an ever greater degree, conservation and wilderness preservation. The impact of the "civilized" multitudes on Colorado's mountains becomes more noticeable each year, and our most resourceful people are needed to implement ways in which we and our mountains can live in harmony.

JOHN L. DEVITT, *President*

Iowa Mountaineers. The club has become increasingly active in sponsoring skiing, backpacking, and mountaineering courses for University of Iowa credit. In January 40 members camped at 11,000 feet in Colorado's Collegiate Range and completed a 10-day cross-country skiing and winter survival course. In March a group undertook a 10-day backpack into Arizona's Grand Canyon. In May and June 80 members completed an intensive one-week rock climbing course, augmented in the fall and spring with 60 members completing intensive weekend rock-climbing courses. The customary number of Sunday dinner hikes was sponsored, with a few of them attracting over 130 participants. The popular travel/adventure film-lectures were continued with the usual high attendance. The club celebrated its 35th anniversary at the annual banquet in April, which attracted over 160 members from eight states. The membership now stands at well over 1,000.

Small groups of club members climbed in many areas of the world in the summer, particularly in Alaska, Europe, and New Zealand. The August summer camp was held in the San Juans in Colorado, where seven major peaks were climbed. The foreign expedition was to Peru. Forty members attended the Quebrada Ishinka Base Camp, from which five major peaks were climbed, including Western, Central, and Eastern Urus, Ishinka, and Tocllaraju. There were over 118 summit registrations despite several days of bad weather and deep, soft snow. Later 17 members climbed Nevado Huascarán, all of them reaching the highest camp near the saddle. Nine of them reached the south summit and four the north peak.

JOHN EBERT, *President*

Mountaineering Club of Alaska. Alaskan mountaineers were again active in the Alaskan, Brooks, Talkeetna, and Chugach ranges. A highlight was the second ascent of Mount Deborah via a new route by Brian Okonek, Pat Condran, Mark Hotman, Dave Pettigrew, Pat Stuart, and Toby Wheeler. (See article in this journal.) The first ascent of the mountain had been 21 years ago. Another impressive event was the winter ascent of Mount Foraker in February-March from the west fork of the Kahiltna Glacier. After an unsuccessful attempt on the difficult south ridge, Steve and Gary Tandy remained on the mountain to climb the slightly easier southeast ridge after the others were flown out. Kevin Apgar, Steve and Sandy Passmore, Ann Widmer, Gerry Schriever, Clyde Helms, and Bill Brant reported five minor ascents, probably all firsts, in the Arrigetch Peaks area of the Central Brooks Range in early August. In June Charlie Hammond (18), Ward Warren (20) and Mark Fouts (16) completed a two-week traverse of the Matanuska and Marcus Baker Glaciers. The termination point was an airstrip in Grasshopper Valley, near Knik Glacier.

Ski touring and hiking have generated significant interest. Ski tours from Arctic Valley Ski Bowl Road to Indian, via Ship Creek and Indian Creek Pass, have become annual events. The annual four-day spring tour from Arctic Valley to Girdwood, via Ship Creek, North Fork Ship Creek, Camp Creek, Raven Creek, and Crow Pass, was aborted this year when the party was struck by an avalanche in the North Fork Lake area. Dona Agosti, the hiking chairman, organized a group of 36 members for a very rewarding five-day backpack tour in Katmai National Monument in July. A non-technical climb of Organ Mountain was made in August from the North Fork Ship Creek Valley and the southeast slope.

The MCA continues to support environmental issues affecting club activities. The club supports pending legislation to establish a Talkeetna Mountains State Park, and is recommending that hunting, trapping, and shooting be banned within the Chugach State Park, a de facto wilderness area just outside the boundary of the Anchorage municipality. The proposal now before the U.S. Board on Geographic Names to change the name of Mount McKinley to its historic name, Denali, is strongly endorsed by the club.

A basic mountaineering course was conducted over five weekends in the spring and summer. Thirty students enrolled, and 10 instructors participated. The students were taught techniques in basic rock and ice climbing and the fundamentals of glacier and alpine travel.

We were saddened by the untimely death of Don Sheldon, the veteran Talkeetna glacier pilot, in early 1975.

The MCA requests information on climbs in the ranges near Anchorage by "outside" groups so that the history of these ranges may remain complete. A note to the club (Box 2037, Anchorage, AK 99510) detailing pertinent points would be appreciated.

WILLIAM A. STIVERS, *President*

The Mountaineers. Climbing techniques and climbing equipment have changed considerably over the past few years. The Mountaineers' Climbing Course has also changed to keep pace with the new techniques and equipment. Changes include new methods of instruction, course and climb-size limitations and an increased emphasis on making experience climbs more instruction-oriented than they have been.

The large demand for climbing instruction has necessitated limiting each Basic class to a maximum of 240 students. This number was determined by considering how many students we can instruct at field trips without decreasing course quality or increasing the number of field trips. Climbing-party size has now been limited to 12 on glacier climbs and 8 on rock climbs. We must schedule and obtain leaders for nearly 100 basic experience climbs each summer for our students to complete their required three climbs.

Changes in climbing technique and equipment have also had a considerable impact on our Intermediate climbing class. We begin with a mandatory field review of many of the most important basic techniques. In 1975, a third day of practice was added to the Intermediate rock climbing. As the use of chocks has become more widespread, our emphasis has been on their use though we have not abandoned piton instruction. Ice-climbing practice has also changed, with more emphasis on developing a well-rounded, flexible technique. Most of the students and instructors find our rescue-methods intermediate field trip to be one of the most enjoyable and interesting.

The Seminar program provides lectures and field trips about once a month during which a single topic is discussed or practiced in detail. Two of the important classroom topics are leadership and teaching skills. Another type of seminar is a "brush-up" trip aimed at former students who have become temporarily inactive or who have been climbing regularly but have not kept abreast of the many new techniques and items of climbing equipment. In 1975, the 275th student graduated from our Intermediate climbing course.

EDWARD L. PETERS, *Climbing Committee Chairman*

Book Reviews

EDITED BY GALEN A. ROWELL

The Seventh Grade, by Reinhold Messner. New York: Oxford University Press, 1974. 160 pages, 30 photos, 1 map. $8.50.

Messner's book seems to have improved a lot since it was published a year or so ago ("Pass the crow, please, George." "Certainly, Marshall: like some more of these delicious feathers?" "Certainly, I'd love some."). A couple of mountaineering eons have passed since then, marked by Messner and Habeler's recent ascent of Hidden Peak in unbelievable style; insult to the injury of their earlier *Eigerwand* jaunt, which was, by comparison, merely amazing. How should we read these omens? This little book will, perhaps, explain it all.

It's an impressionistic piece, a haughty sandwich of interior monolog with old-fashioned climbing narrative. The climbs described here live mostly in Messner's own stomping-ground, the Dolomites. Messner alternates classics with exotic-sounding obscures, and one might as well be another, to any ear but Messner's. Taking turns with these passages are darker studies, strangely borne in italics, which offer us enigmatic musing, incomprehensible chest-thumping and physical-fitness advice.

So built, the book is a peculiar species of tale—more explanation than narrative—with no calibration of text-weight to magnitude of route. Bouldering on a sawmill wall is treated in detail, while the northeast face of Yerupajá is polished off in a clause, with, apparently, total disregard for dramatic effect. Mountaineering literature traditionally goes all out for the chills and chuckles, but this is very strange. Bold or inept? Psychological? Mystical? One hardly knows.

On the nuts-and-bolts level, the prose—a translation—belongs to no recognizable idiom of English. Rather, it might have been collated from the output of a room full of teletypes, then filtered vigorously through a thesaurus. What are we to think of a sentence like this: "While I was climbing, I kept thinking of 'extravagant expressions' such as overhang, straddling, prussik knots and the like."? Is this enigmatic? If not, what? But, while rooting through this strange fuzz, we occasionally turn up an improbable pearl: recalling climbing up the summit waterfall of the Punta Tissi (topping off his solo ascent of the Philipp-Flamm) the Messner mask speaks a familiar tongue: "There are many such ravines in the Dolomites, but for me there is only one like a strangler's hand." Yes, indeed.

We miss here the humane wit and self-mockery of a Tilman, or the love and malapropulous comedy of Mazeaud (who sees his hungover companions "happily chatting and vomiting" on a ledge below,) but we also miss a certain amount of point at the same time. This book is, apparently by design, an illustrated argument about the role of style and the role of difficulty in the concoction of grandeur; about what it may mean to be the world's best living mountaineer. One who expects a good climbing yarn might well look elsewhere, for *The Seventh Grade,* as yarn, is barely readable. It's quite another story; possibly a useful set of program notes for astounding climbs to come. As the man fares, so fares the mask. We plan to be listening when the mask elects to speak again, in however private a voice. Consider this: Messner reflects on the Nanga Parbat ordeal, that "Accompanied by a man like Peter Habeler, I would risk trying an 8000-metre peak, having an equal chance and less risk than when attached to a great expedition with all its customary ballyhoo." Promised then; and now performed. Messner is a practical prophet, as good as his word. Not a bad yarn, at that.

GEORGE LOWE *and* MARSHALL RALPH

Modern Snow & Ice Techniques, by Bill March. Manchester, Cicerone Press: 1973. 76 pages 7 photographs. $3.00.

This is the best manual on ice-climbing technique to hit print since the technical ice revolution began in the mid-sixties. Ten years ago Yvon Chouinard was refocusing his innovative attention from big-wall rock gear onto ice climbing. The droop he forged into the pick of his Simond axe became the model for a whole generation of ice gear that quickly revolutionized the technique of ice climbing. Security *and* speed of front-pointing were both improved so much that a decade later we are still exploring the limits of the possibilities opened up by this advance. Not until now, however, has there been a useful manual written by one of the modern ice climbers about the technique involved.

This is a functional book by a man who knows how: small, inexpensive, and unpretentious, containing the complete essence of modern ice technique in a few well chosen words backed solidly by experience. March is one of the leading Scottish ice climbers, and it is natural that his approach should reflect Scottish ice conditions and attitudes. Scottish ice is steep, often confined in gullies, and harder than the usual Alpine ice but not as brittle as the typical American frozen waterfall. Consequently, March emphasizes front-pointing with short-handled tools and describes placing his points on the ice where Americans will often need to kick harder to set their points in denser ice.

The discussion of front-pointing is excellent, really the heart of the book, beginning with the shape of tools before applying them. March is not afraid to name advantages and shortcomings by brand, and to support the dampening qualities of a good wood handle. There is a detailed discussion of the pros and cons of different methods of tying the axe or hammer to one's body versus the danger of poking holes in oneself, clinched by the wry observation that a sliding wrist loop adversely "affects compass!" However, his drawing (p. 27) of the single axe anchor position incorrectly shows the spike of the axe resting on the ice, a common mistake which weakens the pick's crucial bite into the ice. Just the opposite, pulling gently outward on the bottom of the shaft, will seat the toothed pick most securely. Several photos show this clearly.

French technique is not as well organized. This subtle and elegant way of climbing flat-footed on intermediate slopes of softer ice really deserves a chapter to itself. Instead, March has integrated French techniques into smooth progression with front-pointing, which emphasizes the way technique adapts to steepening angles but not how it changes with the hardness of the ice. I would rather front-point on ice of only 35° to 40° if it is brittle, but I will gladly French-step at 55° when my points will penetrate securely on softer ice or frozen snow. March neglects to mention that a longer axe (70-80cm.) is necessary for good French technique. But we can easily excuse the emphasis on techniques more suited to Scottish winter, as long as we remember French for ourselves on those beautifully crunchy mornings in the Tetons and Palisades.

March's respect for the varied dangers of ice climbing is worth noting, especially by Americans coming to it from the more secure rock. He devotes a lot of space to self-arresting and belaying, while clearly pointing out the limitations of each: self-arrest is as chancy on hard ice as ice-axe belaying is in soft snow. Warnings about uncautious glissading and moving together while roped are well taken. It is impressive to hear a modern hard man's technical excellence balanced by such caution. I would modify his emphasis to rate self-belayed prevention ahead of the self-arrest, scratch sitting hip belay anchored to an ice axe in favor of the more reliable boot-axe belay, and junk the Clog deadman, which can fail suddenly, in favor of the much more reliable fixed-angle MSR snow fluke, Larry Penberthy's redemption for his useless "ice axes."

Five years ago March's countryman Johnny Cunningham said in an interview, "cutting steps in ice is immoral." March adds to this, observing that the chest sling on the hammer, ". . . could be a method of resting on long steep ice pitches or used as a position to place ice screws. Etriers may also be used in conjunction with the hammers which would be used as temporary aid points. Both these methods are unethical and retrogressive as they complicate a fast clean technique of climbing." Bravo. I hope they're listening in Calgary.

Thanks for the book, Bill. It's not elegantly done, but it is packed with well-distilled experience. I learned a lot. It's a pleasure to have a manual to recommend when everything else is out of date.

Doug Robinson

Advanced Rockcraft, by Royal Robbins. Glendale, California: La Siesta, 1973. 96 pp. 26 photos, profuse sketches.

This important book on rock climbing technique appeared more than two years ago. Blame for failure of this journal to review it promptly must rest squarely on the book review editor: me! The two-year wait is not entirely bad, however. It allows us to view the book in a much better perspective. Subtle strengths and faults are not always apparent to a reviewer who receives a pre-publication copy and writes about it from a single, usually hasty reading.

Advanced Rockcraft is the best climbing technique book to appear in the English language. This is partly due to the author's wide knowledge of his subject, partly due to his hard work, and partly due to the structure of the book. It deals with a tight subject in a loose manner. In all too many informative books, editors without first-hand knowledge of the subject try to drape the author's material onto a framework that doesn't quite fit. Square facts are bludgeoned to fit round holes. To its credit, this book has not been tightly edited. The author's gut feelings come through in descriptions of equipment and technique. Photos are not always related to text material, but the frequent, instantly readable sketches by Sheridan cover the subject so well that photos need only be window dressing.

Other reviewers have taken the author to task because his own actions have not always been what he suggests to others. The alternative is to lower ideals because they haven't been attained in the past. That Robbins has used or removed more bolts than he thinks correct in hindsight is not something that needs to be dealt with in an instructional book. For instance, in this bicentennial year we should remember that Jefferson often tried to short cut the very democratic processes he helped to create, but we must be thankful that he didn't feel compelled to water down the Declaration of Independence because he couldn't live up to every word himself. In fact, Robbins handles the chapter on values exceptionally well, refining a few of the unqualified statements he made in *Basic Rockcraft.* The instructions he gives would-be climbers are a careful balance of some social order with enough individual freedom. This is a critical crossroads where most previous books have taken a wrong turn which points the reader, distantly but inevitably, toward the dead-ends of safety fetishism, regimentation, and reliance on equipment instead of self.

Robbins' chapter on "Leading" has absolutely nothing in common with the chapter on "Leadership" in *Freedom of the Hills.* The former deals with the individual gaining self-reliance and the latter discusses how the head person should behave in a group situation. Here, once again, the tight subject of "Rockcraft" gives a helping hand. Leadership on technical rock means the ability to walk the tight rope of one's limits, a combination of skill, self-confidence and self-awareness. Leadership on non-technical mountain outings with large groups usually means following the same guidelines as a den mother.

The most important parts of the book are carefully thought-out comments on each technique and piece of equipment. These are wholly trustworthy and well rounded with caution. Every climber, no matter how experienced, stands to gain something by reading them.

The book's main shortcomings are all peripheral to the text. The index must have been written before the book was complete, since many page numbers are in error, usually by only one digit. The photos are abstruse, showing some of the author's personal world, but not relating to the text, such as a group of climbers posed near a tree captioned only as "The Great Southern Sierra Hinterlands Expedition, 1973." The book ends with a creatively written account of one of the author's climbs, in this case an exception to the adage that a photo is worth a thousand words. The short essay outweighs the value of many photos, focusing the various threads of the book into a final, experiential context.

If you are a serious climber, you must read this book. It comes closer to capturing the soul of rock climbing than any other instructional book available.

GALEN A. ROWELL

The Field Book of Mountaineering and Rock Climbing, by Tom Lyman and Bill Riviere. New York: Winchester Press, 1975. 208 pages, with photos and illustrations. Price: $8.95.

Tom Lyman, an active experienced mountaineer, collaborated with outdoor writer Bill Riviere to produce *The Field Book of Mountaineering and Rock Climbing.* Alas, this is just another instructional manual on mountain travel, equipment, clothing, techniques, and hazards, with appendices on maps and aerial photographs, and a mountain medicine bibliography.

I am sceptical when an author refers to his work as *The* field book to techniques and equipment. And in this case the book is not complete. It is always hard to move from illustration and description to execution; a beginner will find gaps in the description which make this doubly difficult. Illustrations such as the one on page 109 showing a belayer with a single nut for protection are misleading and dangerous. Lyman describes the placement of ice screws in one way and illustrates it in another: in the text he tells us the eye of the screw is turned uphill so that the downward force is exerted directly on the shaft of the screw; the illustration on page 110 shows the eye turned downhill.

One welcome addition to the tried-and-true format is the chapter on conservation in the mountains. Minimum impact wilderness use is an idea whose time has come. The use of stoves instead of campfires in alpine areas and *other heavily traveled mountain areas* has become even more critically important than clean climbing. People must be taught not to mass produce campfire pits and erect megolithic shelters. Many climbing instruction books have been written. Undoubtedly, more will follow. And while the ultimate degree of this proliferation is uncertain, it will probably continue until each publishing house has issued at least one book.

Final recommendation: If you want a general climber's instruction book, save your $8.95 and stick with the "classics".

ROBERT SCHNEIDER

Downward Bound: A Mad Guide to Rock Climbing, by Warren "Batso" Harding, with illustrations by Beryl "Beasto" Knath. Englewood Cliffs: Prentice Hall, 1975. 204 pages, numerous photos and drawings. Price $7.95.

Climbing autobiographies have never become popular in American climbing, probably due to the lack of audience. The scene has never had a public following as in such urban cultures, as France, which has produced many fine mountain memoirs, or Britain, which has also had a goodly number. One event in American climbing certainly did catch the public's fancy: Warren Harding's climb of the Wall of Early Morning Light. Whether this was attention long overdue, a fluke or as Warren says, "Merely the result of a slack period in the overall news scene," it generated a lot of public interest, gave Warren his long overdue fame— though not fortune—(he mock-laments that his first ascent of the Nose twelve years before was eclipsed in the news by the death of the Pope), created widespread fear and loathing in the climbing community, and eventually resulted in this book.

Into this literary void steps the modest Batso, at times unsure for whom he is writing. The climbing community has read his trenchant pieces of satire—directed as much at himself as at others—and loved him for it. Some of this new wit is obviously for them, but the book is basically for wider audiences. It starts with a lengthy discourse on the conduct of climbing, with answers to the question of "How does the rope get up there?" works into climbing "Philo-pharcy" and Warren's life as a rock climber, and climaxes with "the big motha climb" itself. All this is set in play form with members of the audience, ranging from Dr. Sigmund

Fraud and Hairy-Giant Superclimber to Penthouse Pundid and Rather Well-Equipped Young Lady, rising from time to time to pose difficult questions. Warren is right in his element. But the action dragged for me; I've heard too many novice-oriented explanations of how climbing is done. So I watched the reactions of interested but less jaded friends. They seemed to be as enlightened as entertained. Those who have read Warren before will recognize the humor.

What delights me is Warren's sense of proportion, disarming by understatement the usual tendency toward self-important dramatics. He answers the question of "Why climb?" with "It's fun." Then he adds his twist on Mallory's famous enigma: "It's there and we're mad!" When he finally succeeds in getting up the south face of Half Dome after many tries and one close shave, it becomes "an uneventful but tedious six days." And his final judgment on the publicity surrounding the Wall of Early Light is turned not toward climbing, which he doesn't see suffering from its growing popularity, but toward the public, who got "something more positive to talk about than the routine crime, crises and catastrophies that normally dominate the news."

Physical testing is a theme that runs through Harding's climbing and, lightly of course, through this book. Not the gymnastic sort of move strength—he pokes fun at the Yosemite scene focused on free climbing—but endurance, staying power, slogging it through the long haul. Instead of working the high bar or walking the chains set up all over Camp 4, we find Warren up on the Yosemite Falls Trail trying to better his time to the rim and back. His bolting marathon on the last pitch of the Nose is well known, hammering away hour after hour at the overhanging darkness, drilling all night to arrive on the summit at dawn.

I think Warren is truly excited by steep, blank walls. While most of us like to see the features on the walls, preferably set off by surrounding blankness, he sees the blankness of the route, the holes rather than the net which defines them, the gaps. Some choose form as their task, others emptiness. Either way we haul our load of conceptualized style around with us, as surely as our water and salami. Warren sees the rock his own way and climbs accordingly: blankness begets bolts. Being inventive too, and bold, and tired of hammering, he came up with bat hooks, a device guaranteed to keep the interest up.

Climbing ethics is a favorite topic with Warren, a subject he loves to hate. But do not be deceived. He is by no means antiethical. He chastises the early attempts on the Wall of Early Morning Light for starting up the right side of El Cap Tower, which he sees as a route unto itself. His own line further to the right he considered more direct, more in keeping with the character of the route and needing fewer bolts. He turned out to be wrong about the bolts, but the character of the climbing so impressed even Royal Robbins that he decided to quit "erasing" the route. Warren's point is not antiethical then. He is just against other people imposing their ethics on him. He is certainly his own man.

Whatever the future holds for Warren Harding, it is bound to be interesting as he continues to do "my own thing my own way."

DOUG ROBINSON

The Great Days, Walter Bonatti, Translated by Geoffrey Sutton, Victor Gollancz, Ltd., London, 1974, photos, clothbound, 184 pages.

Last spring, as several climbers and a slew of Balti porters trudged up the Baltoro Glacier high in the Karakoram, a porter who was surely old enough to remember pointed out a prominent boulder and declared, "Bonatti climb!" One climber picked up the challenge and comfortably scrambled up it. A short time later, another boulder, this time larger with fewer holds, was noted: "Bonatti climb!" This was also topped, but the moves were slower, tougher. The game grew, the angles went up, and the climbing became increasingly desperate. Finally, the Balti stood in front of a flawless wall, capped by a jutting ceiling. "Bonatti climb," he said in a similar tone. The Baltis, of course, had had their game, but the point is none-the-less well taken. Even in the high, remote Karakoram, Walter Bonatti has become an unquenchable legend.

The Pakistani porter could have recalled Bonatti from the 1954 Italian trip up the Baltoro to K2 (where Bonatti did not reach the summit but did spend a blistering cold night in the open at over 8,000 meters with the Hunza, Mahdi, who, a year before carried Hermann Buhl from the face of Nanga Parbat), or perhaps he remembered him from the 1958 climb on Gasherbrum IV (where he was successful). But the mass of the climbing world knows him for other climbs in other mountains, particularly those of the Mont Blanc range: Walker Spur in winter, the tragedy on the Central Pillar of Freney, his soul-searching solo of the Dru, and the direct route on the north face of the Matterhorn —alone and in winter.

The Great Days is the second collection of the debris of Bonatti's climbing memories, and its essence is much like that of the first, *On the Heights* (1961). Indeed not only does this installment take up where the former left off, but even the first chapter of *Days* is exactly the same as the final chapter of *Heights* (A portent for his third book?).

The Great Days was translated from the original Italian version. I do not read Italian and perhaps it's best that I don't. I'd prefer to believe that Bonatti's graceless, stylized, and often dull prose is the sole result of a disinterested translator. Bonatti's first book was also mighty slow going, but with a different translator. But no matter. One doesn't read this kind of stuff for literary style anyway.

Now in his early 40s and retired for the second time from moun-

taineering, Bonatti is an Italian cultural monument of the stature of some of his mountaineering feats. As a personal memoir *Great Days* fails. Bonatti prefers to stay in the shadows and rarely comes stage front. Other than a passing word, we are left only to speculate about his personal relationship with other climbers, just as we're left guessing about his private life. There are only rare glimpses, such as a teenage climb of Walker Spur using a cotton shopping bag for a balaclava and supplied with a dozen apples bought on credit, or his brusque introduction to adolescence when he saw his schoolboy immortal, Mussolini, as a disfigured corpse dangling from a gasoline pump, or his very quiet and only companion on the Matterhorn, a small, stuffed teddy bear.

As in his first book, we see Bonatti in *Great Days* as the quintessential man of mountaineering, hurling himself into action and controversy as the only antidote to an overwhelming hypocrisy in the mountains. He polishes his purist image seeking purification through pain and chips away at the controversies which have dogged his enigmatic climbing life.

Though a full quarter of the chapters are throwaways, most of *Great Days* is like Diogenes' search; here's Bonatti cramponing about with headlamp aglow, searching for an honest life. And while he justifiably rails against the "morals of the rat race" in contemporary climbing, we muddle through the usual mountaineering litany of horrible bivouacs and impassable overhangs, terrifying winds, bleeding fingers, and unbearably icy nights which are somehow always borne.

But in the end he gets his man. If only Pogo had read *Great Days,* surely he'd be strained to say, "He met his maker, and he was it!" On retirement, Bonatti sums it up: "I imagine them all, the supporters and the detractors, debating the man, the scene, the challenge, the courage, the significance, the pride, the comparable, the soul, infinity, conquest, in short the whole range of subjects which all too often give rise to the empty question, 'Was it worth it?' "

Bonatti inescapably left his profound imprint on mountaineering and his feats are altogether genuine. But in this melancholy judgment of their meaning and in the almost mock-heroic gesture of his retirement, he is clumsily groping for a self he has already sold into servitude, not merely as a superb climber, but rather as a deity.

DENNIS G. HANSON

The Mountains of America: From Alaska to the Great Smokies, by Franklin Russell. Introduction by Edward Abbey. New York: Harry Abrams, 1975 224 pages, 133 photos, 124 in color. Price: $40.00

Not many years ago it was fashionable to talk about cheap Japanese imitations of American goods. I kept quiet after I began using high quality Japanese camera equipment. Now, however, the pendulum is swinging the other way. How long can America keep up with Japan? This is the new question, especially in quality book publishing.

Harry Abrams, the publisher of this book, also published *Himalayas,* the 12 x 17 photographic extravaganza of the world's highest mountains. Abrams has published some of the world's finest art books, and in the case of *Himalayas,* the combination of high mountains and novel photography produced an important work of art. The photographs were all by the same photographer, Shirakawa, and even those who did not like them had to admit that they represented a distinctive style: through the art of photography a man had given his interpretation of a range of mountains. *The Mountains of America,* on the other hand, resembles a book assembled by committee. It has no distinctive style, but the photographs share with *Himalayas* an other-worldly quality. Part of this is due, not coincidentally, to a common publisher that might offer a glint of understanding about the photographs in both books. *Himalayas* has been controversial because people wondered, "Are the colors *real*?" Shirakawa stated in the book that he used no colored filters and his photographs represented the scene as closely as possible. It doesn't take a genius to figure out that Shirakawa had to write those words *before* he was aware of the final reproductions in his book!

Mountains of America solved the *Himalayas* enigma for me. The book uses photographs from a large number of American photographers. While working as a photo editor for another publisher, I had seen several of the originals that were eventually used in *Mountains.* I was particularly familiar with the photos of David Muench, who is probably the top color large-format scenic photographer in the United States today. In *Mountains* I found Muench's images reproduced with the same inky purple shadows and harsh contrasts as in the controversial *Himalayas.* Knowing the originals, the overall effect was not pleasing.

I'm not sure how I would respond to *Mountains* if I had never seen any of the original photographs or the mountains themselves. Few Americans outside the American Alpine Club have been high in the Himalayas to compare the real sunrises with the reproduced purples. Many Americans, however, have visited their native mountains to compare them with the unfamiliar scenes in *Mountains.* The photographs in this book do not give a fair representation of different mountain areas. In the search for the unique image, the commonplace has been lost. The book is a gaudy counterpoint to the Sierra Club standby, *Gentle Wilderness.* The mood of a certain area is not apparent except in the most superficial ways. The emphasis is on ethereal things: streams, clouds, lightning, waterfalls, sunsets. But this soft subject matter is reproduced in grainy harshness. If I had never seen a mountain, and I owned this book, I would probably tilt my head in dog-like bewilderment when I saw the real thing.

The artsy photos are blended with an almost deadpan text on the geography of each region. The subject is too vast, and the book is spotty. Canadian mountains seem to have been included as a token gesture in this bicentennial year. The Rockies have a few quick pages, but Mount Logan, the Selkirks, and the Bugaboos are nowhere to be found.

For the mountaineeer, there are glimpses of many of America's wildest mountains in the photographs. The text is worthless to a climber. For instance, the crest of the Sierra Nevada is described as "such a tumble of rocks that much of it is virtually inaccessible." Even *National Geographic* recognizes that the Pacific Crest Trail runs the length of the range.

This book is a must only for the compulsive collector. My advice? Wait for the Japanese imitation.

GALEN ROWELL

Mountain Sheep and Man in the Northern Wilds, by Valerius Geist, Ithaca: Cornell University Press, 1975. 248 pages, black and white photos, charts. Price: $10.00

Why review a book on sheep in an alpine journal? Because the author has something very unique and controversial to say that resulted from his experiences living in the mountains studying wildlife. After several introductory chapters on sheep behavior in the Cassiar Mountains and human behavior on the Alaska Highway, Geist comes to the point. He postulates that man acquired his humanity, not from easy living in the tropics where food sources were relatively abundant, but from the northern latitudes, especially during the ice ages, when he was forced to become a hunter and, more importantly, to cooperate to survive. He doubts that pre-men were hunters, and considers current 'evidence' of early hunters in Africa to be a distortion of the evidence. He thinks that some hunting did occur, but it was not a predominant way of life. Only later, in the colder latitudes, did cooperative hunters of big game develop "not only the tools and skills but the human attributes, of loyalty, altruism, and discipline."

How nice to think that human character was built at some sort of Pleistocene Outward Bound. Geist never mentions climbing directly, but he presents much for the mountaineer to ponder. He spent seasons living off the land in northern Canada while studying sheep behavior and he came to the conclusion that many human emotions have their basis as "old adaptations or means of survival in a distant . . . physical and social milieu. We are, after all, creatures shaped by past environments and we have lived in the present one only a very short time. We should not be surprised if our present way of life strains and dissatisfies in a nebulous, unfathomable manner, or if it hurts without knowing just where the pain originates."

Geist likens these things to "behavioral appendixes." One of these cravings, inherited from eons of early hunters of big game, is for a set of conditions that closely parallel those of the modern mountaineers: "Picture a man with a short flint-tipped throwing spear four paces from a mammoth. It took no small amount of courage to get that close and go through with the task . . . the foolish would hardly live to tell his tale; the coward would hardly venture within spear throwing distance, nor would he respond to the urgent need, should it arise, of distracting the quarry's attention from his endangered hunting companion. *Such an act requires self-discipline and the ability to calculate one's moves, as well as the need to keep a very level head while only inches from possible death.* These requirements had to be met, not once in a lifetime, but on every hunt, and every week, month, year of a man's life span."

No wonder we have a restless urge to climb. If Geist's theory is right, then we should finally understand why we grow neurotic if we don't see a snowy peak or a cliff for a month. His logic is impeccable. If cold climates made man human, then lack of them should make man as ornery as a polar bear in Florida, and it may accomplish exactly that with Geist's colleagues. He has joined company with Lorenz, Ardrey, and Morris in extrapolating human behavior from animal research. He's on risky ground, but if he's right, that's what made us the way we are.

GALEN ROWELL

Encyclopaedia of Mountaineering by Walt Unsworth. New York: St. Martin's. 1975. 272 pages, 34 photos. $12.95.

This is, quite simply, the worst reference book I have ever seen. Since reference books must be accurate to be usable, the multifold errors in this book render it not only close to useless, but potentially damaging to future mountain literature if it is used as source material.

In an hour of thumbing through the pages I found literally hundreds of errors of fact and omission. Under "Vittorio Sella," we read, "in 1909 . . . Chogolisa was climbed: a height record for the time (25,110 feet)." Sella's expedition failed to reach the top of Chogolisa and I have never seen it published otherwise. Herman Buhl, the famous Austrian climber, was killed trying to make the first ascent in 1957.

We are told that Lionel Terray did not reach the top of Mount Huntington in Alaska, when, in fact, he did. Under "Barry Bishop," we are told, "On 22 May 1963, Bishop, with L. G. Jerstad, became the first American to reach the summit of Mount Everest." No one's ever called Big Jim un-American before. Whittaker reached the top of Everest twenty-one days earlier than Bishop.

Names and numbers cause considerable trouble for this author. Under "Yosemite" we learn that Harding spent 45 days climbing El Capitan the first time. Under "El Capitan," we are told that the same climb took 47 days. One index reference to Mount Logan on page 142 doesn't exist. Names suffer quite often. Leif Patterson comes out "Petterson;" Salathé becomes "Salethe;" Mount Jefferson becomes "Jeffereson. The Rocky Mountains suffer an even worse indignation. They are missing under "R," both in the index and the main text. There are short notes under "Colorado Rockies" and "The Canadian Rockies."

Missing are listings under the names of Ardito Desio and Nick Clinch, who led successful expeditions to the first and second highest peaks in the Karakoram. We do find, however, people like Francis Vaughan Hawkins, a member of the Alpine Club in London "who had a brief but interesting climbing career," before resigning from the AC in 1861.

It is hard to discover any rhyme or reason for the author's entries. Hornbein has a listing, but not Unsoeld. Gary Hemming is described, but John Harlin is missing. Sir Edmund Hillary gets half the space devoted to Ian Clough. Obscure anachronisms appear, such as: "Naismith's Rule . . . The rule is: allow one hour for every three miles on the map plus an additional hour for every 2,000 feet of climbing. . . . Further refinements can be made (see *Mountain Leadership* by E. Langmuir), but these spoil the essential simplicity of the calculation."

Under "K2" we find a run-down of each expedition. For the 1902, 1909, and 1938 expeditions the maximum elevation reached is listed. Not so for the 1939 expedition, which set an altitude record that stood for fifteen years until the first ascent. Heinrich Pfannl is listed under his name for ascents in the Eastern Alps, with no mention that he was on the first expedition to attempt K2.

Descriptions are often hard to follow such as this one locating Yosemite's El Capitan: "It stands on the true right bank of the river about two miles below Yosemite Village, and thus, in driving up the valley, it is one of the first cliffs to be encountered."

The cardinal sin of this book is that it is not objective. Biographies read more like gossip columns than what should be expected from a reference work. We learn that Bonington handled photo coverage of the first descent down the Blue Nile, but Reinhold Messner, currently the world's leading alpinist, is dismissed in a brief paragraph. We are told that Warren Harding's "siege tactics did not meet with universal approval. Harding has always adapted his tactics to meet the situation as he sees it." The author obviously sides with Royal Robbins, whom he describes as "the exponent of the single push theory of big wall climbing as opposed to siege tactics." Harding comes off as an opportunist; Robbins as a saint. In truth, both climbers used siege tactics during a stage in their careers, Harding to a greater extent than Robbins, who tried to avoid them as much as possible. For the last fifteen years, neither Harding nor Robbins have used siege tactics, but this doesn't come through in the bad guy/good guy biographies.

Mixed in with biographies, famous mountains, and tiny cliffs are definitions of climbing words. These are no better than the rest of the book. "Granite," according to the definition, "varies from place to place but is *always* sound to climb upon." Quite a surprise to climbers who have turned back on friable Alaskan granite and rotten desert cliffs!

GALEN ROWELL

Himalaje-Karakorum, by Tom Piaty, ed. Warsaw, Poland, Wiedza Powszechna, 1974. 472 pages of text, with 376 pictures. Hardbound. 140 zlotys ($7.60).

I am quick to declare that I know no Polish, but the language is not an obstacle to understanding and enjoying this Polish book, the fifth of the collection "W. Skalach i Lodach Swiata" ("Amid the Rock and Ice of the World"). This edition covers the achievements of the Poles in the mountains of the globe from 1968 to 1974. The title of this book is therefore misleading, since it is by no means confined to the mountains of Central Asia. There are fifteen chapters, three indexes (with English and Russian summaries) and a chronology, embracing in all an unusually wide geographic area of the mountains of the world, which attests to the extraordinary activity of the Poles.

The great asset of this book, whether one knows Polish or not, is its photographs. There are 367 black and white and nine color pictures of high standards, taken by Poles among the better known ranges of the world as well as among others we rarely see photographed: Semyen (Ethiopia), Alai and Tien Shan (Russia), Altai (Mongolia), Atacama (Northern Chile), Yugoslavian and Bulgarian Alps, etc. If there is anything to complain about in this book it is the total lack of maps, a strange omission indeed. But it is a book of merits, that will please those who dream of traveling and climbing in the least known mountain ranges of the world.

EVELIO ECHEVARRÍA

In Memoriam

MIRIAM O'BRIEN UNDERHILL
1899-1976

It was on a Boston-Maine sleeping car back in the 1920s that I first met Miriam O'Brien. We were on our way to the Glen House, at the foot of Mount Washington, for a week of winter climbing with the "Bemis Crew," an Appalachian Mountain Club group. This was the beginning of a long and happy friendship, of companionship among the hills of New England and Europe and gatherings at home.

Miriam was born in Lisbon, New Hampshire in 1899, was graduated from Bryn Mawr in 1920, studied at Johns Hopkins, and when we met, was working at the Massachusetts Eye and Ear Infirmary. But neither job nor finances kept her from constant summers in Europe from 1926 on. As a child with her mother, she had already made minor climbs in the Alps and was thoroughly at home on our New England hills and cliffs. Miriam's ability as a mountaineer was soon apparent; facile and graceful on rock, her speed on all types of terrain was outstanding. Perhaps her most notable guided climb was the first traverse, in 1928, of all five pinnacles of the Aiguilles du Diable with Robert L.M. Underhill and guides Armand Charlet and Georges Cachet.

Soon Miriam was not content to be a "touriste" and aspired to lead "manless" climbs. In preparation she frequently took the lead from a complaisant guide. In 1929, with Winifred Marples, she led the Peigne and later that summer, the Grépon with Alice Damesme. She started her 1930 season by leading me up an amusing route on Torre Grande in the Dolomites. Later that summer we romped (with guides) over the Leiterspitz when higher Zermatt peaks were snowed in. There were other manless climbs, and after several attempts, a successful ascent of the Matterhorn.

Miriam and Bob Underhill had been mountain companions for several years and in 1930 they became engaged, putting an end to her manless climbing, but not an end to her outstanding career in the Alps. With Bob, she continued a program of spectacular ascents. Her prowess was early recognized. Membership in the Groupe de Haute Montagne, the Ladies Alpine Club, the American Alpine Club came soon. Recognition particularly pleasing to her was the dedication of a new and difficult route on Torre Grande as "Via Miriam." She wrote articles for the *National Geographic* and European and American alpine journals. As her reputation grew, the Ladies Alpine Club, the Appalachian Club and the American Alpine Club conferred on her honorary membership, and when the

Ladies Alpine Club and the Alpine Club (London) merged, she became an honorary member of the latter, sadly when she was too ill to realize it.

Though the Alps were Miriam's particular playground, starting in 1946 she and Bob did pioneering climbing in the ranges of Montana. For six summers they enjoyed this terrain, so different from Europe. She was a charter member of the AMC's "Four-Thousand-Footer Club," those who had climbed all of New Hampshire's peaks of 4000 feet and over. She invented the game of "Four-Thousanders in Winter." Indefatigable in her love for the hills, she was collecting New Hampshire's "Hundred Highest" at the time of her collapse.

Though mountaineering was a vital part of her life, to view Miriam solely as a climber is to overlook many facets of this remarkable woman. She had a facile pen and authored the autobiographical *Give Me The Hills*, a book which, while sufficiently technical to satisfy her peers, is also enjoyed by the non-climber. For five years she was editor of *Appalachia*. Her photography, used to illustrate her writings and her witty lectures, was superb. The Appalachian Mountain Club's *Mountain Flowers of New England* owes much to her color photos of the little mountain blossoms.

I like to remember Miriam as a hostess, first in her parents' home in Dedham, then, after her marriage, in Concord, Massachusetts, and since 1960 in the attractive home the Underhills built in Randolph, New Hampshire, facing the Northern Peaks of the Presidential Range. It was always fun to be with her whether indoors, planning new ventures, reminiscing on past pleasures, just chatting; or out, scaling cliffs or tramping up snowy ridges.

After a long illness, Miriam Underhill died on January 7. She leaves her husband Robert L.M. Underhill and two sons, Robert of Del Mar, California and Brian of Boulder, Colorado.

MARJORIE HURD

BURGE BICKFORD
1906-1975

September 1975 ended almost a lifetime of adventure in the mountains for Burge Bickford.

His first ventures were with his father who was a guide in the Presidential Range of New Hampshire. Joining the Mountaineers in 1936 and with climbing courses behind him, he climbed with even more enthusiasm. As a climbing leader and lecturer and later as Climbing Chairman he contributed much to the development of the present school. His style and ability to relate to young climbers made him most popular and much in demand.

In the Mountaineers Burge served many areas of responsibility beyond the Climbing Committee; Summer Outing Chairman, Board of Trustees, Treasurer, Vice President and President.

He became a member of the American Alpine Club in 1942 and was also active through the years in the Washington Alpine Club, Sierra Club, Wilderness Society, World Affairs Council, Zero Population Growth and East Africa Wildlife Society.

All of us who climb and love our great mountain wilderness have lost a good friend, one who contributed tremendously in our time and to the future as well.   OME DAIBER

CARMIE R. DAFOE, JR.
1920-1975

The mountaineering community in general and the Mazamas and the America Alpine Club in particular have lost a dedicated friend. Carmie R. Dafoe, Jr. was killed in an automobile accident in Moccasin, Montana on June 29, 1975.

Carmie was born June 22, 1920 in Portland, Oregon. He received a B.A. degree (Phi Beta Kappa) from Reed College in 1946 and a J.D. degree (cum laude) from Harvard University in 1949. He served as a captain in the U.S. Army from 1941 to 1945 and 1951 to 1952. His overseas duty included Morocco, Algeria, Italy, France and Germany. He was a partner in the law firm of Lindsay, Nahstoll, Hart, Duncan, Dafoe and Krause in Portland, Oregon.

Carmie's interest in mountaineering started with an ascent of Mount Hood on July 22, 1961. He then joined the Mazamas and entered into their activities with an enthusiasm that did not seem to have bounds. His leadership ability was soon recognized, and he was appointed to the climbing committee where he served first as chairman of the basic climbing school, second as chairman of the intermediate climbing school and finally as chairman of the climbing committee itself.

He was appointed to the outing committee and subsequently served as its chairman. He was elected to the Mazama Executive Council and served two years as President. He also found time to climb extensively and to lead climbs in the Cascades of Oregon and Washington, the Wallowas of Oregon, the Tetons of Wyoming, the Sierra Nevada of California, the Selkirks of British Columbia, the Sawtooth of Idaho, Rocky Mountains of Canada, the Coast Range of British Columbia, Wind River Range of Wyoming, the Olympic Range of Washington, the Beartooth Range of Montana, the Lost River Range of Idaho, the Ruby Mountains of Nevada and the Swiss Alps. He was climb leader of Mazama outings to the Selkirks and the Tetons. He was co-leader of a Mazama climbing outing in Mexico. He was outing leader of Mazama outings to the Rocky Mountains of Canada and the Ruby Mountains.

He was leader of a Mazama expedition to climb Aconcagua in Argentina.

As a leader his planning was meticulous and his concern for the safety of his party was of first importance. He found time in his busy schedule to co-author a climber's guide to the Sawtooths of Idaho and to author a climber's guide to the Ruby Mountains and East Humboldt Mountains of Nevada.

Carmie was a frequent contributor of articles and photographs to the Mazama annual publication. At the time of his death he was chairman of the Mazama By Laws Committee and designated leader of a Mazama climbing outing to the Swiss Alps in 1976. In addition to his Mazama activities, Carmie also became active in American Alpine Club affairs. He was elected in 1966 to the AAC and served as chairman of the Oregon section in 1973-74. In 1973 he was elected to membership in the Explorers Club.

He is survived by his wife, Vera (also an AAC member), a daughter, Janet Dafoe Davis and a son, Barton Dafoe.

KENNETH M. WINTERS

BRUCE ALLAN CARSON
1951-1975

Bruce Carson died on September 4, 1975. He fell through a cornice on the summit of Trisul, a 23,362-foot peak in the Indian Himalayas. Falling through a cornice is not a common way to die in the Himalayas. Climbers are much more often frozen in storms or crushed in avalanches. Yet Buhl died in the Himalayas by falling through a cornice, and so, probably, did my friend Mick Burke, after reaching the summit of Everest alone in October 1975. But at least Buhl and Burke were at or past the prime of their climbing careers. Bruce, in spite of his numerous accomplishments, was still near the beginning of his.

Bruce was a true mountaineer, with a deep passion for climbing. He was also an unusually brilliant rock climber, who could draw the line fine without getting flustered. On the occasions when I climbed with him, I was struck by the natural grace and coolness with which he led the hardest pitches I was capable of following. But Bruce's rock climbing was distinguished by far more than technical virtuosity. He had a creative touch and a self-assurance which set him apart from other experts. He had insight. He early saw the possibilities of hammerless ascents of existing big routes in Yosemite, and carried them out, sometimes alone, sometimes with partners, in the best possible style. Examples of this are his Yosemite ascents of the Rostrum north face, Rixon's Far West, the Nose of El Capitan, the south face of Washington Column, and the Chouinard-Herbert route on Sentinel Rock, the last two solo. All these were not only done without driving pitons but without even taking hammers. This purity of concept and execution informed everything Bruce did.

But his outstanding accomplishment on rock was his solo, hammerless ascent of the west face of Sentinel Rock. It was enough that this was Bruce's first grade six, enough that it was the first solo of the respected route, but that he should deepen the adventure by leaving behind what had formerly been the Yosemite big-wall climber's indispensable weapon, the hammer, was one of those flashes of genius which combine courage and insight in a flare of illumination and spark achievements which are extraordinary, even transcendent, the sort of illumination of genius which makes possible such masterpieces as the Bonatti Pillar.

Yet Bruce was primarily not a rock climber, but rather a mountaineer, and in his short career had already climbed in the mountains of New Guinea, the Pamir, the Yukon, and the Andes before meeting the fatal cornice after reaching the summit of Trisul in the Indian Himalayas.

Bruce had an unusual combination of sensitivity, practicality and strength. I have never met anyone with such a diamond-hard core of integrity. Yet he was gentle and self-sufficient, coming and going as he pleased.

The poignant thing about Bruce's death is his youth. He had the character and qualities which assure success in life. He was what a man should be: strong, gentle, good. With so many villains in the world, it is sad to lose a hero.

ROYAL S. ROBBINS

BRADFORD FULLER SWAN
1907-1976

With a heavy heart we write these lines in memory of Brad Swan, who with gentle irascibility brought wisdom and manners, good judgment and humor to us all. Brad was not a great mountaineer; his alpine accomplishments were minimal. Indeed on one of the few occasions when he donned a rope, he slid off an easy slab. But, then, with typical humor announced that if we would have him, he would henceforth be our haulbag.

Brad climbed and hiked in the Himalaya, the Hebrides, the Antarctic, and the mountains of Western Canada. But his main qualification for election to the American Alpine Club was forty years of service as a volunteer guide and trainer of leaders for camp groups in the alpine areas of New England. No one knew the trails and vistas of the Presidential Range as he did. Few people are aware of the alpine flowers, but he was among that even smaller group that cared to study, describe and preserve their delicate environment.

He was Chairman of the Huts Committee for the Appalachian Mountain Club and served some years as editor of *Appalachia,* the oldest mountaineering journal in the Western Hemisphere. His greatest work, though, was as one of the principal figures behind the establishment of a vigorous mountain leadership program within the A. M. C. For this last labor he was in course named a Corresponding Member of that organization, a barely adequate recognition for one who gave so much.

In the real world Brad Swan was a giant. He served as President of the Rhode Island Historical Society, the Providence Art Club, as historian for the Society of Colonial Wars and was the author of a number of scholarly historical works. A member of many distinguished historical and bibliographical societies, he was also an artist of some taste who created many works in water color.

His ancestry was extremely distinguished, including sixteen Mayflower passengers; among them, John Alden, Myles Standish and William Bradford. Nevertheless Brad prided himself on his standing as a liberal Democrat, and took nobody very seriously.

The Possessor of the finest wine cellar in the Providence Plantations, as the principal arts and drama critic for the Providence *Journal* and *Bulletin,* he was for decades the leading arbiter of taste in one of America's most historic cities. Nothing, however, was preserved from his wit, and as a devotee of Mencken, he laughed at everyone.

Brad Swan was our cook and counselor in the mountains, stooping over smokey heather fires in the rain and enjoying with vicarious glee the tales of ascents made by the younger members of the party. They, in turn, would gather respectfully every evening while he discussed the flowers and birds he had seen that day nearer to camp.

Brad had known for quite some time that without corrective surgery on his weakened aorta, his days would be limited. But, in a decision supported by all his friends, he elected to serve out his time in full intellectual vigor. On his last trip to the mountains he advised us that if he were to die there, that's where he was to stay. And that is where we, who have lost so much, have taken his ashes.

WILLIAM L. PUTNAM *and* ANDREW J. KAUFFMAN

ALFRED ADOLPHE COUTTET
ARMAND CHARLET
GEORGES TAIRRAZ

Alfred Adolphe Couttet and Armand Charlet, two of the most distinguished guides in the history of the French Alps, died at Chamonix during the last year. Although neither was a member of the AAC, both led many AAC members on scores of first ascents and other challenging climbs in the twenties and the thirties. Living in an era when pitons and other hardware were rarely used except to make a rappel easier or safer, they both did free-climbing ascents like the north ridge of the Aiguille de Géant and the Aiguille de la République which are rarely attempted today, even with our wide resources of mechanical aids. Couttet, in particular, was also a man of great depth of character, a philosopher, a lover of nature, a superb photographer and the French national ski champion of 1924. Those of us who had the privilege of climbing behind them and being taught by them will miss them both keenly—as lifelong friends and masters of their profession, at a time when professional guiding in the Alps was at its zenith. Georges Tairraz died in June. He was not only a gifted photographer of the heights but also a licensed member of the Compagnie des Guides de Chamonix. He made the first moving pictures of the traverse of the Charmoz and Grépon in 1927 and had a long and distinguished record of photography in the French Alps. Many of the extraordinary and beautiful pictures of Rébuffat were made by him.

BRADFORD WASHBURN

Proceedings of the Club

SECRETARY'S REPORT FOR THE YEAR 1975, ANNUAL MEETING AND DINNER

*Minutes of the 73d Annual Meeting and Dinner Held at
Providence Heights, Issaquah, Washington, on December 6, 1975*

President Putnam called the meeting to order at 1:30 P.M. There were 127 members present. The minutes of the 1974 Annual Meeting were approved as printed. Mr. Putnam then read passages from the minutes of several of the earliest meetings of the Club and its Board of Directors.

The Secretary reported that the Club is now composed of 1,145 active members and 26 honorary members (of whom 14 are also active members). During the year, 81 active members were elected to the Club. Twelve members resigned, and 13 members were dropped for nonpayment of dues. The Secretary then reported the deaths of the following members: Burge B. Bickford, Carmie R. Dafoe, Jr., and George C. Miles. Bruce Carson, one of the Club's most outstanding young climbers, was killed on Trisul in India's Garhwal in September when a cornice collapsed. They shall be sorely missed.

Treasurer Dodson presented the Treasurer's report. He reported that during the year the Club's bookkeeping function had become internalized and that the investment portfolio had been transferred from Morgan Guaranty Trust Company and put into the hands of Assistant Treasurer Kenneth Henderson. These measures were taken to realize economies while at the same time suffering no diminution in the quality of services provided. Mr. Dodson also reported that it had been necessary to liquidate approximately 15% of the Club's portfolio to repay an outstanding loan and to close the budgetary deficit. He noted that the audit report, normally available at the Annual Meeting, was not yet complete but would be printed in a future News. He further reported that the budget for fiscal 1975-76 is balanced, but a deficit can be avoided only by a strong campaign to increase contributions. He noted that income from rents and the Teton ranch would increase and that costs were anticipated to be 8% less than the previous year. Although the Club's operating structure remains unchanged, Mr. Dodson reported that efforts were being undertaken to achieve even greater economies in terms of the Club's operating costs. In response to Mr. Nicolai's question, Mr. Dodson reported a slight improvement in the Club's net worth from approximately $272,000 to $280,000. It was voted to accept the Treasurer's report.

President Putnam gave the report of the Nominating Committee, which had been distributed previously to members. Those nominated as Directors for terms ending in December 1978 were Henry C. Barber, Dana J. Isherwood, George Henry Lowe III, Joseph E. Murphy, Jr., and T.C. Price Zimmermann. There being no other candidates, the Secretary declared these nominees elected pursuant to the Bylaws.

Professor Zimmermann, chairman of the Conservation Committee, next reported. He pointed out that the committee had been active in pursuing an on-going program to promote awareness among climbers of the need for protecting the mountain environment. As examples, he cited the Khumbu clean-up and Denali Environmental Expedition's work on Mount McKinley in trash removal and control. Professor Zimmermann also reported on the committee's periodic review of wilderness proposals and master plan proposals on public lands. A special ad hoc committee had been particularly active in connection with the Yosemite master plan, under the leadership of R. D. Caughron. Professor Zimmermann commented on the difficulty of determining what level of use creates unacceptable burdens on public lands worthy of protection. He mentioned the pending litigation concerning questions of access on Mount Rainier. Mr. Putnam advised of the appointment of George Hamilton, Director of State Parks in New Hampshire, to head a Club task force to look into the problem of access to the mountains in light of a long-standing commitment to preserve the mountain environment.

Robert Craig, chairman of the Endowment Committee, next reported on efforts to increase the Club's endowment. A serious downturn in the nation's economy had resulted in a 75% fall-off in contributions over the previous year, he reported. Nevertheless, Mr. Craig detected signs of change and was encouraged by the prospect of reversing this trend. He advised that $3,000 had been made available to start the Jon Gary Ullin Memorial Fund. The interest derived from this fund will be made available to underwrite future visits by American climbers to the Soviet Union. He reported that $5,000 had been raised to enable six Russian climbers to visit the United States this past summer, where they climbed extensively in the 'Gunks, Tetons, Pacific Northwest, and Yosemite. As part of a reciprocal exchange program, the Soviet Union will host six climbers from this country next summer, selection of the team to be based on ability and compatibility. In closing, Mr. Craig stressed the importance of having a broad base of support from the membership in making contributions and particularly seeking unrestricted grants. He finally noted that contributions other than cash were equally desirable, including, for example, securities and libraries.

Expeditions Committee Chairman James Henriot reported that the Club had agreed to endorse a number of expeditions, including the 1975 Colorado Noshaq expedition, 1976 Broad Peak expedition, 1976 Mazama

Karakoram expedition, 1976 Alaska expedition to Tilicho, and 1978 Annapurna III expedition. Sponsorship was also extended to the 1976 Indian-American Nanda Devi expedition, and the 1976 Annapurna I expedition, which has since abandoned its objective because of the inability to obtain permission from the Nepalese government. Mr. Henriot noted that the committee was looking into the problem and possibility of expeditions to China and mentioned the Russian invitation for American climbers to participate in climbers' camps in the Caucasus. He also reported on the changes in endorsement and sponsorship criteria adopted by the Board of Directors the previous day.

H. Adams Carter, the editor of the *American Alpine Journal,* explained that work was progressing well on the new Journal and that some very good articles had been received. Mr. Putnam remarked that the Journal was the finest publication of its kind anywhere in the world.

Theodore Vaill, chairman of the Legal Committee, reported briefly on his committee's activities. He commented that several lawsuits affecting climbers were being monitored, particularly the Mount Rainier access litigation and a West Virginia lawsuit involving the failure of a Jümar ascender. Mr. Vaill also reported that releases were being prepared for use by climbers seeking access to private property.

Raffi Bedayn, chairman of the Guide Certification Committee, reported that a decision had been reached early in the year to terminate the certification program, after 30 months of study and the expenditure of several thousand dollars, and to concentrate instead on educational seminars designed to test and improve the competence of mountain guides.

Chairman of the Membership Committee Alex Bertulis reported briefly on the criteria for evaluating candidates for Club membership and stated that in recent years more stress was being placed on an applicant's showing of a sustained interest in mountaineering, rather than on a strong technical climbing record.

Dr. Herb Hultgren, chairman of the Medical Committee, reported briefly on the committee's work during the previous year. Twenty-five physician-climbers worked with the committee in various aspects of mountaineering-related medicine. They participated in a mountaineering-medicine symposium which was very successful, and he noted that future seminars of this nature were being contemplated.

President Putnam next reported on a Bylaw amendment adopted by the Board of Directors the previous day which would reduce the number of affirmative votes required to elect honorary members from all of the Board of Directors but one to all but three. The amendment would also permit the submission of votes by Directors in writing, to avoid the problem of taking up the question of honorary membership at a meeting at which less than 12 out of 15 Directors were present. Mr. Putnam noted that proxies had been returned from members favoring adoption of the Bylaw amendment by a vote of 127-19. It was voted to adopt the amendment to Section 8 of the Bylaws.

There being no further business, at 2:25 P.M., President Putnam declared the meeting adjourned.

AFTERNOON AND EVENING LECTURES
AND PANEL DISCUSSIONS

In the afternoon, nearly 425 members and guests attended two slide programs following the Annual Meeting. Gerry Roach gave an interesting account of the first ascent of Mount Foraker's north ridge. R. D. Caughron and Mike Warburton followed with slides of their new route on Mount Waddington's north ridge and hike out the Franklin Glacier. This new climb was nicely juxtaposed with historical slides of early exploration and ascents in the Waddington area by Phyllis Munday and Fritz Wiessner. In the evening, following the annual dinner attended by 270 members and guests, Galen Rowell presented "The Year of the Baltoro," a comprehensive account of the unsuccessful attempt to climb K2's northwest ridge and the many other expeditions visiting the Baltoro region last summer, including the remarkable Messner-Habeler alpine-style ascent of Gasherbrum I. As with last year's Annual Meeting, two stimulating panel discussions were conducted on different subjects: mountaineering medicine and climbing in the national parks. Also, two excellent films by Steve Marts, *Ascent* and *Taking Time*, were shown on a continuous basis during the Annual Meeting. The next morning, William Putnam presented a film on the Russian climbers' visit to this country, and Mike Warburton gave a refreshing slide lecture on his climb of the Salathé Wall with the Russians. Dee Molenaar completed the weekend's activities with an illustrated talk on Cascade geology.

JAMES WICKWIRE, *Secretary*

CLUB PUBLICATIONS

THE AMERICAN ALPINE JOURNAL, annually from 1929, illustrated. Many back issues still available, as well as a number of indices for many volumes. $8.50

ACCIDENTS IN NORTH AMERICAN MOUNTAINEERING, published every June since 1948 by the AAC Safety Committee. Accounts of mountaineering accidents with an analysis of each. Many back issues available. $1.50

A CLIMBER'S GUIDE TO THE INTERIOR RANGES OF BRITISH COLUMBIA—NORTH, by William L. Putnam. Basically a reissue of the 1971 edition. Covers the Monashee and Cariboo ranges, and those portions of the Selkirk range north of the Arrow Lakes. Revised index, appendix of passes, brief summary of new material, and maps. Sixth edition, 1975. $8.00

A CLIMBER'S GUIDE TO THE NEEDLES IN THE BLACK HILLS OF SOUTH DAKOTA, by Robert F. Kamps. Covers 350 different pinnacles. Guide is handy pocket size. Eight large, separate detail maps. Fifth edition, 1971. $5.50

A CLIMBER'S GUIDE TO THE ROCKY MOUNTAINS OF CANADA—NORTH, by William L. Putnam, Robert Kruszyna and Chris Jones. A complete revision of earlier editions by J. Monroe Thorington. This edition covers the range from Howse Pass northward. Sixth edition, 1974. $8.50

A CLIMBER'S GUIDE TO THE ROCKY MOUNTAINS OF CANADA—SOUTH, by William L. Putnam and Glen W. Boles. Covers the range from the International Boundary northward to Howse Pass. Completely revised from the earlier editions by Monroe Thorington. Sixth edition, 1973. $8.00

CLIMBING IN NORTH AMERICA, by Chris Jones. The first comprehensive history of mountaineering in North America. 360 pages, 200 illustrations. 1976. $14.95

SHAWANGUNK ROCK CLIMBS, by Richard C. Williams. Covers 393 routes on the Trapps, Near Trapps, Sky Top, and Millbrook cliffs. Illustrated. 1972. $7.00

AMERICAN ALPINE NEWS, newsletter of the Club published in the quarters ending in March, June, September and December.
Subscription beginning with the March issue only. $3.00
Back issues each $1.00

Write for order forms and payment instructions. AAC member discount 20 percent on most titles.

The American Alpine Club
113 East 90th St., New York, N.Y. 10028

INDEX

All entries in the American Alpine Club Journal Index are arranged alphabetically. Subject entries are indicated by capital letters. Mountains are entered by their proper name: quotation marks indicate those names which are unofficial. For the sake of brevity references to mountains which have a variety of peaks identified by number, east, west, chico or grande, etc., are all included under the given name of the mountain. The range, and geographic location are given in parentheses, where known. Latin American Cordilleras are filed under Cordillera. The words mount, mountain, peak, pico, nevado, cerro, etc., are generally omitted. Mc and Mac are filed as if spelled Mac. Personal names are filed ahead of geographical names where they are the same. Please send any errors or omissions to the Alpine Club offices.

This index was prepared by Earlyn Church

A

Abiko, Michiko, 50: 480
Adams, Bruce, 50: 429
Adams (Cascades, Wash.) 50: 441, 442
Advanced Rockcraft, reviewed 50: 565-566
Aeberli, Siegfried, 50: 512
Afanassieff, Jean, 50: 512
Affentranger, Irene, 50: 518
Afghanistan, 50: 553
Agier, M., 50: 474
Agnew, C. H., 50: 514
Aguirre, César, 50: 487
Aiguille du Couchant (Baffin Is.) 50: 467
Airoldi, Luigino, 50: 494
Akinori, Hosaka, 50: 530
Alaska Range, Alaska, 50: 277-301, 313-319, 429-433
Albertelli, Giovanni, 50: 488
Alcock, David E., 50: 531
Aldred, Peter, 50: 475
Alhuayco (Cordillera Real, Bolivia), 50: 501
Alippi, Gigi, 50: 515
Alippi, Giuseppe, 50: 515
Aliprandi, Franco, 50: 488
Allen, Kate, 50: 437
Allison, Michael, 50: 429
Alma Negra (Argentina), 50: 502
Alok Chandolo, 50: 523
Alpamayo (Cordillera Blanca, Peru), 50: 480, 481, 482, 484
Altet, Albert, 50: 486, 487
Altitude Effects, 50: 416-428
Altitude Sickness, 50: 407-415
Alvarez, R., 50: 484
Alwood, Stephanie, 50: 457
Amamiya, Tasashi, 50: 520
Ambros, Lluís, 50: 486
American Alpine Club
  Annual meeting, 1975, 50: 583-586
  Secretary's report, 1975, 50: 583-586
  Section reports, 50: 556-557
Ames, Alcides, 50: 481
Amit Sinha, 50: 526
Ammerer, Gustav, 50: 537
Amoros, Jaime Fabrés, 50: 487
Amoros, Rosa, 50: 487
Amy, B., 50: 474
Amy, M. F., 50: 474

Bertulis, Alex, 50: 340-344, 359
Bevan, Jeff, 50: 431
Bhagirath Rana, Narsingh, 50: 515
Bharat Kunta (Garhwal, India), 50: 526
Bharati Banerjee, 50: 527
Biafo Glacier (Himalayas, Pakistan), 50: 531-532
Bianchi, Graziano, 50: 489
Bickford, Burge, 50: 577-578 obit.
Bidhu Sarkar, 50: 527
Bielfeldt, Talbot, 50: 369
Billoro, Sergio, 50: 502
Bindschadler, R. A., 50: 438
Biock, Martin, 50: 526
Biox, Salvador, 50: 485
Bishnu, Bahadur, 50: 515
Bishop, James, 50: 476
Bitterroot Range, Mon., 50: 455-456
Bjørnstad, Eric, 50: 453
Black, Dave, 50: 444, 447, 448, 449
Black, David, 50: 307
Black, Dennie, 50: 480
Black, Donnie, 50: 486
Black, Jim, 50: 447
Black, John, 50: 480
Black, Sam, 50: 486
Blackburn (Alaska), 50: 438
Blake, Steve, 50: 468
Blauth, Krzysztof, 50: 501
Blazina, Aleksander, 50: 485
Bliss, Bob, 50: 459
Blum, Arlene, 50: 525, 556-557
Boardman, Peter, 50: 357
Bocarde, Gary, 50: 435, 440, 441
Boche, Ken, 50: 447
Bodin, Patrice, 50: 512
Bodnar, Dirk, 50: 433
Boissy, Alain, 50: 517
Bonanza (Cascades, Wash.), 50: 340-344
Bonatti, Walter, 50: 359
Bonatti, Walter, his, The Great Days, reviewed, 50: 569-570
Bondurant, Mark, 50: 433
Bonhomme, M. A., 50: 480
Bonington, Christian, 50: 345-357
Bootleg Tower (Day Canyon, Utah), 50: 452
Borgonovo, Danilo, 50: 481
Borowiec, Wladyslaw, 50: 485
Borrett, Jean, 50: 438
Boselli, Felice, 50: 489
Bosina, Erich, 50: 524
Bouchard, John, 50: 507-509

Boundary Range, Alaska-Yukon, 50: 437
Bourbousson, Frédéric, 50: 537
Bourgeois, Jean, 50: 532
Bowne, Thomas, 50: 486-487
Boyd, Dan, 50: 429
Boyd, Jeff, 50: 496
Boyd, Robert, 50: 480
Boyer, Keith, 50: 441, 442
Boyer, Tim, 50: 442
Boysen, Martin, 50: 357, 532
Bradsma, Maynard, 50: 429
Bragg, John, 50: 503, 507
Braithwaite, Paul, 50: 357
Brammah I (Himachel Pradesh, India), 50: 528
Brandstötter, Rudi, 50: 549
Breslin, Zoran, 50: 513
Briet, M. A., 50: 480
Bright, Jim, 50: 369
Brister, D. A. J., 50: 514
Brniak, Marek, 50: 484, 504, 551
Broadhead, Dave, 50: 545
Broad (Himalayas, Pakistan), 50: 536
Broemel, Dave, 50: 486
Brooks, Don, 50: 434
Brooks (Alaska), 50: 433
Brooks Range, Alaska, 50: 435-437
Brosig, Georg, 50: 480
Broughton, Robert, 50: 480
Brown, Belmore, 50: 400
Brown, Darrell, 50: 312
Brown, Douglas, 50: 475
Brown, Elizabeth, 50: 528
Brown, Garret, 50: 433
Brown, Joe, 50: 533
Brown, Simon, 50: 528
Browne, Belmore, 50: 433
Browne, Mike, 50: 496
Bruce, Larry, 50: 334, 503
Bruchausen, Peter, 50: 380
Bruner, Patrice, 50: 467
Brunin, Jane, 50: 482
Brush, Charles, 50: 551
Bruyntjes, Hans, 50: 525
Bubbs Creek Wall (Sierras, Cal.), 50: 447
Buechner, Tom, 50: 478
Bugaboos (Purcells, B.C.), 50: 472
Buizza, Giuseppe, 50: 489
Bumbacher, H., 50: 546
Buni Zom (Himalayas, Pakistan), 50: 548
Burbank, Doug, 50: 465-466
Burke, Alan, 50: 532

Chugach Mountains, Alaska, 50: 437-438
Churen Himal (Himalayas, Peru), 50: 522-523
Cichy, Leszek, 50: 540
Cieplinska-Bojarska, Halina, 50: 536
Ciochetti, David, 50: 480, 481, 482, 487, 488
Cioncka, Henryk, 50: 504
Cirque of the Unclimbables (Logan Mts., N.W.T.), 50: 465-466
Claramunt, Joan, 50: 548
Clarke, Charles, 50: 357, 527
Clarke, David, 50: 357
Clarke, Michael, 50: 525
Claudet, Serge, 50: 481
Clautice, Stephen, 50: 429
Clemenson, Jean, 50: 517
Clevenger, Vern, 50: 444, 449
Clough, Jane, 50: 528
Clough, Nicki, 50: 528
Clyde Palisade (Sierras, Cal.), 50: 449
Coast Range, B.C., 50: 472-474
Cochran, Nan, 50: 489
Cochrane, Susan, 50: 486
Coène, Raymond, 50: 532
Coffey, Mick, 50: 503
Cohen, Geoffrey, 50: 546
Cohen, Michael, 50: 480
Collie, John Norman, 50: 402, 406
Collie, Norman, 50: 400
Collister, Netti, 50: 528
Collister, Rob, 50: 528, 529
Collister, Robert, 50: 551
Colliver, Gary, 50: 446, 447
Colombari, Armando, 50: 533
Colomer, Jordi, 50: 548
Colorado Mountain Club, 50: 558
Colque Cruz (Cordillera Vilcanota, Peru), 50: 496-498
Coman, Ionel, 50: 553
Conde, J., 50: 479
Condoriri (Cordillera Real, Bolivia), 50: 499-500
Condran, Pat, 50: 301
Conness (Sierras, Cal.), 50: 447
Constantin, Bernard, 50: 467
Conti, Mario, 50: 494, 515
Conway, Howard, 50: 499
Cook, Leonard, 50: 429
Copa (Cordillera Blanca, Peru), 50: 481, 485
Copap (Cordillera Blanca, Peru), 50: 485
Corbellini, Tullio, 50: 488-489

Cordier, Patrick, 50: 512
Cordillera Blanca, Peru, 50: 372-374, 376-379, 479-488
Cordillera Chila, Peru, 50: 494
Cordillera Central, Colombia, 50: 478
Cordillera Central, Peru, 50: 493-494
Cordillera Huayhuash, Peru, 50: 488-493
Cordillera Huaytapallana, Peru, 50: 493
Cordillera Real, Bolivia, 50: 499-501
Cordillera Vilcabamba, Peru, 50: 498
Cordillera Vilcanota, Peru, 50: 495-498
Cordillera Yauyos, Peru, 50: 494
Cotopaxi (Ecuador), 50: 479
Coudray, Jean, 50: 523
Couttet, Alfred Adolphe, 50: 581-582 obit.
Covington, Mike, 50: 330, 384-389
Covington, Michael, 50: 457-459, 460, 536
Cox, Brian, 50: 441
Crawford, Clancy, 50: 435
Cremonese, Franco, 50: 502
Cretton, Maurice, 50: 523
Crocker, Clint, 50: 442
Crow, Pieter, 50: 478
Crowley Buttress (Sierras, Cal.), 50: 447
Cruz, Marco, 50: 479
Cuiñas, H., 50: 484
Cuiñas, Héctor, 50: 505
Culp, Bob, 50: 459
Cumberland Peninsula, Baffin Is., 50: 467
Cundiff, Reed, 50: 447
Curnis, Mario, 50: 515
Curtis, Al, 50: 435
Curzio, J., 50: 478
"Cyclops" (Logan Mts., N.W.T.), 50: 325
Czerwinska, Anna, 50: 540

D

Dacher, Michael, 50: 512
Dafoe, Carmie, R., Jr., 50: 578-579, Obit
Daiber, Ome, 50: 577-578
Dailey, David, 50: 440
Dakiya, 50: 520
Dangel, Bob, 50: 462
Darling, John, 50: 528
Danielson, Scott, 50: 429

Da Polenza, Agostino, 50: 489
Darphuntso, 50: 516
Daubas, Charles, 50: 523
Davies, Thomas, 50: 293
Davis, David E., 50: 434
Dawa, 50: 369
Dawson, Lou, 50: 334, 336, 432, 457
Day Canyon, Utah, 50: 452
Deangeli, Bruno, 50: 509
Debi, Ram, 50: 527
Deborah (Alaska Range, Alaska), 295-301, 434
De Gruyter, Philip, 50: 477
De Infanti, Sergio, 50: 546
Dekker, P., 50: 480
Dell Oro, Carlo, 50: 494
Del Pozo, Angel, 50: 485
Del Zotto, Giancarlo, 50: 491
Dellinger, Robb, 50: 445, 448
Demeter, Anton, 50: 553
De Nancques, Philippe, 50: 517
Dengate, Howard, 50: 496
Denkewalter, Paul, 50: 435, 440
DeStavola, Walter, 50: 483
Devasher, Vijay, 50: 369
Devistan (Garhwal, India), 50: 526
Devitt, John L., 50: 558
De Vries, J., 50: 546
Devuderjit Singh, 50: 523
DeWolf, Barton, 50: 462-463
Dey, Sumasher, 50: 369
Dhaulagiri I (Himalayas, Nepal), 50: 520
Dhaulagiri II(Himalayas, Nepal), 50: 520
Dhaulagiri II (Himalayas, Nepal), 50: 520-522
Dhaulagiri V (Himalayas, Nepal), 50: 522
Di Beaco, Bianca, 50: 548
Diablos Parados (Chilean Andes) 50: 501
Diaz, Juan Manuel, 50: 478
Diemberger, Adolf, 50: 549, 553
Dijk, K. E. J., 50: 480
Dilly, P. N., 50: 514
Dipak Pal, 50: 526
Dobrzynski, Jerzy, 50: 485
Dodds, Bob, 50: 459
Doleschel, Grit, 50: 475
Domenech, B., 50: 474
Donahue, Maureen, 50: 505
Donini, Jim, 50: 503, 505
Dorjee, ———, 50: 520
Dorjee Lathuo, 50: 523
Doswald, H.P., 50: 546

Douglas, David, 50: 397
Dovjan, Janez, 50: 513
Dowbenka, Theo, 50: 499
Downward Bound, A Mad Guide to Rock Climbing, reviewed, 50: 567-569
Doyle, Conan, 50: 403
Droker, Rick, 50: 480, 486
Dragontail (Cascades, Wash.), 50: 441-442
Dubacher, M., 50: 546
Duben, Vincent, 50: 480
Dubreuil, Elliot, 50: 445
Duchini, Carlo, 50: 533
Ducroz, Denis, 50: 512
Duff, James, 50: 357
Duke of Abruzzi, 50: 361
Dunham, Fred, 50: 359
Dunagiri (Garhwal, India), 50: 524
Dunn, James, 50: 457, 459
Dunn, Mike, 50. 429
Dupont-Roc, Andrée, 50: 467
Dupont-Roc, Maurice, 50: 467
Dupraz, Jean, 50: 540
Durville, Jacques, 50: 467-468
Duttle, Hans Peter, 50: 467

E

Earth Angel (Long Canyon, Arizona), 50: 453-454
Eastwood, Frank, 50: 509
Ebert, Jim, 50: 486
Ebert, John, 50: 486, 559
Echelmeyer, Keith, 50: 312
Echevarria, Evelio, 50: 477, 478, 479, 484, 501, 504, 575
Echo Rock (Utah), 50: 452
Eddy, Steve, 50: 445, 448, 455-456
Edwards, Ralph, 50: 398
Eekayruk (Brooks Range, Alaska), 50: 435-436
Eggers, August, 50: 400
Eggert, Joe, 50: 475
Eggert, Waltraut, 50: 475
Eggert, Willi, 50: 475
Ehrenfeldt, Ed, 50: 449
Eihlers, Craig, 50: 442
El Sangay (Ecuador), 50: 479
El Toro (Chilean Andes), 50: 501
Eldridge, Harry, 50: 489
"Electra Spire" (Logan Mts., N.W.T.), 50: 325
The Elephant's Perch (Sawtooth Range, Idaho), 50: 455
Elliott, Tom, 50: 436

Embick, Andrew, 50: 320-325
Emmett, Dan, 50: 525
Emrick, Robert, 50: 551
Encyclopaedia of Mountaineering, reviewed, 50: 573-575
Enda, Keiji, 50: 549
Engle, Stan, 50: 486
Estcourt, Nick, 50: 357
Estevez, Luis, 50: 505
"Eumenides" (Logan Mts., N.W.T.), 50: 325
Everest (Himalayas, Nepal), 50: 345-357, 515-516
Ewert, Alan, 50: 429

F

Fabre, José, 50: 485
Facchetti, Andrea, 50: 500
Fagan, Mark, 50: 465
Fairley, Bruce, 50: 464
Fairweather (Fairweather Range, Alaska), 50: 308-312
Fairweather Range, Alaska, 50: 308-312, 438-440
Falsoola (Brooks Range, Alaska), 50: 435-436
Fantin, Mario, 50: 502, 518, 548-549
Farrar, Jamie, 50: 465
Farrell, Peter, 50: 512
Favalli, Pietro, 50: 488
Faylor, Bob, 50: 419
Fearnehough, Pat, 50: 532
Ferenski, Janusz, 50: 536
Ferguson, Rob, 50: 551
Fernández, André, 50: 489
Ferrari, Casimiro, 50: 481
Ferrari, Giuseppe, 50: 500
Feuillet, Pierre-Henri, 50: 475
Fiala, Ivan, 50: 480
Field Book of Mountaineering and Rock Climbing, The, reviewed, 50: 566-567
Fields, Mark, 50: 429
Fiocchi, Giulio, 50: 533
Fisher, Brad, 50: 429
Fisher, Elliot, 50: 489
Fischer, Karl, 50: 550
Fitz Roy (Patagonia, Argentina-Chile, 50:504)
Fiut, Walenty, 50: 478, 484, 493
Fleming, Jonathan W., 50: 513-515
Flores, Maria Elena, 50: 480
Florschutz, Henry, 50: 319
Flouret, Michel, 50: 434
Font, Enrique, 50: 485

Foraker (Alaska Range, Alaska), 50: 277-284, 430-431
Ford, Bud, 50: 480
Foresti, Giovanni, 50: 500
Foresti, Melchiorre, 50: 500
Forrat, Jean-Jacques, 50: 540
Forrest, Bill, 50: 457
Forsythe, Jack, 50: 445
Four Gables (Sierras, Cal.), 50: 448
Fouts, Mark, 50: 433, 437
Fraile Grande (Ecuador), 50: 479
Frank, H., 50: 478
Franzl, Richard, 50: 550
Frehel, Jean, 50: 532
Frésafond, Hélène, 50: 537
Frésafond, Jean-Pierre, 50: 537
Fresno Dome (Sierras, Cal.), 50: 445
Fried, Mark, 50: 480, 486
Fuhrer, Hans, 50: 463-464
Fuhrman, Peter, 50: 527
Fuiten, Roger, 50: 433
Fujii, Yoshiaki, 50: 438
Fujiwara, S., 50: 521
Fuller Butte (Sierras, Cal.), 50: 447
Funk, Terry, 50: 528, 553
Furtner, Alois, 50: 537
Furuichi, Tsyuoshi, 50: 550
Furuzuka, ———— 50: 526
Fyffe, Allen, 50: 357

G

Gaetani, Lodovico, 50: 492
Gálfy, Ivan, 50: 480
Gálvez, C., 50: 500
Ganter, Gerd, 50: 519
Garcia, Emilio, 50: 489
García, Gerardo Blázquez, 50: 518
Garmush (Hindu Raj, Pakistan), 50: 549
Garner, Valentin, 50: 553
Gasherbrum II (Himalayas, Pakistan), 50: 537-541
Gasherbrum III, 50: 540-541
Gaskill, Steven, 50: 308-312
Gaviria, Pancho, 50: 478
Gaviria, S., 50 : 478
Gaviria, Sergio, 50: 478
Gaynor, Mark, 50: 447
Geist, Valerius, *Mountain Sheep and Man in the Northern Wilds,* reviewed, 50: 572-573
Geldhung (Garhwal, India), 50: 526
Gelmi, Angelo, 50: 500
Gentner, Heinrich, 50: 480, 483
Gerdes, Karl, 50: 480

596

Hardy, Tom, 50: 488
Hargesheimer, Randy, 50: 438, 464
Harms, Les, 50: 486
Harrison, W. D., 50: 438
Harsha Muni Nautiyal, 50: 527
Hartmann, Olaf, 50: 496
Hasegawa, Ryoten, 50: 522
Hasfjord, Jerry, 50: 441
Haston, Dougal, 50: 357, 517
Hatakeyama, Masaaki, 50: 429
Haverson, Ian, 50: 478
Havildar, Major Tsering Norbu, 50: 529
Hawley, David, 50: 429
Hawley, John, 50: 480
Howard, Ted, 50: 532
Hayashi, Yasuhide, 50: 549
Hayashibara, Ryuji, 50: 550
Hayes (Alaska Range, Alaska), 50: 295-301, 434-435
Heath, Mike, 50: 439
Heinl, Josef, 50: 502
Henderson, Richard, 50: 475
Henderson, Rick, 50: 516
Hennek, Dennis, 50: 536
Henostroza, Humberto, 50: 485
Herrligkoffer, Karl Maria, 50: 545
Herwick, Peter, 50: 480
Hesse, Mark, 50: 334, 336
Hidden Falls (Col.), 50: 337
Hidden Peak (Himalayas, Pakistan), 50: 541-542
Hidezumi, Komi, 50: 519
Higgins, Molly, 50: 457, 459
Higgins, Thomas, 50: 449
Higgs, David, 50: 509
Higley, Howard, 50: 486
Hildner, Ernest, 50: 486
Hildner, Richard, 50: 486
Hill (Northern Boundary Range, Alaska-Yukon), 50: 437
Hillmaier, 50: 545
Himal Chuli (Himalayas, Nepal), 50: 519
Himalaje-Karakorum, reviewed, 50: 575
Hinckley, Bern, 50: 429
Hippach, Frank, 50: 404
Hiratsuka, Hiroshi, 50: 522
Hiroshi, Maeda, 50: 519
Hisano, Eiko, 50: 515
Hoey, Marty, 50: 555
Holm, Bjarne, 50: 429
Holm, C. M., 50: 441-442, 443, 454, 455
Holden, Peter, 50: 552

Homer, George, 50: 330
Honda (Cordillera Blanca, Peru), 50: 485
Honnilh, L., 50: 518
Horiskey, Joe, 50: 429
Hösle, Ludwig, 50: 550
Hosted, Michael, 50: 553, 528
Hostetler, Charlie, 50: 435
Hotchkiss, Walter, 50: 551
Hottman, Mark, 50: 301
Hou Sheng-fu, 50: 516
Houston, Charles S., 50: 407-415, 416-428
Howard, Everett, 50: 369
Howard, Geoffrey, 50: 402
Huacaña (Cordillera Real, Bolivia), 50: 499
Huacshash (Cordillera Huayhuash, Peru), 50: 492
Huagaruncho (Cordillera Oriental, Peru), 50: 493
Hualcán (Cordillera Blanca, Peru), 50: 482
Huandoy (Cordillera Blanca, Peru), 50: 483-484, 485
Huascaran (Cordillera Blanca, Peru), 50: 376-379, 479-481, 484, 485
Huayna Potosi (Cordillera Real, Bolivia), 50: 499, 501
Hub, Carl, 50: 542
Hubbard, George, 50: 429
Huber, J., 50: 546
Huddleson's Bluff (Idaho), 50: 454
Hudson, Cliff, 50: 433
Hugas, Juan, 50: 480
Huggard, Eric, 50: 429
Hugin (Baffiin Is.), 50: 467
Huila (Cordillera Central, Colombia), 50: 478
Huiyata (Cordillera Real, Bolivia), 50: 501
Humbert, Nöel, 50: 467
Hummler, Thomas, 50: 475
Humphrey, Neil, 50: 464
Humphreys (Sierras, Cal.), 50: 443
Hunt, Peter, 50: 475
Hunter, Diana, 50: 459
Hunter, Jane, 50: 505
Huntley, Dave, 50: 434
Hurd, Marjorie, 50: 576-577
Hurley, George, 50: 459
Hutchison, Hall, 50: 489
"Hydra" (Logan Mts., N.W.T.), 50: 325

I

J

K

Kentz, Steve, 50: 482
Kenya (Kenya), 50: 384-389
Kerns, Matt, 50: 442
Kerr, Matt, 50: 464
Keshab Mukherjee, 50: 527
Kesicki, Marek, 50: 536
Ketil (Greenland), 50: 474-475
Kettle Dome (Sierras, Cal.), 50: 445, 449
Khala Cruz (Cordillea Real, Bolivia), 50: 501
Kichatna Mountains, Alaska, 50: 304-307, 435
Kiene, Helmut, 50: 443
Kimura, F., 50: 521
Kimura, Kazutomo, 50: 429
King, Jeff, 50: 429
King, M. T., 50: 514
King, Simon, 50: 445
King Edward (Can. Rockies) 50: 469
Kirn, Peter, 50: 429
Kishtwar Himal (Himal Pradesh, India), 50: 528-529
Kitchener (Can. Rockies, Alta.), 50: 326-333
Klingshirn, Josef, 50: 499
Knapp, Andrew, 50: 438, 464
Kobayashi, Minoru, 50: 522
Kobayashi, Yasunori, 50: 543
Koblmüller, Eduard, 50: 537
Kochalka, John, 50: 478
Kodaka, Kazuo, 50: 543
Kodama, T., 50: 521
Kogure, Shigehito, 50: 522
Koh-e-Bandaka (Hindu Kush, Afghanistan), 50: 553
Kohe Purwakshan (Wakhan Pamir), 50: 555
Kokubu, Mosako, 50: 480
Kolaczkowski, M., 50: 555
Kolb, Fritz, 50: 370
Komatsu, Kozo, 50: 522
Konno, Akira, 50: 429
Kono, Masaru, 50: 522
Kono, Terayaki, 50: 522
Kor, Layton, 50: 457, 459
Koshtantau (Caucasus, U.S.S.R), 50: 555
Kosiol, Ryszard, 50: 485
Kotnik, Evc, 50: 513
Kovacs, Zotan, 50: 553
Koziol, Ryszard, 50: 480
Krakauer, Jon, 50: 465
Krakauer, Jonathan, 50: 285-293
Krasowski, Roman, 50: 485

Krebs, Stewart, 50: 284
Krenck, L., 50: 370
Kruger-Syrokomska, Halina, 50: 540
Kubirjang, Rai, 50: 515
Kulbe, B. C., 50: 526
Kulis, Janusz, 50: 536
Kumar Khadga Bikram Shah, 50: 518
Kunaver, Ales, 50: 512-513
Kunel, Ernest, 50: 486
Kunga, Pasang, 50: 516
Kunwar Singh, 50: 527
Kuroda, Haruhisa, 50: 522
Kursa, Zbigniew, 50: 504
Kwangde (Himalayas, Nepal), 50: 518
Kyoji, Sugimoto, 50: 526

L

La Mesa (Argentina), 50: 503
Laba, Roman, 50: 499
"Labyrinth" (Logan Mts., N.W.T.), 50: 325
Lacedelli, Compagoni, 50: 359
Lackner, Erich, 50: 512
Lafranconi, Giuseppe, 50: 533
Laili (Himalayas, Pakistan), 50: 543
Lamilla, R., 50: 500
Lanbeck, Bob, 50: 366
Lancashire, Howard, 50: 552
Landry, Werner R., 50: 477
Lane, M. P., 50: 514
Lanfranchi, Gianluigi, 50: 533
Lang, Fred, 50: 480, 486
Lang, Jos., 50: 496
Langar (Himalayas, Pakistan), 50: 546-548
Langmade, Dan, 50: 480, 481, 482, 487, 488
Langton, Nick, 50: 516
Lant, V., 50: 483, 552
Lanzl, Richard, 50: 550
Lapinski, Andrzej, 50: 504, 540
Laritti, Benvenuto, 50: 533
Lasontay (Cordillera Huaytapallana, Peru), 50: 493
Latok I (Himalayas, Pakistan), 50: 543
Latok II (Himalayas, Pakistan), 50: 543
Laurendeau, Cl., 50: 474
Lauria, Don, 50: 536
Lawrence, Dave, 50: 464
Lawrence, Jill, 50: 466
Laxson, Bill, 50: 429

599

Malville, Kim, 50: 486
Malville, Nancy, 50: 486
Manaslu (Himalayas, Nepal), 50: 518-519
Manfreda, Marjan, 50: 513
Manning, Dan, 50: 482
Manson, Laurie, 50: 457
Mantle, Douglas, 50: 429
Mapes, Sandy, 50: 433
Marangunic, Cedomir, 50: 495
Marble Icefall (Col.), 50: 334
March, Bill, *Modern Snow & Ice Techniques,* reviewed, 50: 563-565
March, William, 50: 454
Marchal, Dominique, 50: 475
Marcus Baker (Chugach Mountains, Alaska), 50: 437-438
Markham, Clements, 50: 495
Markov, Gregory C., 50: 439
Marshall, P.S., 50: 525
Marti, Max, 50: 550
Martin, Roger, 50: 507
Martinelli, Giovanni, 50: 518
Martínez, Alfred, 50: 548
Martínez Jerónimo López, 50: 518
Martini, Sergio, 50: 483
Martinson, Craig, 50: 466-467
Marts, Steve, 50: 361
Masahiro Nagaoka, 50: 522
Masaru Takeyama, 50: 530
Masciardri, Fabrio, 50: 491-492
Masciardri, Maria, 50: 491
Masino, Yvon, 50: 523
Mastellaro, Toni, 50: 502
Matheson, Colin, 50: 475
Matkah (Hindu Raj, Pakistan) 50: 548-549
Matsuda, Naohisa, 50: 429
Matsunaga, Toshiro, 50: 434-435
Maude (Cascades, Wash.), 50: 442-443
Mautino, Felipe, 50: 480
Maverna, Carla, 50: 518
Mawenzi (Africa), 50: 509
Mayerl, Sepp, 50: 512
Medina, Sofia, 50: 480
Mehrbani (Himalayas, Pakistan), 50: 551
Mehring, Chip, 50: 312
Mejak, Walter, 50: 548
Mendenhall, John D., 50: 444
Mendenhall, Ruth Dyar, 50: 557
Mendenhall Towers (Juneau Icefields, Alaska), 50: 441
Mention, Dave, 50: 474
Menz, Georg Peter, 50: 502

Mera (Himalayas, Nepal), 50: 518
Mercedario (Argentina), 50: 502
Mercer, John, 50: 495
Meroni, Vittorio, 50: 492
Merrill, Tom, 50: 432
Merz, V., 50: 546
Mesaric, Vladimir, 50: 502
Messer, Reinhold, *Seventh Grade,* reviewed 50: 562-563
Messner, Reinhold, 50: 515, 541
Metcalf, Peter, 50: 313-319
Michaelski, Jerzy, 50: 494
Michelson (Brooks Range, Alaska), 50: 436-437
Michioka, Tokiko, 50: 464
Middle Palisade (Sierras, Cal.), 50: 444
Migden, Douglas, 50: 433
Mikolajczyk, M., 50: 555
Milani, Carlo, 50: 489
Millar, John, 50: 370
Miller, Irene, 50: 435-436
Miller, Jack, 50: 380-383, 505
Miller, Jim, 50: 429
Miller, Keith, 50: 476
Miller, Pat, 50: 487
Millpo (Cordillera Huayhuash, Peru), 50: 490-491
Milne, Rob, 50: 462
Minaspata (Cordillera Chila, Peru), 50: 494
Mingardo, Graziano, 50: 502
"Minotaur" (Logan Mts., N.W.T.), 50: 325
Miori, Albert, 50: 481, 487
Misener, Wayne, 50: 470
Miskil, Brian, 50: 430
Mitchell, Richard, 50: 470-471
Mitkiewicz, Maria, 50: 540
Mitopunta use Yanacaico (Cordillera Huayhuash, Peru)
Mitsuaki Nishigori, 50: 529
Miura, Kohichi, 50: 494
Miyazaki, Tsutomu, 50: 494
Mizohata, Hiromichi, 50: 522
Modern Snow & Ice Techniques, reviewed, 50: 563-565
Morgan, Charles (Chip), 50: 489
Mohan Singh, 50: 527
Molenski, Stan, 50: 452
Moljnir (Baffin Is.), 50: 467
Monteath, Colin, 50: 496-498
Montfort, José María, 50: 551
Monument Valley, Arizona, 50: 453
Moomaw, Sheldon, 50: 480, 486
Moore, Carl, 50: 525

Moore, Malcolm, 50: 441
Moose's Tooth (Alaska Range, Alaska), 50: 285-293, 432
Mora, Gino, 50: 489
Morales, Marcelino, 50: 480
Moreno, Pepe Luis, 50: 478
Morgan, Chip, 50: 482
Morgan, Frank, 50: 525
Mori, Sakae, 50: 549
Mori, Tetsuo, 50: 464
Morioka, Masaaki, 50: 522
Moritada, Kenji, 50: 429
Moro, Kazuhiko, 50: 543
Morozumi, Yasuo, 50: 522
Morrison, Don, 50: 532
Morse, Dick, 50: 429
Mostul, Burl, 50: 487
Mozinski, Jarek, 50: 485
Mountain Sheep and Man in the Northern Wilds, reviewed, 50: 572-573
Mountaineering Club of Alaska, 50: 559-560
The Mountaineers, 50: 560-561
The Mountains of America: From Alaska to the Great Smokies, reviewed, 50: 570-572
Moyano (Patagonia, Argentina-Chile), 50: 505
Mozzanica, Dario, 50: 509
Mozzanica, Ivo, 50: 509
Mrigthuni (Garhwal, India), 50: 526
Mudge, Arthur, 50: 480, 486
Mukerbeh (Himachal Pradesh, India), 50: 527-528
Muko, Ichiyo, 50: 494
Müller, Hanna, 50: 550
Müller, Hermine, 50: 524
Mumm, A.L., 50: 401
Munin (Baffin Is.), 50: 467-468
Muñoz, A., 50: 479
Murray, Hal, 50: 462
Murray, Kathy, 50: 325
Muston, A. J., 50: 514
Mutti, Anchise, 50: 544
Myrabo, Arne, 50: 446

N

Nakajima, Sinichi, 50: 522
Nakajima, Teruhiko, 50: 550
Nakamura, H., 50: 52
Nakamura, Takashi, 50: 464
Nakamura, Teruzo, 50: 429
Namikawa, Kazuyu, 50: 542

Nanda Devi (Garhwal, India), 50: 523-524
Nanda Ghunti (Garhwal, India), 50: 526
Nandaraj, Gurung, 50: 514
Nanga Parbat (Himalayas, Pakistan), 50: 545
Narbaud, Georges, 50: 475
Naik Nim Dorje, 50: 529
Narbu, Sherpa, 50: 514
Nawang Tsering, 50: 528
Needles, (Sierras, Cal.), 50: 444
Negishi, Tomo, 50: 522
Negri, Pino, 50: 481
Nepeomnyashchy, Anotoly, 50: 344
Neubauer, Franz, 50: 475
Nevado del Pulpito (Sierra Nevada del Cocuy, Colombia), 50: 478
Nevado Paloblanco (Sierra Nevada del Cocuy, Colombia), 50: 478
Nevado Pan de Azucar (Sierra Nevada del Cocuy, Colombia), 50: 478
Ngopo Khyen, 50: 516
Nicholson, Ian, 50: 551
Nicola, Pablo, 50: 505
Nicolai, William S., 50: 472
Niewodniczanski, Jerzy, 50: 485
Nigris, Antonio Beorchia, 50: 502
Nima Dorje, 50: 527
Nima Kanchha, 50: 521
Nirvana (Logan Mts., N.W.T.), 50: 325
Nishimae, Shiro, 50: 521
Nishimura, K., 50: 521
Nishimura, N., 50: 521
Nitai Roy, 50: 526
Niut Range, Coast Range, B.C. 50: 472-473
Nogaki, Kengo, 50: 429
Noku, Shizuo, 50: 528
Northumbria (Baffin Is.), 50: 468
Noshaq (Hindu Kush, Afghanistan), 50: 551
Notling, Rick, 50: 436-437
Nose, Mahito, 50: 526
Notchtop (Rockies, Col.), 50: 460, 461
Novia, Dolores, 50: 480
Nowaczyk, Bogdan, 50: 536
Noyes (Can. Rockies), 50: 469-470
Numao, Yoshitata, 50: 520
Nun (Himalayas, India), 50: 529-530
Nuptse (Himalayas, Nepal), 50: 513-514

Portolan, Nino, 50: 502
Porzak, Glenn, 50: 551
Potter, Charles, 50: 429
Potts, Dave, 50: 533
Pozzoli, Edoardo, 50: 489
Prem Chand, 50: 523
Pressl, Fred, 50: 537
Prevedel, Helmut, 50: 542
Price, Mike, 50: 464
Priesner, Fritz, 50: 537
Prithvi Prasad, 50: 527
Prosser, Jonathan D., 50: 531
Prunes, Joaquim, 50: 486, 487
Pschorr, Barbara, 50: 480
Pschorr, Walter, 50: 480
Ptarmigan Towers (Rockies, Col.), 50: 460
Pucahirca (Cordillera Blanca, Peru), 50: 480
Pucaraju (Cordillera Blanca, Peru), 50: 480
Pucaranra (Cordillera Blanca, Peru), 50: 480
Pucarashta (Cordillera Blanca, Peru), 50: 482
Puig, M., 50: 500
Pulpito del Diablo (Sierra Nevada del Cocuy, Columbia), 50: 478
Pumasillo (Cordillera Vilcabamba, Peru), 50: 498
Pumori (Himalayas, Nepal), 50: 517-518
Purcells, B.C., 50: 472
Purian Sar (Himalayas, Pakistan) 50: 549-550
Puscanturpa (Cordillera Huayhuash, Peru), 50: 488
Putnam, William L., 50: 469-470, 580-581

Q

Queen Mary (Can. Rockies), 50: 468-469
Quilindaña (Ecuador), 50: 479
Qualizza, Mario, 50: 546
Quitaraju (Cordillera Blanca, Peru), 50: 482

R

Radin, Pierino, 50: 483
Ragana, Armando, 50: 502
Ragle, Dick, 50: 419
Rainbow Mountains, Nevada, 50: 452

Rainier (Cascades, Wash.), 50: 441
Rainsford, Guy, 50: 369
Rajani Rakshit, 50: 526
Rajuntay (Cordillera Central, Peru), 50: 493
Ralling, Chris, 50: 357
Ralph, Marshall, 50: 562-563
Rams, Ramon Bramona, 50: 548
Ranjit Rit, 50: 526
Ranrapalca (Cordillera Blanca, Peru), 50: 372-374
Rattan Singh, 50: 527
Ratti, J., 50: 474
Rauzi, Alberto, 50: 518
Ravenhill, T.H., 50: 408
Rawlinson, Ken, 50: 468
Raymond, Alain, 50: 540
Raymond, C.F., 50: 438
Rearick, David, 50: 457
Redman, Earl, 50: 429
Reenstra, William, 50: 486
Regnault, Martine, 50: 467
Reid, Roger, 50: 509
Reilly, John, 50: 486
Reilly, Tom, 50: 486
Reiser, Eugen, 50: 550
Reismüller, Erich, 50: 526
Renaud, Raymond, 50: 523
Renshaw, R. M., 50: 524
Reynolds, A., 50: 433
Reynolds, Eric, 50: 434
Rhodes, Mike, 50: 357
Richards, Ronnie, 50: 357, 532
Richert, J. K., 50: 480
Ricker, John, 50: 488, 495
Rieder, H., 50: 546
Rinzing, 50: 528
Ritacuba Blanco (Sierra Nevado de Cocuy, Colombia), 50: 478
Ritipampa del Quelccaya (Cordillera Vilcanota, Peru), 50: 495
Riva, Giancarlo, 50: 494
Riviere, Bill, *Field Book of Mountaineering and Rock Climbing* reviewed, 50: 566-567
Rizzi, Giuseppe, 50: 500
Roach, Barbara, 50: 284
Roach, Gerard, 50: 277-284
Robert, Alain, 50: 517
Roberts, Alan, 50: 509
Roberts, David, 50: 465
Roberts, Dianne, 50: 361
Roberts, Eric, 50: 509
Roberts, Jack, 50: 445, 447
Roberts, Jimmy, 50: 518

Robbins, Royal, 50: 578-580
  Advanced Rockcraft, reviewed,
  50: 565-566
Robinson, Bill, 50: 470
Robinson, Doug, 50: 563-565, 567-569
Robinson, John, 50: 429
Robinson, Roger, 50: 429-430
Rocca, Alfredo, 50: 488
Rocco, Guido, 50: 488, 544
Rocco, Tullio, 50: 544
Rocky Mountains, Col., 50: 457-458
Rodarmor, William, 50: 380
Rodzinski, Ryszard, 50: 504
Rolands, Clive, 50: 532
Romano, ——— 50: 481
Romanzof Mountains (Brooks Range, Alaska), 50: 436
Rose, Millie, 50: 486
Rosende, P., 50: 500
Rosiak, Kasimier, 50: 480, 485
Roskelley, John, 50: 499
Ross (Kerguelen Island, Indian Ocean), 50: 509-512
Rotter, Peter, 50: 499
Rourke, Michael J., 50: 372-374, 376-379, 479-480, 481, 482, 483-484, 485, 487, 488
Rowell, Galen A., 50: 361, 443, 444, 566, 570-575
Rowland David, 50: 442
Royrvik, Ola, 50: 429
Rozniecki, Marek, 50: 494
Rubens, Dea, 50: 545
Ruckhaus, Michael, 50: 312
Rüdi, Marcel, 50: 550
Ruhl, Steven, 50: 312
Ruhland, Wolfgang, 50: 475
Russell, Diane, 50: 459
Russell, Franklin, *The Mountains of America* reviewed, 50: 570-572
Russell (Sierras, Cal.), 50: 448-449
Russignaga, Charles, 50: 467
Rutkiewicz, Wanda, 50: 540
Ruwenzori, Uganda-Congo, 50: 509
Ryan, Tim, 50: 444
Ryn, Zdzislaw, 50: 504

S

Sabat, Francesa, 50: 548
Sad Ishtragh (Darrah-e-Qalat, Afghanistan), 50: 553
Saeed Ahmed Malik, 50: 540
Sáez, J., 50: 479
Saganek, S., 50: 555

St. Elias (St. Elias Range, Alaska-Yukon), 50: 463
St. Elias Range, Alaska-Yukon, 50: 438, 463
Sajama (Chile), 50: 499
Salcantay (Cordillera Vilcamba, Peru), 50: 498
Saleki, Mischa, 50: 551
Salembier, Martine, 50: 467
Saltoro Kangri (Himalayas, Pakistan), 50: 542
Salvetti, Celso, 50: 491, 492
Samdrub, 50: 516
Sanavio, Massimo, 50: 544
Sánchez, E., 50: 479
Sanford (Wrangell Range, Alaska), 50: 438
Sankat Ali Mondal, 50: 527
Santa Cruz (Cordillera Blanca, Peru), 50: 480
Santon, Francesco, 50: 483
Sara Urco (Ecuador), 50: 479
Saraghrar (Himalayas, Pakistan), 50: 548
Sarapo (Cordillera Huayhuash, Peru), 50: 488-489
Sardar Pemba Norbu, 50: 521
Sasakane, Shiro, 50: 522
Sasaki, Takanori, 50: 429
Sato, Hideo, 50: 548
Sato, Toshihiko, 50: 543
Satoru, Takashi, 50: 529
Saunders, Dennis, 50: 472
Savenc, Franci, 50: 502
Savic, Boris, 50: 429
Savidge, Dick, 50: 477
Sawtooth Range, Idaho, 50: 455
Sawyer, ———, 50: 401
Scalettaris, Aldo, 50: 546
Schäfler, Otto, 50: 475
Schaller, Rob, 50: 359
Scharl, Werner, 50: 475
Schauer, Robert, 50: 542
Schell, Hanns, 50: 542
Schell, Leselotte, 50: 542
Schibli, Hans, 50: 546
Schlick, ——— 50: 519
Schlunegger, Peter, 50: 463
Schmatz, Gerhard, 50: 550
Schmatz, Hannelore, 50: 550
Schmitt, Dennis, 50: 437
Schneider, Bruce, 50: 480, 486
Schneider, Robert, 50: 366-567
Schnait, Beyerlein, 50: 545
Schnait, Margaret, 50: 545
Schoening, Pete, 50: 359

605

606

Thuermer, Angus, 50: 319
Thui Group (Hindu Raj, Pakistan), 50: 545-546
Thurnbichler, Herman, 50: 550
Tinaut, A., 50: 479
Tirch Mir (Hindu Kush, Pakistan), 50: 550-551
Tirokwa (Baffin Is.), 50: 466, 467
Tocllaraju (Cordillera Blanca, Peru), 50: 485, 486
Tokosha Mountains, Alaska, 50: 433-434
Tolima (Cordillera Central, Colombia), 50: 478
Tollenaar, H., 50: 480
Tombstone Range, Yukon, 50: 465
Tomo, Odanaka, 50: 526
Tompkins, Doug, 50: 536
Torre Egger (Patagonia, Argentina-Chile), 50: 505-507
Torres, Patricio, 50: 479
Torrico, Emilio, 50: 489
Toss Valey Kulu (Himachel Pradesh, India), 50: 528
Totem Pole (Monument Valley, Arizona), 50: 453
Toyoma, Akie, 50: 480
Trachsel, Hans Peter, 50: 504
Trango Tower (Himalayas, Pakistan), 50: 532-533
Trapmann, Dieter, 50: 475
Trasker, Joseph, 50: 524
Trimble, Phillip, 50: 525
Tripan Singh, 50: 527
Trisul (Garhwal, India), 50: 525-526
Tsering Tobgyal, 50: 516
Tucker, David, 50: 472-473
Tumbling Glacier (Can. Rockies, B.C.), 50: 470
Tupungato (Argentina), 50: 502
Turnweather (Baffin Is.), 50: 468
Tuttle Creek (Sierras, Cal.), 50: 445-446
Twin Owls (Rockies, Col.), 50: 459
Twin Pillars (Greenland), 50: 476
Twomey, Arthur, 50: 496

U

Uchida, Yoshihiro, 50: 550
Uekawa, K., 50: 521
Uls (Baffin Is.), 50: 468
Ulta (Cordillera Blanca, Peru), 50: 482
Umeki, Eiichi, 50: 552

Underhill, Miriam O'Brien, 50: 576-577, obit.
Unsoeld, William F., 50: 516
Unsworth, Walt, Encyclopaedia of Mountaineering reviewed, 50: 573-575
Upernivik Is., Greenland, 50: 475
Urdok I (Himalayas, Pakistan), 50: 542
Uribe, Andrés, 50: 478
Uruashraju (Cordillera Blanca, Peru), 50: 488
Urganowicz, Rogdan, 50: 448
Urus (Cordillera Blanca, Peru), 50: 486, 487

V

Valadez, Steve, 50: 516
Valencot, Francois, 50: 540
Valley of the Gods (Utah), 50: 452-453
Vallunaraju (Cordillera Blanca, Peru), 50: 487
Valmaggia, Italo, 50: 491, 492
Valsecchi, Amabile, 50: 533
Valsecchi, Emilio 50: 494
Vance, Joe, 50: 486
Vance, Joseph A., 50: 480
Vancouver (Yukon), 50: 462-463
Vandiver, Chris, 50: 446, 447
Van Helbergen, A. C. A., 50: 480
Van Hollebeke, Terri, 50: 442
Van Horne, William, 50: 398
Vais, Erich, 50: 524
Vargas, Joaquim, 50: 480
Varoli, G., 50: 484
Vawter, John, 50: 477
Veclani, Francesco, 50: 488
Vellay, Gérard, 50: 475
Vennum, Walter, 50: 437, 445, 449
Vértigo (Sierra Nevada de Mérida, Venezuela), 50: 477
Vieiro, Guillermo, 50: 484, 505
Villaret de Chauvigny, Bernard, 50: 540
Vincent, John, 50: 531
Vineta, Francisco, 50: 485
Virk, Dilsher Singh, 50: 527
Viscarret, T., 50: 477
Vogler, Peter, 50: 502, 512
Von Allmen, Ernst, 50: 504
Von Känel, Hans, 50: 550
Von Känel, Paul, 50: 504

609